HOLOCAUST CITY

D0209427

HOLOCAUST CITY

The Making of a Jewish Ghetto

TIM COLE

ROUTLEDGE
NEW YORK & LONDON

Published in 2003 by
Routledge
29 West 35th Street
New York, NY 10001
www.routledge-ny.com

Published in Great Britain by
Routledge
11 New Fetter Lane
London EC4P 4EE
www.routledge.co.uk

Routledge is an imprint of the Taylor & Francis Group.
Printed in the United States of America on acid-free paper.

10 9 8 7 6 5 4 3 2 1

Library of Congress Cataloging-in-Publication Data

Cole, Tim, 1970–
    Holocaust city : the making of a Jewish ghetto / Tim Cole.
        p. cm.
    Includes bibliographical references and index.
    ISBN 0–415–92968–7 (hardback) — ISBN 0–415–92969–5 (pbk.)
        1. Jews—Hungary—Budapest—Social conditions—20th century. 2. Jewish ghettos—Hungary—Budapest—History—20th century. 3. Hungary—Social policy—History—20th century. 4. Hungary—Social conditions—1918–1945. 5. Hungary—Ethnic relations. 6. Human geography—Hungary. 7. Urban policy—Hungary. 8. Holocaust, Jewish (1939–1945)—Hungary. I. Title.

    DS135 .H92 C65 2003
    940.53'1853912—dc21   2002153070

FOR MY PARENTS,
ROGER AND CHRISTINE COLE

CONTENTS

PREFACE

I loved playing with LEGO blocks as a kid. On Sunday afternoons my brother and I dragged the old plastic ice-cream containers full of colored bricks into the back room and built our own world. For a while we always built towers, one of which touched the ceiling but the next morning lay in ruins on the carpet. The bright plastic blocks are still at my parents' house, in the same old ice-cream containers, up on the top shelf in my old bedroom, from where they are brought down when the grandchildren visit. I got thinking back to those Sunday afternoons and the obsession of an eight- and a ten-year-old with LEGO, with the opening at the Jewish Museum in New York of the controversial art show "Mirroring Evil." It opened in the spring of 2002, just as I was coming to the end of writing this book. Among the many pieces exhibited are the provocative works of the Polish artist Zbigniew Libera titled "Correcting Device: LEGO Concentration Camp." This was not the first time they had been exhibited, far from it. First created in 1996, Libera's works had been causing controversy for a number of years.

As the exhibition curator, Norman Kleeblatt, recounted in the excellent catalogue that accompanied the exhibition, Libera's work had first come to his attention some years before. It was one of a number of pieces reflecting what he saw to be a shift in artistic representations of the Holocaust. For Kleeblatt, Libera was one of "a new generation of artists who look at these events in a radically different—indeed disturbing—way. They turned from what has become a standard focus on the often anonymous victims and instead stared directly at the perpetrators."[1] The result of this shift from the victims to the perpetrators was clear in Libera's seven-box limited edition of LEGO sets that could be used to construct the concentration-camp scene shown on the cover. Viewers were being invited to do nothing less than "to envision the possibility of building their own concentration camp."[2] In one, a crematoria with three chimneys can be constructed. In another a concentration camp modeled on Auschwitz I, complete with guard towers, barbed wire, and gallows, can be built from what are essentially generic LEGO blocks.[3]

What I think is particularly powerful about Libera's provocative work is that he has purposefully chosen to allow the viewer to construct Auschwitz from something as everyday as LEGO bricks. Now, of course, the gallery visitor can choose to construct something else. That is after all the great attraction of LEGO building bricks to generations of kids, my brother and I included. They are an ultimately flexible tool in the hands of a child's imagination. But Libera is surely suggesting that the human imagination can think up places like Auschwitz,[4] as well as places of great aesthetic beauty. And his suggestion is, I think, that the means for not just thinking up but also constructing both places of terror and places of beauty lie within easy reach. As the art critic Ellen Handler Spitz rightly suggests, the power in Libera's work is that "his realistic toy constructions join terms we prefer to keep apart: like carefully planned construction and wanton destruction . . ."[5]

In using such ordinary building blocks from this ubiquitous child's toy to create such extraordinary structures, Libera raised, I think, the kinds of questions that I seek to address in this book. They are questions that continue to be at the very forefront of thinking about the Holocaust. In short, face-to-face with a place like Auschwitz, the nagging question is who on earth would build such a place, and why on earth would they build it. As James Young reflects in his essay written for the exhibition catalogue, "for these artists, the only thing more shocking than the images of suffering victims is the depravity of the human beings who caused such suffering."[6] But it is not just a new generation of artists who have confronted such issues, it is also a new generation of academics. I think that the work of Robert Jan van Pelt, which I refer to in the first chapter of this book, is one striking example. As I will explore, van Pelt is one of the first to point to the fact that Auschwitz was constructed by trained architects and engineers, rather than simply appearing. And thus he raises disturbing questions about the involvement of these professions in constructing the architecture of the Holocaust.

Perhaps more than anyone else, the historian Christopher Browning has explored the disturbing question of just how ordinary the motivations of those involved in implementing the Holocaust were in his groundbreaking study *Ordinary Men*. Although Browning examined specifically the actions and motivations of one Reserve Police Battalion—number 101—in Nazi-occupied Poland, his study has been taken as having a much broader relevance when thinking about why anyone would implement the Holocaust. His suggestion is that the reasons behind the involvement of the middle-aged Germans he looks at were ordinary in the extreme. And in a haunting section at the close of the book, he suggests that

> the collective behavior of Reserve Police Battalion 101 has deeply disturbing implications. There are many societies afflicted by traditions of racism and caught in the siege mentality of war or threat of war. Everywhere society conditions people to respect and defer to authority, and indeed could scarcely function otherwise. Everywhere people seek career advancement. In every modern society, the complexity of life and the resulting bureaucratization and specialization attenuate the sense of personal responsibility of those implementing official policy. Within virtually every social collective, the peer group exerts tremendous pressures on behavior and sets moral norms. If the men of Reserve Police Battalion 101 could become killers under such circumstances, what group of men cannot?[7]

Browning points to such ordinary motivations as concerns with career advancement and peer pressure leading to such extraordinary acts as the mass murder of Polish "Jews."[8] And Libera raises the disquieting issue that something so seemingly innocent as a LEGO block can be built into something so terrifying as a concentration camp. Both address a set of questions that haunt me the more I research the Holocaust. At the back of my mind there is an image of an engineer working diligently in an office in Berlin, creating the most efficient door possible for a crematoria oven to be erected in a place in Poland called Auschwitz. It is that image which has stuck with me through the time spent researching and writing this book. In it, I take a group of ordinary men involved in municipal government in Budapest, Hungary, and try to get inside their heads as they implement ghettoization of the city's "Jews" during 1944. And I also try to get inside the heads of some of the "non-Jewish" neighbors, living in the same apartment buildings as "Jews" restricted to the place of the ghetto in 1944. What I'm interested in is how something so ordinary as the very spaces and places of a city was manipulated during 1944 to create distinct "Jewish" and "non-Jewish" space. In short, I'm interested in how a city became a Holocaust city, and ultimately I'm interested in that question which obsesses anyone who encounters the Holocaust: Why?

Tim Cole
Bristol
September 2002

ACKNOWLEDGMENTS

Many people have helped me as I've spent over a decade asking the questions how and why the city of Budapest became a Holocaust city. Three people have been especially important. My parents, Roger and Christine Cole, to whom this book is dedicated, have taught me by their example that there are no such things as bad questions. Their nonconformist approach to life has influenced me profoundly. Without their example, help, and support I would never have started out on the long path of intellectual inquiry, of which this book is one result. The other person who is a constant inspiration, as well as my companion on that path, is my wife, Julie. I first met her in Budapest in the summer of 1991, a few days after arriving in the city to embark upon learning Hungarian. And this book will be published just as she has our first child. Her love and friendship have meant so much to me over the last eleven years.

Alongside the love and support of my parents, and Julie, I feel privileged to have had so much help during the years since first starting out researching the Hungarian Holocaust. One important group has been friends in Budapest, Cambridge, Bristol, and Washington, D.C. In particular, I am very grateful to three friends—Ádám Szabados, Laci Sümegi, and Tamás Hámor—who offered their hospitality in Budapest and introduced me to their city and their country. In Cambridge, I am especially grateful for the friendship of my housemates Matthew (and Karen) Sleeman and Jeremy Lindsell, who shared the excitement and anguish of postgraduate study. It was Matthew who first got me thinking about doing a Ph.D. in the Geography Department at Cambridge on the Budapest ghetto, and who introduced me to Graham Smith who became my Ph.D. adviser. Graham was a wonderful adviser, who was always ready to offer advice and, perhaps most important, gave me self-belief that my ideas were worth exploring and expressing. One of my regrets is that Graham tragically died before that Ph.D. research ever resulted in a book.

Whilst all research is a somewhat lonely task, it is also something which makes one realize that academia is a communal exercise. Although much of this book is based on research in a number of Hungarian archives, my thinking has been influenced by the wealth of secondary literature on the Holocaust. Robert Jan van Pelt's groundbreaking work on the architecture of Auschwitz has been particularly influential, as the opening chapter of this book reveals. The seminal work of Raul Hilberg has also been particularly significant for this Holocaust scholar, as for many. Perhaps more than anyone's, the extensive writings of Randolph Braham have been hugely influential. Whilst there are places—as will become obvious—where my thesis differs from that of Braham's, his work on the Hungarian Holocaust remains a tribute to decades of scholarship. I trust that my own contribution will supplement in a small way the rich contribution that he has made.

I have been fortunate to benefit, throughout the last few years, from the advice and help of a large number of archivists and librarians in Budapest, Cambridge, Oxford, Washington, D.C., and Bristol. I am also very grateful to Ian Agnew for drawing up the figures. I have also enjoyed being part of the academic communities in the Geography Department at the University of Cambridge, in the Center for Advanced Holocaust Studies at the United States Holocaust Memorial Museum (USHMM), and in the Department of Historical Studies at the University of Bristol. My three years at Cambridge were made possible through a Ph.D. studentship from the Economic and Social Science Research Council, and my year at the USHMM through the funding of the Resnick family. I was the Pearl Resnick Postdoctoral Fellow in the year that the donor of the fellowship, Pearl Resnick, sadly passed away. I am grateful both for her vision and for her generosity in funding academic research.

In the process of writing this book, I have already published a number of articles and essays in which some of the ideas developed here first saw the light of day. I reference these in the bibliography. In addition, many of the ideas here have benefited from being aired with colleagues both informally and more formally at research seminars and conferences in both Europe and America. I am grateful for the constructive feedback of colleagues, in particular, Andrew Charlesworth, Christian Gerlach, and Jonathan Steinberg, as well as those who have said that they plain think I'm wrong. I don't think I'm claiming here to be right, but I am saying that there are all sorts of questions that seem to me to be worth asking.

My final thanks are due to my editor at Routledge, New York: Ilene Kalish. I first met Ilene after she published the American edition of my earlier book. She has been very patient in seeing this manuscript into press, and her comments have been invaluable. Of course, all mistakes are mine, and the rather dull sections are undoubtedly those that Ilene pleaded with me to change!

ONE

ARCHITECTURAL SOLUTIONS, SPATIAL SOLUTIONS, AND FINAL SOLUTIONS

Alice Lok Cahana is one of five Hungarian Holocaust survivors featured in Steven Spielberg's documentary *The Last Days*. In the movie, she returns to Auschwitz-Birkenau some fifty or so years after being taken there in the summer of 1944. After looking around at the decaying structures of the camp, Alice turns to her son, who has accompanied her on this trip, and tells him, "What [a] vast landscape you are seeing here . . . Somebody had to plan it. Somebody had to be an engineer. Somebody had to really put on a map, this kind of deficiency."[1] Her body language and words suggest that she still cannot comprehend that architects, engineers, and cartographers actually spent hours diligently planning *this* place.

Her apparent disbelief that people would actually plan and construct a place like this reminded me of the words of the historian Simon Schama, who reflected that "In our mind's eye we are accustomed to think of the Holocaust as having no landscape—or at best one emptied of features and color, shrouded in night and fog, blanketed by perpetual winter, collapsed into shades of dun and gray; the gray of smoke, of ash, of pulverized bones, of quick lime."[2] And yet, as Schama suggests with his words, the Holocaust does have a landscape, and, as Alice struggled to convey to her son, that landscape was man-made. Not only were there architectural blueprints for Auschwitz-Birkenau,[3] but these were drawn up by "fully qualified architects," including the Bauhaus graduate Fritz Ertl, rather than simply by ideologically driven amateurs.[4]

I was recently reminded again that the Holocaust had its architects, engineers, and cartographers as I was looking through documents from the Hungarian county archives. Amongst the paperwork produced in implementing ghettoization in one of the counties in southern Hungary in May 1944 were a series of sketch maps in which the precise locations of the county's ghettos were mapped out.[5] As these maps show so visibly, decisions were made about where to locate ghettos. And as the architectural blueprints for Auschwitz-Birkenau show so clearly, decisions were made about where to house, and murder, the "Jews" deported from those ghettos to Auschwitz-Birkenau. That these decisions were made is a reminder of the physical implementation of the "Final Solution of the Jewish Question."

This book is about that physicality and about some of those decisions. In particular it is about the physicality of ghettoization in one city—Budapest—and the series of decisions made about where to locate the ghetto by one group of decision makers—Budapest municipal officials. It is a study of where officials decided to house "Jews" in the city when they implemented a policy of segregating "Jews" and "non-Jews." And in asking the question where, I am interested in also getting at the bigger question why. What I want to suggest is that the former is one way to uncover the latter. This book is an attempt to get inside the heads of local officials and ordinary Hungarians in Budapest and, by looking at the profoundly spatial decisions they made, try to work out what motivated them to do the things they did.

Implementing ghettoization in a city like Budapest meant deciding to put Budapest's "Jews" in one part of the city, rather than another. In short, planning and implementing ghettoization was, in part at least, an act of urban planning. As the "Final Solution of the Jewish Question" was implemented in occupied Europe, a multitude of architects, engineers, and cartographers implemented smaller architectural and spatial solutions. In the case of Budapest, this amounted to a physical reshaping of the city in 1944–45. But before I turn to think about the spatial decisions which municipal officials in Budapest made during the Second World War, I want to start with architecture, and in particular the groundbreaking work of the architectural historian Robert Jan van Pelt, and then shift to think more about geography, and, in particular, notions of place and space. There is much to be gained, I think, from drawing upon these two disciplines' concerns with physical structures and spatiality in rethinking the Holocaust. Van Pelt's work has clearly reinvigorated our understanding of Auschwitz in particular and the concentration and death camps in general.[6] My hope is that this study of the spatiality of the Holocaust will reinvigorate our understanding of the Budapest ghetto in particular and Holocaust ghettoization in general, and ultimately, that it will offer at least a glimpse into the question of why ordinary men would do the seemingly extraordinary in a Holocaust city.

ARCHITECTURAL SOLUTIONS

Despite (or perhaps precisely because of) the role played by architects in offering architectural solutions in the concentration and death camps, there has been, by and large, a failure on the part of the architectural profession to address this particular legacy. There is, for van Pelt, something profoundly disturbing about such disciplinary amnesia. He acknowledges that "it seems easy to commit these flimsy and shoddy buildings to the garbage-heap of architectural history,"[7] and yet calls for a disciplinary response to the architecture of Auschwitz. However, the tendency within architectural history has been to ignore the "flimsy and shoddy buildings" of the concentration and death camps, and focus instead on what has been seen as the "true" side of Nazi architecture—the monumental architecture of Nazi architects such as Albert Speer.

This focus can be seen in two seminal works published in the late 1960s and early 1970s—Barbara Lane's *Architecture and Politics in Germany 1918–1945* and Robert Taylor's *The Word in Stone*[8]—which both stressed the ideological commitment of Nazism to heroic monumentalism. Through the use of durable materials, particularly granite, and by building on a massive scale, the regime created structures that were seen to be entirely appropriate for, and representative of, the planned Thousand Year Reich. By focusing on these monumental buildings, Lane and Taylor both chose to study what van Pelt has termed "the architectural and urban delusions of Germania,"[9] and Andrew Charlesworth has memorably termed the "heart" rather than the "anus" of Nazi planning.[10] And in doing that, they essentially bought into Nazi propaganda, which offered up architectural monumentalism and suppressed the architecture of the concentration and death camps. An example is a publication produced for foreign consumption in 1941, titled *A Nation Builds: Contemporary German Architecture*, which detailed architectural developments in the Nazi rebuilding of Germany.[11] Covering not only the monumental state architecture but also military and domestic architecture, this book, unsurprisingly, makes no references to concentration camps. But what is surprising is when that silence is carried over into contemporary architectural history. And that silence is particularly pronounced given the central place afforded to the Holocaust, and Auschwitz, within contemporary perceptions of Nazism.[12] Reading Lane and Taylor, one critic expressed surprise that neither "so much as mentions the concentration camp, the one building type, above all, which for most of us represents the quintessence of Nazi ideology."[13]

Concentration camps are mentioned in Alex Scobie's *Hitler's State Architecture*, published in 1990. However, in a work that points to Roman influences in the monumental architecture of the Nazis, Scobie's only reference comes at the close of the book, in an acknowledgment of the use of slave labor in the creation of these monumental structures.[14] Although the book as a whole focuses on Speer's plans for Nuremberg and Berlin, Scobie's last sentence hints at the broader context, concluding that

> buildings like the Congress Hall in Nuremberg and the *Volkshalle* in Berlin,
> inspired by the Colosseum and the Pantheon, respectively, were not merely sym-
> bols of tradition, order, and reliability, but signaled a far more sinister intention
> on the part of the autocrat who commissioned them: a return to "Roman" ethics,
> which recognized the natural right of a conqueror to enslave conquered peoples in
> the most literal sense of the word, a right already made manifest even within the
> sphere of architecture by the creation of concentration camps, whose inmates
> were forced to quarry the stone for the Reich's buildings.[15]

While acknowledging the existence of concentration camps, which were the "home" to the slave laborers quarrying stone for Nazi monumentalism, Scobie does not consider the architecture of the camps themselves. That architecture had not been examined on its own terms until the recent work of Pressac and, more significantly, van Pelt (in a series of essentially theoretical reflections published in 1993 and an empirical study of Auschwitz cowritten with the social historian Debórah Dwork, published three years later). Rejecting what they see as the "demonization" of Auschwitz as a place somehow outside of human history, van Pelt and Dwork demonstrate that Auschwitz was "just another place which became what it did by ordinary people using standard procedures: requisition forms, transportation vouchers, planning permissions, bills of sale, bills of receipt."[16] Their painstaking research into the evolving shape of this complex of labor, concentration, and death camps—"step by step, blueprint by blueprint"[17]—gives an insight into the bureaucratic and architectural development of this place where Alice Lok Cahana and some 400,000 other Hungarian "Jews" were taken in the early summer of 1944.

Yet until van Pelt's work—and also that of Pressac—the architecture of the camps themselves remained a glaring gap within architectural history (and therefore, by extension, the newly developing field of Holocaust studies). This tendency toward silence within architectural history is in part a result of the divorcing of these two aspects of Nazi architecture: the architecture of Nazi monumentalism and the architecture of the concentration and death camps. Now, of course, there is little doubt that there are significant differences between the two. There is a striking sense of the creation of distinct "Aryan" and "non-Aryan" architectural space in Nazi-occupied Europe. Reading *A Nation Builds*, alongside van Pelt's work on Auschwitz, makes that distinction all too clear. Both describe, in some detail, Nazi barrack design. But the barrack blocks designed for "Aryan" soldiers are in many ways another space entirely from the barracks designed for "non-Aryan" prisoners. In outlining the former, the author of *A Nation Builds* notes that

> The term "barracks" has become synonymous with a human habitation devoid of comfort and beauty and designed merely to fulfill the function of sheltering large groups of men in the most economical and elementary way possible. Today the new army and air force barracks provide officers and soldiers with homes which, however simple they may be, embody the best features of a model "*Siedlung*" [settlement]. And in order that the lives of officers and enlisted men shall not be devoid of the enrichment of life which works of art provide, assembly rooms and mess halls are decorated with murals, sculpture and ornamental ironwork . . .[18]

The contrast with the barracks designed for prisoners in Auschwitz-Birkenau, which van Pelt describes, could not be more marked. Within the "non-Aryan" space of Auschwitz,

> the theoretical interest in the minimum dwelling and the *Existenzminimum* [subsistence level], which had fuelled so much of the most enlightened architectural discourse in the late 1920s, found at last a most practical implication in the design of the barracks that were to house the slave population. . . . [T]he architects of Auschwitz designated the standard design of army horse stables as a proper solution to the housing problem in the camp. Within these flimsy and

shoddy constructions people were forced to live in a situation of abject degradation. They were heaped up as if they were goods in dirty and cold spaces too small to hold even the volume of their bodies.[19]

The—limited—adaptation of horse stables for "non-Aryan" living space fitted within an ideology that classified "non-Aryans" as subhuman and portrayed "Jews" as vermin.

The same sense of contrast can be seen when comparing the description of "Aryan" housing with the ghetto conditions faced by East European "Jews." *A Nation Builds* described the new style of mass house building:

> The need for more sun and air and for uncluttered space, plus the new building materials and labor saving devices, are basic elements which have determined the new style. There is a tendency to use large windows, combined with sun terraces and porches which unite indoors with out-of-doors; this and the effort to simplify existence, to do away with dust cluttering ornament, are functional reasons for the simplification of style which characterizes the new house.
>
> However in developing a style which derives from a new attitude towards life, it is significant that the love for tradition has not been abandoned. Designers of modern domestic architecture in Germany have been able to combine traditional forms with new materials and new needs. The pointed roof and gabled window, the plaster and wood of the typical German farm house are elements which have frequently been retained. The ability to combine features which the wisdom of the race has discovered to be of permanent value, with modern needs and building materials, is what differentiates the contemporary home in Germany from the more starkly theoretical version of the modern house developed elsewhere.[20]

Such concerns with sun, air, and "uncluttered space" were turned on their heads in the creation of "Jewish" ghettos, where intentional overcrowding operated as a self-fulfilling prophecy. As van Pelt notes,

> The ghettos and camps created a situation in which it became unavoidable that the crime would catch up with the retribution. When the Germans concentrated more than 400,000 Jews in an area of 403 hectares in Warsaw, they created a biological time-bomb. With a population density of 110,880 per square kilometer, the starving population tried to manage as best it could. Most people lived in utter degradation. For the Germans the common deprivation was a proof of Jewish depravity.[21]

There was clearly an architecture for "Aryans" and an architecture for "non-Aryans," and, more broadly, distinctive "Aryan" and "non-Aryan" spaces. And ultimately the difference between these spaces—as Francis Aldor recognized as early as 1940—was that the Nazis were creating "non-Aryan" *Todesraum* [death space] in Poland while in the process of creating "Aryan" *Lebensraum* [living space].[22]

However, to isolate two distinct spaces and architectural styles is not to argue that these two were not in various ways linked. Indeed, van Pelt suggests that there were surprising commonalities between the housing being built in Germany for the "Aryan" worker (and described so glowingly in *A Nation Builds*) and the barracks being built in occupied Poland for the "non-Aryan" prisoner. Despite the real and seeming contrasts, both were examples of an architecture of surveillance. For "while Nazi propaganda made much of the 'clarity, beauty and harmony' of the several hundred settlements created by the Labor Front, it failed to mention that the price for the little red-roofed houses was the loss of all privacy."[23] The result was that the "Aryan" worker was subjected to an architecture of surveillance and control, albeit of a different form and magnitude from that experienced by the "non-Aryan" prisoner subjected to the gaze of the guard towers at Auschwitz-Birkenau.

These concentration-camp guard towers were more than simply the products of an architecture of surveillance. They can, the art historian Paul Jaskot suggests, be seen as monumental structures in their own right.[24] And this is where a real blurring takes place between the Nazi architectural extremes of heroic monumentalism and concentration-camp flimsiness. For, within a single concentration camp, there could be both monumental and "flimsy" architecture. As Jaskot notes, writing about the Flossenbürg concentration camp—located northeast of Nuremberg—"as with other camps, the buildings used by the prisoners were flimsy structures and, in the case of the barracks, purchased from private firms. But the SS acquired better materials and organized a careful process of design for the camp administrative buildings, walls and watch towers."[25]

In the case of the walls and watch towers in particular, the monumentalism of their design was due in large part to the fact that they looked two ways—both into and out of the camp. Thus alongside their role as sites of surveillance, they were also a monumental façade. This was most obviously the case at Flossenbürg and Mauthausen—located northeast of Linz—where the ready availability of stone meant that durable structures were created with attention paid to form as well as function. At Flossenbürg, considerable concern was given to the architectural detailing of guard towers,[26] and at Mauthausen the two sides of the camp exposed to the public gaze were created with towers and walls which "projected a loose ideological relation to the defensive structures of the Middle Ages."[27] The monumental façade on these two sides of Mauthausen contrasted markedly with the merely functional use of electrified barbed-wire fencing on the two sides not open to public gaze.[28] But this sense of a monumental façade being created at concentration and death camps was not restricted to the stone structures created at Flossenbürg and Mauthausen. It was common to other camp architecture. Although made of brick and plaster, the entrance gateway at Auschwitz-Birkenau shared a concern with form and function, with Jaskot suggesting that it "projected the institutional authority of the SS," alongside serving a functional purpose of surveillance.[29]

But the entrance gateway at Auschwitz-Birkenau and walls and watch towers at Mauthausen did more than project the power of the SS, alongside serving as functional means of imprisonment and surveillance. They also served to hide and camouflage the realities of the camps from both the victims themselves and the bystander.[30] Thus the walls of Mauthausen offered to the public gaze a castlelike edifice with its accompanying historical connections, which *also* hid the activities of the camp itself from the onlooker. And the role of camouflage played by these monumental façades was not aimed simply at the bystander but also the victim, as the infamous mock railway station complete with its fake clock at Treblinka makes clear. This layer of camouflage at Treblinka was overlaid with another layer—the shielding of the camp with the "natural barrier to sight" afforded by the dense Polish forest.[31]

This dual function of being a backdrop for performance and a barrier which hides is central to the façade. As Henri Lefebvre points out in his important theoretical work *The Production of Space*, "walls, enclosures and facades serve to define both a scene (where something takes place) and an obscene area to which everything that cannot or may not happen on the scene is relegated: whatever is inadmissible, be it malefic or forbidden, thus has its own hidden space on the near or the far side of a frontier."[32] And thus, "a façade admits certain acts to the realm of what is visible, whether they occur on the façade itself (on balconies, window ledges etc.) or are to be seen from the façade (processions in the street for example). Many other acts, by contrast, it condemns to obscenity: these occur behind the façade."[33]

And it is those two functions—site of performance and means of camou-flage—which can be seen in the widespread use of the monumental façade in Nazi architecture, "with its pomp and brutality even more pronounced, its monumentality more oppressive than ever."[34]

Whether the façade of the Nuremberg Party Rally Grounds or the façade of Auschwitz-Birkenau, the Nazi façade served both to define and demarcate space. In the case of the latter, the monumental gateway was both backdrop and attempted camouflage to the imprisonment and killings that took place in the camp. It defined and demarcated *Todesraum* [death space]. It is striking that, generally speaking, Nazism created "appropriate" (and inappropriate) death spaces behind—at times monumental—façades. Camps were designed as demarcated genocidal space. But there were also the forests of eastern Poland and the occupied Soviet Union that offered their own leafy façade behind which killings had a certain place (of hidden-ness). Of course there were vast numbers killed without any concern for a façade, but it is remarkable—given the context of the war—that in the spring and summer of 1944, hundreds of thousands of Hungarian "Jews" were taken by train several hundred miles to the death camp of Auschwitz-Birkenau, to be gassed and cremated behind the camp's façade. Auschwitz-Birkenau was seen to be an "appropriate" death space.

That the two Nazi architectures shared concerns with surveillance and the centrality of the façade is not the end of the connections between these seemingly oppositional categories. As Alex Scobie hinted at, and Paul Jaskot and Michael Allen have so clearly shown, forced labor under SS con-trol was critical for quarrying out the vast quantities of stone required by the monumental architectural designs.[35] Thus the "heart" and "anus" were linked—and linked through the harsh conditions suffered by slave laborers. Jaskot notes that at the camp of Flossenbürg, "thousands of prisoners lost their lives in the forced-labor quarries, realizing the political function of the camp. Yet this forced labor also served an architectural function: the largest single patron for Flossenbürg granite was Albert Speer's office for the rebuilding of Berlin."[36] In short, there were far more connections between these seemingly disconnected sides of Nazi architecture than either archi-tectural historians such as Lane and Taylor have articulated or Albert Speer maintained in his defense at the postwar Nuremberg trial.[37]

The question of connections between these two Nazi architectures is one with more than simply academic significance. After all, it was asked with particular intensity in West Germany in the late 1970s and early

1980s, within the context of what Gavriel Rosenfeld terms the "Architects' Debate."[38] Emerging prior to and then running parallel with the *Historikerstreit* (Historians' Debate) of the mid-1980s, this Architects' Debate shared a concern with the historicization of the Nazi past in contemporary Germany. Essentially the debate involved modernist and post-modernist German architects exchanging the expletive "fascist," with each in turn dubbing the other's work as inextricably linked to the problematic history of the Third Reich.

In an attempt to unhinge monumental and neoclassical forms from the Nazi past, postmodern German architects sought both to point to the diversity of Nazi architectural styles and to question the link between the monumental architecture of the regime and the architecture of the death camps. Thus in seeking to rehabilitate the work of Albert Speer, Leon Krier asserted that Speer's "neoclassical architecture was always the civilized and proper side of the empire of lies. It was its aesthetic and ethical façade."[39] But Krier went further than simply disconnecting neoclassicism from the death camps. He sought to discredit modernist architecture by seeing in the death camps the epitome of modernity, reminding modernists that the Nazis' crimes "were not committed in a monumental environment but in demeaning industrial barracks and camps."[40] Indeed for Krier "industrial civilization is unable . . . to create meaningful and beautiful places. It erects suburbs, zones, transportation systems . . . and concentration camps. It is always concerned with mass housing . . . mass transport . . . and mass extermination. Auschwitz-Birkenau and Los Angeles have the same parents."[41]

In giving Auschwitz-Birkenau and Los Angeles the same parent—modernity—Krier shared the wider tendency to compare Nazi Germany with other places and times so central to the very public *Historikerstreit*. Not surprisingly, therefore, his claims were seen as sharing the apologetic tendencies of neoconservatism. It was stressed that there was not only a need to look behind the neoclassical façade, where Wilhelm Kücker noted "that people froze and starved,"[42] but also a need to come to terms with the widespread use by the Nazis of slave labor in the building of the monumental structures in Berlin and Nuremberg. As I have suggested, the connections between the two architectures are even more far-reaching than that, given in particular the shared concern with the façade.

Yet the façade was, by definition, only the public face of the concentration and death camp. Behind the monumental façade was concentration-camp "flimsy," which was characterized above all by a concern with the functional. The architecture of the barracks at Auschwitz-Birkenau described above by van Pelt makes that very clear. And it is that functionality which has caused the death camps to be described in the language of the industrial as being little more than factories of death. This is expressed most forcefully in Henry Feingold's oft-cited description of Auschwitz as

> a mundane extension of the modern factory system. Rather than producing goods, the raw material was human beings and the end product was death, so many units per day marked carefully on the manager's production charts. The chimneys, the very symbol of the modern factory system, poured forth acrid smoke produced by burning human flesh. The brilliantly organized railroad grid of modern Europe carried a new kind of raw material to the factories. It did so in the same manner as with other cargo. In the gas chambers the victims inhaled noxious gas generated by prussic acid pellets, which were produced by the advanced chemical industry of Germany. Engineers designed the crematoria; managers designed the system of bureaucracy that worked with a zest and efficiency more backward nations would envy. Even the overall plan itself was a reflection of the modern scientific spirit gone awry. What we witnessed was nothing less than a massive scheme of social engineering.[43]

Feingold's view of Auschwitz as part of "the modern factory system" is one that has been taken further by those who cast the Holocaust as expressive of modernity unleashed.[44] Giving Auschwitz the parent of modernity, as writers such as Zygmunt Bauman have done, is of course more acceptable outside of the German context within which Krier was writing. The historicization implicit to such comparative history does not hold the same apologetic tendencies that it did in the German cases of the historians' and architects' debates. Whilst there are clearly problems with reducing the Holocaust to the extremes of modernity, it is striking that the sheer functional nature of much of the death-camp architecture (although not all, as I have suggested with regard to the importance of the façade) does resonate with the description of industrial architecture given in *A Nation Builds*:

> Entirely utilitarian in its purpose, and without the need for expressing a spiritual idea as is the case with public buildings or domestic architecture, the modern German factory is an exemplification and justification of the theory that function and material determine form. Although in many instances the effort is to fit the factory to its local background, nevertheless it is its stark utilitarianism and use of

new building materials that have given the modern German factory its distinctive and distinguished style.[45]

Such a concern with functionality—at least in part—does make sense when thinking about the architecture of the concentration and death camps. Alongside a concern with the façade lay a series of functional—and essentially "technical"—questions posed and answered by "experts." Thus the question of where to house the inmates at Auschwitz-Birkenau was answered "in the shape of the largely unmodified horse stables (known as *Pferdestallbarakken* OKH-Typ 260/9 and designed to house fifty-two horses) which the architects of Auschwitz adapted to house a thousand prisoners."[46] And the question of how to deal with "the problem of corpse disposal" at Auschwitz-Birkenau was answered by a "combination of the design-skills of *Amtsgruppe* [Office group] C, the *Zentralbauleitung* [Central Building Authority] and outside firms" that drew up plans for the crematoria.[47]

In writing here of "the problem of corpse disposal," the choice of language used by van Pelt is, I think, quite self-conscious. It stresses the almost clinical sense of bureaucratic detachment by engineers and architects focused upon devising a functional solution to a purely technical problem—in this case, "the problem of corpse disposal." This "problem" was effectively the last in a line of "problems" addressed by "experts." And it was of course, a "problem" entirely of the Nazis' own making. The problem was the numbers of "Jews" killed by mass gassing, which itself was a solution to an earlier "problem," which . . .

Within the catchall category of the "Final Solution to the Jewish Question," there were, along the way, numerous intermediary solutions to detailed questions, of which corpse disposal was the final of the final solutions. But there were plenty of other questions posed and solutions proffered by a host of "experts." As Raul Hilberg has noted of the numerous "specialists" engaged in the destruction process—"accountants, lawyers, engineers, or physicians"—

The questions with which these men were concerned were almost always technical. How was a "Jewish enterprise" to be defined? Where were the borders of a ghetto to be drawn? What was to be the disposition of pension claims belonging to deported Jews? How should bodies be disposed of? These were the problems pondered by the bureaucrats in their memoranda, correspondence, meetings and discussions.[48]

In large part this book is a narrative that exposes the questions posed and solutions proffered by one group of "experts": municipal officials in Budapest. The questions revolved around the segregation of "Jews," and the solutions concerned a series of ghettoization measures. These municipal officials, alongside the engineers who designed the crematoria ovens and the architects who designed the crematoria chimneys,[49] can be grouped together, I think, under Lefebvre's memorable phrase "doctors of space."[50] The assumption of these doctors of space was that there was a pathological space, which demanded a spatial cure. They imagined a series of "Jewish questions" in spatial terms, each of which demanded spatial solutions.

A difficult question is the extent to which those spatial solutions were essentially functional, rather than intentional, solutions.[51] There is a need to ask whether spatial cures were—for these doctors of space—more than simply the functional solutions offered by experts. Certainly van Pelt would seem to suggest that in the case of the architects of Auschwitz, there was an ideological intentionality to the manipulation and creation of space in the camp. He argues that "the German architects designed the camps in such a way that their tectonics and their rites would destroy purposefully the inmates' sense of meaning and direction . . . Auschwitz was created to annihilate the spirit and exterminate the body."[52] Evidence for this architectural intentionality comes in part, van Pelt suggests, from the postwar memoir of a Polish Auschwitz inmate who tells of "how the physical (architectonic) environment of these barracks spoke to her with the commanding voice of revelation."[53] In her memoir, *Twenty Months at Auschwitz*, Pelagia Lewinska writes that "at the outset the living places, the ditches, the mud, the piles of excrement behind the blocks, had appalled me with their horrible filth . . . And then I saw the light! I saw that it was not a question of disorder or lack of organization but that, on the contrary, a very thoroughly considered conscious idea was in the back of the camp's existence. They had condemned us to die in our own filth, to drown in mud, in our own excrement. They wished to abase us, to destroy our human dignity, to efface every vestige of humanity . . . to fill us with horror and contempt toward ourselves and our fellows."[54]

I am not sure, however, that van Pelt uses this source critically enough. What is striking is that the source is a postwar memoir, and thus offers us a victim's, rather than a perpetrator's, perspective on the architectural space of Auschwitz. This certainly suggests that the space was both perceived and experienced by the victim as intentional. And once perceived as intentional there was resistance. However, it is problematic to suggest, as van Pelt does, that the way in which a space was experienced by the victims matched the original intentions of the perpetrators. Offering a particular solution could, and did, create by-products, which are by definition significantly different from the major original intentions. However questioning, van Pelt's use of this particular survivor memoir is not to deny that spatial solutions could and did have ideological intentions rather than being "merely" functional answers to technical questions. It is quite clear from the propaganda function afforded to the Warsaw ghetto—which both featured in a propaganda movie and was the destination of organized bus trips—that intentionality and functionality were intertwined. However, the basis to explore this is not primarily in the memoirs of survivors but in the memos and plans drafted by the doctors of space.[55] The perspective of the victim is an indispensable part of the story of the Holocaust, but in this book I aim to examine the meanings given to ghettoization by the doctors of space involved in decision making in Budapest.

And in doing so, I am particularly interested in laying bare the spatiality so often implicit rather than explicit within writing on the implementation of the Holocaust. There is after all something inherently architectural and spatial about the implementation of the "Final Solution of the Jewish Question." There is a physicality to the Holocaust. As van Pelt's work has demonstrated, a camp like Auschwitz has an architecture. And it also has a geography. It is a real (and imagined) place of destruction. But it is also more than a—the—place where the Holocaust was implemented, it is also a *space* through which the Holocaust was implemented. And this is where I want to turn from my initial reflections on architectural history to thinking geographically about the Holocaust. Because in this book I am interested in examining how geographical concerns with place and space can be utilized when considering the Holocaust, and so bring the spatial much more to the fore.

SPATIAL SOLUTIONS

Geographers—like architectural historians—have been rather reticent in studying the Holocaust.[56] Indeed, the historical geographer Andrew Charlesworth suggests a similar level of disciplinary resistance to that signaled by van Pelt. He tells of one of his own colleague's reactions to teaching the first course on the Holocaust within a geography department in a British university: "One geographer with a visible sign of distaste has asked me how I can take students to a place like Auschwitz-Birkenau. No such distaste would have been expressed if I had taken them through the monumental imperialist landscapes of Berlin."[57]

Whilst in general terms there has been a turning away from the death camps within geographical writing, there are a number of exceptions. A few geographical studies have touched upon the spaces of the Nazi concentration camps and ghettos, although they do not fully develop what geographies of the Holocaust might look like. They do, however, provide a useful starting point, and I explore three—essentially overlapping—perspectives below. These perspectives are suggestive of a number of possible approaches that I intend to develop with regard to Holocaust ghettoization in chapter 2, and which then permeate the narrative developed in the subsequent chapters in this book.

There is an importance to thinking geographically about the Holocaust, that is broader than simply an importance to the discipline of geography. As is the case with architectural history, disciplinary resistance impacts two ways. Not only does a failure to engage with the Holocaust have implications for the discipline itself but it also results in disciplinary gaps within Holocaust studies. This field has tended to be dominated by the work of historians, resulting in an emphasis upon chronology. That stress can be seen above all in the dominance of the "intentionalist versus functionalist" debate in the 1980s and early 1990s, which was in essence a peculiarly historical debate, given its focus upon the precise dating of decisions.[58] Whilst I do not want to jettison that concern with chronology (I teach in a history department, after all), geography's concern with space has, I think, much to offer the increasingly interdisciplinary field of Holocaust studies in terms of helping us unpack the spatiality inherent in the implementation of the "Final Solution of the Jewish Question." It reawakens us to the historically specific places where the Holocaust was implemented and the ways in which the Holocaust was implemented through space.

The first element is more obvious, I think—that the Holocaust was implemented in historically specific places. In short, to take the words of the geographer Doreen Massey,

> geography matters. The fact that processes take place over space, the facts of distance or closeness, of geographical variation between areas, of the individual character and meaning of specific places and regions—all these are essential to the operation of social processes themselves. Just as there are no purely spatial

processes, neither are there any non-spatial social processes. Nothing much happens, bar angels dancing, on the head of a pin.[59]

That the Holocaust did not occur on a pinhead hardly needs stating. In the literature, there is recognition that the "Final Solution of the Jewish Question" was implemented within the complex and variegated history and geography of Second World War Europe. The twin ideas of time *and* place are very much present in Raul Hilberg's classic study *The Destruction of the European Jews*, which remains, four decades later, the definitive Holocaust study.[60] Although Hilberg was interested in the unfolding of an essentially similar destruction process, he was sensitive to national and chronological differences. His account combines an essentially chronological narrative with country-by-country studies.[61] And Hilberg reveals a concern with the geography of Europe—in particular with his focus upon the role played by the rail network in the deportations.[62] The theme of rail transportation is one discussed seemingly endlessly by Hilberg and Lanzmann in the celebrated film *Shoah*, which Lanzmann himself described as "*un film de topographe, de geographe.*"[63]

The twin ideas of time and space that play such a role in Hilberg's work can also be seen as central to other comparative studies of the Holocaust. In particular, the fact that the relative numbers of "Jews" killed varied from country to country has resulted in studies which explore national differences in terms of factors such as differing geopolitical relationships vis-à-vis Nazi Germany and differing histories of native antisemitism and collaboration.[64] And those differentials in mortality are in general the starting point for national and local studies that seek to narrate and explain place-specific experiences of the Holocaust. To give only one example, Bob Moore's useful study of the Netherlands starts with Moore's noting that "Jewish" mortality in the Netherlands was 73 percent, compared with 40 percent in Belgium and 25 percent in France, prompting him to ask the question: "How could such a huge difference have arisen between apparently similar states, and more importantly, how could the Netherlands compare so unfavourably with her nearest Western European neighbours?"[65] And in answering that question throughout the remainder of the study, Moore focuses upon local factors of this place-specific episode. That focus within national and local studies could be multiplied again and again. In short, within Holocaust studies there is recognition that "geography matters" as far as national differences and concerns with place go.

Perhaps more than anything else, Martin Gilbert's *Atlas of the Holocaust*[66] and the USHMM-published *Historical Atlas of the Holocaust*[67] have provided historians with powerful visual reminders of the geography of the "Final Solution." That geography is also present in Gilbert's travelogue *Holocaust Journey*.[68] Rather than being arranged chronologically—as ironically this book essentially is—Gilbert's text is arranged geographically. It does self-consciously begin in Berlin, with a sense of origins, but then travels through the ghetto and concentration-camp sites in the Czech Republic and Poland. It is, after all, the narrative of a journey made by Gilbert and his graduate students, and journeys don't obey the classic chronological approach (which starts with the Nazi rise to power in 1933 and then moves on year-by-year to the end of the war) so beloved by historians.[69] Instead, Gilbert and his students follow the landscape of destruction (rather than the timeline of destruction), and what is striking is how far-reaching that landscape is. Gilbert and his students don't make it into Hungary or Romania, or the Soviet Union, or the Netherlands and France. Indeed, they really cover only Poland in depth, and yet even here their journey to the places of destruction takes two weeks. As one student commented on this experience of traveling kilometer-upon-kilometer through Europe, "when one spends hour upon hour visiting Jewish community upon Jewish community, and ends the day at the site of their mass murder, one becomes deeply conscious of the scale of the *Shoah*. And that was one road, to one camp, in one country."[70]

These words—"one road," "one camp," "one country"—reveal a growing awareness of location and a grappling with the places that formed the backdrop to the concentration, deportation, and extermination of European "Jews." But they also reveal a consciousness of scale in two main ways. Firstly, they acknowledge that the Holocaust was implemented at the scale of "one road" to the scale of "one camp" to the scale of "one country"—in essence, that the Holocaust took place at a variety of scales from the local through the national (and beyond). And within that, secondly, the words recognize that there wasn't one country, let alone one camp or one road, but that "Jews" were taken along many roads, and railroads, leading to a number of camps in occupied Europe. Grasping that sense of many roads is one way of mentally mapping out the sheer physical scope of the Holocaust, which was played out in (and through) multiple European landscapes.

And that is where a second, and less obvious, element emerges—that the Holocaust was implemented *through* space. Recognition of the many roads, and railroads, which led (in some cases after hundreds of kilometers) to death camps (*Todesraum*) is recognition of physical distance (and proximity). And distance was something that did not simply have to be overcome. It was also something that could, and did, play a central role in ensuring the hidden-ness of destruction. In short, distance was not simply something passive to be overcome but also something active, which could facilitate and not simply hinder. And that is because, as human geographers have stressed, space is not simply passive but active. All of that can be seen, I think, in Doreen Massey's words relating to class relations, which stress that distance is something other than simply a logistical concern. And her words—while written within the context of a work of economic geography—are words that can be usefully rewritten in the process of exploring what a geography of the Holocaust might entail.

For Massey,

> space is not a passive surface on to which the relations of production are mapped, nor yet simply a negative constraint (in the sense, for instance, of distance to be crossed). The fact of spatiality is an integral and active condition. In relation to production, spatial form and spatial strategy can be an active element of accumulation. Capital can make positive use of distance and differentiation.[71]

These ideas, which Massey develops with regard to capital and the active role of space, can be rewritten with regard to racism, and in particular the antisemitic racism of the Holocaust, and so read:

> *space is not a passive surface on to which the "Final Solution" is mapped, not yet simply a negative constraint (in the sense, for instance, of distance to be crossed).[72] The fact of spatiality is an integral and active condition. In relation to the "Final Solution," spatial form and spatial strategy can be an active element of segregation and destruction. (antisemitic) Racism can make "positive" use of distance and differentiation.*

And perhaps nowhere does that idea of (antisemitic) racism making "positive" use of distance and differentiation appear more marked than in the ghettos and concentration camps of Holocaust Europe. With the restructuring of the spaces of the urban and rural environment—segregating the "Jew" in ghettos within major cities, and constructing death camps in rural areas proximate to rail networks—the Holocaust emerges as a profoundly spatial historical event. The relationship between "Nazi" and "Jew," between

"Perpetrator" and "Victim," was one constructed in, and *through*, space. Annihilating the "Jew" was a spatial process from start to finish. The "Final Solution of the Jewish Question" was not implemented simply within the space of the wartime city of Budapest, for example, but through the manipulation and restructuring of the wartime city of Budapest. And yet that spatiality remains very much implicit, rather than explicit, within most historical writing on the Holocaust.

In part this is the result of an essentially geography-*frei* Holocaust studies which assumes that "geography is an inert, fixed, isotropic back-drop to the real stuff of politics and history."[73] And yet the challenge of recent work within human geography is to see space not simply as the stage where the Holocaust is enacted but as an actor central to the implementation of the "Final Solution of the Jewish Question." In short, the challenge is to consider space not simply as where things happen but as part and parcel of things (not) happening. As the work of a number of geographers has pointed out, there is a need both to recognize the importance of examining space as "socially constructed" *and* to recognize that "social processes are constructed over space."[74]

That first idea is central to the work of Henri Lefebvre, whose writings on the "production of space" I have already referred to with reference to the façade. Lefebvre asks rhetorically, "What is an ideology without a space to which it refers, a space which it describes, whose vocabulary and links it makes use of, and whose code it embodies? . . . what we call ideology only achieves consistency by intervening in social space and in its production, and by thus taking on body therein. Ideology per se might well be said to consist primarily in a discourse upon social space."[75] Writing within an essentially Marxist framework, Lefebvre suggested that "the idea of producing . . . today extends beyond the production of this or that thing or work to the production of space."[76] That space is socially produced points to the usefulness of thinking in terms of Nazi or Holocaust space. As I've already considered, Nazism created certain concrete spaces characterized by the use of the façade—the site of the Nuremberg rallies, Auschwitz (as van Pelt has examined in detail), ghettos—but it also made a fetish of abstract space through notions of, for example, *Lebensraum*.

That these real and imaginary places and spaces were produced is critical in coming to terms with the physicality and spatiality of the Holocaust. But there is a need to think about space as more than simply a social product. For space is society, in the human geographer Edward Soja's words, "not as its definitional or logical equivalent, but as its concretization."[77] And thus, as another human geographer, Derek Gregory, suggests, like Massey writing in the context of a concern with class rather than "race," "the analysis of spatial structure is not derivative of and secondary to the analysis of social structure: rather each requires the other. Spatial structure is not, therefore, merely the arena within which class conflicts express themselves but also the domain within which—and in part through which—class relations are constituted . . . "[78]

These are also words that can be rewritten, with antisemitism rather than class relations in view:

> *The analysis of spatial structure is not derivative of and secondary to the analysis of social structure: rather each requires the other. Spatial structure is not, therefore, merely the arena within which antisemitisms express themselves but also the domain within which—and in part through which—"Jewish"/"non-Jewish" relations are constituted.*

At present within the literature, this focus upon space as an active agent through which the Holocaust is implemented remains undeveloped. It is hinted at in Michael Freeman's *Atlas of Nazi Germany*. There he signals that mapping out some of the geographical dimensions of the Third Reich involves more than simply "the compilation of some sort of 'place' inventory" or "focus on distributional patterns in space." Rather, drawing upon the work of Soja amongst others, he signals that mapping out the Third Reich involves grappling with "the dialectics of space" which necessitates treating space as "an active not a passive construct in social production and reproduction."[79] However, in practice the atlas fails to follow through with such an engagement with space as an active element. Thus, when Freeman maps out National Socialist schools, he does little more than sketch a "place inventory." And yet, in this particular case, there was a clear fetishization of space, with the self-conscious locating of *Ordensburgen* (Order Castles) in the symbolic and sacred Teutonic spaces of the border regions and East Prussia.[80] Such fetishization of space is something that suggests that the places where these schools were located were not merely neutral backdrops. In short, space was active and not merely passive.

Something of that does come through in the work of three geographers who touch on Holocaust space in passing. They all explicitly identify the Nazi concentration camp (and in a couple of cases the ghetto) as one example of a distinctive space (of modernity) variously described as "pariah landscapes," "landscapes of exclusion," and "spaces of domination." Situating the concentration camp within a broader geographical category places it within a longer history of spatial strategies of separation and exclusion. I think it is worth briefly sketching out these three ways of looking at the space of the concentration camp before turning to think about the themes that these works point to.

PARIAH LANDSCAPES, LANDSCAPES OF EXCLUSION, AND SPACES OF DOMINATION

The American geographer W. A. Douglas Jackson makes explicit reference to both the Nazi concentration camps and ghettos as examples of what he dubs "pariah landscapes."[81] Jackson suggests that these "spatial expressions of exclusion" have taken a number of different forms but share a concern with physical and spatial separation and banishment, noting that

> the historic record affords examples where perceived differences are not only unacceptable to the majority, but also physical separation or segregation is the sought-after solution, unless outright genocide is practiced. The unacceptable, the rejected, are society's pariahs, and their spatial separation from society may take the form of banishment to a colony, a camp, an institution, a ghetto, or a reservation. These latter entities may be designated pariah landscapes.[82]

His suggestion is that Nazi Germany provides an extreme example of a regime engaged in the creation of "pariah-scapes,"[83] and he describes the Nazi death camps as "the most extreme and cruelest form of spatial banishment that a society and its leadership can devise."[84]

A similar sense of spaces of separation can be seen in the work of the British geographer David Sibley, who uses the term "landscape[s] of exclusion" to describe the process of assigning less desirable space to marginalized social groups.[85] Like Jackson, he recognizes that power is exercised in and through space, with the creation of the "Other" being followed up by situating them in an imaginary or real "elsewhere."[86] While he explicitly references Nazi Germany as an example of a regime with "programs of exclusion which are starkly expressed in spatial terms and connect with clearly articulated ideologies,"[87] Sibley's major focus is upon "more opaque instances of exclusion."

Drawing upon Sibley's work in particular, the British geographer Steve Pile notes the creation of "spaces of domination" (which he contrasts with "spaces of resistance")[88] in the course of the exercise of sociospatial control. Making explicit reference to the concentration camp as an example of such a space,[89] Pile sees "spaces of domination" to be both "spaces of purification and exclusion."[90] It is in and through these "spaces of domination" that "many oppressive practices of authority seek to control and regulate people's use of space, ultimately confining people to highly circumscribed spaces— whether the cloister, the prison, the concentration camp, the housing estate, the township and so on."[91]

Underlying all three essentially overlapping concepts—"pariah land-scapes," "landscapes of exclusion," and "spaces of domination"—are a number of common features. Firstly, all three focus upon "spatial expressions of exclusion." Thus they show a concern with the creation of real and imaginary spaces and places that in one sense or another are deemed to be beyond the pale. Secondly, they reveal a concern with the exercise of sociospatial power. They see control being exercised *through* the creation and mainte-nance of real and imaginary spaces, and thus assume that these are spaces of territoriality.[92] Thirdly, they suggest that the drawing up and policing of boundaries and borders is an essential part of "spatial expressions of exclu-sion." Their work points to a need to focus upon the imaginary or real boundary and the policing of that boundary.

These three ideas—taking space and place seriously, the exercise of power through space and not simply in space (territoriality), and the border/wall/ boundary as central to ideas of demarcation and separation—are ones which I think are useful to those of us who are engaged in writing about the Holocaust. In this book, I want to explore how these ideas can reinvigorate writing on Holocaust ghettos by developing a case study of the Budapest ghetto(s). But I think that they have a broader significance. They can be use-ful, I think, in exploring not just ghettos and concentration camps most obvi-ously but more generally the spatiality and territoriality so central to the implementation of the "Final Solution of the Jewish Question."

As I've suggested, aside from a few partial attempts, that exploration has not really been done. But spatiality and "race" have been examined in other contexts. It is perhaps unsurprising that all three writers—Jackson, Sibley, and Pile—make explicit reference to the spatiality of apartheid.[93] This, after all, is an area that, unlike the Holocaust, has been studied in some depth by geographers.[94] For example, Jennifer Robinson has stressed the "spatiality of apartheid power" and argued that "the organization of urban space into racially segregated living areas was central to the persistence of the racial state."[95] Glen Elder has described apartheid as "a geographical process," noting that "forced removals, evictions from ancestral homes, and the active destruction and re-invention of neighborhoods and communities are just some ways that geographical processes were experienced by South Africans living under apartheid."[96] Taking one particular apartheid place—the mining compound—Jonathan Crush points out that "the architecture of the compound provides important clues about the spatial exercise of power."[97]

In laying bare the geographies of exclusion so central to the exercise of apartheid power, geographers have picked up on the words of South African Prime Minister Balthazar Vorster, who in 1973 expressed—albeit naively—the central role played by space within apartheid. In these famous words, Vorster claimed that the only difference he would experience if he were to be reclassified as "black" would be geographical relocation.[98] While of course being classified as "black" was about so much more than simply living in a particular designated place, it is clear that the creation of landscapes of exclusion was central to the exercise of power in apartheid South Africa. Apartheid was—as geographers have rightly noted—a profoundly spatial experience.

Whilst so explicit in the case of South Africa, the creation of racialized landscapes of exclusion has also been studied by geographers within liberal democracies. In particular, racialized residential segregation in Britain has been studied by Susan Smith,[99] and David Sibley's work on "landscapes of exclusion" focuses on the marginal status afforded to British gypsy communities.[100] The idea that "geography matters" with regard to questions of "race" is not something new in geographical research.[101] Peter Jackson writes that "many forms of racism have an explicitly territorial dimension that requires us to examine the complex interweaving of social relations and spatial structures . . . we should be sensitive to the reciprocal relationship between society and space, recognizing both the spatial expression of social processes and the spatial constitution of society."[102]

However, within the field of Holocaust studies there is a need to restate the contention that geography matters. It is not simply a case of reasserting that the "Final Solution" was implemented within space. (Being a geographer is surely about more than drawing maps.) Rather, there is a need to explore the manipulation and restructuring of space within the implementation of the

"Final Solution," and, more than that, the way in which space both empowered and restricted the implementation of the "logic" of the "Final Solution." In chapter 3, I want to start exploring the first—and more accepted—aspect of thinking geographically about the Holocaust. Taking a sense of place seriously, I want to examine wartime Hungary in general, and Budapest in particular, as the places where the "Final Solution of the Jewish Question" was implemented in 1944–45. In doing this I am interested in thinking about the Holocaust's implementation in space, as well as examining the sense of a number of scales that this implies.

But before doing that, I want, in the next chapter, to explore what I think is the more untried approach of thinking geographically about the Holocaust. I am interested in reflecting upon what it might look like to examine the Holocaust as an event implemented through space. I will not attempt to touch on all of the implications of the recent work of human geographers for Holocaust studies, but will take one particular element of Holocaust space—the ghetto—and explore what a concern with teasing out the spatiality inherent in ghettoization might look like. It is the place of the Holocaust ghetto that is the main focus of this book, and in particular the place of the ghetto in Budapest and the role of the doctors of space who created its various incarnations during the course of 1944.

TWO

ASKING SPATIAL QUESTIONS OF HOLOCAUST GHETTOIZATION

One way to reexamine the critical Holocaust question of motivation—the big question why—is to examine just where the doctors of space charged with implementing ghettoization planned and located ghettos. This seems, to me at least, to be one area where geographical concerns have something to offer to a relatively geography-*frei* Holocaust studies. It is striking how little concern there has been with issues of space and place within the existing literature on Holocaust ghettos. Despite the profoundly spatial nature of Holocaust ghettoization, the tendency within the historiography on Holocaust ghettos has been to focus on themes other than the physicality of the ghettos themselves. As early as 1949, the sociologist Samuel Gringauz, in a study of the Kovno ghetto, identified what he saw as three emerging methodological approaches to studying Holocaust ghettoization, which he termed the "historical-sociological," the "historical-morphological," and the "historical-philosophical"[1]—none of which focused upon the spatial.

Although rather a mouthful, the distinctions that Gringauz pointed to are, I think, useful in highlighting three very different ways in which Holocaust ghettoization has been examined in the last fifty or so years. The first approach, which was adopted by Gringauz in his own work, has tended to see the ghetto as "a sociologically relevant experiment of a Jewish community under specifically abnormal and extraordinary living conditions." By contrast, the second approach has tended to see the ghetto as a place less of Jewish history than of Holocaust history. In these terms, ghettoization was significant as, again in Gringauz's words, "one of the forms of mass destruction in the great Jewish catastrophe of 1939–1945." The third trend in the literature identified by Gringauz was the attempt "to find continuity between the distantly separated beginnings and end of the movement and to discover a spiritual or ethical principle in this continuity" (with European Jewry being created in, then emerging from, and finally being destroyed in the ghetto).[2]

Although this third approach has been considerably less influential in the historiography, the other two have dominated the scholarly literature on Holocaust ghettos. In essence, the differences between these two dominant approaches to Holocaust ghettoization can be distilled to a focus upon the victims versus the perpetrators; a focus upon the ghetto as "Jewish" place versus the ghetto as part of the Holocaust process; and the adoption of the methodology of social and cultural history versus the methodology of political and institutional history.[3] Neither has taken the spatiality inherent to ghettoization that seriously.

THE GHETTO AS "JEWISH" PLACE

For Gringauz, it was the "historical-sociological" approach which held an attraction, and which he adopted in his own study of Kovno. The life span of this ghetto offered Gringauz the opportunity to undertake a "sociology of Jewish inner life."[4] Clearly writing in the context of the emerging state of Israel, Gringauz concluded that "the Jewish sociological experiment of the ghetto community, as exemplified by Kovno, has shown that an autonomous Jewish national concentration is capable of creating the kind of social, moral and spiritual values which a Jewish diffused community could never create."[5] The contemporary context was made explicit in a later article, where Gringauz wrote that "the ghetto of the great catastrophe is the only instance of a full-fledged Jewish community outside the state of Israel."[6]

In the early years of the state of Israel, the "Jewish" ghettos of the Nazi era could be examined as examples of Jewish communal life, essentially removed from their specific and terrible Holocaust context. For Gringauz, these ghettos offered one of the few points of comparison that could be made with the newly established "Jewish" state, given that they were characterized by "Jewish" concentration rather than the dispersal of the Diaspora. Thus the ghetto's significance was not that it was part and parcel of the Holocaust, but that it was in essence a city-within-a-city—a territorial experiment in "Jewish" self-government. In the immediate postwar context, it is perhaps not surprising that for Gringauz, the ghettos were not so much Holocaust ghettos as "Jewish" ghettos first and foremost. As an increasing number of writers have shown, the Holocaust as a distinct event was accorded relatively slight attention in the immediate postwar era in Israel, Europe, and America. Other concerns were far more pressing. In Israel, the process of establishing a new state, and in Europe and America the emergence of the Cold War, which necessitated a redrawing of allies and enemies, pushed the Holocaust to the periphery.[7] Written in this context, Gringauz's early work on ghettos viewed the Holocaust as almost a footnote to what was seen to be the real significance of the ghetto: the antithesis of Diaspora assimilation.

With the emergence of the Holocaust as distinct event, generally traced as taking hold from the 1960s onward, and particularly with the trial of Adolf Eichmann in Jerusalem, such a divorcing of "ghetto" and "Holocaust" became more or less inconceivable. However, the approach that Gringauz had dubbed "historical-sociological" continued to be an influential methodology. Indeed, in the aftermath of the Eichmann trial, which did so much to raise awareness of the Holocaust both in Israel and abroad, "historical-sociological" studies of Holocaust ghettos became even more significant. Studying the inner-life worlds of the wartime Jewish ghettos was central in countering Hannah Arendt's controversial claims made in the wake of the Eichmann trial.[8] In a series of essays originally written for *The New Yorker* and subsequently published with the subtitle *A Report on the Banality of Evil*, Arendt raised a furor with her claims of mass passivity by ordinary Jews and collaboration by their leaders. For Arendt, both contributed to the scale and success of the Nazi exterminations.

Such controversial claims were immediately challenged, and subsequently countered in the literature, in particular through "historical-sociological" studies of the ghettos. Whilst the wider context of the Holocaust was central to such studies, the focus was upon "Jewish" rather than Nazi German actors—upon the victims rather than the perpetrators. And in focusing on the victims, these studies challenged Arendt's broad-brush attack. The role of the Jewish Councils was explored most fully by Isaiah Trunk in his massive study of the *Judenrat* in Poland and Lithuania. His nuanced suggestion that there was a need to recognize local differences and the context within which the "Jewish" leadership operated can, I think, be seen as a direct response to Arendt's work.[9] Arendt's work was also challenged in a series of ghetto studies the historian David Cesarani describes as having " . . . revealed a high level of cultural activity and a remarkable spiritual resistance that signified defiance of Nazi efforts to dehumanize and humiliate the Jews."[10] Drawing upon ghetto diaries, postwar memoirs, and oral history accounts, this picture of the vitality of Jewish life in the ghettos[11] differed markedly from the fatalism of Arendt and the compliance thesis of Hilberg.[12] Martin Gilbert undoubtedly had Arendt et al. in mind when he wrote in his introduction to Tory's Kovno ghetto diary that

> from the fall of 1942 to the summer of 1944, the Jewish Council in the Kovno Ghetto acted on a daily basis to ensure the preservation of as much of Kovno Jewry as possible: to feed, to guard, to maintain morale, to protect. We know about similar activities in other ghettos; Tory's diary is a full and sustained account of them. It therefore enables the reader to see the absurdity of the often reiterated suggestion—made by those who ignore the conditions of all Europe's captive peoples under Nazi rule—that Jews participated in their own destruction. They participated in a desperate, prolonged, and tormented struggle to survive.[13]

Perhaps more than anything, the Warsaw ghetto revolt assumed a central symbolic role in offering a writing of the ghetto alternative to Arendt's. This ghetto has been seen to offer the antithesis to Arendt's thesis, and it is that history, alongside the attraction of the Warsaw ghetto uprising to Israeli society, which has made it the ghetto most thoroughly studied.[14] It was of course a large ghetto, and in existence for a considerable period of time. But there is more than simply a commonsense explanation for why it has emerged as the definitive Holocaust ghetto (to match Auschwitz as the definitive Holocaust concentration and death camp). There is also an ideological explanation, very much rooted in Israeli society and politics of the 1950s and 1960s,[15] and the response and reaction to Arendt's influential text.

However, whilst clearly an important strand within the literature of the last half century, approaching the ghetto in "historical-sociological" terms has—in the long run—been of less significance than studies which have adopted what Gringauz dubbed the "historical-morphological" approach. In short, within Holocaust studies the ghetto has been studied not simply—nor primarily—as the place of the victim, but as a part of the destruction process implemented by the perperatator. In these terms, the ghetto has been seen not primarily as a "Jewish" place, but as a Holocaust place.

THE GHETTO AS HOLOCAUST PLACE

This approach can be seen perhaps most clearly in the metanarratives of the Holocaust, of which Hilberg's has been the most influential. In his work, ghettoization was seen as a major element in the "concentration" so central to the Nazi destruction process.[16] Hilberg made explicit in his text that

> we are not going to discuss here the complex changes which the institution of the ghetto imported into the Jewish communities; that is a subject which belongs to Jewish history, not to the history of the anti-Jewish destruction process. In this book we shall be interested in the ghetto only as a control mechanism in the hands of the German bureaucracy. To the Jews the ghetto was a way of life; to the Germans it was an administrative measure.[17]

Within such an approach, the focus was much more on ghettoization as process than the ghetto as place, and indeed for Hilberg "ghettoization" encompassed far more than simply the creation of the physical places called ghettos. It was a five-step process involving "the severance of social contacts between Jews and Germans, housing restrictions, movement regulations, identification measures, and the institution of Jewish administrative machinery."[18] The ghetto was therefore an element of ghettoization, and ghettoization was an element of concentration—and for Hilberg, "a transitional measure"[19]—and concentration was one element in the Nazi destruction process.

Seeing the ghetto as part and parcel of the Nazi destruction of European "Jews" has characterized the literature generated by the field of Holocaust studies. The main point of departure has been over the precise role played by ghettoization in the radicalization of the Nazi destruction process. At the height of the functionalist versus intentionalist debate in the 1980s, the ghettos established in Poland in the early years of the war played a crucial role in the debate about the authorship and dating of, and motivation for, the implementation of a policy of Europe-wide mass murders of the "Jews."

GHETTOIZATION AND THE QUESTION WHY

A foreshadowing of the intentionalist position can be seen in Philip Friedman's early writings on ghettos. In a 1954 article, Friedman explicitly adopted the language of Gringauz, and acknowledged that his approach was "the historico-morphological method."[20] For Friedman, the ghettos planned and established by the Nazis in Poland from 1939 onward were a "step towards genocide."[21] He interpreted Reinhard Heydrich's 21 September 1939 order to the chiefs of *Einsatzgruppen* units in newly occupied Poland to concentrate "Jews" in cities with a "Jewish" population of more than 500 in proximity to a railway junction—or at the very least a railway line—as a prelude to deportation and extermination. Heydrich himself had spoken of ghettoization as a temporary measure to be implemented prior to the "ultimate goal." Whilst acknowledging that at this stage the precise nature of that "ultimate goal" remained somewhat hazy, Friedman claimed that "it is quite possible that the plan for the physical annihilation had already been spelled out."[22] In the light of such an understanding, ghettoization was seen as being implemented in Poland with extermination as the ultimate goal.

And yet, within an intentionalist approach, ghettoization was seen as more than simply a staging post on the journey to death. Ghettoization was also seen as part and parcel of the overall destruction process. Friedman argued that "there is indirect evidence . . . that the 'concentration' of the Jews was intended as a preparation for gradual extermination, as originally conceived, by hunger, cold, disease, epidemics, forced labor and, finally, by the murder operations called 'actions.'"[23] In a similar vein, Lucy Dawidowicz wrote that "the only institution comparable to the Nazi ghetto was the Nazi concentration camp. . . . Death bestrode the Nazi ghetto and was its true master, exercising its dominion through hunger, forced labor and disease."[24] Ghettoization was thus interpreted as a self-consciously implemented exterminatory measure.

In marked contrast, functionalist writers interpreted ghettoization as a policy envisioned apart from extermination, suggesting that exterminatory policies were adopted only when ghettoization policies were seen by local actors to be failing. In contrast to Friedman's assumption that Heydrich's "ultimate goal" in implementing ghettoization was destruction, Hans Mommsen argued that "the primary motive was revealed in the executory provisions of Heïnrich Himmler's decree for the *Reichsgau Wartheland*: 'The purging and protection of the new German areas' was designed to provide housing and employment prospects for the ethnic German settlers."[25] However, once established, these ghettos presented increasingly intolerable conditions. It is in this context that Martin Broszat argued that a decision was made to implement exterminatory policies as a solution to the starvation, disease, and overcrowding of the ghettos. He posited that "epidemics and a high mortality rate [in the ghettos] suggested the possibility of 'helping nature along' in a systematic fashion."[26] Thus, ghettoization was viewed by Broszat not as prelude to destruction, but rather as a crucial element in the radicalization of Nazi anti-"Jewish" policy. He noted that ghettoization was a "form of self-confirmation and self-fulfilling prophecy," given that "epidemics in the ghettos made them a threat to the health of the general population."[27] Ghettoization as self-fulfilling prophecy was—Broszat argued—"exploited not only by Hitler and Himmler but also by Goebbels and Ribbentrop and by the district military and civil administration chiefs."[28]

In a critique of what he saw to be the excesses of intentionalism and functionalism, Christopher Browning offered a middle path. In an important article on the Warsaw and Lódz ghettos first published in the mid-1980s, Browning suggested that "neither of these approaches [intentionalism or functionalism] adequately explains either ghettoization policy or its relationship to the subsequent program of systematic mass murder." In contrast to intentionalist approaches, he claimed that "ghettoization was not a conscious preparatory step planned by the central authorities to facilitate the mass murder nor did it have the 'set task' of decimating the Jewish population." In contrast to functionalist approaches, Browning argued that "left to themselves, most local authorities followed a course of normalization, not radicalization. In the end only renewed intervention from Berlin induced an abrupt change of course from the policies of normalization to which they inclined." Advocating an approach sensitive to questions of both time and space, Browning suggested that "ghettoization was in fact carried out at different times in different ways for different reasons on the initiative of local authorities."[29]

Taking the ghettos in Lódz and Warsaw by way of example, Browning argued that whilst the two ghettos "were created at different times for different reasons"—in the case of the former as "a strictly temporary device for extracting Jewish wealth,"[30] and in the case of the latter as a measure to limit the spread of epidemic[31]—once both ghettos were in existence, the German authorities in both cities were presented "with identical problems." These "problems" were essentially the "imminent starvation" of the population of the closed ghettos.[32] In this context, Browning signaled how tensions amongst the local German authorities were played out between those who favored a rational exploitation of the productive potential of the ghettos—dubbed "productionists"—and the "attritionists," who argued for their deliberate attrition.[33] In both Lódz, in the autumn of 1940, and Warsaw, in May 1941, productionist arguments prevailed, meaning that "the ghetto was not to be starved to death but made into a productive entity."[34] During 1941–42, however, these policies were replaced by policies of ghetto liquidation emanating from Berlin. Thus, Browning argued that during 1941 a decision was made—in Berlin—to kill Europe's "Jews," which amounted to the ultimate victory of attritionist approaches.

Within the last decade or so, the heat has very much gone out of this debate, which was for a time so central to Holocaust studies. Instead of an attempt to write metanarratives, the focus has shifted to local studies that explore the complexity of the implementation of the Holocaust and the interrelationship of a host of actors at both the center and the periphery. This study is very much along those lines, targeting as it does the implementation of Holocaust ghettoization in Budapest by local officials. However, whilst the intentionalist versus functionalist debate no longer holds a position of dominance, the questions of motivation which it addressed are still pertinent ones. They are central to this study, and indeed are central to historiography more generally, involving the asking of that most immediate of questions when confronted with the past: Why?

The question why has been—and continues to be—asked with regard to the implementation of ghettoization. Within the context of the intentionalist versus functionalist debate it was asked particularly of the implementation of ghettoization in Poland in the critical years of 1940–41. With a shift away from that debate to questions of center and periphery, it is an appropriate question to ask outside of this specific chronology and geography—even of a place and time as far removed as Budapest in 1944. Of course, it is an obvious and easy question to ask, but far more difficult to get an answer to. Questions of motivation lie at the very heart of historical research, but the problems of uncovering motivation mean that historical debate follows any attempt to answer the question why. There are, after all, critical methodological questions as to which sources afford us the best opportunity to uncover intentionality, and that is before we even start asking epistemological questions about whether authorial intention is uncoverable. And once we have identified potential sources, there are further methodological questions about the nature of those sources and what the best reading of them is. And that is where historical debate follows.

I think something of that can be seen in Browning's work on ghettoization, which I have just referred to. Using the paperwork of the perpetrators, Browning identified the motivation underlying ghettoization in Lódz and Warsaw to be concerns with extracting "Jewish" wealth and limiting the spread of "Jewish" epidemic, respectively.[35] However, other historians have offered alternative readings of these documents that suggest Browning has taken the language of the Nazi officials he studied too much at face value. A number of historians have contended that these pronouncements are best read as propaganda (that is, justification) rather than intention (that is, motivation).[36] In the specific case of Lódz, Lucjan Dobroszycki has pointed out that Nazi officials articulated a variety of reasons for ghettoization in a variety of contexts. Thus, "in their internal correspondence, whose function was to help convince themselves, and in their public pronouncements, which were chiefly for propaganda purposes, the Nazis put forward other reasons for isolating the Jews—that they represented a criminal element, were the bearers of contagious diseases, were unwilling to work, and so forth."[37] In a similar vein, Israel Gutman noted in his study of the Warsaw ghetto that "the claim that the Jews constituted a danger to the health of the population at large—which was not entirely unfounded—was consciously blown out of all proportion to serve as a convenient tool of the Nazi propaganda campaign to convince the Poles, as well as the Germans, that the Jews were being segregated out of concern for the Jewish masses of Warsaw."[38] This is a view shared by Friedman who saw the justification of ghettoization on the grounds of health measures as a German propaganda move.[39]

Browning himself has countered such criticisms, which he sees—in the case of the Warsaw ghetto—belying a simplistic thesis that "the Nazi reference to epidemics was a mere pretext to justify ghettoization, which in turn was a conscious preparatory step for total annihilation." To argue thus, Browning suggests, "presumes both a uniformity of view among the various German agencies in Poland and a continuity in Jewish policy from 1939 to 1941 that is impossible to reconcile with the reality of the German occupation regime in the General Government."[40] His dismissal of such criticism is essentially grounded in a broader moderate functionalist critique of the intentionalist approach of a writer such a Friedman.

However, I don't think Browning's critics can be dismissed so easily. Their comments have a certain bite to them, given that there is the tendency in Browning's writings on the motivations behind ghettoization to blur rhetoric and reality. There is surely a need for a more critical reading of the textual sources that give us an insight into what the implementers of ghettoization—the doctors of space—said.[41] But perhaps more significantly, there is a need to study the landscapes of the ghettos themselves, which provide an insight into what the implementers of ghettoization actually *did*, not just what they *said*. This is one area where a stress upon the physicality and spatiality of Holocaust ghettoization is potentially helpful. It necessitates looking beyond textual sources, to engage in the mapping and landscape study of ghettos.

GHETTOIZATION, THE QUESTION WHY, AND THE QUESTION WHERE

In some ways, Friedman came close to adopting that sort of approach in his 1954 article. In stressing the physical realities of ghetto formation, he turned the focus away—somewhat—from the study of purely textual discourses, to the study of discourses in space. Friedman juxtaposed official statements and newspaper articles, which he viewed primarily as sources of propaganda and "German explanations of the need of segregation,"[42] with sources which he saw as revealing "the true reasons for ghettoization."[43] These sources are both textual and nontextual—the physical landscapes of the ghettos themselves. Thus Friedman argued, on the one hand, that "the true reasons for the setting up of the ghettos emerge from allusions made by high officials in private conversations or in conferences held by the Nazi party," and on the other hand, that "the purpose of the ghettos became apparent from *the manner of their formation*."[44]

That focus upon the ghetto landscape as a source in its own right was repeated by Friedman in 1960, in his *Guide to Jewish History*, coauthored with Jacob Robinson. They noted there that "a careful examination of the ghetto maps is . . . of utmost importance in the study of the trends and objectives of Nazi ghetto planning," and suggested that

> . . . a comparison of the ghetto maps with the city maps can help the student to decide whether there was a Nazi master-plan to locate the ghettos in the periphery of a town, in its dilapidated and overpopulated suburbs, or in those sections which were destroyed by military operations. A comparison of the ghetto area with the "Aryan" section of a town will show the relationship between density of population and available living space for Jews and non-Jews, and thus reveal a pattern of overcrowding the Jewish ghettos. A study of the ghetto and city maps will indicate whether gardens, squares and other recreation areas were permitted

in the ghetto area. The ghetto maps themselves will show the non-Jewish enclaves (e.g. the Gypsy ghetto in Lódz) and intimate why they were placed there by the Nazis. On September 21, 1939, Reinhard Heydrich recommended that the ghettos be placed near railroads in order to facilitate the deportations of the Jews. The ghetto maps may indicate whether this recommendation was accepted by local authorities. This does not exhaust their usefulness. They also reveal a peculiar feature of Nazi ghetto planning: the simultaneous creation in several towns of two or even three ghettos, with either no communication between them, or with very little . . . The maps also show the frequent changes the Nazis made in the ghetto areas, almost all of which were meant to worsen the existing facilities, narrow the available space, or move the inmates to new sites . . . [45]

To be fair, Browning does engage in something of this landscape study of the ghetto, writing, for example, of the significance of boundary changes in the Warsaw ghetto.[46] However, his work on the Warsaw and Lódz ghettos contains no attempt to map out the ghettos, nor any attempt to examine motivation in terms other than the discourse adopted by the perpetrators. He is not alone. Robinson and Friedman's words, noting that the sources available for the study of ghettoization are not simply the textual discourses of the actors involved—which must be read critically, with an awareness of discourses of propaganda—but the ghetto landscapes *themselves*, have fallen upon deaf ears in the field of Holocaust studies, dominated as it is by the historian's obsession with written texts. The mapping out of Holocaust ghettos as a way to reconsider motivation is something that has not really been taken on board by historians, and, indeed, the mapping out of ghettos, period, remains rather sketchy. Even in such a geographical text as Martin Gilbert's *Atlas of the Holocaust*, there is only one detailed ghetto map,[47] and it is a map of "The Warsaw Ghetto Revolt, 19 April 1943," which is not so much a mapping of the ghetto as it is a mapping of the revolt.

Things are perhaps changing somewhat, with the publication of a number of books containing ghetto maps. In his more recent book, *Holocaust Journey*, Gilbert does include maps of the Theresienstadt, Krakow, Warsaw, and Piotrkow ghettos.[48] And in the USHMM-published *Historical Atlas of the Holocaust*, there are maps of the ghettos in Warsaw, Lódz, Krakow, Minsk, Bialystok, Vilna, Lvov, Riga, Kovno, Odessa, Theresienstadt, and Budapest.[49] These have been joined in a number of recently published Hungarian works with excellent maps of the ghettos in Budapest,[50] Szeged,

Kecskemét, Makó, and Szentes. [51] In part this book is a contribution to the mapping out of the ghettos. Central to the text are a number of mappings of ghettoization in Budapest both as planned and as implemented.

However, there is a need to do more than simply draw maps, given that geography is about much more than simply cartography. There is a need for readings of those mappings along the lines suggested by Friedman and Robinson, because it is through those kinds of readings that crucial questions about motivation can be addressed. In short, there is a need to ask questions such as where, and how, alongside—and as a way in to exploring—the question why. This means examining the precise location of the ghetto—the where of the ghetto—within the larger place of the city. Doing so is to take seriously the notion of the ghetto as a spatial product which is located in a particular place by doctors of space for functional and ideological reasons (drawing selectively on the spatial history of the city). I want to briefly return to the three themes which I highlighted in the first chapter—taking space and place seriously, territoriality, and the place of the boundary in demarcation—and think about how these might reinvigorate our thinking about Holocaust ghettoization.

GHETTO SPACE, AND THE GHETTO AS PLACE: GHETTOIZATION AND "JEWISH PRESENCE" AND "JEWISH ABSENCE"

One of the central ideas that a concern with the spatiality of ghettoization involves is taking the location of ghettos seriously. In short, it is to recognize that the doctors of space involved in implementing ghettoization in the locality made decisions over where the ghetto boundaries were drawn and where they were not drawn within the Holocaust city. Questions of location have been asked by Holocaust historians investigating ghettoization. A clear example is in Hilberg's pioneering work, where, for example, he notes the decision to locate the ghetto in Lódz in "a slum quarter."[52] This location was significant, Hilberg suggests, given the role of ghettoization in facilitating appropriation and not simply concentration and segregation.[53] Thus he writes that

> As the Jews moved into the ghetto, they left most of their property behind. This "abandoned" property was confiscated. It can readily be understood now that the choice of the ghetto location was of utmost importance to the success of the

operation. As a rule, the preferred ghetto site was a slum, for in that way the better houses, apartments and furniture were left behind. But this solution also had
its difficulties, because the slums were often filled with warehouses and factories.[54]

Implicit in Hilberg's text here is a sense of ghettoization involving both
the creation of spaces of "Jewish absence" and the creation of spaces of
"Jewish presence," which I want to suggest is one important way of reading
mappings of Holocaust ghettoization. Holocaust ghettoization, by definition, is about the drawing of boundaries (whether physical façades or imaginary dividing lines) which separate "Jews" from "non-Jews." The boundary
created by ghettoization acts as both a means of inclusion and a means of
exclusion. On the one side it keeps the "Jews"—the "Other"—in the place
of the ghetto, whilst on the other side it excludes the "Jews" from the "non-
Jewish" spaces of the remainder of the city. Ghettoization can therefore be
a means of gathering all the "Jews" in the city together in one particular
place ("Jewish presence"), and/or it can be a means of making the remainder of the city *judenfrei* ("Jewish absence").

Of course in reality ghettoization involved both. Putting the city's
"Jews" in one place necessarily meant that the remainder of the city was
made *judenfrei*. (And making the remainder of the city *judenfrei* necessarily
meant putting the city's "Jews" in one place.) That can be seen in Hilberg's
words above. In the case of Lódz, ghettoization involved both policies of
appropriation (which is primarily about "Jewish absence") and concentration (which is primarily about "Jewish presence"). Whilst both are achieved
through the location of the ghetto, I think that it is useful to highlight and
separate the two out. Making such a distinction explicit is significant
because the shifting prioritization of ghettoization as a means of exclusion
("Jewish absence") and a means of inclusion ("Jewish presence") reflects
changes in motivation on the part of the doctors of space implementing
ghettoization.

The interrelationship between the ghetto as place of "Jewish absence"
and place of "Jewish presence" is one that is paralleled in a number of other
Holocaust interrelationships highlighted by Hilberg in his writing on concentration. Thus, for example, he notes that the "anti-mixing decrees"
adopted in Germany

fell into two categories, one based on the assumption that the Germans were too
friendly with the Jews and that such friendships therefore, had to be prohibited in

the interest of German purity and National socialist ideals. The other category was based on the opposite assumption that the Germans were so hostile to the Jews that segregation measures were required for the maintenance of public order. There is a simple explanation for this contradictory reasoning. The former category comprised measures which, for their administrative effectiveness, had to be enforced against Germans; the latter consisted only of injunctions against Jews.[55]

The former can be seen, I think, as concerned primarily with "Jewish absence," the latter as concerned primarily with "Jewish presence."

Within the antimixing degrees, therefore, it is possible to see concerns with both "Jewish absence" and "Jewish presence." However, when seen alongside later developments, these measures emerge as *primarily* concerned with "Jewish absence." Writing in the context of Germany, Hilberg notes that "antimixing decrees constituted the first phase of the ghettoization process. Most were drafted in the 1930s, and their aim was limited to social separation of Jews and Germans." This was followed by what Hilberg sees as a "second phase," whereby "the bureaucracy attempted a physical concentration by setting aside special Jewish housing accommodations."[56] There would seem to be a different emphasis within these two elements of what Hilberg terms "ghettoization," with a concern for "Jewish absence" being central to the first phase and a concern for "Jewish presence" being more central to the second phase. There is of course a concern with "Jewish absence" in this second phase also, for example, the initial prioritizing of the vacating of their apartments by Jewish doctors.[57]

I think the idea of "Jewish absence" and "Jewish presence" is also implicit in Hilberg's writing on the implementation of ghettoization in Poland. Here he identified a twofold plan, which again is characterized by a concern with "Jewish absence" being followed by a concern with "Jewish presence." With the implementation of the Heydrich plan for the concentration of Polish Jews, Hilberg writes that "in the course of the first phase, approximately 600,000 Jews were to be shifted from the incorporated territories to the *Generalgouvernment*" and so make way for ethnic Germans.[58] This was to be followed by a second phase, whereby "these 2,000,000 Jews [in the *Generalgouvernment* were to] be crowded into closed quarters—the ghettos."[59] Now of course both phases of this planned concentration involved elements of "Jewish absence" and "Jewish presence." In the first phase, the creation of spaces of "Jewish absence" in the incorporated territories resulted in the creation of spaces of increased "Jewish presence" in the

Generalgouvernment. However, there does seem to be a priority given to creating "Jewish absence" [and "ethnic German presence"]. Likewise, the corollary of creating intentional places of "Jewish presence"—ghettos—meant creating spaces of "Jewish absence." However, in this second phase, there does seem to be a prioritizing of "Jewish presence."

Hilberg adopts—as I've noted—a fluid definition of ghettoization which involves a series of measures of concentration and segregation far broader than simply the creation of closed "Jewish" quarters or ghettos. Within this broader definition of ghettoization, there is, I think, a usefulness in thinking in terms of the twin concerns of the creation of "Jewish absence" and "Jewish presence." But these twin concerns also provide a useful framework for thinking about ghettoization much more narrowly defined as the creation of closed "Jewish" quarters. Certainly in the case of the creation of ghettos in Budapest, it is possible to signal shifting concerns with ghettoization being envisioned primarily as a means of creating "Jewish absence" at times, and as a means of creating "Jewish presence" at other times. And behind such shifting priorities lay shifting motivations.

The value of reading the ghetto landscapes in terms of concerns with "Jewish absence" and "Jewish presence" is in providing another way to get to the questions of motivation—the why—so central to historical study. Thus, taking the ghetto landscape itself as a source has real potential. But stressing the physicality and spatiality of Holocaust ghettoization allows us to do more than map out the ghetto and read the ghetto landscape. Stressing the physicality of ghettoization also acts as a reminder of the central place of territoriality in the implementation of the Holocaust. This is to reiterate in many ways my concerns in the last chapter to explore the implementation of the Holocaust not simply in space but also through space. And one of those spaces through which the Holocaust was implemented was the ghetto. The ghetto was a territorial solution to a series of "Jewish questions"; as Hilberg notes, these included both appropriation and concentration in the case of Lódz, and thus were questions concerned with both "Jewish absence" and "Jewish presence."

TERRITORIALITY AND THE EXERCISE OF POWER
THROUGH GHETTO SPACE

Territoriality is an important concept within geographical writing—in particular, within political geography.[60] Defined by Robert Sack as "a spatial strategy to affect, influence, or control resources and people, by controlling area,"[61] territoriality is about the exercise of power through the control of space. It is—Sack argues—in short, "the primary spatial form power takes."[62] Sack gives, by way of an example, a scene at home where a child is attempting to "help" a parent do the dishes in the kitchen. In order to stop him or her, the parent can put all the dishes out of reach of the child and so limit his or her access to them, or the parent can tell the child not to go into the kitchen. It is this latter decision which is, for Sack, an example of a territorial solution, given that it involves controlling access to a particular space.[63] Thus, critical to territoriality is power and control being exercised in and through space. Of course, power and control can be exercised in other, nonterritorial ways—as the kitchen illustration suggests—but with territoriality, power is exercised through demarcating and guarding a particular place. Territoriality is only one means of exercising control, but it is a means particularly prevalent, Sack suggests, in modernity.[64]

Within modernity, territoriality—the spatial expression of power—can be seen operating at a variety of scales from the global to the local. Something of that variety comes through in the early call of the geographer Edward Soja for political geographers to

> explore systematically and comparatively the great variety of political organizations which have a spatial expression. These include not only Germany and Australia, Idaho and Silesia, Detroit and the Tyrol; they must also involve the Bushman band and the Ashanti confederacy, the Indian caste and the African lineage, Mayan and Yugoslav village communities, medieval guilds and American corporations, the ghetto and the gang.[65]

Of course, writing in the United States in 1971, Soja thought of the "ghetto" in terms of the racialized urban landscapes of contemporary America. However, the "ghettos" of another place (Central and Eastern Europe) and another time (1939–45) also deserve study in terms of an explicit awareness of the implementation of territorial solutions.

During the Holocaust, territoriality clearly played a key role in Nazi efforts to exert control over Europe's "Jews." Not all control involved territorial solutions, but territoriality was central to solutions such as ghettoization, involving as it did an attempt to demarcate and control "Jewish space." And such territorial solutions had their advantages to the perpetrators, particularly in terms of allowing for greater degrees of control. As Sack comments, "it is easier to supervise convicts by placing them behind bars than by allowing them to roam about with guards following them. Controlling things territorially may save effort."[66] However, territorial solutions also had—as the doctors of space whom I examine in this book were well aware —their costs.

That the Holocaust ghetto was a marked example of the territorial exercise of control is something that is certainly implicit—if not explicit— in the literature. I think that is what Hilberg is really suggesting, in his important analysis of Isaiah Trunk's *Judenrat*, when he refers to the ghetto as a political entity. His description makes clear that by political he is refer- ring to the exercise of power through territoriality. Thus Hilberg writes that

> the principal characteristic of the ghetto was the segregation of its inhabitants
> from the surrounding population. The Jewish ghetto was a closed-off society, its
> gates permanently shut to free traffic, so much so that Trunk labels as relatively
> "open" those of the ghetto communities (in smaller cities) that dispatched labor
> columns daily to projects outside the ghetto limits.[67]

This latter reference to "open" ghettos suggests that ghettos could—and did—vary in their degree of territoriality, by which I mean their degree of spatial control. As Sack notes, "territories can occur in degrees. A cell in a maximum-security prison is more territorial than a cell in a county jail, which is more territorial than a room in a halfway house."[68] The degrees here are degrees of control. And what I think is significant when bringing territoriality to the fore in discussing Holocaust ghettoization is that it forces us to ask about the nature of the solutions being adopted—were they territorial or nonterritorial and why?—and also in the case of the territorial solutions, the degree of territoriality being exercised. As this study of Budapest suggests, territorial solutions were adopted in the course of 1944, and the degree of territoriality increased. However, there were also nonter- ritorial solutions advocated, which in some ways were seen as having fewer costs than territorial solutions.

Now the thing about territoriality is that in essence it is a neutral con- cept. It is not implicitly bound up with antisemitism, although antisemitism could and did make use of territorial solutions. In the case of Budapest, as I will examine in chapter 8, it is striking that in the winter of 1944, territori- ality was central to attempts to rescue "Jews" and not simply destroy "Jews." Thus territorial solutions were being proffered by both the Nyilas puppet government *and* a host of neutral powers with legations in Budapest. In part, I think, the adoption of territorial solutions by the latter was about continuing a tradition in which territoriality had played such a central role in controlling the city's "Jews" over the course of the preceding year. If you like, territoriality was the language being talked vis-à-vis the "Jews."

This brings me to the third element, which I think is useful to examine when taking another look at Holocaust ghettoization with a spatial awareness. This is the need for a renewed focus upon the role and nature of the boundary—the ghetto wall. As Sack makes clear, "territories require constant effort to establish and maintain. . . . Circumscribing things in space, or on a map . . . identifies places, areas or regions in the ordinary sense, but does not by itself create a territory. This delimination becomes a territory only when its boundaries are used to affect behavior by controlling access."[69] Thus central to territoriality is the drawing up and policing of borders, to exclude the territorial transgressor. And central to ghettoization is the drawing up and policing of the ghetto wall.

GHETTO WALLS, GHETTO BOUNDARIES

The ghetto wall—the façade—formed an apparently impermeable divide between one world and another—between "Jew" and "non-Jew," between *Todesraum* and *Lebensraum*. In the words of Jean Améry, "the ghetto wall was . . . the demarcation line that separated the Jews from the human being."[70] In this sense the boundary afforded by the wall both kept "Jews" within the ghetto ("Jewish presence") and kept "Jews" out of the remainder of the city ("Jewish absence"). It was thus a wall, which was about control and exclusion. As Yi-Fu Tuan has noted more generally about boundaries, "generally speaking, every human-made boundary on the earth's surface— garden, hedge, city wall, or radar 'fence'—is an attempt to keep inimical forces at bay. Boundaries are everywhere because threats are ubiquitous: the neighbor's dog, children with muddy shoes, strangers, the insane, alien armies, disease, wolves, wind and rain."[71] Tuan's talk of "disease" is a reminder of Browning's work on Warsaw, in which he suggests that it was the fear of epidemics that first led to the constructing of the ghetto wall, and the subsequent policing of that wall. The difficulties of policing the boundaries of the ghetto led to the relocation of the wall in the center of streets to prevent openings being made in the backs of houses along the boundary and thus allow for more effective policing.[72]

As such forced resiting of the wall suggests, what might at first appear to be an impermeable boundary was in reality far more permeable. As Emil Apfelbaum wrote,

> In the view of their inventor, the Warsaw ghetto walls, peppered with broken glass at the top, were meant to serve one and only one aim. The aim was mass murder, which was committed by means of mass hunger. That was the sense and essence of the modest brick-and-glass composition. But the wall-maker must have been slightly disappointed when he learned that his scheme had gone awry. Nurtured by the pathological soil of the ghetto enclosure, it had grown to become one of the pathological paradoxes of life: smuggling, an essentially negative phenomenon, was our salvation. That force was in constant motion, around the clock. Smuggling put a brake on mass starvation, slowed down its tempo and made it less all-embracing.[73]

The ghetto wall ensured control over what went into and what came out of the ghetto. Thus there was complete control over the entry of such essentials as fuel and foodstuffs, all of which had to go in through the ghetto wall. However, this wall was not—in reality—entirely impermeable. Foodstuffs came not simply through the gateways into the ghetto in official transports, but also over the wall in the pockets of smugglers. Smuggling played a critical and paradoxical role in the ghetto. On the one hand it resulted in the creation of a new class of well-to-do through "illegal" activities. On the other hand it was a means of penetrating the ghetto walls and undermining the territorial solution being applied to the "Jews" in the ghetto, which quite literally was a lifeline.[74] Thus in the words of Dr. Israel Milejkowski, head of the hospitals in the Warsaw ghetto: "the smuggler with his blood and sweat, gave us the possibility of existence and work in the ghetto."[75] And smuggling offered not simply food to eat but also a means of resistance, undermining as it did the finality of the territorial solution. In the words of one ghetto rhyme:

Hitler won't be able to cope
With the English fleet
And with the Russian sleet,
With American dollars
And Jewish smugglers.[76]

This potential permeability of the ghetto wall meant that the boundary was a source of anxiety which necessitated policing by the perpetrators, whilst also being a source of opportunity for the victim. The ghetto wall was a liminal space, which had both a sense of definiteness to it and a sense of ambiguity. Such is the problematic nature of the boundary when one is attempting final territorial solutions. And thus examining the boundary and, in particular, contestation and policing of the boundary are critical aspects of thinking about the Holocaust ghetto. As will be seen in this study, planning, implementing, and policing ghetto walls is central to the story of ghettoization in Budapest.

Before I focus upon ghettoization—first as it was implemented nationally in Hungary (chapter 3) and then in more detail as it was implemented locally in Budapest (chapters 4 through 8)—I want to continue the idea of the ambiguous nature of boundaries and think about the drawing up of imaginary boundaries so central to the process of defining the "Jew." Now you might be wondering why I've been using quotation marks every time I write the word "Jew" over the course of the last few pages. In large part, this is a self-conscious strategy to highlight that the "Jewish question" being "solved" in territorial and nonterritorial ways was a "question" entirely of the Nazis' own making.

POSTSCRIPT: DEFINING THE "JEW"

I get nervous when I see "Jewish question" or "Jewish problem" without quotation marks, because it seems to suggest that there really was a Jewish question that needed answering, and a Jewish problem that demanded a (final) solution. And I also get nervous when I see "Jew" or "Jewish" without quotation marks, because it seems to suggest that there was an unproblematic Jew in Europe for whom a final solution could be designed. And yet as Hilberg has noted, the vital forerunner to exterminating the "Jew" was defining who was and wasn't a "Jew."[77] And that process of definition was far from simple or uncontested. The problematic and contested nature of defining the "Jew" came in particular because such definition involved an attempt to draw (imaginary) boundaries between the "Jew" and the "non-Jew" in Hungary. That boundary drawing has its own history, which is worth exploring briefly, prior to examining the kinds of physical boundaries created in the implementation of territorial solutions to the "Jewish question."

In what Randolph Braham has described as "the first major anti-Jewish law in post-World War One Europe,"[78] legislation was enacted in Hungary in 1920 to restrict "Jewish" access to higher education, and thus to the professions. However, the so-called *Numerus Clausus* law made no reference specifically to "Jews." As Katzburg notes, the law "makes no mention of the term "Jew"—but the intention was obvious."[79] By focusing on remedying perceived "Magyar" underrepresentation, rather than "Jewish" overrepresentation, the law neatly sidestepped the need to explicitly define who the "Jew" was and was not.

While the word "Jew" was used explicitly in the so-called First Anti-Jewish Law of 1938, there was no attempt at a thoroughgoing definition of who the "Jew" was.[80] In legislation that limited "Jewish" participation in the media, the professions, and financial, commercial, and large industrial concerns to 20 percent, the assumption was that the "Jew" was a member of the "Israelite faith." However, whilst the law did not define who the "Jew" was, it did define who the "Jew" was not. In attempting to draw boundaries between the "Jew" and "non-Jew" the blurring of these boundaries was officially acknowledged in the creation of a series of exempt categories—if you like, jews who weren't, for legislative purposes, "Jews." Exempt from the scope of the law were converts to Christianity and those with a history of distinguished service in the First World War.[81] These two categories of jews continued to be liminal cases. As I will explore in chapter 8, converts in particular—"Christian Jews"—were discussed as a group requiring their own distinct territorial solution.

Whilst the 1938 law defined only those jews who weren't "Jews," the 1939 law—the so-called Second Anti-Jewish Law—offered the first detailed definition of who the Hungarian "Jew" was. In legislation "concerning the restriction of the participation of the Jews in public and economic life," the "Jew" was defined as a member of the "Israelite faith" or a person with at least one parent or two grandparents who were members of the "Israelite faith" when the law came into effect.[82] Thus for the first time in Hungarian legislation, "Jewishness" was defined not simply in personal religious affiliation, but in terms of the pseudoracial category of ancestry. Alongside this defining of the "Jew," the law also defined the jew who wasn't a "Jew." Exemption continued along the lines of conversion and service to the nation, with the latter category being expanded to include distinguished performances in the political, academic, religious (Christian), and sporting arenas alongside the military.

With the issuing of the so-called Third Anti-Jewish Law in 1941, a new, and broader, definition of the "Jew" was introduced. In legislation prohibiting marriages between "Jews" and "non-Jews," the "Jew" was defined as a member of the "Israelite faith" or a person with two (or more) grandparents who had been born as members of the "Israelite faith." Thus the critical relationship was not that of the parent but the grandparent—and the grandparent's status *at birth*. This definition was tempered somewhat by an exemption measure agreed upon after the bill received opposition in the upper house of parliament. This provided that the jew who had been born a "Christian" to parents who were "Christians" at the time of their marriage was not "Jewish," regardless of the status at birth of their grandparents. Thus there was space for exemption for the convert. However, whilst being permitted to marry a "non-Jew," these converts were forbidden from marrying a "Jew" or someone in the same category as themselves (a jew). Such regulations—reminiscent of the Nuremberg Laws—sought to achieve a certain fixed distinction between "Jews" and "non-Jews."[83] Thus there was an attempt in the long run to obliterate the liminal space created by the "Jewish" convert—by the jew. By marrying the "non-Jew," the convert, it was believed, would be assimilated into the category of "non-Jew," and thus be quite separate and distinct from the category "Jew." In essence there was an attempt to create a binary category, with a clear boundary between the two. Hungarians would either be "Jews" or "non-Jews."

This attempt to create a clear imaginary boundary between "Jews" and "non-Jews" was made visible in April 1944. In the aftermath of the Nazi German occupation of Hungary in March 1944, legislation was introduced which required the "Jew" defined along the lines of the 1941 law to wear a ten-centimeter-wide canary-yellow star on his or her outer clothing in public places.[84] Thus the "Other" was to be made visible. It was this visible "Other"—in bureaucratic shorthand, "the Jew obliged to wear the distinguishing sign"—who was subjected to the territorial solutions which I want to examine in the subsequent chapters of this book.[85] In short, territorial (and nonterritorial) solutions were enacted not against the jews of Budapest but the "Jews" of Budapest—a bounded category created through a history of definitional legislation.

It is to stress that the victims were a constructed group that I utilize quotation marks throughout. Whilst it is potentially irritating to editor and reader alike, I adopt this strategy to emphasize that the category "Jew" is historically and geographically situated. Therefore neither a contemporary definition nor the definition of Nazi Germany fits when writing of the "Jew" persecuted in the 1940s. Rather, there is a need to acknowledge that there is a specific history to the attempts to create an imagined boundary between the "Jew" and "non-Jew." Those imaginary boundaries became—in the course of 1944—physical boundaries, as territorial solutions were planned and implemented by Hungarian doctors of space.

But there is more to my use of quotation marks around the word "Jew" than such concerns with stressing the history of defining and constructing the "Jew" in Hungary. There is also a looking to the present, as well as a looking to the past. My looking to the present is recognition of the dangers of writing about the "Other" in an unproblematic manner. This was picked up on by Henry Louis Gates, Jr. in an important piece on "writing 'race'" published in 1985. Using quotation marks to write of "race," Gates sought to emphasize that "race, as a meaningful criterion within the biological sciences has long been recognized to be a fiction" and therefore that "when we speak of 'the white race' or 'the black race,' or 'the Jewish race' or 'the Aryan race,' we speak in biological misnomers and, more generally, in metaphors."[86] It is in the same vein that I write "Jew" in quotation marks to stress that notions of the "Jewish race" are biological misnomers created by late-nineteenth- and early-twentieth-century racial antisemitism. In doing this, I seek to escape from an unreflective writing which—to cite Gates again—unthinkingly means to "engage in a pernicious act of language, one which exacerbates the complex problem of cultural or ethnic difference, rather than to assuage or redress it."[87]

But my writing of the Hungarian "Jew" does more than look to the present. It also looks to the past, and attempts to afford those subjected to territorial and nonterritorial solutions as a "Jew" the (posthumous) freedom to rewrite their own identity. The category "Jew" was after all not simply accepted by all those thus dubbed by Hungarian officialdom. As the poet István Vas reflected on his own conversations with his fellow "Jewish" poet Miklós Radnóti (who was killed during the Holocaust),[88]

> If I try to recall what we talked mostly about, I remember only the Jewish question. . . . My own point of view was this: if you were born a Jew, you had a choice. Either you said, "I want to be a Jew" or you said, "I don't want to be a Jew." Personally, I took the second choice. But it is quite impossible to say "I am not a Jew." Yet that is precisely what Miklós said: let Hitler do as he likes, let the whole world turn upside down, still I am not a Jew. Miklós was right, at least as far as

he was concerned, and he showed it with his martyr's death. Although they killed him as a Jew, he died as a non-Jew. His last eclogues, elegies, postcards were written not by a Jew, nor by an ex-Jew trying to free himself of his Jewishness.

Rádnoti's desire to choose for himself his own identity is one that I seek to create space for in my own writing of the "Jew." Yet the tendency in the writing and remembering of the Holocaust is to talk only in terms of a monolithic Jewish victim group. There is an irony in this, not lost on Andrew Benjamin when he describes the list of names in the *Gedenkbuch*—the list of German "Jewish" deportees from Berlin:

> They are grouped in a way in which they would never have been grouped. Neither Synagogue congregation lists nor burial lists nor even a list of professions would have held them all. Berlin's Jews were, for a significant part, secular and assimilated. Their Judaism lay in what are usually described as cultural ties and affinities. Even a census that would have demanded the registration of religion could not have incorporated them all. Urban life is, in general, too varied and too cosmopolitan. Some would have married out, others would have disavowed their Judaism, still others may not have even known—or for that matter would not have cared to know—that they were Jews. It would have needed a special occurrence to bring all Berlin's Jews together and to allow them all—for the most part all—to be named. They came to be named in a book that marks their mass death. They can all be named insofar as the *all* who were named are dead.[89]

I can't make those dead live again, but I can give those killed as "Jews" the freedom to choose their own identity.

THREE

HOLOCAUST GHETTOIZATION AND THE SPECIFICS OF TIME AND PLACE: HUNGARY, 1944

If one aspect of thinking geographically about the Holocaust is to recognize that territorial "solutions" were applied to the "Jewish Question," another is to acknowledge that those territorial "solutions" were both time *and* place specific. What such thinking implies for this study of the territorial decisions made by doctors of space in Budapest in 1944 is the need to investigate Hungarian wartime relations with Nazi Germany. In particular, there is a need to examine the vexed question of collaboration at a variety of scales—the actions of national and local government as well as the role played by ordinary Hungarians during the implementation of the Holocaust. Now to explore those themes is to engage with both a contentious historiography and a contentious public debate over the Holocaust past in the Hungarian present. As I want to suggest in the final chapter of this book, the ways in which the Holocaust is—and is not—remembered and represented in contemporary Hungary are very much live political issues. And this sense of contemporary debate is reflected in a contentious historiography, which I will attempt to navigate in this chapter, before turning to look more specifically at the spatiality of ghettoization in Budapest.

THE GERMAN OCCUPATION AND THE HUNGARIAN HOLOCAUST

Given that the marking with a yellow star, ghettoization, and deportation of Hungarian "Jews" took place only in the final full year of the war—

1944—there has been a tendency in both general and specialist literature to emphasize the primacy of the German occupation of 19 March 1944 in determining the fate of Hungary's "Jews." Although Hungary was a wartime ally of Nazi Germany, it was only with the Nazi occupation of this ally state, the majority of historians claim, that the relative safety enjoyed by Hungary's "Jews" was abruptly ended. Typical of such an interpretation is Hilberg's suggestion that prior to the occupation,

> the Hungarian Jews were living on an island. But the island was not surrounded by water; it was a land-island enclosed and protected only by a political boundary. The Jews depended on that boundary for their survival, and the Germans had to break the barrier down. In March 1944, the Hungarian frontiers began to crumble. The Germans overran the country, and catastrophe overtook the Jews.[1]

Such a view is repeated in the more specialist literature on the Hungarian Holocaust, with István Deák writing that it was only after the German invasion that "the road lay open for the extermination of the Jews."[2] A similar approach can be seen in the works of Randolph Braham, who more than anyone else has offered the authoritative writing on the Hungarian Holocaust. For Braham, "the destruction of Hungarian Jewry . . . was to a large extent a concomitant of this German military decision"[3]—the decision to invade Hungary.

This prevailing view in the historical literature—that the German occupation of Hungary led to the destruction of the Hungarian Jews—reflects the alibis offered in the postwar memoirs written by the Hungarian political elite of the interwar years. For example, Miklós Kállay, who was prime minister between 1942 and 1944, claimed that prior to the German occupation, the physical survival of the Jews was guaranteed. He wrote of consistently refusing German demands in 1942 and 1943, claiming, "I gave various ingenious reasons for refusing to send the Jews into ghettos and forbidding the introduction of the Yellow Star and the handing over of the Jews to work for the Germans."[4] What is striking is that the implied suggestion of this former prime minister, that if Hungary had managed to retain its independence then its "Jews" would have remained safe, has essentially been reiterated in the historiography.

However, Hungary is seen not to have managed to retain its independence, with serious implications for its "Jewish" population. As Braham claims, "Ironically, it appears in retrospect that had Hungary remained a militarily passive but vocally loyal ally of the Third Reich instead of engaging in provocative, essentially fruitless, and perhaps even merely alibi-establishing diplomatic maneuvers, Hungarian Jews might have survived the war relatively unscathed."[5] Of course such a statement is an exercise in counterfactual history. Unlike the scientist, the historian simply cannot withdraw one variable to see what would have happened if. . . . Yet, the statement does reveal Braham's stress upon the German occupation in explaining the mass destruction of Hungarian "Jews," and it also reveals Braham's understanding that the occupation of the previous ally Hungary was the result of Hungarian attempts to withdraw from the war.

Here there is more of a parting of the ways between historians. While there tends to be some degree of consensus over the role of the occupation—although I will highlight dissenting voices below—there is disagreement between, for example, Braham and Deák over the role that the "Jewish question" played in the German decision to invade their ally in March 1944. For Deák, "the Final Solution of the Hungarian Jewish Question was the alpha and omega of the Germans' policy toward Hungary, one which they saw as closely tied to their other policy goal, the reactivation of Hungary's participation in the war."[6] Thus, whilst acknowledging the role played by Hungarian attempts to extricate themselves from the war and sue for peace with the Western Allies,[7] Deák lays greater stress upon the unsolved "Jewish question" as the reason for the German occupation.[8]

Whilst Braham saw the unsolved "Jewish question" as "not negligible" in the decision to occupy Hungary in a work published in 1961,[9] in his later writings he tempered this approach somewhat and argued that as a causal factor of occupation, the " 'unsolved' Jewish question" was "important," but "not the determining one."[10] More critical for Braham were Hungarian attempts to come to separate terms with the Western Allies and withdraw from the war. As he saw it, "the evidence now available indicates that these military and geopolitical factors, rather than the unsolved Jewish question, were the determining elements underlying the occupation decision."[11] Such a position can also be seen in John Conway's comment that the occupation was "largely to prevent any defection by the Hungarian authorities from the Axis to the Allied side."[12] This fitted with German Foreign Minister Ribbentrop's own explanation of events during his postwar trial, when he justified the occupation on the grounds that Hungarian troops were being withdrawn and news was received in Berlin of Hungarian attempts to negotiate surrender.[13]

The differences between an approach like Deák's on the one hand and Braham's and Conway's on the other are in essence the differences between seeing the implementation of the Holocaust in Hungary as the reason for the German occupation and seeing it as the result and by-product of the German occupation. With both, the occupation itself is seen as critical in determining what happened to Hungary's "Jews" within the matter of a few short months. However, as I have suggested, there is an important parting of opinions over the question of German intentions in occupying this ally state.

In support of Deák's interpretation, there can be little doubt that Hungary was consistently subject to German pressure to implement a more "satisfactory" solution of the "Jewish question," particularly from 1942 onward. In the so-called Luther memorandum of 6 October 1942, German Foreign Ministry demands were made for the elimination of "Jews" from cultural and economic life, the marking of "Jews," the evacuation of "Jews" to the east with the stated aim of the total "solution of the Jewish question" and the disposal of "Jewish" property.[14] Further demands were presented by the German minister in Budapest, Dietrich von Jagow, on 14 October 1942.

However, the official Hungarian response was one of intransigence. Whilst Jagow was informed that Prime Minister Miklós Kállay would deal with the issues raised by the Germans within his speech to the party conference a little over a week later, no mention was made of the marking or "resettlement" of the Hungarian "Jewry" in the speech, and Kállay criticized those who saw the "Jewish question" as the root of all of the nation's problems. He did, however, mention "his government's determination to eliminate all Jews from key positions in the country's socio-economic life and to solve the acute housing shortage."[15] In discussion with Jagow on 27 October 1942, Kállay further elaborated that the solution of the "Jewish question" within Hungary remained an internal matter and one problematic because of the sheer number of "Jews" involved.[16] Given their central role in the Hungarian economy, the German "solution" of the "Jewish question"—resettlement—was not deemed transferable, especially in the context of an economy geared to the war effort.[17] Similar sentiments were expressed on 2 December 1942 when the Hungarian representative in Berlin, Döme Sztójay, brought the Hungarian government's response to the measures recommended in the Luther memorandum. Alongside the argument against resettling "Jews" on economic grounds, it was pointed out that the sovereign Hungarian nation had been the first to implement "anti-Jewish" legislation excluding Hungarian "Jewry" from the spiritual and cultural life of the country.[18] In essence, this was a declaration that a distinct Hungarian "solution" to the "Jewish question" already existed.

Such perceived Hungarian intransigence resulted in German opprobrium. In discussion with Sztójay on 15 January 1943, Luther issued a warning that Hitler was determined, "come what may, to remove all Jews from Europe while the war is still on," and that the German government could not look at the "danger" of the Hungarian sheltering of Jews "in the long run . . . without action."[19] During Kállay's visit to Rome in April 1943, Jagow contacted Ribbentrop with the suggestion of German intervention in a Hungary where the "Jews" were regaining their "negative" influence. He recommended the replacement of Kállay by a more pro-German government, including the former premier Imrédy.[20] Goebbels's diaries reveal an increasing frustration over the failure of the Hungarian government to "solve" the "Jewish question." For example, after the meeting between Hitler and the Hungarian regent Miklós Horthy in April 1943, Goebbels noted in his diary, a few weeks later, that

> The Jewish question is being solved least satisfactorily by the Hungarians. The Hungarian state is permeated with Jews, and the Fuhrer did not succeed during his talk with Horthy in convincing the latter of the necessity of more stringent measures. Horthy himself, of course, is badly tangled up with the Jews through his family, and will continue to resist every effort to tackle the Jewish problem aggressively. . . . The Fuhrer made every effort to win Horthy over to his standpoint but succeeded only partially.[21]

Frustration was also revealed in the end-of-mission report drawn up by Edmund Veesenmayer in late April 1943. Hungarian sheltering of the "Jew" was seen as an attempt to protect "Hungarian interests," and he viewed the "Jews" within Hungary as the enemy of the Reich, along with "the aristocracy with family relations to the Jews." Veesenmayer argued, however, that given the standing of Horthy, it was preferable to work with him rather than against him. The real target emerged as the Kállay government, with the suggestion that change would come about in the Hungarian attitude to the "Jewish question" only through increased German pressure. Béla Imrédy and László Bárdossy were put forward as potentially more favorable candidates to replace Kállay.[22]

A similar picture of German frustration emerged in Veesenmayer's second report, of 14 December 1943. He reiterated the constant bugbear that the Hungarian government had failed to carry through measures against the "Jews," but also informed his superiors of attempts being made by Kállay to sue for peace with the Allies and extricate Hungary from the war.[23] During early 1943, German dissatisfaction with Hungary over the solving of the "Jewish question" had been the constant theme of discussion between Sztójay and members of the German Foreign Office in Berlin, and Jagow and members of the Hungarian government in Budapest. However, with increasing Hungarian moves to sue for peace, the "Jewish question" became overshadowed toward the end of 1943 by the issue of Hungarian attempts at surrender and the geopolitical consequences of such a move.

And it is here that Braham's and Conway's position seems more convincing. It is these attempts at suing for peace with the Western Allies that led to growing German anger at Hungary's position and ultimately brought about occupation. These attempts had been gaining momentum since 1943. In January 1943, the Hungarian army was devastated at Voronezh.[24] This Soviet breakthrough and the German defeat at Stalingrad in February 1943 shook the early confidence of the Hungarian leadership in German victory. Accordingly, attempts were made to loosen the ties with the Third Reich and reorientate Hungary toward the Western Allies. Attempts were redoubled with the Italian surrender of late summer 1943 and the military victories of the Western Allies in Italy, North Africa, and the Far East and the continued success of the Soviet army. Increasingly vocal calls for withdrawal from a costly and futile war were being voiced by members of the political center and left.[25] However, these voices were not the only ones: from the extreme right came calls for continued involvement and a hardening of attitudes vis-à-vis the Jewish community. "Secret" negotiations—although known to Berlin—on 17 August 1943 between Horthy, Kállay, and a number of senior and trusted politicians ended with agreement that Hungary seek to sign a separate peace with the Western Allies (rather than with the feared Soviet Union). In January and February 1944, Hungary sought to withdraw from the war.[26]

These attempts came as the Red Army was pushing westward, meaning that the surrender of Hungary would leave German forces in Central and Southern Europe open to encirclement and potentially rapid defeat. Therefore, Germany simply could not afford to lose Hungary to neutrality, let alone to the side of the Allies.[27] The German response was the preparation of plans for the potential occupation of Hungary.[28] These plans for the "restricted occupation" of Hungary were signed and issued by Hitler under the code name "Operation Margarethe I" on 12 March 1944.[29] Troops were to be deployed along the border, under the pretence of preparations for a new eastern offensive, and two SS units were to be mobilized. Horthy was summoned to Schloss Klessheim, where at an 18 March meeting with Hitler, he was informed of the planned occupation but given assurances that German troops would leave Hungary as soon as an "acceptable" government was formed. The occupation itself began prior to Horthy's returning to Budapest. On Sunday, 19 March, a parachute regiment of the Brandenburg Regiment seized key positions within Budapest, followed up by the land invasion of eleven divisions under the command of Field Marshal von Weichs. There was little resistance, and Horthy replaced Kállay with a premier (the former Hungarian ambassador in Berlin, Sztójay) and cabinet more favorable to Germany. Given the success of the operation, the majority of German troops were withdrawn in April 1944 and reassigned to service on the front.

That this occupation was the occupation of an ally state raises the question of how enthusiastic an ally Hungary ever was. That issue was central to a divided postwar historiography, which was heavily politicized. For some writers, Hungarian attempts to withdraw from the war in 1943–44 were the last efforts of a country that had been an "unwilling satellite" of Nazi Germany for some time. This phrase—coined by John Montgomery in 1947[30]—was used by émigré writers to describe a nation which they saw to be "hardly . . . an obsequious, loyal ally of Nazi Germany, but rather a country that given its geographic location and understandable zeal for a change in the territorial status quo, acted honorably and at times even thwarted Hitler's foreign and domestic programs."[31] Such a view contrasted with the Communist historiography of postwar Hungary, which dubbed Hungary the "last ally," rather than the "unwilling satellite."[32] This literature pointed to the visit of Hungarian Prime Minister Gyula Gömbös to Hitler in 1933—the first visit by a foreign premier to the new leader of the German nation—and the place of Hungary by 1945 as the last of Germany's wartime allies to remain loyal, to stress a long history of friendly relations between Hungary and Nazi Germany.

The reality was perhaps a little more complex than these two politicized positions allowed for. The entire interwar period had seen contestation between radical and more moderate rightists within the relative political stability of the virtually unopposed rule of a series of conservative coalition governments under the regency of Horthy. From the appointment of Count

István Bethlen as premier in 1921, the values and personnel of the coun-terrevolution (values in direct opposition to the short-lived Communist—and "Jewish"—Béla Kun regime in the aftermath of the First World War) were established in power in Hungary for the entire interwar period. However, whilst at one level the period was characterized by relative stabil-ity, at another level the interwar period was marked by contestation amongst the political elite, within the boundaries of the accepted values of counterrevolution. Historians have pointed to Horthy's attempting to play off pro-German and anti-German forces against each other.[33] Thus, Macartney sees the rapid succession of premiers as evidence of Horthy's control, arguing that "during a number of most critical years the authority of the Regent was incomparably the most important political factor in Hungary."[34] In thus writing, there is in effect a restating by historians of the self-portrayal given by Horthy in his *Memoirs*. There he wrote of his replac-ing of Premier Bárdossy by Kállay as an attempt "to regain Hungary's free-dom of action and to return, if possible, to a state of non-belligerence. . . . The extreme right wing of Parliament, which consisted of the Premiers Bárdossy and Imrédy and their adherents and of course the Arrow Cross [*Nyilas*] adherents, demanded an intensification of the war effort, while the left wing, consisting of the Smallholders Party under Bajcsy-Zsilinszky and the Social Democrats, demanded more or less openly that we should with-draw from the war."[35]

The increasingly rapid succession of premiers was characterized by Hilberg in terms of the alternating appointment of "pro-Germans" and "reluctant collaborators":[36]

1921–1931	Count István Bethlen	
August 1931–September 1932	Count Gyula Károlyi	
October 1932–October 1936	Gyula Gömbös	
October 1936–May 1938	Kálmán Darányi	
May 1938–February 1939	Béla Imrédy	pro-German
February 1939–April 1941	Count Pál Teleki	reluctant collaborator
April 1941–March 1942	László Bárdossy	pro-German
March 1942–March 1944	Miklós Kállay	reluctant collaborator[37]
March–August 1944	Döme Sztójay	pro-German
August–October 1944	General Géza Lakatos	reluctant collaborator
October 1944–February 1945	Ferenc Szálasi	pro-German

Although it is rather too neat to see the rapid changeover of personnel in these years in binary terms—what Braham has memorably termed the " 'pendulum' theory of Hungarian history"[38]—it is clear that the interwar and wartime periods saw years when Hungarian governments were more, and less, reluctant friends of Nazi Germany. The result was, Hilberg suggested, that "as Prime Ministers changed, the fate of Hungarian Jewry changed also. There was a close correlation between the succession of Hungarian rulers and the pacing of anti-Jewish action. The moderate Prime Ministers slowed down and arrested the catastrophe; the extremists hurried it along. The destruction process in Hungary was therefore an erratic development in which periods of near tranquility alternated with outbursts of destructive activity."[39]

For many historians, the close ties with Nazi Germany advocated by those on the radical right were primarily motivated by a desire to redress the hated post–First World War Trianon Treaty which had cut approximately two-thirds of Hungary's territory and three-fifths of Hungary's population.[40] This raises the question of what role Hungarian attempts to undo the terms of the Trianon Treaty played in the Nazi alliance in general and the implementation of antisemitic measures in particular.

TRIANON, THE NAZI ALLIANCE, AND ANTISEMITIC MEASURES

During the interwar period, Hungary's first diplomatic maneuvers had been directed not toward Germany but Italy. The signing of an Italo-Hungarian Treaty of Friendship and Arbitration in April 1927—when István Bethlen was prime minister—has been described as the "first momentous break in Hungary's diplomatic isolation."[41] With the shift to the right associated with Gyula Gömbös's becoming prime minister of Hungary in October 1932, there was talk of the development of a "form of German-Italian-Hungarian partnership."[42] With the 1938 *Anschluss*, Hungary became a neighbor of the Third Reich. However, whilst diplomatic relations between the two nations were strengthened, there was a continued reluctance on the part of Hungary to translate this relationship into a military alliance.

Whilst not committing to a military alliance with Germany, Hungary did gain from German expansionism.[43] Through the First Vienna Award in 1938, Hungary was granted pre-Trianon territory from Czechoslovakia. Regent Horthy rode at the head of his troops—over the bridge at Komarom—into the newly acquired Hungarian territory, amidst scenes of great excitement. However, the nature of the award was partial and, as Dreisziger noted, "it was amply evident that all this was partly a handout from Hitler, a favor granted by a great power to a small one. Later it became increasingly obvious that Hungary's continued enjoyment of that favor was conditional on good behavior. The German leaders would never forget—and would from time to time remind the Hungarians—that when Germany had wanted Hungary's military cooperation, it was not offered."[44]

In 1939 further revision of the Trianon borders was achieved, with the Hungarian occupation of Sub-Carpathia on the basis of secretly granted German consent. However, there remained official, adamant rejection of a German-Hungarian military partnership. Prime Minister Pál Teleki wrote to Hitler in July of 1939, with regard to possible German-Polish conflict, that "Hungary could not, on moral grounds, be in a position to take armed action against Poland."[45] The pressing of territorial claims in Transylvania—the symbolic heart of the Magyar lands—in 1940 achieved further Trianon border revision, as did the acquisition of former Yugoslavian territory in 1941. In the case of the latter, a request that Hungary participate in the March 1941 attack upon Yugoslavia and allow German troops to pass through Hungarian territory was proffered with the promise of the return of the Bácska, the Banat, and access to the Mediterranean port of Fiume. After discussion in the Council of Ministers, Horthy forwarded a favorable response to Hitler. In the event, the land regained was less than that promised. The Allied warning of the severing of diplomatic relations and declaration of war on Hungary if she participated in the German attack on Yugoslavia brought about the suicide of Prime Minister Teleki on 2 April. Four days later the Germans attacked, using Hungary as a route of passage. One day after, Hungarian troops occupied the Bácska.

These years of partially successful revision of the Trianon borders are seen as being achieved at the price of increased dependency upon, and debt owed to, the Third Reich, with Dreisziger arguing that "it was through this process of piecemeal and on the whole peaceful revision that Hungary, slowly and almost imperceptibly, drifted into the Axis orbit."[46] Thus Hungary is seen as—somewhat naively—pursuing territorial revision whilst oblivious to the facts of being inevitably dragged into the Axis.[47] Ultimately, official Hungarian entry into the war came in June 1941 with the declaration of war against the Soviet Union. The immediate causus belli was an unprovoked attack on the town of Kassa, allegedly by Soviet planes, on 26 June 1941.[48] Following the declaration, Hungary committed to the deployment of seven occupation divisions on the Eastern Front, followed by a further nine light divisions.

Parallel to being drawn into the war as a result of its attempts to undo the hated Trianon Treaty, Hungary has also been portrayed as being drawn into enacting increasingly harsh antisemitic legislation as a result of its concern with territorial acquisitions. This has particularly been the case with regard to the three major acts of antisemitic legislation issued in 1938–41. An entire—and dominant—historiography has seen these as essentially functional acts of Hungarian governments concerned with placating their antisemitic ally. Such thinking comes across clearly in the work of both Hilberg and Braham. In his 1961 study, Hilberg suggested that the changing pace of antisemitic legislation in Hungary should be understood in the context of the "debt" owed by Hungary to Germany for a series of territorial acquisitions, arguing that

> the earliest [anti-Jewish] law was drafted in 1938, when Hungary approached the Reich for help in the realization of Hungarian plans against Czechoslovakia. The second law was presented to Ribbentrop in 1939, at a moment when the Budapest government was pleading with the German Foreign Office for its support in the liberation of Hungarian minorities in Romania and Yugoslavia. A third sequence of measures was taken when Hungary joined Germany in the war against Russia.[49]

Braham argued in a similar vein that both the 1938 and the 1939 antisemitic legislation reflected "not only the anti-Semitic policies of the Hungarian governments of the period, but also Hungary's symbolic gratitude to the Third Reich for the political and diplomatic assistance received in the reacquisition of these territories."[50]

Katzburg offered a rather more nuanced approach, suggesting that the "proximity" of the 1938 law to the *Anschluss* was "deceptive," and that "it was not the *Anschluss* which prompted the Hungarian government to introduce the bill." Rather, he argued that "the idea of restrictions on the Jews was conceived in 1937."[51] However, he did suggest that "German involvement was probably more decisive" in the case of the Second "Anti-Jewish Law" of 1939, and that the Law of 1941 "was introduced under direct German pressure."[52] Hungarian antisemitic legislation is thus represented primarily as a sop to the Nazis,[53] offered by a pragmatic Hungarian government in the business of placating an ally busy redrawing post-Versailles borders.

A rather different view is offered by Vera Ranki, in a recently published work, which is, to my mind, equally problematic and insightful. Where Ranki is important is in pointing to Hungarian antisemitic legislation and practice as something other than simply the merely functional response of a government concerned with appeasing their antisemitic ally. Instead she stresses the strength of Hungarian antisemitism in the interwar period in its own terms, and perceives it as intentional rather than merely functional. Thus, rather than antisemitic legislation being introduced to curry favor with the Germans and regain lost territory, Ranki points to the centrality of the Trianon Treaty in changing the way that "Jews" were perceived in Hungarian society.

Under the terms of the Trianon Treaty, Hungary's borders were radically redrawn, with the country losing two-thirds of its former territory and three-fifths of its former population. It is perhaps impossible to overestimate the impact of this treaty upon interwar Hungarian politics and society. Flags were flown at half-mast for the next eighteen years, "*nem, nem, soha*" ("no, no, never") came to dominate Hungarian discourse, and revision of the hated Trianon Treaty became a political staple. But more important, Ranki suggests that this radical redrawing of Hungary's borders had a considerable impact upon the relationship between the "Jewish" and "non-Jewish" population within a shrunken Hungary. In essence Hungarian nationalism shifted—in Ranki's words—from being one of "inclusion" to being one of "exclusion," and thus the "Jews" found themselves effectively "excluded" from the nation.[54] As Raphael Patai suggests in his history of Hungarian "Jews," "their [Hungarian "Jews'"] position within the body of the nation had undergone a veritable sea change as a result of the Trianon Peace Treaty, which at the stroke of a pen transformed Hungary from a large, multinational state into a small one in which the Jews remained as the only population element viewed, in Hungarian eyes, as significantly 'other.'"[55]

Prior to the 1920 Trianon Treaty, ethnic "Hungarians" made up less than half of the population of Hungary. In this context of an "inclusive" nationalism engaged in a process of "Magyarization" in the periphery, Hungarian-speaking "Jews" were seen to be a part of the "Hungarian" nation. However, after Trianon, the "Jew" became—quite literally—expendable. In the interwar period, ethnic "Hungarians" made up around 90 percent of the population of Hungary. In this context of an "exclusive" nationalism, "Jews" found themselves "outsiders" and an increasingly vilified

"Other." The Hungarian "Jews" who had effectively been accepted as the "middle class" during the modernizing period in the late nineteenth and early twentieth centuries, were now attacked as an alien and privileged socioeconomic elite.

That attack came early, with the implementation of the so-called *Numerus Clausus* Law in September 1920. Although the "Jew" was not explicitly mentioned by name within the text of the law, it was clear from the parliamentary debate in the run-up to adoption that the law aimed to counter what was perceived to be "Jewish" overrepresentation within the universities (and, by extension, the professions).[56] That same discourse of "Jewish" overrepresentation can also be seen in the implementation of the so-called First and Second "Anti-Jewish Laws" in 1938 and 1939, which limited "Jewish" involvement in public and economic life.[57] Thus this antisemitic legislation can be situated within a different history. Rather than being situated within the history of German demands on a Hungary indebted to her antisemitic ally for territorial revision, they can be situated within a history of Hungarian antisemitism developing out of a newly exclusive definition of the Hungarian nation.

Now of course both histories are important to what is happening in Hungary in the 1930s and 1940s. What is more difficult to decide is how to weave together these two different stories—one longer term and rooted around shifting ideas of the nation, the other shorter term and rooted around geopolitics. And in many ways the sense of historiographical debate that surrounds the Hungarian Holocaust is about the stress given to one of these factors or another. Whilst both Braham and Deák do reference native antisemitism, their stress is, as I have shown, quite clearly upon the occupation as the central factor in explaining the Hungarian Holocaust. And that is, as I have suggested, the generally accepted position. What is interesting about Ranki's recent work is that she bucks that trend and explicitly rejects Braham's suggestion that Hungary's "Jews" might have survived if the Hungarian government had conducted itself with greater diplomatic astuteness. Rather, she argues, "that Hungarian institutions participated fully in the deportation of the Jews, and . . . Hungarian society accommodated the 'Final Solution' *because* they were immersed in decades of state-sponsored and social antisemitism, and that this, together with antisemitic and extreme right-wing government policies *inevitably* led to the Holocaust in Hungary."[58] Ranki does admit that the German occupation was a "catalyst."[59] Yet she continues to argue that "the ideological, historical, political and social developments, inevitably led to the Holocaust in Hungary."[60]

Now, with all this talk of "inevitability," Ranki offers her own teleology—albeit a teleology without the German occupation. She offers a seemingly inevitable Hungarian Holocaust, once antisemitic governments emerge in interwar Hungary. And to suggest that is of course equally problematic as a teleology that sees the Holocaust to be inevitable post-Nazi German occupation. The tendency in Ranki's writing is to lapse into a theoretical monocausality, which the complexity of historical reality does not fit at all easily with. As the esteemed Hungarian historian who shared the same surname, György Ránki, wrote, "to say that anti-Semitism automatically led to the Final Solution is a gross oversimplification."[61] However, where I think Vera Ranki's work is important is in drawing attention once again to the question of how the domestic developments in 1920s and early-1930s Hungary linked with the implementation of the "Final Solution of the Jewish Question" in 1944.

This really poses a couple of questions. Firstly, to what extent should antisemitism in Hungary be seen as having its own native history? In essence, it is to ask whether Hungarian antisemitism can be understood and explained in its own terms, not solely in terms of foreign influences. Of course it is impossible to artificially separate Hungary from the realities of its interwar geopolitical context. But there is perhaps a need to try to think of Hungarian antisemitism in its own terms, given that Hilberg's and Braham's influential writings on the Hungarian Holocaust have tended to stress the question of Hungarian-German relations in the late 1930s and early 1940s to such an extent (in part I think because of their use of German sources). As Asher Cohen notes, "in Hungary between the wars, a widespread and multiform anti-Jewish campaign of indoctrination was launched," which he sees creating "the aggressive public opinion whose practical results were clearly seen after March 1944."[62] Such developments—which are worthy of much more detailed study—cannot be explained solely in terms of Hungarian wooing of Nazi Germany with a view to reversing the hated Trianon treaty. There is surely much more to interwar Hungarian antisemitism than that.

Secondly, to what extent should the Holocaust in Hungary be seen as a history of continuity and to what extent should it be seen as a history of change? In essence, was the Nazi occupation the great dividing line after which the Holocaust could happen? Or are there greater continuities between the interwar and post-March 1944 period? Of course the period after March 1944 was markedly different in so many ways. The months after the occupation did see the implementation of policies of marking, ghettoizing, and deporting Hungarian "Jews" with terrifying rapidity. However, there is a danger in therefore assuming that, postoccupation, there is an entirely new history characterized by the discontinuity of the German occupation.

There do appear to be elements of continuity between the pre–March 1944 and post–March 1944 periods. Not only were three "Anti-Jewish Laws" passed in 1938, 1939, and 1941 by the Hungarian Parliament, but there were also a series of expropriations and other measures taken against "Jews" prior to the Nazi occupation.[63] During the premiership of Kállay, "the total and immediate expropriation of the estates belonging to Jews" was implemented.[64] But it was more than "Jewish" property which came under the control of the Hungarian state—it was also "Jewish" life. As Braham himself has so clearly shown, there were a significant number of "Jewish" deaths—Braham estimates 63,000—prior to the occupation. Close to 20,000 of these were the so-called "alien Jews"—although it is clear from recent research that a significant number of these "Jews" were indeed Hungarian "Jews"—who were expelled from the country in 1941 and executed.[65] A further 42,000 were "Jewish" males of military age who were placed into special labor battalions, where they frequently suffered poor conditions and physical abuse.[66]

And there is also a danger, I think, in assuming that postoccupation, there was an inevitability to the Holocaust's taking place. To assume so is to fail to examine the precise nature of postoccupation government at both the national and the local level. Rather than assuming that the entry of German actors into the scene ensured the most radical—and terrible—solving of the "Jewish question," there is a need to examine the roles of Hungarian as well as German actors. There was often more continuity at the level of Hungarian officials than would be expected. And those officials played critical roles in implementing policies such as ghettoization. That raises the question of how "Hungarian" the Hungarian Holocaust was: to what extent were Hungarian actors free to make their own decisions, and to what extent were they merely carrying out German orders? And if they were doing something other than merely carrying out German orders, then what motivated them to do what they did? It's those kinds of questions that this study of Hungarian doctors of space is asking.

THE "HUNGARIAN-NESS" OF THE HUNGARIAN HOLOCAUST

Although the German occupation of March 1944 heralded a change in political personnel at the level of the prime minister and cabinet, there is a danger of overstating the political changes wrought in March 1944, particularly at the level of local politics. At the national level, March 1944 did see the victory of radical rightists under Sztójay. And with his appointment, the suggestion is that the coast was clear for the radical implementation of the "Final Solution of the Jewish question." Not only was Sztójay seen to be pro-Nazi, but ultimately the head of what Braham saw as essentially a quisling government.[67] However, Braham does acknowledge that "one of the Germans' primary objectives throughout the occupation period" was to be the retaining of the "façade of Hungarian sovereignty."[68] Thus the destruction of the Hungarian "Jew" took place in a world of Council of Ministers discussions with a discourse of careful consideration as to the "legality" of measures adopted.[69] As Yeshayahu Jelinek argues, "although satellites, it would be a major mistake to consider the East European states as powerless in face of German supremacy."[70]

A critical question in the aftermath of the German occupation is where power in Hungary lay—at a variety of scales from the national through the local. In March 1944, the occupation was not simply an invasion of German military forces, but also an "invasion" of Nazi German personnel,[71] headed up by Veesenmayer who assumed the position of plenipotentiary of the Greater German Reich and minister in Hungary. His task was to be one of overseeing political and economic decision making within the nation and providing political directives to Higher SS and Police Leader Otto Winkelmann, although, initially at least, there was "considerable jurisdictional friction" between the two.[72] Included in Veesenmayer's brief was the directing of "police duties in connection with the Jewish problem."[73] Amongst his staff were several with previous experience in "anti-Jewish" actions.[74] The civilian advisers grouped around Veesenmayer were mirrored by a grouping of SS and Gestapo officials around Winkelmann. Under Winkelmann's jurisdiction came, amongst others, the special commando of Office IV under the immediate command of Adolf Eichmann. Eichmann was accompanied by a commando squad numbering 150 to 200. Eichmann is seen by much of the historiography to have put all his years of experience of deportations to the test with the implementation of the "Final Solution" in Hungary at a remarkably rapid rate.

This can be seen most clearly in a short work written by Braham at the time of the arrest and trial of Adolf Eichmann. There he portrayed Eichmann planning the implementation of the "Final Solution" upon the country's "Jewish" population prior to the occupation, and gathering together a team of experts for an SS conference at Mauthausen on the first weekend in March 1944 where "the blueprint for the 'final solution' was discussed in the minutest detail."[75] Eichmann is then seen as quickly implementing this "master plan" upon his arrival in Budapest. In flamboyant language, Braham wrote that

> Eichmann himself saw his life's dream come true. He finally had a chance to test his well-oiled death apparatus on a massive and grandiose scale in a lightning operation. And, indeed, the "master," as Heinrich Mueller, his immediate superior had called him, proved to have been at his best in Hungary. Having the benefit of years of experience in the deportation and extermination program as directed centrally from Berlin, he could now test his efficiency in the field. Within the course of three months he cleared Hungary (excepting Budapest) of Jews![76]

Such a description makes sense when you think of the context within which Braham was writing. In the context of Eichmann's historic arrest and trial, Braham was explicit that his "primary purpose" was to present "a succinct . . . account of the destruction of the Hungarian Jewish Community during World War II, with special emphasis on the role of Eichmann and his collaborators."[77] In contrast to Eichmann's trial claims that he was merely a small cog in a bigger machine, Braham argued that his work "belies this claim" and "shows that Eichmann and his German and Hungarian collaborators, far from being 'mere cogs' were actually among the originators of, and the ones primarily responsible for the destruction of Hungarian Jewry."[78] Such a German-centric—and specifically Eichmann-centric—approach makes complete sense when one thinks of the context in which Braham wrote, and also when one thinks about the sources Braham drew upon—primarily documents from the German Foreign Office Inland II section. The result is that Braham adopted a German "top-down" approach which, whilst acknowledging, for example, that ghettoization was carried out by Hungarian police and gendarmerie, stressed that this took place under "the over-all supervision and guidance of the Eichmann *Sonderkommando*."[79]

However, with a *Sonderkommando* numbering less than 200, the cooperation of native instruments of state power was vital in ensuring the successful implementation of the "Final Solution of the Jewish Question." And this was recognized by Braham in his two-volume history of the Holocaust in Hungary published some twenty years later, where Braham made greater use of Hungarian sources and, accordingly, greater attention was paid to the interaction of German and Hungarian actors.[80] In particular, the undersecretaries of state in the Interior Ministry, László Endre and László Baky, were represented by Braham as willing and active accomplices. Thus responsibility for the Hungarian Holocaust was shared between Eichmann and Hungarian government officials such as Endre and Baky. Yet, whilst stressing the role of Hungarian officials, Braham's emphasis was still upon the occupation as the critical event, and thus his stress is upon change (the German occupation) rather than continuity (Hungarian antisemitism) in explaining ghettoization and deportation. This can be seen in Braham's recent statement—written in 1999—that, "while the antisemitic policies and exclusionary legislative actions of the pre-1944 Hungarian governments made the draconian Holocaust-related measures more acceptable, the historical evidence indicated that it was the German occupation that sealed the fate of Hungarian Jewry."[81]

Yet, even though Braham clearly stresses the primacy of the German occupation, he—along with all other scholars—does acknowledge the important, if not vital, role played by Hungarians. As György Ránki asked rhetorically, "how can one dismiss the major role of the Hungarians? How can one ignore that ultimately Hungary was one of the countries where organized anti-Semitism became a part of government policy, where anti-Semitic laws appeared as a part of legislation . . . ?"[82] Indeed, Ránki suggested that "the German occupational regime could clearly function only if it could rely absolutely upon the Hungarian civil service. Without the assistance of the various ministries, of the provincial and the municipal administration, as well as that of the police, the gendarmerie, and the army—without all of this help, the entire Nazi occupation machine would have become incapable of operating within a few days . . ."[83]

There is general agreement that Hungarian complicity was crucial to the rapid ghettoization and deportation of the country's "Jews." And it was not simply the Interior Ministry officials Endre and Baky who were involved in the implementation of the logic of the "Final Solution," but the hundreds of local officials who oversaw ghettoization and other policies and the hundreds of gendarmes who oversaw the deportations. Yet the tendency in working primarily from the German sources and adopting an approach that lays greater stress on external rather than internal factors is to portray power emanating from the center and to portray Hungarian officials as simply carrying out German orders.

However, as a number of historians have noted on the basis of examining Hungarian sources, the actions of Hungarian officials in 1944 were not simply limited to carrying out Nazi German orders but also included a willingness to take the initiative in implementing antisemitic measures after the German occupation. Thus Elek Karsai, in a study of the Hungarian administration, concludes that "if any local administration deviated from the national directives, they were aimed at exceeding the target: either by implementing the government decrees ahead of schedule or by taking more severe and harsher measures than required. There are by far less instances of milder measures put in force."[84] And this initiative taking by local officials was, Béla Vágo argues, crucial to the success of the venture. He suggests that

> although the major catastrophe occurred only after the German occupation of the country . . . all that happened in the country after that day was perpetrated not only with Hungarian connivance, but mainly by Hungarians who zealously exploited the new opportunities, and partly took over the initiative for the de-Jewification and the deportation. This policy was supported by the majority of the Hungarian people. Without this willingness, collaboration and local initiatives, the German occupation itself could not have led to the destruction of Hungarian Jewry.[85]

These suggestions of local initiative in the implementation of antisemitic measures go somewhat against the grain of the emphasis in Braham's dominant writing on the Hungarian Holocaust. His stress, as I have suggested, is upon the role of the "group of dejewification experts composed of members of the Eichmann-*Sonderkommando* and a number of Hungarians" in implementing a policy such as ghettoization,[86] whilst portraying city officials as simply carrying out orders. Typical of his approach are comments such as "while the unrealistic deadline set by the Minister of the Interior [for drawing up lists of "Jewish" places of residence] could not possibly be met, the local authorities lost no time in implementing the decision" and "in response to the orders of Baky and Béla Jurcsek, who doubled as Minister of Agriculture and Minister of Supply, the mayors of the local communities asked the local Jewish communal leaders to prepare lists of all the Jews in their particular communities on the excuse that the sugar and soap ration coupons were being replaced by new ones."[87] Both suggest an approach that is very much top-down. Yet, Braham loses something of the dynamic of the relationship between national and city scales, which was not simply a one-way process of blind acceptance.

In contrast to Braham, Vágo lays greater stress on the role played by local actors, and thus sees the Hungarian Holocaust as more than simply a German import, applied from the top down. His argument is that "although policy after March 19, 1944 was suggested and directed by the Nazis, the methods and details were worked out by the local authorities, and instructions were sent to the different organs mainly by the Under-Secretaries of State in the Ministry of Internal Affairs [Interior Ministry], and also by a few other Ministries . . ."[88] This view of "methods and details" being "worked out by the local authorities" is brought out by Karsai, writing on the role of the local administration in the implementation of the Hungarian Holocaust. With particular reference to the implementation of ghettoization in the locality, Karsai writes that "the middle and lower ranking authorities of administration implemented the directives of the Ministry of the Interior in whatever way they saw fit, and used their own judgement to give them actual content."[89]

That local officials took initiative and shaped anti-"Jewish" policies in the locality can be seen in Judit Molnár's study of Szeged. There she points out that an official announcement restricting "Jewish" access to steam baths in the city *predated* the Interior Ministry legislation of 2 May 1944. As early as 28 April 1944, the local press had carried just such an announcement grounded in concerns about public health.[90] Moreover, the Interior Ministry regulations, when published, were contested within the locality by the city's Works Committee. They requested that the Mayoral Office not implement the designation of certain days and hours for "Jewish" bathing out of fears that such legislation would result in the spread of infection. The result was that when the ghetto was established, "shower-baths" were set up within the ghetto area solely for "Jewish" use, in order to meet these local concerns.[91]

That there were clear examples of both initiative being taken in the locality and national orders being contested in the locality is, perhaps, not that surprising. From the time of the Austro-Hungarian Empire, the principle of local autonomy had been enshrined in Hungarian politics. Under legislation enacted in 1870, individual counties were granted a degree of administrative independence and decision-making power.[92] It should be noted that the following decades did see power increasingly shift away from the locality to the center;[93] however, the continuing tension between central and local power was personified in the existence of both lord lieutenants and deputy lord lieutenants in each county. Lord lieutenants were central government appointees, while their deputies were elected locally for their ten-year period in office. Although lord lieutenants had considerable power, Karsai suggests that in the interwar period, day-to-day decision making was left more or less to locally elected officials.[94] A similar personification of centrally and locally appointed individuals can be seen in Budapest with the coexistence of the lord mayor and mayor. Although the lord mayor was, from 1934, the appointee of the regent,[95] Budapest's mayors, on the other hand, continued to be locally elected and responsible for day-to-day decision making in the capital.

POLITICS AT THE LOCAL SCALE—BUDAPEST, 1944

In the wake of the German occupation, Veesenmayer informed Berlin that Prime Minister Sztójay was committed to maintaining the administrative autonomy of Budapest.[96] This commitment was seen by the writers of an *Actio Catholica* report as being shared by László Endre, who they described as an "adherent of autonomy."[97] However, this autonomy was to be terminated if measures were not carried through with due speed and comprehensiveness. In particular, Veesenmayer noted that the newly appointed lord mayor of Budapest, Tibor Keledy, was to "thoroughly comb" the city administration. In effect, the maintenance of local autonomy was dependent upon the "right" type of people being officeholders in the locality.

Keledy had been appointed lord mayor of Budapest on 8 April 1944, following the resignation of the previous lord mayor, Tivadar Homonnay. Keledy had been a municipal official in Budapest prior to being appointed mayor of Kolozsvár, when the city was reincorporated into "rump Hungary" after the Second Vienna Award.[98] His appointment as lord mayor of Budapest was greeted with approval by the rightist press.[99] That he was the "right" kind of man was confirmed by his acceptance speech, in which he described the damage done to the nation in general, and Budapest in particular, by a "foreign mentality" [i.e., the "Jews"].[100]

Keledy's appointment as lord mayor was but one example of the more or less wholesale replacement of lord mayors/lord lieutenants in the postoccupation period.[101] There was nothing very unusual about such replacements. The constitutional practice in interwar Hungary was that the resignation of the national government was followed by government-appointed local officials offering their resignation to the incoming government.[102] Therefore, with the resignation of Kállay and the appointment of a new government under the leadership of Sztójay, a wave of resignations in the locality was to be expected. This process was reported by Veesenmayer when he wrote to the German Foreign Ministry on 10 May that "the purging of the Hungarian provincial administration was satisfactorily underway."[103]

However, the historian Judit Molnár, writing on the situation in Szeged, concludes that the number of replacements and resignations in the locality were surprisingly few.[104] Whilst there was an extensive replacing of lord lieutenants,[105] Molnár notes that deputy lord lieutenants and mayors "were not affected until the end of June, by which time the deportations were complete."[106] The two changes that did take place at these administrative levels within the Szeged area were both the results of promotions rather than resignations.[107] Thus whilst accepting that there was a widespread changing of the guard at the highest levels of local administration, Molnár points to continuity—as far as the implementation of ghettoization was concerned—at the crucial levels of deputy lord lieutenant and mayor.

Molnár's suggestion of little in the way of change at these levels of local administration in the Szeged district until the end of June seems also to hold true for Budapest, where there clearly was continuity, as well as change, of key city government personnel. The main change was the appointment of a new mayor. The existing mayor, Károly Szendy, "retired" (or, rather, was pensioned off) at the 12 April General Assembly. His replacement was Ákos Doroghi Farkas, who was appointed on 14 April but only officially elected mayor by a clear majority of the City Council meeting in emergency session on 19 May 1944.[108] Doroghi Farkas's credentials made him an ideal candidate for the position of city mayor. Coming from the far right of the governing Magyar Élet Párt (Hungarian Party of Life— hereafter M.É.P.) and as one of the founding members of the Hungarian Institute for the Researching of the Jewish Question (along with—among others—László Endre),[109] he was clearly the right kind of man. He had been chief councilor in the presidential section of the municipality since 1934, later moving to the business administration section, and had unsuccessfully attempted to gain election to the position of deputy mayor in the 29 March 1939 election.[110] At the M.É.P. party conference held at the City Hall on 20 June 1944 by the party's city leadership, Doroghi Farkas was welcomed warmly and wished well in his taking up high office "in historic times."[111]

The "strong spirit of national race-protection" central to the Hungarian extreme right was seen as the very "ideological basis of the life and work of the Municipal Authority."[112]

However, whilst the appointment of Doroghi Farkas as mayor was clearly a case of a significant change of personnel in Budapest politics, both the existing deputy mayors, Dr. László Bódy and Dr. Endre Morvay, remained in place, as did most of the district councilors. Indeed, given the time lag between the retirement of the previous mayor and the election of Doroghi Farkas, Bódy assumed the role of acting mayor during the interregnum. Although both he and Morvay were members of the ruling M.É.P., neither could be seen as members of the extreme rightist grouping of Doroghi Farkas et al. Thus, in April 1944, their continuing in their positions was by no means certain.[113] Bódy was referred to as "the Jew's great friend" in a letter of congratulation—upon his Interior Ministry appointment of 15 April 1944—from a friend of László Endre. The writer of the letter saw him as a member of the "city hall jungle," headed up by "the Freemason Szendy" and "controlled by Jewish Budapest."[114]

Bódy himself later suggested to the "Jewish" leader Ottó Komoly that the reason why he had not been appointed mayor in Budapest was "that I did not want to issue and sign the decree relating to the concentration of the Jews."[115] Komoly's reply is revealing. His statement "I was aware of this right away when I saw that there was only one applicant, Doroghi Farkas, for the position of Mayor, whereas I knew that you were the most suitable candidate for the position" suggests that the appointment of Doroghi Farkas over Bódy was greeted with some surprise by interested onlookers. Clearly, Doroghi Farkas's appointment was not the norm. His predecessor, Szendy, had first been elected deputy mayor (in May 1934), before being elected mayor (in December 1934). However, such a pattern of progression was not to be practiced in the context of the changes within municipal government in March–April 1944. Rather, Doroghi Farkas "leapfrogged" Bódy in the uncontested election of the city's new mayor. It would seem that the new government had a clear preference for Doroghi Farkas over Bódy. And yet, it does seem that Bódy played an important role in issuing "anti-Jewish" legislation, particularly during the period prior to Doroghi Farkas's official "election" on 19 May, and, as I suggest in chapter 7, this included clear acts of initiative.

What is perhaps most significant about such examples of initiative on the part of local officials, significant numbers of whom were in office prior to the Nazi occupation, is that it becomes impossible to explain them simply in terms of Nazi influence. Thus the whole strand of historiography that stresses the impact of German pressure upon Hungary at the diplomatic level becomes somewhat redundant when one is seeking to explain such seemingly unilateral actions taken at the local level. At the local level there seems to me a need to take on board the historiography which points to domestic developments from the 1920s onward and considers the role of Hungarian antisemitism. Of course, there is a need to acknowledge more fully than Vera Ranki does that the occupation is crucial to our understanding of the antisemitic measures implemented in mid-1944. However, there has perhaps been a tendency to lay too much stress upon the German influence, at the neglect of examining the meanings and motives of Hungarians—including ordinary Hungarians.

The role of ordinary Hungarians is important, given the tendency during the Communist period to exonerate the masses. Károly Balla, in the context of a war crimes trial held in Cluj in 1946, noted the tendency to exonerate "ordinary Hungarians" and protested:

> Please tell me where . . . the notion of "Hungarian people" ends, and where the "hordes of Hungarian Fascists" starts. This question torments me because here I fear a terrible mystification and here I suspect that I am going to be misled again, exactly as before, when we were driven into the ghetto by lies, then put into cattlecars and sent to the gas chambers. Let us not allow ourselves to be deceived again, and let us reject the illusions created by the tales we are being fed on. If we swallow these tales once more, we shall again pay a heavy price for doing so.[116]

Within the Communist historiography, the tendency was to dismiss whatever popular support there was for the native National Socialist movement, as a phenomenon largely associated with the support of the "bourgeoisie" and "the numerically considerable backward stratum of urban and village semi-proletarians and proletarians who were void of any class consciousness."[117] In terms of such an interpretation, the "liberation" of a people still under the "shackles" of fascist rule by the victorious Red Army, which marched into Budapest in January 1945, assumed a heightened importance.

Very much against the grain, István Bibó, in the immediate postwar period, did draw attention to the role of Hungarian society at large in the implementation of the logic of the Holocaust in his seminal 1948 essay "The Jewish Question in Hungary after 1944." There Bibó bravely suggested that "the anti-Jewish legislative measures were supported, if not by a clearly visible majority, then at least by a force more massive than their opponents."[118] What Bibó saw to be a "slippage" from the 1930s onward resulted in the events of 1944, which for Bibó provided evidence of "the moral decline of Hungarian society."[119] The opportunities for upward mobility which "non-Jews" seized hold of in 1944 Hungary provided, Bibó claimed, "an appalling picture of insatiable avarice, a hypocritical lack of scruples, or at best cold opportunism in a sizeable segment of this society that was profoundly shocking not only to the Jews involved, but also all decent Hungarians."[120]

In many ways Bibó's willingness to address full-on the "Hungarianness" of the events of 1944, and to link these to developments in the interwar period, was exceptional rather than the norm in the immediate postwar era. Rather than casting the Hungarian Holocaust as essentially a German—or fascist—product (something from outside), there is, it seems to me, a need to try to understand the complex interplay between longer-term domestic factors and shorter-term external factors which provide the context to the events of 1944, and the complex interplay between Hungarian and German actors at a variety of scales in implementing the "Final Solution of the Jewish Question."

Before turning to examine the detailed implementation in Budapest of one element of that final solution—ghettoization—under the leadership of Doroghi Farkas, I want to reinvestigate more generally the place of ghettoization within the Hungarian Holocaust, and specifically the motivation behind implementing ghettoization. In essence I want to ask the question why with regard to Hungarian ghettoization, before in the remainder of the book suggesting that actually asking the question where might be a good way to try to uncover critical questions of motivation and reinvigorate our understanding of Holocaust ghettoization.

HOLOCAUST GHETTOIZATION IN HUNGARY AND THE QUESTION WHY

The result of the stress within the historiography of the Hungarian Holocauast upon its inevitability after the Nazi German occupation in March 1944 has been that the question why has been seen as rather redundant. This has clearly been the case within the literature on ghettoization. The generally accepted view is that the establishing of ghettos in Hungary—as part and parcel of the Nazi destruction process—was more or less "inevitable." With the occupation came, according to Randolph Braham, whose work dominates the field, the implementation of a Holocaust "master plan worked out by the German and Hungarian dejewification experts"[121] that called for ghettoization, followed by deportation. Cohen adopts a similar approach in pointing to the postoccupation implementation of ghettoization and "mass evictions" as elements of "the process . . . characteristic of the German policy during the period of the Holocaust."[122] The suggestion is that the "normal" elements of the Nazi destruction process were "exported" to Hungary after the occupation. As Braham puts it, "the Eichmann *Sonderkommando* followed the well-tested approach which had been employed successfully in other Nazi-occupied countries . . . marking the Jews, placing them into ghettos, and deporting them . . . "[123] As all this talk of "master plans," "characteristic" elements, and "well-tested approaches" makes clear, there is not seen to be anything unusual about what happened postoccupation, including ghettoization. What is seen to be unusual is the rapidity with which it all happened. As Braham notes, "in no other country was the Final Solution program—the establishment of the *Judenrate*, the isolation, expropriation, ghettoization, concentration, and deportation of the Jews—carried out with as much barbarity and speed as in Hungary."[124]

Certainly the speed with which Hungary's "Jews" were subjected to a raft of anti-"Jewish" measures after the German occupation is striking. From 5 April, Hungarian "Jews" were required to wear a ten-centimeter canary-yellow star on outer clothing in public places. The day before, 4 April, ghettoization was first discussed at a meeting of Hungarian and German officials. This meeting resulted in the issuing of a confidential ghettoization order, signed by Secretary of State in the Interior Ministry Baky, on 7 April. [125] Three weeks later, ghettoization was officially sanctioned by ministerial decree.[126] A further three weeks or so later, mass deportations commenced. Between 15 May and 8 July 1944, 437,402 "Jews" were transported from ghettos in provincial Hungary to Auschwitz-Birkenau, where the majority were gassed and cremated on arrival.[127]

Given the speed with which these by-now-familiar measures were implemented, and the speed with which the "Jews" from provincial Hungary—Alice Lok Cahana amongst them—were taken to Auschwitz-Birkenau, it is understandable that the literature on the Hungarian Holocaust tends toward teleological explanations. As I have suggested, the dominant historiography sees the Nazi occupation as sealing the fate of

Hungarian "Jews," with the Nazis bringing with them the characteristic elements of their "Final Solution of the Jewish Question": marking with the yellow star, ghettoization, deportation. This assumes Hungary to be essentially virgin soil on which the Nazi destruction process is rapidly carried out. In such a view, ghettoization was simply the inevitable forerunner to mass deportations. The short-lived ghettos established in Hungary need little more explanation than as simply functional gathering points en route to Auschwitz. Ghettos were established because the Nazi destruction process was implemented in Hungary—end of story.

Now given the speed with which things happened in Hungary, and the short-lived nature of all the ghettos but those in Budapest, such assumptions seem well grounded. Chronologically, the German occupation *was* more or less immediately followed by a series of anti-"Jewish" regulations including ghettoization. And chronologically, ghettoization *was* rapidly followed by mass deportations from provincial Hungary to Auschwitz-Birkenau. However, chronology alone is no explanation. I want, very briefly in the closing pages of this chapter, to begin to question what appears to be an overly teleological approach in the existing literature.[128] In the chapters that follow, I hope to develop this questioning of the historiographical orthodoxy through a study of the decision making of the doctors of space who implemented territorial policies in the locality.

In one sense, therefore, this work is a work of revisionist history—revisionist in the sense that it questions the existing literature on the Hungarian Holocaust. However, it is perhaps worth stating explicitly that it is not "revisionist" in the way in which that word has come to be used in discussions of the Holocaust. Within Holocaust studies, revisionism has become essentially synonymous with denial. (That two such radically different terms have become effective synonyms does perhaps say something about Holocaust studies.) In this study I am *not* engaging in a revisionism that equates with denial. In questioning what I see to be overly teleological explanations of the Hungarian Holocaust, I am not attempting to escape from the realities of what Hungarian "Jews" experienced in 1944. They were marked with a yellow star, placed into ghettos, and deported—Budapest's "Jews" aside—to Auschwitz-Birkenau. There, hundreds of thousands of Hungarian "Jews" were subjected to mechanized mass murder in gas chambers. To question the inevitability of all of this is not to claim that it did not happen. It is rather to suggest that in some senses at least it did not "need" to happen (as teleological explanations tend to assume). It is to refuse to accept simple (and simplistic) explanations for why Hungarian "Jews" were subjected to the "Final Solution of the Jewish Question" and in their place to attempt to confront the Hungarian Holocaust in all its complex (and complicated) horror (and banality).

Whilst the historiographical consensus sees deportation as the "logic" underlying ghettoization, such assumptions were challenged in Carlile Macartney's two-volume history of modern Hungary published in 1957. There he wrote that "the Ghetto Order [issued on 28 April] (which was put into operation immediately) had been drafted [in early April] when there was still no thought of deportations."[129] Macartney saw initial ghettoization plans as not providing "either for massacre, deportation out of Hungary, nor even, on paper, for spoilation, *but only for segregation inside Hungary*, and it is possible that those who drafted it—and perhaps at the time even Baky and Endre—were thinking only in those terms."[130] Whilst acknowledging that ghettoization was officially ordered at the end of April "just as the deportations were sanctioned," Macartney saw this to be "probably a coincidence," albeit a "coincidence" which "greatly facilitated the planning of the further action."[131] Thus rather than simply viewing the implementation of ghettoization in April 1944 as part and parcel of the Nazi "master plan," Macartney saw it as an element of the radicalization of anti-"Jewish" policy in Hungary. For Macartney, the 4 April meeting where ghettoization was discussed was a radicalizing catalyst, where "the threads which were soon to lead to the ghastly 'final solution' ran disastrously together."[132]

Now this interpretation of ghettoization contrasts quite markedly with Braham's view of the 7 April order as spelling "out the procedures to be followed in the ghettoization, concentration, and deportation of the Jews."[133] It is somewhat surprising that Braham makes no attempt to engage with Macartney's alternative interpretation, despite his quite extensive use of Macartney's work elsewhere. There can be little doubt that Macartney's work is problematic, given his pro-Horthy line. However, there is a big difference between adopting a critical reading of Macartney's thesis and simply dismissing it out of hand, or just ignoring it. What Macartney does force is a reconsideration of the dominant historiographical interpretation of Hungarian ghettoization offered by Braham. I would tentatively suggest that Braham's overly teleological interpretation of the April ghettoization legislation is flawed in two main ways. Firstly, it relies upon a problematic translation of the 7 April ghettoization order, and, secondly, it fails to engage with the two ghettoization texts in their entirety.

GHETTOIZATION TEXTS—
7 APRIL AND 28 APRIL GHETTO ORDERS

In *The Politics of Genocide*, Braham used the translation of the 7 April ghetto order first published in Lévai's 1961 *Eichmann in Hungary*.[134] This translation differed quite significantly from Lévai's earlier translation in 1948, *Black Book on the Martyrdom of Hungarian Jewry*, and signaled a clear shift toward an interpretation much more centrally based upon ghettoization as the intentional prelude to deportations to concentration camps. Whilst the phrase "*a zsidóságot . . . a kijelölt gyûjtõtáborokba kell szállítani*" had been translated as "the Jews will be taken to prearranged assembly centers" in 1948, by 1961 it became "the Jewry . . . is to be transported to assigned concentration camps."[135] Rendering "*gyûjtõtáborok*" as "concentration camps" conjures up images of Auschwitz, which the more neutral—and arguably much more appropriate—translation "assembly centers" simply does not.

Within the context of both the Eichmann trial and the domestic political situation in Hungary in the early 1960s, the changes to the later translation make sense. However, the danger in uncritically adopting this later translation—as Braham does—is that it means uncritically accepting the agenda behind this work. Writing at the time of the Eichmann trial, Lévai offered an unashamedly Eichmann- and German-centric picture of the implementation of the "Final Solution" in Hungary, with the "sincere hope that what I have done will help justice in meting out a deserved punishment for the most cold-blooded genocidal arch-fiend of all times."[136] Lévai's "arch-fiend" Eichmann had decided by early April 1944 that "the time had come to start the process of deportation,"[137] hence the intentionalism which comes through in his 1961 translation of the 7 April ghettoization order.

Aside from the problematic translation of a number of key phrases, the full text of the ghettoization order itself challenges Braham's teleological reading. Rather than supporting an interpretation that sees the ghettoization plans of early April as the intended prelude to widespread deportations to "concentration camps," the text itself represents the transportation of "Jews" to "assembly centers" as the prelude, *not* so much to mass deportation,[138] *as* to relocation of part of the Jewish community "later," within urban ghettos. The "*gyûjtõtáborok*" envisioned by the 7 April Interior Ministry regulations were both temporary and of a pragmatic nature. The longer term goal was the relocation of the "Jewry" into specifically designated "Jewish" buildings or ghettos in each locality. However, Braham—and he is not alone in this[139]—is highly selective in his choice of which elements of the document he refers to. Whilst he cites the entire text of the 7 April document, he skates over the vast majority of the text in his interpretation.[140]

The focus of the main body of the text is upon the sheer logistical problems of shifting large numbers of persons around the city. In particular, what emerges is a concern over the potential for temporary homelessness (especially for the "non-Jewish" population) during the lag time between moving out of one property and moving into another which had to be vacated by the time of new occupation. Therefore the order stipulated that "Jews" were to be transported to transit camps, and then at a later point (once these buildings had been vacated by their "non-Jewish" inhabitants) accommodated in "Jewish" buildings or ghettos, assigned to them by the police authorities.[141] Those "non-Jews" vacating what were to become "Jewish" buildings were to be compensated with the provision of "residences of a similar value and similar rent" made available by the fact that "Jews" were required to move first into temporary transit camps before relocating into urban ghettos.

Alongside this concern with the pragmatics of ghettoization, it is clear that ghettoization was also viewed as an opportunity for the appropriation of "Jewish" wealth. "Jewish" homes and shops were to be sealed, "Jewish" foodstuffs and livestock were to be used "to cover the requirements of the army and public security organs, and secondly those of the local population," and money and valuables were to be handed over to the National Bank. The "Jews" were to be transported to the transit camps by train "as prisoners," and only permitted to take with them luggage weighing up to fifty kilograms, two changes of underwear, and food for no more than 14 days. Such regulations meant that more remained for appropriation.

This discourse of ghettoization as socioeconomic measure is detailed quite fully within the 7 April ghettoization order and was central to the Ministerial articulation of ghettoization at the end of April. However, these socioeconomic elements to ghettoization legislation are ignored by Braham when he considers the 7 April order, and dismissed by him when he notes the 28 April Ministerial decree. This decree came twelve days after the (theoretically "illegal") concentration of the "Jews" began in Carpatho-Ruthenia, and therefore Braham effectively bypasses the 26 April Council of Ministers discussion and the 28 April decree, making only passing reference to them on one page of his two-volume work.[142] In assuming that deportation (to Auschwitz) lay behind the 7 April ghettoization order, Braham dismisses the title of the later decree, "Concerning the Regulation of Certain Questions Relating to the Jews' Apartments and Living Places," as simply "camouflage."[143] Thus, insofar as he does engage with the 28 April decree, he does so only to highlight articles 8 and 9, which include—in his opinion—"the crucial provisions of the decree relating to the concentration of the Jews."[144] However, that leaves articles 1 to 7, which form the main body of the decree, to be interpreted; these deal in large part with the appropriation of excess "Jewish" housing for the purposes of meeting the accommodation needs of officialdom,[145] and are remarkably detailed for mere "camouflage."

Speaking before the Council of Ministers on 26 April, Interior Minister Jaross represented the "solving of the Jewish question" as an opportunity to create a "healthier situation" in the sphere of housing.[146] He pointed to "Jews"—because of their better economic status—living in "substantially more favorable housing conditions" than "non-Jews," especially in the cities and larger villages.[147] The economic issue of "Jews" enjoying "substantially more favorable housing conditions" was repeated in an article of 28 April in the rightist *Esti Ujság*. Referring to the issuing of the ghettoization decree published that morning, the evening paper gave statistical evidence to prove that "Jews" in Budapest lived in "substantially more favorable housing conditions" than "non-Jews." In particular, the better housing conditions amongst "Jewish" workers—compared with their "non-Jewish" colleagues—was highlighted.[148] This perceived long-term inequality in provision was seen, by Jaross, to have been compounded by the housing shortage due to the wartime decrease in construction.[149]

Such language vis-à-vis the "Jew" was not new. As Patai notes in his study of Hungarian "Jews," there was a longer history to the claims of officialdom that "Jews" were overrepresented within a variety of socioeconomic spheres. For him, "the year 1937 was memorable in that it signaled the beginning of Hungarian governmental engagement in fostering anti-Jewish sentiment by publicizing information that showed the overrepresentation of Jews in landownership, industry, the press and publishing, and higher-income groups in general."[150] In 1944, at the time of the implementation of ghettoization, overrepresentation in the sphere of housing was added to this list.

Of course the difficult question is what we should make of such a discourse: Should it be viewed as evidence of the causes *or* the rationalizations of ghettoization? For Braham socioeconomic discourses were not merely "rationalization" but ultimately "camouflage." And yet the evidence from

Budapest, which I want to look at in some detail in the subsequent chapters, suggests that socioeconomic concerns—alongside a number of other concerns—were central not simply to the discourses adopted by the city officials who implemented ghettoization but also to their practices. In particular, socioeconomic considerations underlay officials' concerns with ghettoization as a means of creating "Jewish absence."

Rather than adopting a simplistic teleological and "top-down" approach that sees ghettoization as a Nazi given, I intend to adopt a "bottom-up" approach that seeks to examine the complex history of the evolution of ghettoization policies within the context of taking seriously the relative autonomy of local officials implementing ghettoization. Far from being unproblematic, it is clear from archival sources that ghettoization was contested, and the shape of the ghetto in Budapest, both as it was planned and as it was implemented, was in a state of constant flux from late spring 1944 onward. Indeed, the very term "ghettoization" itself needs to be interpreted in a fairly fluid manner, with recognition of the evolutionary nature of the concept.

FOUR

PLANNING AND IMPLEMENTING
GHETTOIZATION, APRIL–MAY 1944

On the day that ghettoization on a national scale was first being discussed by Hungarian and German officials—Tuesday, 4 April 1944—a form of "ghettoization" was already being ordered and implemented in Budapest. Coming, as it did, prior to the issuing of the confidential ghettoization order (7 April) and the official ministerial decree sanctioning ghettoization (28 April), this was clearly a case of initiative being taken in the locality and a form of ghettoization being implemented apart from plans issued from the top down. The precise events are not easily reconstructed, given some discrepancies between sources and the rather problematic nature of the sources themselves,[1] but it is possible to sketch out what in effect was the first act of ghettoization in Budapest. Certainly Bernard Klein saw the appropriateness of speaking of this as "actually the beginning of the ghetto, since the Jews were evicted from certain sections of the town."[2]

It would seem that on 4 April, the Jewish Council was ordered to provide 500 "Jewish" apartments in Budapest for use by "non-Jewish" bomb victims within twenty-four hours.[3] This order came after two nights of back-to-back Allied bombing raids. Previously untouched by aerial bombardment, Hungary had in many ways got off lightly in experiencing the destruction of war. Although casualties had been extremely heavy during the ill-fated battle on the Don, civilian Hungary had been little affected by a war fought away from Hungarian territory. In Budapest, in particular, life went on almost as normal prior to the air raids of April 1944. The impact of the destruction wrought upon Budapest was therefore considerable, coming as it did after years of relative normality.[4] Whilst the bombing was focused particularly upon strategic sites, such as the marshaling yards of Pest and the aircraft and armaments works in Csepel and Horthy Liget, residential areas were not entirely spared. In particular the heavy bombing on the night of 3 April resulted in bomb damage to a large number of domestic properties and, according to the official state news agency, in 1,073 deaths and 526 injuries.[5]

In this context of bomb damage to residential properties, 500 "Jewish" apartments in Budapest were appropriated by city and interior ministry officials. This was not the first time that "Jewish" apartments had been seized. In the aftermath of the occupation, a number of properties had been appropriated for the use of German army and administrative personnel. However, both the scale of the operation and the intended recipients now differed. The intention was that the apartments were to be handed over furnished and ready for immediate use by "non-Jewish" families made homeless by the bombing, with the members of the requisitioning groups instructed to ensure that sufficient furniture and crockery remained.[6] Ultimately it seems that the figure of 500 apartments in twenty-four hours was compounded with a request for another thousand properties, following further bombing raids on the night of 4 April.[7]

The seizure of "Jewish" apartments for the use of "non-Jewish" bomb victims, amounted to the creation of spaces of "Jewish absence" in Budapest, in particular in those parts of the city where the bomb damage had been particularly marked. The clear focus was upon the seizure of "Jewish" apartments—the creation of explicit "Jewish absences"—rather than the relocation of the city's "Jews"—the creation of implicit "Jewish presences." However, the flip side of appropriation was that those "Jews" who were forced to vacate their apartments were to be given new apartments elsewhere. And this amounted to the creation of increased "Jewish presences," particularly, it would seem, in the traditional "Jewish quarter" in the VI and VII districts. Certainly the rightist paper *Függetlenség* reported on 7 April that the "Jewish" leadership was working toward the (re)settling of "Jews" roughly in a "Jewish quarter," in an area of the city located between Podmaniczky u. and Wesselényi u. In this article dealing with the provision of "Jewish" apartments for "non-Jewish" bomb victims, this action was explicitly seen to be the development of a "ghetto."[8] Thus prior to the issuing of national legislation, a form of "Jewish" ghetto was being developed in Budapest as a by-product of appropriation.

This initial restructuring of "Jewish" living space in Budapest fitted within a longer history of appropriation, rather than being a staging post on the way to some form of Nazi "Final Solution." This longer-term tradition of antisemitic attitudes and actions was overlaid with the specific context of the start of Allied bombings. In the aftermath of these, the "Jew" as enemy within was to be punished for an alleged part in the Allied bombings, by being forced to provide apartments for the victims of this treachery. But the Budapest "Jew" was also seen in terms of longer-held antisemitic stereotypes of wealth and privilege. Thus the 7 April *Függetlenség* article justified the appropriation of "Jewish" flats and villas for bomb victims in terms of what was perceived to be the long-standing "problem" of the inequality of housing provision. According to this article, the "Jew" being turfed out of these apartments was the privileged "Jew" who was childless and yet living in "6, 8, even 10 roomed flats and villas."[9]

Although hundreds of properties in the city were vacated specifically for the use of bomb victims, it would seem that a relatively large number of these properties remained empty. Diámant, Freudiger, and Link's claim that "85 per cent of these dwellings remained unoccupied for months"[10] is impossible to verify. However, it is clear that several months later a significant number of the flats requisitioned in April remained empty. Correspondence relating to the VIII and IX districts reveals that by the end of July 1944, thirty-three apartments in the VIII district remained empty—and in the case of this district these were the majority of those seized—and thirty apartments in the IX district remained unused.[11] That seized apartments remained empty suggests that appropriations justified on the basis of the needs of "non-Jewish" bomb victims were clearly about—as the article in *Függetlenség* made clear—something more than the need for housing in a city at war.

That something approaching a "ghetto"—a site of "Jewish presence"—was developing in the VI and VII districts as a result of these appropriations for bomb victims began to be questioned in the rightist press from 16 April onward. On that day, *Magyarság* highlighted what it saw to be the potential geostrategic dangers of segregating the city's "Jews" within one area of the city.[12] Its stated fear was that by placing Budapest's "Jews" in a ghetto, the rest of the city would be opened up to Allied bombing. The assumption was that the city's "Jews" were fifth columnists who would be spared by the British and American bombers. These concerns, which I think are best dubbed geostrategic, were echoed again and again in a variety of sources both during 1944 and afterward. Indeed, such is the significance of this discourse which linked Budapest's "Jews," Allied bombing, and ghettoization that I give a brief history of the discourse, which spans both the primary and secondary literature, in the next chapter.

These geostrategic concerns expressed in the pages of *Magyarság* were responded to by one of the secretaries of state in the Interior Ministry, László Endre. He noted that there were plans afoot to concentrate the city's Jews in a number of closed Jewish quarters—rather than simply one ghetto—to be located throughout the city.[13] This press interview response of 16 April assumed a more concrete form on 9 May, with the drawing up of plans to create seven "Jewish quarters" or "ghettos" throughout the city.[14] Although never implemented, these 9 May plans offer an intriguing insight into the thinking of the doctors of space engaged in implementing ghettoization in Budapest.[15] These plans differed from both the initial form of "ghettoization" adopted in April 1944 and the subsequent "dispersed ghettoization" adopted in June 1944.[16] In mapping out what was ultimately an imaginary geography of ghettoization, I want to examine the meanings given to ghettoization in Budapest in early May 1944.

By 9 May 1944, of course, ghettoization in provincial Hungary was under way. These 9 May plans came after not only the officially sanctioned ministerial ghettoization legislation issued on 28 April 1944 but also the implementation of ghettoization in the peripheral districts of the country. The "Jews" of northeastern Hungary and those living along the Hungarian-Croatian/Serbian border and in northern Transylvania were placed into ghettos between mid-April and early May 1944.[17] Deportations from these early ghettos to Auschwitz-Birkenau commenced in mid-May.[18] Thus the broader context to the 9 May ghettoization plans in Budapest differed significantly from that of the earlier ghettoization measures of 4–5 April 1944. Ghettoization was now a policy in its own right rather than simply the byproduct of a policy of appropriation, and thus there was far greater concern with the ghetto as an explicit place of "Jewish presence." And ghettoization was now a policy legislated nationally, if implemented locally.

MAPPING OUT THE GHETTOIZATION PLANS OF 9 MAY 1944

It is clear from the text of the ghettoization plans that those drawing up the proposals were operating in terms of a series of guiding principles from the center. As I have already suggested, the nationally issued ghettoization decree provided the broad parameters for ghettoization (e.g., ghettos to be set up in towns with populations of over 10,000), whilst the specifics were left to mayoral officials in the locality. In essence, ghettoization in the abstract was legislated at the center, whilst ghettoization in the concrete was enacted at the locality. Although it was ultimately local officials who were involved in reshaping the living space of their particular town/city, they did so in terms of the broad guidelines issued by the Interior Ministry.

In the case of the anonymous mayoral officials in Budapest who mapped out the Budapest ghettos in May 1944, these centrally issued guidelines can be seen both to be the ghettoization legislation of 28 April and further guidelines specific to Budapest itself. At the outset, the Interior Ministry aim that the "Jews" be settled in a particular "part of the town," street, or house was stated. The prime concern can be seen with the creation of places of "Jewish presence," which resonates with the thrust of the 28 April legislation. However, there was recognition that the resettling of "Jews" was to be done in such a way as to ensure the spatial separation of the city's "Jewish" and "non-Jewish" populations, and thus that the ghetto was to be about "Jewish absence" as well as "Jewish presence."

Whilst this concern with "Jewish presence" drew upon the Interior Ministry legislation, another two principles stated at the outset by these doctors of space who mapped out ghettoization in Budapest suggest a number of other, and certainly in one case Budapest-specific, concerns, which reflected a concern with ghettoization as the creation of spaces of "Jewish absence." Firstly, "Jews" were to be resettled from the city's main streets and squares into side streets. Here a concern with explicit "Jewish absence" came to the fore, with its corollary of implicit "Jewish presence." Secondly, mention was made of what I have been dubbing geostrategic concerns. The placing of the city's "Jews" in a single part of the city was seen as potentially opening up the "non-Jewish" remainder of the city to enemy attack. In essence there was a concern with the potential implications of "Jewish absence."

Those concerns with ghettoization as both explicitly and implicitly being about the creation of "Jewish presence" and "Jewish absence" can be seen clearly in the proposed ghettos mapped out by these doctors of space. Taking the general guidelines fed down from the Interior Ministry, they acted in the locality to imagine a city reshaped in order to separate "Jewish" and "non-Jewish" living space. They imagined a city in which the "Jew" was to be removed from certain places and relocated to certain places. This was to be a city in which there was the creation of *judenfrei* space as well as the creation of "Jewish" ghetto space.

The plans of these doctors of space were that the city's "Jews" be relocated to seven minighettos spread throughout the city. Rather than being housed within every apartment block in these ghetto areas, "Jews" were to live in specified buildings within those seven identified ghetto areas. Thus "Jewish" absence and presence were to operate at a number of scales. Firstly, there was to be the creation of "Jewish" presences and absences at the scale of the city, with the concentration of the city's "Jews" into seven designated ghetto areas and the removal of the "Jew" from the remainder of the city. But then within these designated ghetto areas there was to be another scale of presences and absences. "Jews" were to live in certain apartment buildings and not others. So in a sense there was the imagining of spaces of absence within spaces of presence, as well as spaces of presence within spaces of presence. I think it is worth exploring both scales—the city and the ghetto area—in order to explore some of the assumptions underlying these plans.

PRESENCES AND ABSENCES AT THE CITY SCALE

At the scale of the city, both Buda and Pest were to be redrawn in terms of ghetto areas and the corollary of *judenfrei* space. In Buda, three ghetto areas were imagined—in the II, XI, and XII districts. In Pest, four ghetto areas were imagined—in the V, VI & VII, IX, and XIII districts of the city (see figure 1). The largest of these was located in the VI and VII districts of the city, in an area that made sense in terms of the interwar "Jewish" demography of the city. This area was the traditional "Jewish" quarter of the city, home to the major synagogues and community organization offices. A smaller ghetto area located in the V district also made demographic sense, sited as it was in Új Lipótváros, which had a sizable middle-class "Jewish" population. However, the remaining five ghetto areas made little sense in terms of where the "Jew" already lived in the city. In particular, the proposed ghettos in the IX, XI, and XIII districts were in areas with "Jewish" population densities well below the average for the city as a whole. Thus ghettoization was imagined not simply in terms of legislating existing "Jewish" and "non-Jewish" residential patterns in the city. Rather, "Jews" were to be moved into areas where there were previously low levels of "Jewish" residency. This was to be the case in, for example, the IX, XI, and XIII districts of the city, where the May plans involved taking the "Jew" to the ghetto,

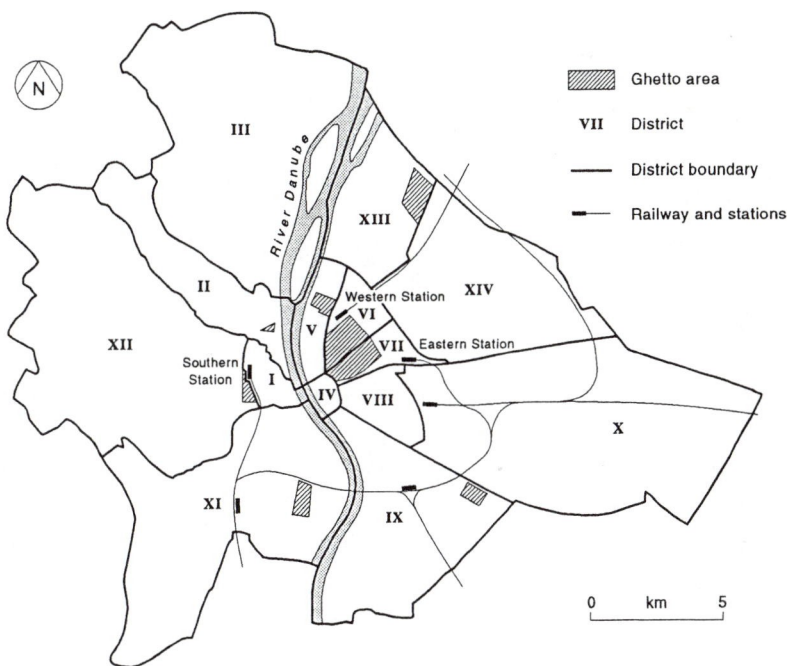

Figure 1. Imagining "Jewish presences" (9 May 1944). © Tim Cole.

rather than taking the ghetto to the "Jew," as was the case in the V and VI & VII districts of the city.

That the "Jew" was to be taken to the ghetto in the case of the proposed ghetto areas planned for the IX, XI, and XIII districts fitted with László Endre's earlier press comments about ghettoization and enemy bombing. These locations would seem to have been chosen largely for geostrategic reasons, situated as they were within the industrial ring of the city, which had been bombed so consistently throughout April. All three were in immediate proximity to a number of important war-related industrial complexes, with the two in the XI and IX districts being close to the Csepel works. The two small ghettos planned for the XII and II districts could be seen as offering some sort of geostrategic protection to the Castle Hill, home to, among other government buildings, the Interior Ministry where Endre himself worked. Perhaps more important, these bordered on the city's southern railway station. It is striking that all of the proposed ghetto sites were located in the environs of either railway stations or railway track and junctions.[19] The ghetto in the V district was close to Budapest's western railway station, the other side of which was the VI & VII district ghetto. This also bordered on the eastern railway station. The XIII district ghetto bordered on two minor railway stations and a number of major rail junctions, the IX district ghetto bordered on a minor railway station, and the XI district ghetto lay close to the main track leading out of Budapest to the southwest.

It does seem that these 9 May plans for explicit "Jewish presences" at the city scale reveal a concern with geostrategic considerations. The choice of ghetto sites fitted squarely with Endre's comment to *Magyarság* on 16 April that "we will concentrate an appropriate number of Jews close to everywhere we expect to be attacked by the terror bombers, for example factories, railway stations . . . "[20] The seemingly surprising choices of ghetto sites in view of the prevailing demographic distribution of "Jews" throughout the city makes sense when the location of factories and railway stations is considered. As has been pointed out, geostrategic considerations linked to allied bombing are mentioned at the outset as an Interior Ministry principle governing the implementation of ghettoization. However, when attention is shifted from presence to absence, it is clear that factors other than geostrategy were at play.

There was more to this mapping of separate living space in early May 1944 than simply a policy of creating explicit "Jewish presences." Alongside a concern with putting the "Jew" in their place ("Jewish presence") was a concern with removing the "Jew" from those parts of the city which were not their place ("Jewish absence"). Now in part, of course, the corollary of creating seven ghetto areas was that the spaces between became implicit places of "Jewish absence." The I, III, IV, VIII, X, and XIV districts were effectively to be made *judenfrei* and therefore, according to the logic of geostrategic concerns, potentially open to bomb attack. But the creation of spaces of "Jewish absence" was not simply the by-product of designating seven ghetto areas. Rather it was an explicit policy in its own right, and one motivated by issues other than geostrategy.

Prior to spelling out where the "Jew" was to be relocated to at the city scale, the authors of the 9 May memo outlined the main streets and squares which the "Jew" was to be removed from, in both Buda and Pest (see figure 2). For these doctors of space, the concern was not simply with creating ghettos where "Jews" were to be housed, but with expelling the "Jew" from places that were to become *judenfrei*. And indeed, in the logic of the memo, it is where the "Jew" was to be relocated from that preceded concerns with

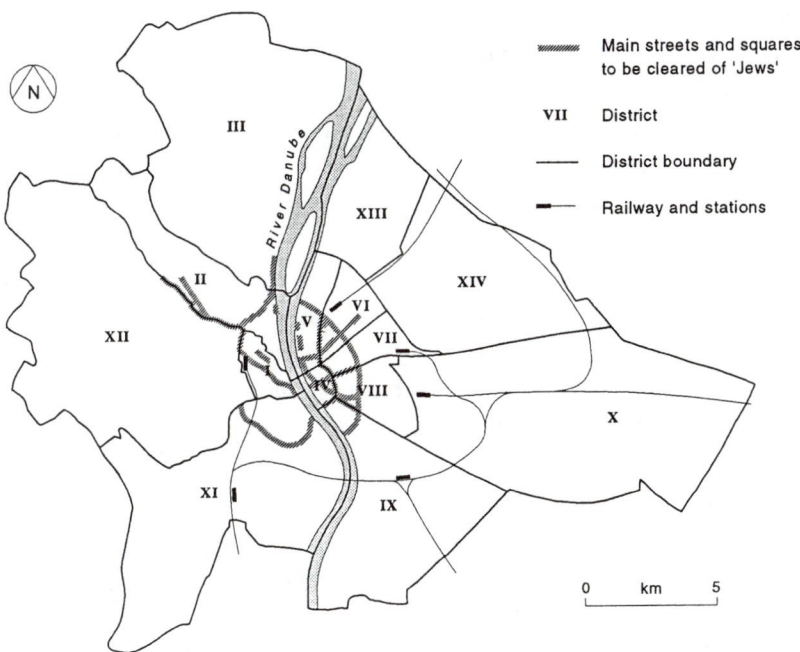

Figure 2. Imagining "Jewish absences" (9 May 1944). © Tim Cole.

where the "Jew" was to be relocated to. With this concern about removal of "Jews" from the living space of the city, the 9 May memo echoed the concerns with vacating "Jewish" apartments so central to the events of early April 1944. By 9 May, of course, creating something approaching a ghetto (which is explicitly stated in the memo) is more than simply a by-product of appropriation. It is clear that it is an end in itself. But appropriation clearly played an important role in this remapping of the living space of the city. The issue was not so much the freeing up of "Jewish" apartments for "non-Jewish" bomb victims, as was true, along with other issues, of the events of early April, set within the specific context of the start of Allied bombings. Rather, there was a different agenda at play, which saw in ghettoization the possibility for restructuring the city on a massive scale.

   Ghettoization offered city officials the chance to make decisions about where "Jews" would both live and not live, and it is clear from the memo that this opportunity was seized upon in such a way as to punish the "Jew." Ghettoization was viewed as an opportunity to advantage the "non-Jew" vis-à-vis the "Jew" in terms of housing provision. Thus, those imagining this newly structured city along antisemitic lines envisioned the removal of "Jews" from places, which they named and described.

Firstly, the main streets and squares of both Buda and Pest were to be "completely cleansed" of "Jews."[21] The nineteen major streets and eight main squares in central Pest and the thirteen major streets and five main squares in central Buda were no longer to be the home of the city's "Jews." No longer were "Jews" to live in the prestigious residences along, for example, Andrássy út or the Nagykörút. Rather these were to be "cleansed." The language used is striking. It suggests a notion of streets and squares somehow dirtied—metaphorically at least—by the presence of "Jews" and needing to be cleansed or purged of that dirtying presence. For those doctors of space mapping out ghettoization, there was more to explicit absences than ensuring that the prestigious—and visible—spaces of the nation's capital were made *judenfrei*. This act was imagined to be the cleansing of a city metaphorically dirtied by the "Jew."

Rather than being housed in prestigious and visible space, the dirty "Jew" was to be relocated to diseased and hidden space. This was clearly stated in the course of the memo as a guiding "principle" for implementing ghettoization. Thus, alongside specific references to named streets and squares which the "Jew" was to be removed from and specific ghetto areas which the "Jew" was to be moved to, these doctors of space wrote in more general terms of the kinds of places which were to be made *judenfrei* and "Jewish" houses. Budapest's "Jews" were to be removed from houses which were "healthy, with good air and well situated," and moved into houses in narrow, dark streets, which were poorly situated and yet with expensive rents.[22] In contrast, Budapest's "non-Jews" were to be relocated into modern flats with low rents.

Clearly those drawing up the plans not only acknowledged that ghettoization impacted the city's "non-Jewish" as well as "Jewish" population, but also realized that ghettoization could be implemented in such a way as to "punish" the city's "Jews" *and* benefit the city's "non-Jews." Thus ghettoization was imagined specifically as a way of restructuring the city's housing stock along antisemitic lines. Here was the opportunity for the history of housing provision in the city to be overturned in one moment. Certainly, the language of the memo suggests such a radical agenda at work. The present living conditions of the city's "Jews"—in healthy and well-situated houses—is explained in terms of assumptions about the economic power of the wealthy "Jew."[23] However, this advantage was to be overturned dramatically through the intervention of these officials, who had the power to assign living space in ways not restricted to what they perceived to be historical economic realities.

And so they seized the moment and offered a radical restructuring of the city. Ghettoization quite clearly had a strongly socioeconomic dimension, or at least the opportunities afforded by ghettoization included the socioeconomic. Not only was the symbolic heart of the city to be cleansed from the dirtying presence of "Jews," but the perceived unfair distribution of housing was to be remedied by the relocation of "Jews" from what was perceived to be their privileged living space into second-rate accommodation. This was nothing less than the imagining of a spatial revolution along antisemitic lines. It was an opportunity for history to be overturned through the legislative act of ghettoization. This moment was clearly visualized to offer the opportunity to do something much more than simply gather the city's "Jews" together in one place for ease of deportation. It was imagined as a revolutionary act in its own terms.

The shape that the ghetto took, as imagined by these "doctors of space" in Budapest in May 1944, was therefore about more than simply the means to an end, or a way to save the city from Allied bombers. The city's "Jewish" and "non-Jewish" populations were to be separated not only spatially but socioeconomically through space. The manipulation of housing space provided the opportunity to bring about a bigger agenda of socioeconomic restructuring, already achieved, in part, through the confiscation of "Jewish" businesses and wealth. This coming together of three agendas—spatial separation, geostrategic concerns, and socioeconomic concerns—can perhaps be seen most clearly in the designation of the severely bomb-damaged Mária Valéria *telep* [settlement] in the IX district as ghetto space. This could in no way be described as a traditional "Jewish" area of the city. Indeed, it was quite the opposite. Yet it fitted the bill in terms of being of geostrategic importance, and also being an area of particularly poor quality housing. And so, the "Jew" was to be taken to the ghetto, constructed in this place that made no sense in terms of the interwar demography of the city.

PRESENCES AND ABSENCES AT THE GHETTO AREA SCALE

As I have already noted, there were to be "Jewish" absences and presences within the boundaries of these planned ghetto areas, of which Mária Valéria *telep* was but one. Rather than being housed within each apartment block within an essentially closed ghetto, "Jews" were to be housed within the houses designated for "Jews" within the broad ghetto areas designated for "Jews." In essence what you see is two layers of designation of "Jewish" living space. Firstly, at the city scale, a broad division of the city into seven designated "Jewish" areas dispersed within an overall "non-Jewish" city was imagined. But whilst "Jews" were to live only within those seven ghetto areas, "non-Jews" were not only to live in the remainder of the city (the *judenfrei* spaces between the ghetto areas) but also to be permitted to remain within the loosely defined ghetto areas, although in separate houses from "Jews." The result of such plans was that the city's "Jews" were to live in "Jewish" houses in one of seven ghetto areas, whilst the city's "non-Jews" were to live in "non-Jewish" houses within one of the seven ghetto areas as well as in the large parts of the city made entirely *judenfrei*.

Alongside two layers of designation, therefore, there were also two layers of division. The city itself was divided into "Jewish" and "non-Jewish" space through the drawing up of these seven ghetto areas. But then within these seven ghetto areas, all of the apartment buildings themselves were to be divided up into "Jewish" and "non-Jewish" houses. This fitted with the Interior Ministry aim that the "end result" of ghettoization be the separation of "Jew" and "non-Jew" at the scale of the house.[24] This second layer of division was not specified in the 9 May plans but was to be completed—by 10 May—after studying the 1941 census data in order to ascertain where the "Jews" already lived in the city.[25] Thus it would seem that the pragmatics of recognizing where "Jews" already lived was to play a part in determining designation at the micro scale. In essence, here it was to be a case of taking the ghetto to the "Jews" with recognition that this would involve a minimum of forced relocations.

But the process was also to be guided by socioeconomic concerns, as I have already noted. The clear principle was that the houses specified for "Jews" within these ghetto areas were to have expensive rents and be poorly situated. In contrast, the houses specified for "non-Jews" in both these ghetto areas and the city at large were to be those with low rents and well equipped. In short, the "Jew" was to be punished and the "non-Jew" rewarded through this exercise of remapping the living space of the city along racial lines. It is clear that at both the scale of the city and the scale of the ghetto area, socioeconomic concerns can be seen as influencing the shape of the ghetto as it is imagined in Budapest. And this fitted, I would suggest, with the broader concerns articulated in the nationally issued legislation, which I examined briefly at the close of the previous chapter.

Seeing ghettoization as offering the opportunity to create a "healthier situation" in housing was, I would suggest from looking at these ghetto plans of 9 May, more than simply "camouflage," as Braham claimed.[26] It was not the only concern of these doctors of space engaged in mapping out the ghetto, but it was a significant concern.

What I think these plans suggest is that ghettoization was being seen as more than simply a short-term measure and gathering together of the "Jews" prior to deportations. At least at the local level, these doctors of space saw ghettoization in rather different terms, and continued to do so throughout May 1944. As correspondence between the locality and the center from the end of May 1944 would indicate, ghettoization was being seen in radically different ways by local and national officials at this relatively late date. As I have already suggested, initial ghettoization plans in Hungary seemingly were made apart from deportation. Certainly the development of something approaching a ghetto in Budapest in April 1944 was not about mass deportations. But even the national legislation would seem to be about other concerns, specifically socioeconomic. Now of course the context in Hungary changed. Mass deportations to Auschwitz-Birkenau commenced from provincial Hungary from 15 May onward. However, the difficult question is when the goal of ghettoization shifted. What I think is striking in the case of Budapest is that knowledge of the "final" goal of ghettoization was not received by all actors at the same time. So, at the end of May 1944, it would seem that national officials were seeing ghettoization as a short-term and temporary measure, whereas local officials were still seeing it as a longer-term and more permanent measure.

THE CHANGING MEANINGS OF GHETTOIZATION, LATE MAY 1944

At the end of May 1944, significant changes were made to the ghetto as imagined in the 9 May plan. These changes emanated from the center—the Interior Ministry—and were then passed on to the locality—the lord mayor and mayor in Budapest. On 26 May, two major shifts in planning ghettoization were communicated by the Interior Ministry. Firstly, the results of a meeting held in the Interior Ministry housing department that morning were communicated to the lord mayor. At this meeting, mayoral proposals concerning ghettoization were discussed. One can only assume that these were the 9 May plans, which I have examined in some detail above. At this meeting, the decision was made to implement a door-to-door survey of all of the city's inhabitants and then make a decision as to which houses to designate either "Jewish" or "non-Jewish" on this basis, rather than the 1941 census statistics as envisioned within the 9 May plans.[27]

This decision made sense in the light of the other information communicated by Endre to the lord mayor on the same morning. He stressed that the designation of "Jewish" and "non-Jewish" houses was to be based on three principles: majority occupation, status of owner, and cost of rents. It would seem that the earlier plans of 9 May to create seven ghetto areas and then designate "Jewish" houses within those areas had been shelved. Now, houses throughout the city could be designated "Jewish" houses if "Jewish" inhabitants were in the majority and the owner was "Jewish." And the corollary of this was that houses throughout the city could be designated "non-Jewish" if the owner was "non-Jewish" and also if the rents were cheap.[28] Interestingly, specific reference is made only to cheap rents being a major criterion of designating a house for "non-Jewish" use. There was no explicit referencing to cost of rents determining "Jewish" designation, although of course this can be inferred implicitly. There was perhaps significance to this. Rather than explicitly seeing ghettoization as a means of punishing the "Jew," the focus was instead on ghettoization as a means of benefiting the "non-Jew" or at least not harming them. There appeared to be a concern with the implications of ghettoization for the "non-Jewish" population, which was to become an increasingly significant issue at the end of May and during June 1944 as ghettoization in Budapest was implemented.

But there was also a shift away from the grand plans of ghettoization as a means of reshaping the city in dramatic fashion. The concerns of the end of May seem to be largely driven by pragmatism rather than utopianism. As far as the Interior Ministry was concerned, ghettoization was to be a temporary measure rather than a major restructuring of the city's housing stock, as was being planned by city officials on 9 May. These less ambitious plans for the opportunity afforded by ghettoization can be seen also in the explicit changing of policy such that no longer were the main streets to be "emptied" of "Jews."[29] There was to be an attempt to decrease the number of "Jewish" houses on main streets, but this was to be done "as far as possible" rather than to be a central plank of ghettoization plans.

There had been important shifts in policy between 9 May and the end of May, and these shifts were very much Interior Ministry–driven.

Ghettoization was being imagined rather differently. Whereas on 9 May, segregation had been imagined taking place at two scales, the city scale and the ghetto area scale, now it was being mapped out at one scale only. Here was arguably a more pragmatic solution to the challenge of ghettoization, which effectively aimed to take the ghetto to the "Jew"—and the corollary, to keep the ghetto away from the "non-Jew." This seems to have been motivated by a desire to minimize the relocations inevitably resulting from ghettoization and to ensure "non-Jewish" support from both house owners and renters impacted by the policy. I want to think about this shift in perception of the ghetto some more in the next chapter, but for now, what is significant is that this concern with the pragmatics of majority occupation on the part of Endre was linked with a concern for the very rapid implementation of ghettoization in Budapest. And it is here that a degree of contestation over the meanings given to ghettoization can be seen between national officials like Endre and officials in the locality. At the end of May 1944, there were markedly differing timescales being imagined for implementing ghettoization, which gave rise to a degree of bureaucratic resistance on the part of officials in the locality.

CONTESTED TIMING

Alongside informing the lord mayor of the new criteria for designating "Jewish" houses, Endre's intervention on 26 May also set out the new timescale within which designation and relocation were to be completed. Under Endre's plan, all houses in the city had to be designated for "Jewish" and "non-Jewish" use by 31 May. "Jews" were then to be given twenty-four hours to move into houses designated for their use. Thus by the end of 1 June, the city's "Jews" were to live only in "Jewish" houses. "Non-Jews" were to be given a longer time to relocate to houses designated for their use, with 30 June being set as the date when all relocations associated with ghettoization were to be completed.

This timescale, which was communicated to the lord mayor on 26 May, quite clearly did not meet with his approval. Lord Mayor Keledy challenged what he saw as the telescoping of ghettoization into thirty-one days, in a lengthy letter written to Interior Minster Jaross on 31 May. In writing to Jaross, Keledy effectively sidestepped the more junior Endre, who was the normal point of contact in the ministry with regard to ghettoization. In what can be seen as an act of bureaucratic resistance, Keledy expressed his concern with Endre's timescale and portrayed ghettoization as an administrative problem rather than an opportunity.

For Keledy, there was absolutely no way that Endre's plans for the rapid implementation of ghettoization could be achieved. Moreover, not only was such a compressed timescale unachievable, but it also presented, the lord mayor suggested, the danger of alienating public opinion. Thus in his letter to Jaross, Keledy took Endre's timescale and significantly extended it at every stage. He rejected the possibility of designating houses on the basis of door-to-door surveys by 31 May. His estimation was that once the registration forms had been collected on 2 and 3 June, "at least a week" would be needed for the city's statistical office to collate data and the mayor to draw up a list of designated houses. Thus, 10 June was seen to be the earliest possible date for the publication of such a list and the start of relocations.

What is interesting is that in this area, Keledy effectively won out over Endre's earlier plans. In a later telephone conversation between Endre and Keledy, Endre agreed to extend the deadline for designations to 10 June.[30] However, in the remainder of his proposals, Keledy's challenge to Endre's timescale was unsuccessful. Here—the deadlines for relocations of "Jews" and "non-Jews"—it was the center that won out rather than the locality. And what is striking is how radically different the timetables which the two imagined were.

For the lord mayor, 10 June was to be the first possible day that "Jews" could begin moving out of their apartments. However, he rejected the practicalities of "Jewish" relocations being completed within twenty-four hours, and "non-Jewish" relocations being completed within thirty days, which was the timescale that Endre was working to. Keledy's timescale was altogether different. He imagined that the whole process of ghettoization in Budapest would take three months to complete, *not* thirty days. Thus the implementation of ghettoization was to begin on 10 June 1944, but not be completed until September.

His suggestion to Jaross was that a three-month rolling program of relocations be adopted. In the first month—June—"Jews" would move out of houses on the city's main streets. At this stage, Keledy was still operating under the 9 May assumption that "cleansing" the main streets and squares of "Jews" was central to ghettoization plans. As I've noted, he was only informed of a shift in policy by Endre during a telephone conversation later that day. During the second month—July—"Jews" were to move out of all other houses. During the third month—August—"Jews" were to move into

"Jewish houses" vacated by their previous "non-Jewish" tenants. These "non-Jewish" tenants would—at this stage—have been able to move into repaired and disinfected flats, vacated by "Jews" during the first two months of relocations.

For Keledy, such a lengthy timetable was necessary because of the practical difficulties which segregating the city's population presented. He expressed considerable concern about finding the transportation and workforce needed to undertake the massive number of relocations in the short period of time outlined by Endre. It would, he suggested, be simply impossible in the context of the city at war. And more than that, it would also create opposition from "non-Jews" forced to move from houses now designated for "Jewish" use. Keledy expressed considerable concern about the implications—in particular, the material implications—of ghettoization for the city's "non-Jewish" population. For those "non-Jews" who must leave their apartments, he pointed out the financial costs of moving their furniture, as well as the financial costs of repairing and disinfecting the former "Jewish" apartments into which they moved. His prediction was that even the longer timescale which he suggested would result in complaints from "non-Jewish" residents, and he rather ominously washed his hands of any political responsibility for the potential trouble which not allowing a proper timescale for relocations would create.

What is striking in his lengthy and detailed letter is the portrayal of ghettoization as a bureaucratic problem that needed a solution, rather than an opportunity for socioeconomic engineering on a grand scale, which I think, lies behind earlier plans. And, linked to this, ghettoization was portrayed as a policy with very real costs for the "non-Jewish" population of the city, and thus needed to be undertaken in a manner which limited the impact upon "non-Jews" to the absolute minimum. For Keledy, the way to soften the blow for the city's "non-Jews"—the group about whom he expressed his concern—was to adopt his proposed rolling timetable for relocations and to ensure that "non-Jews" were allowed to rent the best possible apartments. This he saw as a potential sop to prevent "non-Jewish" unrest against the costly policy of ghettoization—costly, as Keledy saw it, for Budapest's "non-Jewish" population.

Whereas Keledy was successful in persuading the Interior Ministry to push back the date for designation to 10 June, he was unsuccessful in his attempt to extend the final dates for relocations into September 1944. Informing the mayor of his telephone conversation with Endre on 31 May,

Keledy specified that there was to be a "short time limit" for "Jews" moving into designated houses, and that they would not be allowed to take their furniture with them. The fact that "Jews" were to leave their furniture in their vacated apartments was seen to limit the technical problems associated with moving that had so occupied Keledy's complaint to Jaross. The relocation of "non-Jews" was seen as a matter that could wait until later, with the immediate concern only finding temporary accommodation for those living in houses designated for "Jews."

The two letters—to the interior minister suggesting a timescale of three months, and to the mayor informing him that ghettoization was to be accomplished in a "short time limit"—could not be more different. It is clear that the conversation Endre had with Keledy on 31 May was critical in changing his assumption of ghettoization. It would seem that after this conversation, Keledy understood ghettoization—likely for the first time— as a temporary measure to be enacted in a short time period. Prior to this conversation with Endre, Keledy seemed to imagine ghettoization in very different terms, seeing it as something permanent enough to be enacted over the course of three months. What Endre said to Keledy is impossible to state with confidence. What can be deduced, however, is that Endre said enough to radically change the way Keledy viewed the separation of the city's "Jewish" and "non-Jewish" populations.

What you see on 31 May 1944 is a conflict between how ghettoization is being imagined in the locality and at the center. However, that short-lived conflict emerged not because Keledy had changed his mind, but rather, I would suggest, because the Interior Ministry had. Although impossible to pinpoint accurately, a shift in thinking in the Interior Ministry would seem to have occurred at some point in May 1944. It was communicated to Budapest's lord mayor only at the end of the month, and subsequently by the lord mayor to the mayor of Budapest at the start of June 1944.

What is striking about Keledy's letter of complaint to Jaross of 31 May 1944 is that the thrust of Keledy's argument fitted in many ways with the ministerial ghettoization order issued on 7 April 1944. Both show a fundamental concern over the pragmatics of relocations, and in particular that of "non-Jewish" tenants in apartment blocks designated for the "Jew" moving into already vacated "Jewish" flats. The ghettoization decree made provision for "Jewish" vacation of flats—within a thirty-day period—preceding "non-Jewish" vacation of "Jewish houses," with "Jews" being housed in temporary transit camps during the time lag. In essence, the lord mayoral proposal of a "rolling" implementation of ghettoization, starting with "Jews" vacating their properties, fitted with the approach of the Interior Ministry in April 1944.

Thus the thrust of Keledy's complaints at the end of May, concerned as they are with the pragmatics of ensuring that "non-Jews" were not left homeless in the process of implementation, did resonate with the approach to ghettoization adopted by the Interior Ministry in April 1944. However, his plan that the ghettoization process would finally be completed by September at the earliest did not fit with the new realities that Budapest's "Jews" were slated for deportation during July 1944.[31]

This change in plans, that ghettoization was to be a rapidly implemented measure prior to mass deportations, would seem to be unknown at the local level at the end of May 1944. Keledy's pressing for a three-month timescale was presumably a result of his ignorance of the shifting realities, rather than an act of intentional resistance to deportations. It would seem that at the end of May, the lord mayor in Budapest was thinking of ghettoization rather differently than those in the Interior Ministry. But, it would seem from his intervention, the change in thinking of those in national government was a recent development. Certainly Keledy's claim was that at a Council of Ministers meeting held on 10 May, no objection was raised by either the prime minister or members of the cabinet that the implementation of ghettoization in Budapest would take at least three months. Thus Keledy's claim—based on a report given by the mayor—was that his proposals penned at the end of May fitted with the sentiments of the national government expressed (through silence at least) a few weeks earlier.

What Keledy seems to have been unaware of was that there was a shift in national attitudes toward ghettoization, and thus his argument drawing on the sentiments of 10 May no longer cut ice nationally at the end of May 1944. He was clearly informed of this shift in attitudes by Endre on 31 May, and subsequently informed the mayor of the new realities of rapid ghettoization. While the timescale was to be telescoped, the implications of ghettoization for the city's "non-Jewish" population continued to be a matter of concern to officials in the locality. Indeed, as I want to suggest, these concerns markedly changed the shape of the ghetto implemented in Budapest in June 1944.

But Keledy's fascinating letter points to much more than simply a recognition that ghettoization affected the "non-Jewish" population as well as the "Jewish" population. It also suggests two significant issues worthy of further research. Firstly, as I have noted, it would seem that there was a shift in attitudes toward ghettoization at a national scale between April 1944 and the end of May 1944. But I would go further than that, and suggest that if Keledy's reporting of the 10 May meeting is correct, then it would seem that there was a shift in attitudes toward ghettoization in Budapest at a national scale between 10 May 1944 and the end of May 1944. Now whether this shift in attitudes took place during this timescale for the country as a whole is another matter, requiring research in the provincial archives. As I have noted, deportations to Auschwitz-Birkenau began on 15 May 1944, from Carpatho-Ruthenia. The critical question is whether the change in thinking that seems to have taken place as far as Budapest's "Jews" were concerned during mid-to-late May was a broader shift in thinking vis-à-vis the entire Hungarian "Jewry."

The second thing that Keledy's intervention points to is that knowledge was not necessarily gained by all actors at the same time. It would seem that different attitudes were being held at the national and local levels, at least as far as Budapest is concerned. The conversation between Endre and Keledy on 31 May was critical in conveying new knowledge. On the basis of this new knowledge, Keledy's calls for a three-month timescale were jettisoned. Instead he wrote to the mayor informing him that ghettoization was to be rapidly implemented in Budapest. He passed on Endre's desire that once "Jewish" houses were designated on 10 June, they were to be marked with a yellow star—which could at this stage be a paper wall sticker—on 11 June. Relocations were to take place rapidly, and were to be restricted to within—rather than across—districts for "policing reasons." And it was quite clear that the whole process was to come under national government scrutiny. It is this process of implementing ghettoization, and the physical shape that the ghetto took in Budapest, which I now turn to.

FIVE

IMPLEMENTING GHETTOIZATION, JUNE 1944

During the course of May 1944, there were important shifts in the perception of ghettoization, with the Interior Ministry clearly playing a leading role in directing these changes. Of foremost importance was a telescoping of the timescale within which ghettoization was to be completed. But, in addition, at the meeting held at the Interior Ministry on 26 May, the Budapest ghetto was given a new shape. Rather than segregation being planned at two scales, that of the city and then the ghetto area as was the case with the 9 May plans, it was to be implemented at one scale—that of the apartment building. And the specifics of which apartment building was to be designated for "Jewish" and which for "non-Jewish" use were to be determined on the basis of a citywide survey, rather than census data.

This survey was implemented at the very beginning of June 1944. It was a massive undertaking. On 1 June, tax officials in the city distributed registration forms to the caretakers of each of the city's close to 34,000 houses and apartment blocks. These were to be completed and then collected the following day, with the caretaker or owner of each property signing for the accuracy of the information given. It was made clear to the city's population that this registration was being undertaken in the run-up to the implementation of ghettoization in Budapest.[1]

The nature of the questions posed on the registration form, fitted with the new criteria under which ghettoization was to be implemented, was spelled out by Endre on 26 May. Then, Endre had signaled that designation was to be undertaken on the basis of three principles: majority occupation, status of owner, and costs of rents. Completing the form called for information relating to all three. On the front, the names of all owners of the property had to be given, as well as whether they were required to wear the yellow star—in other words, whether they were legally "Jewish." On the rear, the names of all tenants had to be given, along with their status—whether they were "Jewish" or not, whether they were still living at the property, and how much rent they paid. As can be seen, the criteria spelled out by Endre formed the basis for this massive investigation of all of the city's properties and tenants.

But the form also sought further information, which added to the criteria spelled out by Endre on 26 May.[2] Most significantly, the age of the building was to be given. Specifically, the caretaker or house owner was to stipulate whether the building was built before or after 1935. Thus modern apartment buildings—less than nine years old—were to be highlighted. This information picked up on earlier criteria, made explicit in the 9 May plans, which linked the age of building to the level of rents in determining whether a property was to be designated for "Jewish" or "non-Jewish" use.[3] Then, as now, the ideal property for the "non-Jew" was perceived to be the modern property with low rents. And thus, it would appear that in order to determine this happy combination, the rough classification of the property as modern or not modern was sought.

It would seem it was on the basis of this hurriedly collected information that the precise shape of ghettoization in Budapest was determined by city officials. Certainly *Esti Ujság* reported this to be the case.[4] It is clear that officials at the national level were involved in overseeing this process. Not only had they largely determined the information asked in this mass registration, but Endre had communicated his desire, in his conversation with the lord mayor on 31 May, that the ghettoization plans emerging from this survey be discussed with him and other officials. These officials included representatives of the Finance Ministry, the chief police officer, and the chief medical officer as well as representatives from the relevant departments at the city level. A meeting chaired by Endre was held at the Interior Ministry on 9 June to discuss the implementation of ghettoization in Budapest.[5] According to *Esti Ujság*, this meeting was but one of several that had taken place "between government elements and the city leadership" over a number of weeks, at which the implementation of ghettoization had been discussed.[6] What specifically concerned those ministerial representatives who attended were the opportunities presented by ghettoization to free up "Jewish" housing ("Jewish absence"). Not only could apartments be provided for "non-Jews" living in newly designated ghetto houses, but also the planned influx of 15,000 workers in the war industries could now be housed in the city. For the Finance Ministry officials present, their main concerns were with the pragmatics of what "Jews" could and could not take with them when they vacated their existing apartments.[7]

Thus it is clear that national ministerial officials—and, in particular, Endre in the Interior Ministry—played a significant role in shaping the guiding principles that governed the implementation of ghettoization in Budapest. However, the specifics of which houses were to be included in the ghetto list seem to have been determined by local officials, who processed the forms collected on 2 June. At least as far as the IV district was concerned,[8] it appears that the practice of city officials was to write the numbers of "non-Jewish" and "Jewish" tenants in the top left-hand corner of the June 1–2 registration form. If "non-Jewish" tenants were in the majority, then the shorthand "*K*" (*Keresztény*—"Christian") was penciled in the top right-hand corner and the property was designated for "non-Jewish" use. If "Jewish" tenants were in the majority, then the shorthand "*Zs*" (*Zsidó*—"Jew") was penciled in the top right-hand corner and the property designated for "Jewish" use. Thus in the end, the implementation of the specifics of ghettoization was about the bureaucratic banality of pencil sums on the front of a registration form and the penning of the shorthand "*K*" or "*Zs*."[9]

That the information collected on 1–2 June formed the basis of the detailed shape of the ghetto can be seen quite clearly in the case of the apartment block at Váci u. 50, in the city's IV district.[10] This building was included in the list of properties for "Jewish" use in the initial ghetto list issued on 16 June, although "Jewish" tenants were in fact in the minority. The designation called forth protest from the building's "non-Jewish" owners and "non-Jewish" tenants, who pointed out that as well as having "non-Jewish" owners, the entire ground floor of the building was used by a "non-Jewish" business and four of the six tenants in the building were "non-Jews." However, on the registration form collected from Váci u. 50, only the details of two "Jewish" tenants had been filled out, and not the details of any of the building's "non-Jewish" tenants. The official processing the form had therefore penciled "2 Jews" in the top left corner and the shorthand "*Zs*" in the top right corner. Here was a building that, according to the incomplete information offered on the registration form, had a clear majority of

"Jewish" tenants, and thus was designated for "Jewish" use. What is interesting is that the "non-Jewish" status of the owners given on the form was deemed of lesser importance than the seeming majority "Jewish" occupation of this pre-1935 building.

This designation on the basis of the 1–2 June survey was contested by the apartment building's "non-Jewish" owners and tenants. The additional information they offered in their letter of 17 June was checked by an official from the IV district on 20 June, who confirmed that the two "Jewish" tenants were in fact in the minority. On the basis of this new information, the decision was made to cancel the yellow-star status of the property in the "definitive" second list of designations issued on 22 June—which I want to examine in much more detail in the next chapter. In this case, the changing designation reflects the changing nature of the information provided. The constant was the principle of majority residence on the basis of the registration of the building's tenants.

However, whilst the reckoning of majority residence by a city official formed the basis for designations, it would seem that other factors also played a role in determining which properties were identified for "Jewish" and "non-Jewish" use. This can be seen clearly when the list of designated houses posted up on 16 June is compared with two lists of "Jewish houses" drawn up by the Jewish Council.[11] These undated lists each contain the details of the 525 apartment houses in the city "with the greatest percentage of yellow-star tenants" and are described as Hungarian Jewish Association proposals with regard to "designated Jewish houses." They raise the question of the extent to which the Jewish Council played a role in determining the shape of the ghetto in Budapest, which I want to think about a little later.

For now, the lists are useful in giving the proportion of "Jewish" flats in each property proposed. What emerges from studying them alongside the 16 June list of ghetto houses is that plenty of properties in Budapest where "Jews" formed the majority of occupants were not designated for "Jewish" use in mid-June. For example, to take just one street in the V district—Honvéd u.—two houses featured on the Jewish Council list (numbers 16 and 18) and three on the 16 June ghetto house list (numbers 16, 38, and 40). It is clear from the Jewish Council list that Honvéd u. 16 had a majority (70 percent) of "Jewish" tenants.[12] Hence its inclusion in the 16 June list was understandable. However, what is harder to explain is why the neighboring house, Honvéd u. 18, that also had a majority (72 percent) of "Jewish" tenants did not feature on the 16 June list.[13] Such an example is far from isolated, and points to the principle of majority occupation as not being the sole criterion governing the drawing up of the list of "Jewish" houses. Those other factors outlined by Endre at the end of May—the status of the owner and the level of the rents—as well as the age of the building would seem to have also played a role.[14] Certainly, *Esti Ujság* suggested that in the run-up to the designations, "Christian" houses would be those with "Christian" owners, a majority of "Christian" tenants, "relatively cheap rents," modern, and well situated. The corollary was that "Jewish" houses were to be those with "Jewish" owners, a majority of "Jewish" tenants, high rents, old, and on narrow streets.[15] At least some of the socioeconomic principles so clearly visible in the 9 May plans were still of significance.

However, ghettoization as realized on 16 June contrasted markedly with ghettoization as planned on 9 May. Rather than being housed on narrow side streets in seven ghetto areas, the city's "Jews" were to move into 2,639 apartment buildings spread throughout the city.[16] The details of which buildings were to be inhabitable by the city's "Jews" were posted up on the city's streets and published in the press. These buildings were to be marked with a large yellow star, on a black background. All "Jews" in the city were instructed that they must move into these buildings by 21 June. Each family was entitled to only one room or, if the family was large and/or the rooms in the apartment were small, a maximum of two rooms.

COMPARING GHETTOIZATION AS IMAGINED (9 MAY) AND GHETTOIZATION AS IMPLEMENTED (16 JUNE)

Within a little over a month, there had been a significant shift from segregation being envisioned at the scale of distinct ghetto areas to segregation being implemented at the level of individual apartment buildings only. To a degree, the 9 May plans envisioned ghettoization in Budapest in dispersed terms. Thus rather than planning a single ghetto, the doctors of space mapped out seven rough ghetto areas within which houses were to be designated for "Jewish" use. However, the implementation of ghettoization on 16 June took the idea of dispersed ghettoization a stage further. The city's "Jews" were quite literally to be housed throughout the city. As the mapping of the 16 June yellow-star houses in the XI district reveals, the eighty-one properties for "Jewish" use were dispersed throughout fifty-nine separate streets in the district, not the small number of streets mapped out on 9 May as the district's ghetto area (see figures 3 and 4).

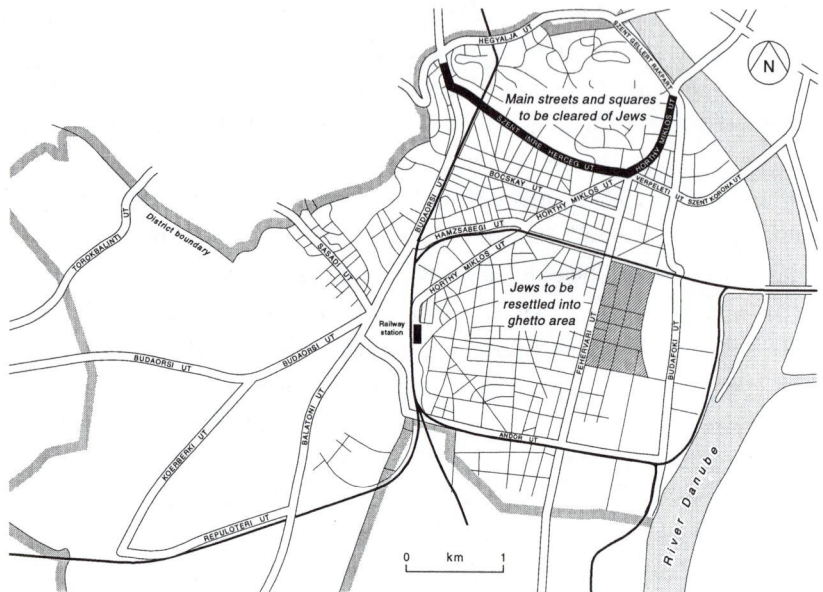

Figure 3. Ghettoization as imagined in the XI District (9 May 1944). © Tim Cole.

Figure 4. Ghettoization as implemented in the XI District (16 June 1944). © Tim Cole.

It is clear that there was a wholesale rejection of the 9 May plans at the level of both "Jewish presences" and "Jewish absences." Apartment buildings were designated not only on streets outside the seven ghetto areas imagined in early May, but also on the main streets and squares which the earlier plans had aimed at "cleansing" of the "Jews." These shifts in thinking can be seen in the case of the XI district. Not only were a mere two of the eighty-one yellow-star houses in the district situated in the ghetto area that had been mapped out under the 9 May plans, but far more houses (seven in total) had been designated on the main streets which were previously to have been "cleansed" of "Jews."

This picture is repeated elsewhere. The geostrategically significant areas in the II, IX, XII, and XIII districts—like this one in the XI district—that had been envisioned as housing a ghetto area did not feature to any great extent in the 16 June list. Indeed the planned Mária Valéria *telep* ghetto area in the IX district did not feature at all in the 16 June list. This complete absence is understandable when the nature of this planned ghetto area is considered. It was, as I noted, a place that made absolutely no sense in terms of where "Jews" lived in the city but complete sense in terms of geostrategic importance and being an area of poor-quality housing. It could therefore be imagined as ghetto space under the 9 May plans, which redrew the city along socioeconomic lines within a framework of geostrategic concerns. However, the criterion for designation had shifted by 16 June, and now majority occupation was the major concern. Thus it was to be primarily a case of bringing the ghetto to the "Jew" rather than bringing the "Jew" to the ghetto, as would quite clearly have been the case with the designating of Mária Valéria *telep* as ghetto space. Now, the very criterion adopted—majority occupation—meant that a place such as Mária Valéria *telep*, which in no way could be seen as a traditional "Jewish" area, would never be designated for "Jewish" use.

Rather, it was the places in the city where the "Jew" already lived that were by and large designated for "Jewish" use on 16 June. This was the inevitable result of a shift in policy toward the pragmatics of "Jewish" majority occupation determining not simply which houses within one of seven designated ghetto areas were to be "Jewish" houses but which houses in the city as a whole were to be "Jewish" houses. This shift in thinking meant that ghettoization as it was implemented on 16 June was in effect shaped by the realities of "Jewish" demography in the city as much as (if not more than) by the hands of doctors of space. Whilst in early May, ghettoization was clearly being seen as an opportunity to overturn the history of "Jewish" residential patterns in the city, by mid-June, ghettoization was, in some ways at least, a legislating of the history of "Jewish" residential patterns in the city.[17]

THE DEMOGRAPHIC CONTEXT TO GHETTOIZATION

Thus, ghettoization as it was implemented in June 1944 took place not in a vacuum but within a demographic context, which can be seen in the inter-war census statistics.[18] These revealed that "Jewish" residential patterns in the city were characterized by clustering within certain districts rather than uniform distribution across the city. In the city as a whole, "Jews" made up 15.8 percent of the population according to the 1941 census. However, the proportions of "Jews" living in each of the city's fourteen main administrative districts did not hover around the 15.8 percent mark (see figure 5). Far from it. At one level, "Jews" tended to live in Pest rather than Buda. Thus while making up 15.8 percent of the city's total population, "Jews" accounted for only 6.1 percent of Buda's population but 18.9 percent of

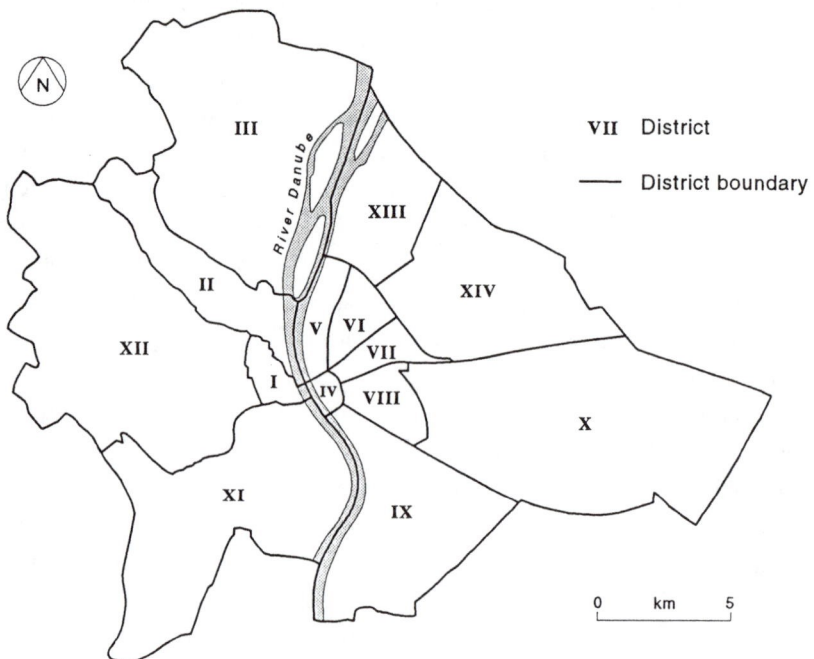

Figure 5. Administrative districts in Budapest (1944). © Tim Cole.

Pest's population. The result was that nine out of ten "Jews" living in Budapest in 1941 lived on the Pest side of the Danube.[19]

But even within Pest, there were marked "Jewish" population clusters. It was the four central districts of central Pest—the V, VI, VII, and VIII districts—which accounted for three-quarters of the total "Jewish" population of the city.[20] In the most "Jewish" of these districts—the VII—"Jews" accounted for 35.5 percent of the district's population. In contrast, in the X district of Pest, "Jews" made up only 3.4 percent of the district's population. What is striking is that this district—the tenth—had the smallest proportion of "Jews" to the population of any individual district not simply in Pest but in the city as a whole. No district in Buda, which had a relatively small "Jewish" population compared with Pest, had such a low proportion of "Jewish" residents.

District	"Jewish" Population as % of Total Population in District (1941)
I	4.1
II	7.5
III	8.3
XI	3.8
XII	5.5
Buda	6.1
IV	14.3
V	34.4
VI	31.6
VII	35.5
VIII	16.6
IX	7.8
X	3.4
XIII	6.3
XIV	18.9
Pest	18.9
Budapest	15.8

This clear "Jewish" clustering at the city scale can also be seen at the district scale. "Jews" were neither equally dispersed throughout the city's districts nor equally dispersed within those districts. At the subdistrict level (each district was further subdivided into smaller administrative units) a distinct pattern of "Jewish" clustering can also be seen. On the basis of statistics from 1920, it is clear that the spread of "Jewish" residential patterns was much more uneven than those of "Catholics," "Lutherans," or "Reformed."[21] In 1920, these religiously defined populations made up 22.9 percent ("Jewish"), 59.6 percent ("Catholic"), 4.6 percent ("Lutheran"), and 10.6 percent ("Reformed") of the city's population, respectively. What is striking when one examines population percentages at the subdistrict level is how much greater "Jewish" overrepresentation and underrepresentation were compared with these other groups. Thus, in Buda, "Jewish" presence ranged from 1.2 percent of the population in subdistrict 25 in the III district to 24.9 percent in the almost neighboring subdistrict 22/a (Óbuda), also in the III district.[22] This marked range compared with the narrower range of other groups. The "Lutheran" presence in Buda ranged from 3.1 percent of the population in subdistrict 22/a in the III district to 10.3 percent in subdistrict 19 in the II district.[23] The figures for the "Reformed" presence ranged from 6.9 percent, again in subdistrict 22/a in the III district with its relatively large "Jewish" population, to 15.5 percent in subdistrict 12 in the I district.[24] For the majority "Catholic" population, the range was from 59.2 percent in subdistrict 19 in the II district to 83.2 percent in subdistrict 27 in the III district.[25]

The extreme of the range of "Jewish" presence at a subdistrict level was even more marked in Pest. Here, "Jewish" presence ranged from a mere 1.6 percent of the population of subdistrict 77 in the X district to 62.4% of subdistrict 51 in the VII district.[26] In contrast, the "Lutheran" population density ranged from 2.3% in subdistrict 51 in the VII district to 7.8 percent in subdistrict 78 in the X district.[27] The "Reformed" population density ranged from 4.7 percent, again in subdistrict 51 in the VII district with its large "Jewish" population, to 17.3 percent in subdistrict 85 in the X district.[28] The Catholic population ranged from 27.6 percent in the "Jewish"-dominated subdistrict 51 in the VII district to 79.5 percent in subdistrict 36 in the V district.[29]

In short, "Jewish" residence patterns in the city were marked by distinct "presences" and "absences" at a variety of scales. Whether the city was divided into Buda and Pest, into the fourteen major administrative districts, or into the one hundred subdistricts, the city's "Jews" were dispersed unevenly throughout the city. Indeed, the Jewish Council–generated lists of properties I have referred to above would suggest that at the level of apartment blocks it is also possible to point to the uneven distribution of the city's "Jewish" population.

This history of clusters of "Jewish" presence and absence in Budapest formed the backdrop to the implementation of ghettoization in large part on the basis of majority occupation. Given that the ghetto was being taken essentially to the "Jew," it is not surprising in the light of this demographic context that of the 2,639 apartment blocks designated for "Jewish" use on 16 June, the majority (2,057) were in Pest. Almost half of the properties designated were located in the four central districts, V, VI, VII, and VIII, that housed around three-quarters of the city's total "Jewish" population. In these central districts, the norm was large apartment blocks, rather than the smaller family homes common in the outlying districts of the city.[30] Therefore, this figure of half of the buildings designated amounted to considerably more than half of the total number of apartments designated.

In order to take into account these differences in housing type between the central districts (fewer, larger apartment blocks) and the outlying districts (more, smaller properties), it is worth examining the numbers of buildings designated on 16 June in each district as a proportion of the total number of properties in that district.

District	Total number of Properties (1941)	Number of Properties Designated on 16 June 1944	% of Properties Designated on 16 June 1944[31]
I	788	35	4.44
II	2,597	157	6.05
III	4,342	226	5.20
XI	3,113	81	2.60
XII	3,551	83	2.34
Buda	14,391	582	4.04
IV	534	48	8.99
V	1,195	372	31.13
VI	1,546	321	20.76
VII	1,593	439	27.56
VIII	2,034	156	7.67
IX	1,484	48	3.23
X	2,581	67	2.60
XIII	2,067	106	5.13
XIV	6,458	500	7.74
Pest	19,492	2,057	10.55
Budapest	33,883	2,639	7.79

The clustering of yellow-star properties is marked in terms of absolute numbers, but more significantly in terms of the proportion of buildings in an individual district designated. Thus, within the V, VI, and VII districts of Pest, the proportion of properties designated was relatively high (31.13 percent, 20.76 percent, and 27.56 percent, respectively). In the V district, close to one in three buildings was designated a yellow-star house on 16 June. Now of course these high percentages of designated properties made sense in light of "Jewish" demography patterns. As I've noted in the earlier table, in these three districts, the "Jewish" population—in 1941—made up 34.4 percent, 31.5 percent, and 35.5 percent of the total population in the district, respectively.

However, whilst placing the proportions of buildings designated alongside the proportions of "Jews" for each district reveals a degree of fit, it is clear that the figures don't match exactly. At the scale of the city, ghettoization did involve a considerable degree of concentration for the city's "Jewish" population. Thus, although making up 15.8 percent of the city's population, on 16 June only 7.79 percent of the city's properties were designated for "Jewish" use. Ghettoization therefore meant the allocation of living space for the "Jew" at a level of around half that of the "Jewish" presence in the city. However, this concentration was not uniform. As the table below reveals, the proportion of properties designated in each district were not roughly half the figure of the proportion of "Jews" in that district. Whilst the demographic realities of interwar Budapest shaped ghettoization in the broadest possible terms, where the "Jew" was to live in the city was not decided at the scale of the city or district, or even subdistrict or street. It was decided at the scale of the individual building, and therefore the picture that emerged when looked at from the district scale did not fit so neatly.

When looked at from the city scale, it is clear that the proportion of properties designated on 16 June was far from uniform. In Buda, where "Jews" made up 6.1 percent of the population, 4.04 percent of properties were designated. In Pest, where "Jews" made up 18.9 percent of the population, the percentage of properties designated (10.55) was relatively lower. It was in Pest where there was particularly marked uneven distribution of yellow-star houses. On the one hand, in the V district, roughly one in three residents was "Jewish" and roughly one in three buildings was designated for "Jewish" use. In contrast, in the XIV district, a little under one in five residents was "Jewish," yet fewer than one in ten buildings was designated for "Jewish" use.

District	"Jewish" Population as % of Population in District (1941)	Properties Designated as % of Properties in District (16 June 1944)[32]
I	4.1	4.44
II	7.5	6.05
III	8.3	5.20
XI	3.8	2.60
XII	5.5	2.34
Buda	6.1	4.04
IV	14.3	8.99
V	34.4	31.13
VI	31.6	20.76
VII	35.5	27.56
VIII	16.6	7.67
IX	7.8	3.23
X	3.4	2.60
XIII	6.3	5.13
XIV	18.9	7.74
Pest	18.9	10.55
Budapest	15.8	7.79

Such statistics had serious implications for the city's "Jews" on 16 June, 1944. As was made clear, the "Jew" was to move within—not between—districts,[33] and thus differences between districts led to differing "Jewish" experiences of concentration. In the I district of Buda, the proportion of properties designated for "Jewish" use actually exceeded the ratio of "Jew" to "non-Jew" in the district. Thus, whilst the June 16 "dispersed ghettoization" in the I district was to involve forced relocation, this relocation was *not* to amount—in theory at least—to a greater concentration of the "Jewish" vis-à-vis the "non-Jewish" population. Now in the I district, the absolute size of the "Jewish" population was small relative to that in other districts in the city. However, in the V district—home to 15 percent of the city's "Jewish" population—a similar picture of June 16 "ghettoization" as forced relocation, yet *not* concentration, emerges. As I've noted, in practice, approximately every third house was designated in a district where approximately one in three inhabitants was "Jewish."

In marked contrast, the sizable number of "Jews" living in the VIII district—home to 13.57 percent of the city's "Jewish" population—experienced the allocation of approximately half the number of properties in relation to their proportion within the district. Thus, ghettoization meant both forced relocation *and* concentration, as was also the case for the XIV district "Jewry" mentioned above. These examples of ghettoization as concentration mirrored the statistics for the city as a whole. Yet it is clear that at least on paper, ghettoization meant different things for the "Jewry" of different districts of the city. I want to think some more about experiencing ghettoization a little later in this chapter, and some more in the next.

Although there were significant differences between districts, very broadly speaking, ghettoization built upon the realities of where "Jews" were already living. The importance given to majority occupation meant that the "Jew" was housed where the "Jew" already was. Now of course the corollary of this was that the "Jew" was not housed where the "non-Jew" already was. And here, shaping the ghetto around majority occupation fitted with the concerns over the implications of implementing ghettoization upon the city's "non-Jewish" population. Those concerns can be seen in the lord mayor's intervention at the end of May 1944, but also go back to the very earliest nationally issued ghettoization orders.

Perhaps the clearest example of the principle of ghettoization being about the designation of where the "Jew" already was came with the designation of "Jewish" institutions (see figure 6). In addition to the designation of some 2,639 residential properties as inhabitable by "Jews" on 16 June, regulations were simultaneously issued dealing with twelve "Jewish" institutions. At this stage there were no plans to move elderly or sick "Jews" from homes or hospitals dispersed throughout the city. In the language of the legislation, "naturally Jews were not to be thrown out" of these institutions.[34] Rather, these "Jewish" institutions also were to be marked with a yellow star. It was the ultimate example of "ghettoization" being about the creation of "Jewish presences" along the lines of historical "Jewish presences."

It would seem that the situation had come full circle from the beginning of April 1944, when the creation of something approaching a ghetto had been the by-product of the creation of explicit "Jewish absences" in the city. By mid-June, the priority was on the creation of "Jewish presences" rather than the explicit creation of "Jewish absences" (save to some degree at least in the "modern" apartment building with low rents). And the creation of these "Jewish presences" was determined largely by pragmatic concerns about how to undertake mass relocations within a limited timescale in a city at war. These concerns, which, as I've suggested, were primarily about

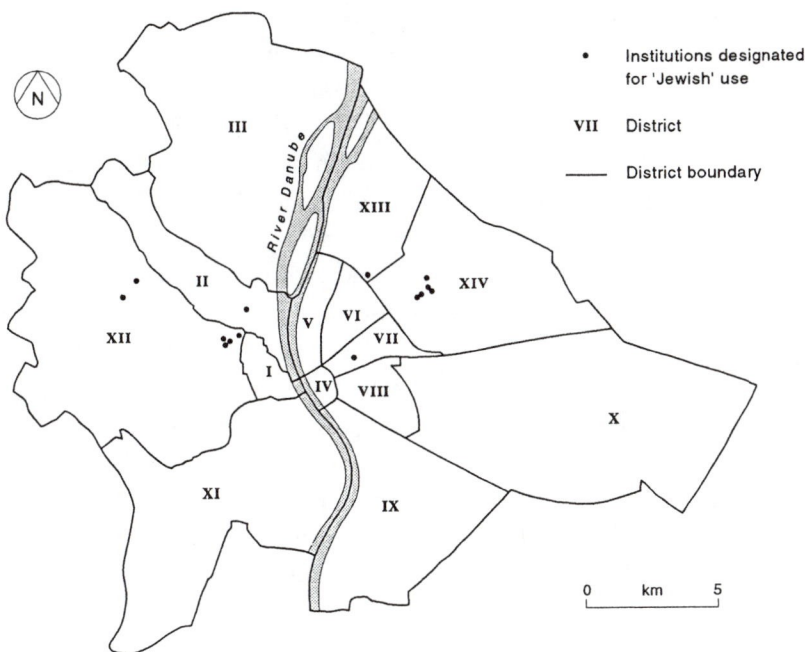

Figure 6. Designating "Jewish" institutions (16 and 22 June 1944). © Tim Cole.

the implications of segregating living space upon the "non-Jew," meant that the principle of designating the buildings where "Jews" already lived (*and* "non-Jews" did not) was of more concern than geostrategic and socioeconomic considerations. However, these concerns—so visible in the 9 May plans—were still present. Or perhaps more significantly, the discourses of geostrategy and socioeconomics were still being articulated in June 1944. As I've already noted, the discourse of the "Jews," Allied bombing, and the Budapest ghetto has its own complex history, which tends to blur the distinctions between primary and secondary sources.

A BRIEF HISTORY OF THE DISCOURSE OF "JEWS," ALLIED BOMBING, AND THE BUDAPEST GHETTO, 1944 TO THE PRESENT

Within the historical writing on the Hungarian Holocaust, the implementation of dispersed ghettoization (as a relatively unusual form of Holocaust ghettoization) in Budapest in June 1944 has been seen as a result of fears that housing the city's "Jews" in a single ghetto would open up the remainder of the city to Allied bombing. As I've suggested, this concern was being articulated in April 1944, when "Jews" were being rehoused after their homes had been confiscated for use by "non-Jewish" bomb victims. Such concerns do seem to have been significant in determining the shape of the 9 May ghetto plans, with the placing of ghetto areas close to factories, railway stations, and other potential bomb targets. However, by 16 June, the "Jew" was not to be housed specifically next to potential bomb targets (to form a protective shield of sorts) because the principle of majority occupation held sway. But, in housing the "Jew" essentially where the "Jew" already was at the scale of the apartment building, the end result was that "Jews" were dispersed throughout the city. So, in one sense at least, it could be argued that although not being specifically used as a protective shield, the implementation of dispersed ghettoization did ensure that large areas of the city were not made *judenfrei* and therefore open to Allied bombing.

However, whilst ghettoization as it was implemented in June 1944 can be seen in such terms, the harder issue is to what extent concerns with geostrategy did drive the decision to place the city's "Jews" in more than twenty-five hundred apartment buildings rather than in a closed ghetto. Now of course such a decision can be seen to be motivated by a concern not to make large parts of the city *judenfrei* and therefore open to Allied bombing. However, such a decision can also be seen—and I think more convincingly so—as a pragmatic choice of limiting the number of relocations involved in ghettoization, and in particular in limiting the number of relocations of "non-Jews."

But if this is the case, and I would suggest that the concerns being articulated in April and May 1944 suggest that this may be so, then why has the historiography of the Hungarian Holocaust opted for an explanation of dispersed ghettoization in terms of fears of Allied bombing? Here I would suggest that it is fruitful to think of these explanations as a discourse that has a history stretching from 1944 right through to the present day. What I would suggest is that contemporary historians have essentially rearticulated this discourse. So in a sense the contemporary historiography has become a continuation of the earlier discourse, which means that those texts become in essence primary sources, alongside, say, newspaper sources from 1944. The classic divisions between primary and secondary sources so central to traditional historical methodology are seemingly highly permeable in the case of the history of this discourse.

During 1944, links were being drawn between the Allied bombing of Hungarian cities (and, in particular, Budapest) and Hungarian "Jews" in general and Budapest's "Jews" in particular. The central perception was that the "Jew," as the enemy within, was to blame for the Allied bombings. As the historian Nicholas Nagy-Talavera, in a study of the representation of the Second World War within the Hungarian rightist press, concluded, "Jewish responsibility for the strategic bombing of Hungary by the United States Air Forces was an axiom for the Fascist press."[35] And as the Hungarian historian Péter Róbert has pointed out, the start of the bomb attacks on Hungarian cities provided fodder for the antisemitic press, which pointed to the "Jew" as both inspiring and directing the bombing.[36] It was claimed that Budapest's "Jews" living in the VI district were signaling from their rooftops to the Allied bombers.[37] With the "Jew" portrayed as coperpetrator of the bombings, it was seen to be entirely appropriate that the "Jew" be punished for the destruction that the bombings wrought from April 1944 onward.

These calls for retribution underlaid the confiscation of Jewish apartments for "non-Jewish" bomb victims in Budapest in early April 1944, as well as calls for the killing of one hundred "Jews" for each "Hungarian" killed by Allied bombs.[38] It also underlaid the decision to apply the policy of evacuation introduced in April 1944 only to the "non-Jewish" inhabitants of Budapest and the surrounding suburbs. When evacuation was implemented, certain categories of "non-Jews" were also excluded. However, the exemption of workers involved in the war industries, transport workers, and doctors, and the like was being done for very different reasons than the exemption of the city's "Jews."[39] "Jews" were to stay in the city as an act of punishment. They were to remain in Budapest to face enemy bombing, which it was suggested they—as fifth columnists—were ultimately behind. And they were not to be given access to bomb shelters.[40]

Alongside this discourse of the "Jew" as coresponsible for the bombing, and developing out of it, was the idea that the "Jew" was being spared by their coperpetrators, the Allies. "Proof" of this was offered by, amongst others, the rightist paper *Virradat*, which published an "interview" with captured American pilots in mid-May 1944. In response to the question "Do you also bomb those houses where Jews live?" the captured American pilots replied, "No, we leave them alone."[41] As a number of historians have suggested, the power of this myth was its seeming to fit, to some extent at least, with the reality of which parts of the city suffered the most during the bombings. Whilst the air raids were aimed primarily at factories and railways and thus the working-class neighborhoods surrounding these sites, these were the very places in the city where the "Jew" tended not to live (as I've noted in this chapter and the previous one). Thus both Macartney and Braham suggested that the demographic realities of where "Jews" lived in Budapest lent credence to suggestions that the allies were sparing "Jewish" areas of the city.[42] It would seem that such conclusions were not limited solely to Budapest but were articulated in the rightist press in the cities of Győr, in western Hungary, and Pécs, in southern Hungary as well.[43]

These arguments that the allies were intentionally sparing the "Jews" were being articulated in the rightist press at the same time that ghettoization plans were also being discussed. As I've already noted, an article in the rightist paper *Magyarság* specifically highlighted the potential geostrategic dangers of segregating the city's "Jews" in mid-April 1944. This article came in the aftermath of the confiscation of "Jewish" apartments and rumors that there were plans to concentrate the city's "Jews" in the area bordered by Dob u. and Podmaniczky u. Such plans were, *Magyarság* claimed, seen by "many" to be "disastrous as the terror bombers (under the orders of the Jews) will spare that area and drop their bombs only where "non-Jews" live!"[44] As I've already noted, Endre's response was to assure the interviewer that the plan was not to construct a single "closed Jewish quarter" but rather to "concentrate an appropriate number of Jews close to everywhere we expect to be attacked by the terror bombers, for example factories, railway stations."[45] And these words can certainly be seen to underlie the 9 May ghetto plans which I've discussed in some detail in the previous chapter.

This article of April 1944 was the first of a number of rightist press reports linking the myth of "Jewish" responsibility for the air raids to an assumption that the Allies spared the "Jews," and thus to an argument that concentrating the "Jews" in one place would open the remainder of the city to Allied attacks. The importance of utilizing the "Jew" as a potential geostrategic pawn when implementing ghettoization was reemphasized in mid-June when dispersed ghettoization was implemented. Not only did an article in *Esti Ujság* approve of the decision not to adopt a policy of "complete separation" in Budapest—as had been the case in the provincial towns "where a separate area has been designated for them [the "Jews"]"[46]—but the paper itself claimed some responsibility for the decision to implement a policy of dispersed ghettoization. The adoption of this policy was seen by the paper to be in part driven by the pragmatics of the sheer size of Budapest's

"Jewish" population, but also by awareness of the dangers of placing the "Jews" in a single ghetto area. And it was here that the paper claimed for itself some role within the decision, arguing that "from the beginning," the paper's "point of view was that the Budapest Christian and Jewish populations must take their share of the Anglo-Saxon air terror . . ."[47]

Now what is interesting is that it was not only the rightist paper *Esti Ujság* that claimed a role in ensuring that ghettoization when implemented was to be in a dispersed form, because of geostrategic concerns. Samu Stern, the president of the Jewish Council, also claimed a similarly influential role for himself. In what must be interpreted as a self-justifying postwar memoir, Stern claimed that

> the Council started a rumor that the ghetto, if there should be one, would not be shelled by the Anglo-Saxons, who would on the other hand destroy the other quarters of the city with an even greater fury. This rumor, although absolutely invented and unlikely, was spread on a wide scale, *and had the expected effect.* The commander of the capital's air-defense services himself protested against the concentration of the Jews into a single quarter, and, in consequence, Endre saw no other way than to give up the idea of the ghetto. Conferences took place throughout June, till at last they came up with the idea of concentrating the Jews in houses identified by Yellow Stars as "Jewish houses."[48]

His claim intentionally went against the more widely held view that the BBC was broadcasting such opinions.[49]

However, Stern's claims that it was the Jewish Council that created the discourse linking Allied bombing and Jewish ghettoization conflicted with the wartime claims of three other leaders of the Hungarian "Jewish" community. One of these, Fülöp Freudiger, was, like Samu Stern, a member of the Jewish Council. But he did not claim any authorship for the discourse linking Allied bombing and "Jewish" ghettoization and, in fact, dismissed it as wartime propaganda. The report written by Freudiger and two fellow leaders in the country's Orthodox community who escaped with him to Romania in August 1944 offered a very different view from that subsequently painted by Stern. For Freudiger, Diámant, and Link,

> every bombardment gave rise to the most ridiculous stories, with one theme only, namely that the Jews has signaled to the bombers, or had given the enemy information by wireless. With a complete lack of discrimination the most ridiculous

and stupid statements were made and published, all in order to strengthen the hatred against the Jews. Unfortunately it has been proved again and again that no propaganda is ever too stupid and clumsy not to appeal to the lowest instincts of the population.

The following case serves as an example: it was stated that English and American pilots dropped dolls and toys filled with explosives in order to kill children. This story was published and elaborated upon for days in the newspapers. Finally an explanation was given by an official source to the effect that traces of collaboration had been discovered between Hungarian Jews and English and American pilots, as a number of still empty dolls had been found at a Jewish merchant. The question as to how these dolls, after having been filled, reached the pilots flying at an altitude of 8,000 to 9,000 meters remained open! But in any case the alleged and hypocritical indignation was great. One can only admit with deep anger that even this idiotic and stupidly impudent statement was believed by many.[50]

For Freudiger, Diámant, and Link, the discourse was dismissed as rumors and propaganda, rather than as the result of an intentional act on the part of the Jewish Council to influence the shape of ghettoization in Budapest. And yet, they did see it, naive as it was, having an impact upon the decision-making process in June 1944.[51]

The prevalence of this discourse, at least amongst some of the city's population, was commented on by Raoul Wallenberg in a dispatch from Budapest in mid-July. He noted in a section reflecting more generally upon "the reaction of the Hungarians" to the persecution of the "Jews" that

I might mention, in this connection, that the presence of Jews is sometimes thought to constitute protection against bombing raids. Those who hold this view appear to believe that the scattering of Jews into about 2,600 Jewish houses all over Budapest, instead of concentrating them in ghettos, is a deliberate act, and that this is also the reason why the Jewish workforce has been forbidden to seek shelter during air raids.[52]

For Wallenberg, this discourse was offered by some as a post-facto explanation for the implementation of dispersed ghettoization in the city. Yet, within the subsequent historiography, the discourse has attained a dominant explanatory value in accounting for why Budapest's doctors of space implemented ghettoization along dispersed lines. Thus it is offered in the historiography not as a post-facto explanation but as an explanation of causation.

There appear to be two major lines of transmission of this discourse into the contemporary historiography. One is through the influential post-war writings of Ernõ Munkácsi and Jenõ Lévai, which are drawn upon heavily by Randolph Braham. The other is through the use made by Carlile Macartney and Raul Hilberg of the press reporting of 1944. However, in both cases, what seems to have happened is that the discourse adopted by Munkácsi and Lévai, and the rightist press in 1944, respectively, have simply been repeated within the historiography and given explanatory value.

In the case of Munkácsi and Lévai, their postwar works are somewhat problematic. Written by a prominent leader of the Pest "Jewish" community and a "Jewish" journalist, respectively, they are a mixture of postwar memoir, collection of documents, and early historical/journalistic accounts of the events of 1944. As a number of historians have noted, this mixture of memoir/documentary/history/journalistic account makes them equally invaluable and problematic.[53] Asher Cohen's comments on the difficulties of using Lévai's works holds true for Munkácsi as well when he notes, with what I think can be seen as the characteristic frustration of a historian, that Lévai's "books contain no footnotes, and in most cases Lévai does not cite his sources. In numerous cases these works contain errors of fact which in part cannot now be verified. There is no doubt that the abundant material in Lévai's book, written soon after the events, are important sources of information. Nevertheless . . . I have used this source with caution."[54] However, the caution he advocates is rather lacking from Braham's work, which dominates the field.

Braham in his chapter on the "Fate of the Jews of Budapest" starts off by more or less repeating Munkácsi's explanation of the rejection of a single ghetto in Budapest word for word. Munkácsi had written in 1945 that initial German plans for the creation of a large ghetto within the "Jewish" quarter in the VII district were rejected on the grounds that they would offend the "non-Jewish" residents of that area and leave the rest of the city open to Allied air attacks.[55] And Braham essentially repeated this in 1981, explaining that a single ghetto was rejected on the grounds of "Christian" sensitivities and fears "that if the Jews were segregated, the Allies would then concentrate their bombing exclusively upon the Christian-inhabited territories."[56]

This explanation that dispersed ghettoization was adopted in Budapest because of fears of opening up the city to Allied bombings had also been offered in the influential postwar accounts of the journalist Jenõ Lévai, whose works are also used heavily by Braham. For Lévai, "when the question of creating a ghetto arose, the Commander of the Budapest Air-raid Defenses, influenced by the threats broadcast by the British wireless, protested against such concentration of Jews. It was therefore decided not to concentrate the Jews in one single place, but separately in houses marked with a yellow star."[57]

Although not drawing upon Munkácsi's or Lévai's work directly, the British historian Macartney had essentially reiterated this argument in his study of wartime Hungary, suggesting that the creation of yellow-star houses—as opposed to a distinct ghetto—met both pragmatic and geostrategic concerns.[58] In Raul Hilberg's classic, *The Destruction of the European Jews*, this view of plans for a single ghetto in Budapest being rejected primarily because "the Hungarians were afraid that the establishment of a closed Jewish district would invite Allied retaliatory air raids upon the non-Jewish sections of the city" was again repeated, thus gaining the status of orthodoxy.[59]

Both Macartney's and Hilberg's works drew heavily upon contemporary press reports, and thus the line of transmission for them is not Munkácsi and Lévai but the rightist press in the period. Macartney acknowledged that the "authority for the overwhelming majority of statements of facts of public nature, and the source of almost all quotations from public speeches, articles, etc., is the Hungarian Press of the relevant dates."[60] Hilberg drew not on the Hungarian-language press but on the German-language press—in his section on Budapest, particularly *Deutsche Zeitung* and *Donauzeitung*, which he saw to contain "an extraordinary amount of information about Jewish matters."[61] However, to see the wartime Hungarian and German press as a source for "authority" and "information about Jewish matters" betrays a somewhat naive acceptance of this material at face value.

In the immediate aftermath of the German occupation of 19 March 1944, press censorship was heavily enforced in Hungary.[62] Control of the press had been in the hands of Antal Ullein-Reviczky, who had permitted the continuing publication of nonrightist papers.[63] Indeed, Juhász suggests that at the end of 1943 the circulation of anti-Nazi papers exceeded that of pro-Nazi papers.[64] However, after the occupation, the press and official news agency came under the jurisdiction of Government Commissioner Kolosváry-Barcsa, described by Macartney as "an extreme anti-Liberal and anti-Semite from the Right Wing of the M.É.P."[65] Centrist and leftist papers were suppressed, resulting in a situation where the remaining press was either in the hands of the government (*Pester Lloyd, Magyarország*) or an assortment of rightist groups (the M.É.P. controlled *Függetlenség* and *Esti Újság;* Milotay influenced *Új Magyarság;* Imrédy's influence was seen in *Virradat* and *Nemzetőr,* the National Socialists controlled *Magyarság;* the Nyilas Party controlled *Összetartás).*⁶⁶ To note the heavily censored nature of the Hungarian press is not to dismiss the importance of press reports as source material. However, it is to point to the need for a critical reading of the wartime press as a potential source of discourses of propaganda rather than discourses of policy. And I would argue that the discourse of the "Jews," Allied bombings, and the Budapest ghetto is just one such case in point.

What is striking is that there was a marked flexibility to the press discourse linking Allied bombings and Budapest's "Jews." Whilst in late April, May, and June 1944 the tendency in the press was to link the realities of Allied bombing to the need to implement dispersed ghettoization, given the assumed usefulness of the "Jew" as a human shield, by July 1944 the tendency was to link Allied bombings to calls for deportation. The "Jew" was no longer being seen as potentially useful to "non-Jews," but in need of punishment.

The flexibility of the discourse over time can be seen with the articulation of two very different versions in the same paper, *Magyarság,* in April and July 1944, respectively.⁶⁷ In April, *Magyarság,* as I've noted above, questioned Endre on the wisdom of placing the "Jews" in a single ghetto, on the grounds that this would open the remainder of the city up to Allied bombing. By July 1944, however, *Magyarság* was calling for the deportation of all of Budapest's "Jews" who stood accused of turning "upon us the American gangster-bombers"⁶⁸ and of bearing "the primary responsibility" for the Allied air attacks.⁶⁹ Yet mass deportations, even more so than the adoption of a single ghetto, would surely have opened the city up to Allied bombings. However, by July 1944, the earlier logic of the "Jew" as "geostrategic" pawn had been long forgotten. Circumstances had changed, and particularly in the context of the decision to halt deportations (which I will discuss more in chapter 8), the "Jew" as enemy within was seen as deserving punishment, not clemency. In many ways, the discourse in July 1944 had come back full circle to the earliest articulation of the "Jew" as the enemy within and therefore deserving punishment.

It is interesting that the Israeli historian Yehuda Bauer links Horthy's decision to halt deportations in July 1944 to the much-articulated issue of

Allied bombing, suggesting that "when, on 2 July, American aircraft bombed the Budapest railway station, Horthy saw in it a Jewish act of revenge. It was, as he himself said to the Germans, a factor in his decision to stop the deportations."[70] Thus, here the assumed link between the "Jews" and the Allies is seen as precipitating halting the deportations from Budapest, in the hope of limiting the bombings. The "Jews" are thus seen as pawns, although in a different manner than in the earlier period.

As this example suggests, there is a need to recognize the flexibility of the discourse of the "Jew" and Allied bombing over time, and to therefore offer a critical reading of it, and to acknowledge that this twisting and turning discourse has its own history. And that history includes the historiographical literature which has tended to restate the discourse of the potential value of the "Jew" as a human shield within historical texts seeking to explain the dispersed nature of ghettoization in Budapest.

However, what is striking when examining the discourse adopted by officials in June 1944 when ghettoization was implemented is that there was little mention of geostrategic concerns.[71] Although present in the 9 May plans, these concerns were not expressed in mid-June. Rather, the discourse adopted was that of the April ghettoization decree which saw the ghetto as, in part, a means of separating the "Jew" and "non-Jew," but also as a means of "freeing up a large number of flats and their allocation for those without flats."[72] There was a repetition of the arguments forwarded by Jaross when presenting the ghettoization decree to the Council of Ministers, with the antisemitic stock phrase "because of their material strength, the Jews live in exaggerated housing conditions . . ." cropping up again. The result of ghettoization was to be that the "Jews" in the city would find themselves "in flats more suitable to their proportion and social values." The corollary of this was to be the ending of the housing shortage faced by "Hungarian workers." This discourse of ghettoization as a means of redistributing access to housing—and being a redressing of the balance—which was being articulated in May 1944 was also being used in the run-up to the issuing of the 16 June regulations.

However, by June 1944, the deportation of the Budapest "Jewry" was being planned by Interior Ministry officials for July. Thus, ghettoization had become the means to an end, and primarily about gathering together the "Jew" for ease of eventual deportation from the city. In this context, the major concerns appeared to be the practical problems thrown up by relocating the "Jewish" population in the city at war and the impact of ghettoization upon the city's "non-Jewish" population. As I've suggested, the attraction of designating properties on the grounds of majority occupation was that it meant designating not simply where the "Jew" already lived but also where the "non-Jew" did not live. However, it was still estimated that ghettoization would involve the moving of 40,000 "Jewish" families and 12,000 "non-Jewish" families,[73] the implications of which were not lost upon either officials or observers.

EXPERIENCING GHETTOIZATION: THE XI DISTRICT

What the 16 June ghettoization plans actually involved in terms of relocations can perhaps best be seen by looking at the XI district in some detail. The survival of detailed surveys for this district allows for some sense to be gained of what ghettoization in mid-June meant for Budapest's "Jewish" and "non-Jewish" populations.[74] As I have already noted, the implementation of dispersed ghettoization on 16 June meant that a total of eighty-one properties on fifty-nine streets in the XI district were designated as "Jewish" houses. However, in practice, of the eighty-one properties designated, three were being used by German forces, one by the Hungarian army, one was a former "Jewish" school, two were officially sealed, and one simply did not exist.[75] Thus eight designated properties were in practice not available for "Jewish" occupancy. With one apartment building being in fact two, the "Jew" in the XI district was thus in practice to be restricted to a total of seventy-four yellow-star houses, containing 476 apartments. With a "Jewish" population of 2,154 in the district,[76] this amounted to on average just over four and a half persons in each apartment.

The properties did not entirely make sense in terms of majority occupation. Of the seventy-four houses, just under half of them (thirty-six) had a majority of "Jewish" tenants. In a further sixteen, the proportion of "Jewish" to "non-Jewish" tenants was 50:50. In twenty-two of them, "non-Jewish" tenants made up the majority, in some cases quite considerably. This was in particular the case in the largest apartment buildings. Thus in the three large apartment buildings designated as "Jewish" houses on Budafoki út (26/b. 32/e, 107), "Jews" were in the minority (five of twenty-four apartments, six of twenty, and four of eighty-four) in all three. A similar picture can be seen in the six large apartment buildings designated as "Jewish" houses in Horthy Miklós út (20, 28, 33, 37, 47, 52). Here "Jews" were in the minority (eight of thirty apartments, two of twenty-four, two of nine, seven of twenty-seven, nine of twenty-seven, and twelve of thirty-six) in all six buildings. It was only in the small villa properties, often with only one or two apartments, that "Jews" made up a majority of tenants. This was recognized by the district councilor who noted that in a district with such a low percentage of "Jewish" inhabitants (the figure he gave was 5.5 percent), the proportion of "Jews" in the large apartment blocks was never 50 percent, but only up to a maximum of between 20 and 30 percent.[77]

The implications were that the 16 June designations impacted a relatively large number of "non-Jewish" tenants in larger apartment buildings such as these in the XI district. For the district as a whole, ghettoization on 16 June meant that 322 "non-Jewish" tenants/families were to leave their apartments while 151 "Jewish" tenants/families were to remain where they were in their apartments. The greatest number of relocations was of course to be of the "Jewish" families in the district who were to move from their homes into these seventy-four designated buildings. This was to be completed within a matter of days. The list of ghetto houses was published on the Friday (16 June), and the relocations were to be completed by 8 o'clock on the Wednesday evening (21 June).

By 20–21 June, just prior to the deadline, 134 "Jewish" families had moved into thirty-nine of the yellow-star houses in the XI district, and 40 of the 322 "non-Jewish" families living in yellow-star houses had moved out of sixteen houses.[78] In essence, the vast majority of "non-Jewish" families still remained in their "Jewish" designated properties, and the vast majority of "Jewish" families remained in their nondesignated homes. Whilst relocation was one response to the issuing of the June 16 ghettoization decree, it is clear—in the case of the XI district at least—that the more common response was to adopt a policy of wait-and-see. Another response, which I want to think about a lot more in the next chapter, was that of active contestation of designations.

However, as I've noted, for 134 "Jewish" families in the XI district, the period from 16 to 21 June 1944 was a time of moving from their existing homes into yellow-star houses in the district. It is clear that this process was overseen by the Jewish Council. The job of relocating the city's "Jewish" population into officially designated "Jewish" living space had been given to the Jewish Council. "Jews" were firstly encouraged to move in with friends and relatives, and then to report these details to the council. However, those who could not find suitable accommodation for themselves were to be allocated a room within a yellow-star house by officials in the Jewish Council housing department. In order to facilitate this, the Jewish Council established 216 makeshift housing offices throughout the city, overseen by the council's central housing department under the leadership of Rezső Müller.[79]

In Buda, four main offices were established, one of which was located in the XI district in the entrance hall of the Bocskay u. synagogue. This was led by Zoltán Szerényi, who seems to have been a chartered accountant living in the district.[80] Under this main office were four suboffices located in apartments and houses in the district.[81] A further suboffice in the XI district came under the jurisdiction of one of the main offices located in the II district. Something of the role of these suboffices can be seen in the reference to Dr. Gyula László, leader of the suboffice for district 202, in a report submitted to the XI district councilor on 20 June 1944.[82]

Within the subdistrict that lay in Dr. Gyula László's jurisdiction, one of the houses designated for "Jewish" use on 16 June was Kikinda köz 9. This family house, with three rooms and servants' quarters, was occupied by the "Jewish" owner's three-member family. The Jewish Council's housing department had allocated this home to a further four "Jewish" families on 15 June. Since the allocation came prior to the official issuing of the list of yellow-star houses, it is clear that the Jewish Council had been made aware of which houses were being designated and had begun allocating families to these. This would seem to support Braham's claim that "thanks to Szentmiklóssy's [mayoral official in charge of housing] co-operation, Müller's department [in the Jewish Council] was ready with operational plans when the decrees were published, and had obtained complete statistical data on the number of vacancies and the number of Jews in each Yellow-Star house."[83]

However, these four families did not move into the house, as Gyula László had received new orders on 19 June which advised that no "Jews" should move into designated houses with less than three flats until further instructions were received. This ruling was applied by László at the housing subdistrict level, meaning that the planned relocations did not take place into Kikinda köz 9, containing as it did only one apartment. Therefore, it would seem that the Jewish Council was informed not only of the 16 June designations prior to their official issuing, but also something of the criteria of the 22 June redesignations—which I will look at in the next chapter—prior to their official issuing. Ultimately, the yellow-star status of Kikinda köz 9 was canceled on 22 June, requiring the owner and his family to move into one of the eighteen properties which remained for "Jewish" use in the

XI district. However, the four "Jewish" families the council had lined up to move into the house were saved from moving twice in a matter of days.

Whilst it is clear that the Jewish Council oversaw the relocation of "Jews" into yellow-star houses once they had been designated, it does not seem that the council had much influence in the process of designation. As I have suggested, this was overseen by Endre in the Interior Ministry, with the detailed shape of the ghetto being determined by the readings of the 1–2 June registration forms by officials in the mayoral housing department. It is significant, I think, that Jewish Council Chairman Samu Stern, in his postwar account, made no reference to council involvement in the designation of properties. Indeed, he explicitly stated that—unlike the situation in April when the Jewish Council had been called upon to provide apartments for bomb victims—"designation [of yellow-star houses] was not our job." Rather, designation is shown to have been in the hands of Szentmiklóssy, chief of Budapest's Housing Affairs Office, who was portrayed by Stern as a man of "good will."[84] Stern's silence over Jewish Council involvement is all the more significant when one considers the self-justificatory nature of his postwar memoir and his claims, which I've mentioned earlier, to having influenced the broad shape of ghettoization by creating the rumor that the Allies would spare the "Jews."

However, Stern's fellow council member Freudiger did claim that the Jewish Council played a role in the specific nature of the designations. In the coauthored report I've referred to earlier, Freudiger noted that "the Central Council was ordered to work out the plans" for ghettoization at the end of May. The result was that "a plan was made by the Central Council according to which the Jewish population of Budapest, about 200,000 people, were within six weeks to be installed in 3500 houses." Following the intervention of Endre—who "wrote on the document: '2500 houses, 2 days'"—the Jewish Council is represented as "only with the greatest difficulty" managing "to raise the number of houses to 2700 and to prolong the delay to five days."[85]

In his postwar account, Lévai painted the council as playing an active role in drawing up plans for ghettoization in Budapest, claiming that "Endre urged the mayor to invite the co-operation of the Executive Committee [i.e., the Jewish Council]" and that the first lists of designated properties were prepared "with the Committee's assistance."[86] This raises the question of whether the two lists of houses I've mentioned above are the results of just such Jewish Council cooperation. Certainly, the Hungarian historian Ágnes Ságvári sees them to be significant in determining the shape of the ghetto, reproducing a shortened and combined form of the lists she describes as "the first lists of those houses in which tenants required to wear the star, live in the greatest proportion," where "they ordered the settling of other Jews."[87]

However, these lists appear to have had little impact on the eventual choice of apartment blocks for designation. Whilst many of the houses featuring on the Jewish Council lists do feature in the 16 June designations, nothing in the way of a consistent pattern emerges. The V district provides an example. Of the 102 V district houses noted on the first list, 78 also featured in the 16 June designations. Of the 110 V district houses noted on the second list, 82 also featured in the 16 June designations. It is a case of houses designated on one list being omitted on the other. Those properties included on both lists arguably are there by dint of the shared criteria of choice being "Jewish" majority occupation, rather than due to any direct link between the two designations. It is impossible to tell whether these proposals were demanded by the Interior Ministry or offered by the Jewish Council. Whatever their status, the Jewish Council lists amount to a partial registration, which seems to have been quietly confined to the Interior Ministry archives.

Arguably the most vocal articulation of Jewish Council involvement in the specifics of drawing up the list of ghetto houses on 16 June came in the rightist press. In the aftermath of designation, the rightist press started a vocal campaign against designations. There was particular concern over the plight of "non-Jewish" inhabitants, with recognition that ghettoization was "not merely a Jewish affair, but closely affects the Christian population also."[88] The rightist press reminded the authorities that they "should not forget that Christians do not willingly leave yellow-star houses, but are forced to by the regulations."[89]

Much was made of examples of well-situated, modern apartment buildings being designated for "Jewish" use on 16 June, and behind this was sniffed a "Jewish" conspiracy. Thus, *Esti Ujság* claimed that the Jewish Council had played a part in the choice of apartment blocks to be designated and that "the Jews who know the greatest part of the Budapest apartment blocks well, arranged for themselves those apartment blocks with rooms of the largest dimensions."[90] The rightist press offered up the complaints of "non-Jewish" readers" that "Jews" had gained for themselves "well-situated villas" yet had "forced Christian inhabitants into the darkest and unhealthiest situated houses"[91] as evidence of a Jewish Council conspiracy to arrange the best properties for the city's "Jews."

Here is evidence of another discourse being variously articulated in June 1944—that of Jewish Council masterminding of the precise shape of the ghetto. In reality, it seems that the Jewish Council were largely involved simply in the process of arranging relocations into a ghetto shaped by other's hands (and ultimately, as I've suggested, shaped by the history of "Jewish" residence patterns in the city). However, it is clear that in the aftermath of 16 June this discourse of a "Jewish" conspiracy was one of the many complaints being raised against the shape of the ghetto. The precise shape of ghettoization was heavily contested in mid-June 1944 and ultimately led to the issuing of a reshaped ghetto on 22 June. It is that contestation and reshaping which I now want to turn to.

SIX

CONTESTING GHETTOIZATION, JUNE 1944

The implementation of a territorial solution of the "Jewish question" in Budapest in the shape of 2,639 "Jewish" houses was contested more or less immediately. Criticism of the houses designated for "Jewish" use was voiced in the rightist press in mid-June. According to Lévai, none other than Ferenc Rajniss, the editor of the notoriously antisemitic paper *Magyar Futár*, as well as *Esti Ujság*, ironically found himself living in a house— Kossuth Lajos tér 18—which was designated for "Jewish" use on 16 June. Failing to see the irony of this, Lévai notes that Rajniss immediately moved into the Gellért Hotel and protested what he saw to be a "Jewish" conspiracy in the pages of his paper.[1] But it was not simply in the pages of the press that the precise shape of the ghetto was being contested. Rather, a significant number of ordinary Hungarians—both "Jewish" and "non-Jewish"— petitioned the mayor in the aftermath of the designations. By 20 June, Budapest's mayor was reported by *ÚjMagyarság* as estimating that between 300 and 400 complaints had already arrived at the City Hall concerning the precise shape of ghettoization, and I have located some 600 or so surviving petitions in the archives of the City Council.[2]

In his only comments on this contesting of ghettoization in Budapest, Braham is right to note that "the overwhelming majority of the pleaders were Christians requesting that their buildings not be designated as Yellow-Star houses; Jews usually had the opposite request."[3] Of the 600 or so petitions in the City Council's archive, the largest single group (just over 200) are requests from "non-Jews" for cancellation of yellow-star designation and the second-largest group (just over 150) are requests from "Jews" for yellow-star designation. The third-largest group of petitions (over 100) came from those in mixed marriages requesting that both partners be permitted to remain together. The regulation of "Jewish" living space—which ghettoization entailed—threatened to split up mixed marriages and families. Whilst marriages between "Jews" and "non-Jews" had been outlawed since 1941, it was not until the implementation of ghettoization in the capital that the "Jew" and "non-Jew" spouse were to be physically separated.

Alongside the contesting of the designating of residential properties, the period 16–22 June also saw the contesting of designated institutional space. Two "Jewish" institutions omitted from the 16 June list of designated institutions petitioned for yellow-star status. Both the Buda Jewish Women's Association home for the elderly (II Keleti Károly u. 22) and the Weiss Alice hospital for mothers (XIII Bókay tér 4) were added to the places in the city where the "Jew" could live after 22 June 1944[4] (see figure 6). With the "Jewish" institutions in the city, therefore, the process of designation and redesignation occurred simultaneously with the process of designation and redesignation of "Jewish" apartments. The implementation of ghettoization in the city amounted to the total restructuring of all "Jewish" living space in Budapest. However, the response of mayoral officials to requests for designation of institutional space appears to have been more positive than the response to requests for designation of residential properties. Presumably this was in large part because designation of the former had little impact on the "non-Jewish" population of the city.

But with the designation of apartment buildings, ghettoization impacted in myriad ways "non-Jews" and "Jews" who contested designation. I think that something of the complexity of this contestation of ghettoization in mid-June 1944 can be seen by examining ten of the properties that featured in petitions submitted to Budapest's mayor.[5] Four of these apartment buildings—V Pannonia u. 44, VI Király u. 82, VI Lendvay u. 15, and VIII Rákoczi út 51—had been designated for "Jewish" use on 16 June. Another six apartment buildings—V Koháry u. 16, V Szent István Park 10, VI Eötvös u. 42, VII Erzsébet körút 15, VII Hársfa u. 57, and IX Ráday u. 37—had not been designated as part of the ghetto. The status of all ten was contested in mid-June. In the case of the former group of properties, there were calls for cancellation of yellow-star status and in the case of the latter calls for yellow-star status. However, what is particularly interesting about these ten properties—and this is why I've chosen to examine them in depth—is that they featured in more than one petition, with the mayor, often explicitly, being called on to mediate in the contestation of the status of an individual apartment block between differing parties. Thus in the case of these ten apartment buildings, it was not simply the original designation that was contested but the subsequent petitioning by one group with an interest in the property. In short, these ten properties were contested sites in mid-June 1944.

What is striking is that this contestation did not simply divide along the fault lines of "Jew" versus "non-Jew," as Braham's brief comments would suggest. In five of the ten apartment buildings I want to look at, contestation was between "Jews" and "non-Jews," with "Jews" calling for designation of their particular building and "non-Jews" calling for cancellation. As I've already noted, such petitioning makes up the majority of the challenges to the shape of the ghetto submitted to the mayor in mid-June. However, contesting ghettoization, in some cases at least, brought about coalitions between "Jews" and "non-Jews," as well as divisions within the "non-Jewish" population. Thus, in addition to being called upon to mediate between "Jews" and "non-Jews," the mayor was also called upon to mediate between three other groups divided by ghettoization. Firstly, these contested sites point to conflict between owners and tenants, secondly, between "non-Jews," and thirdly between "non-Jews" and coalitions of "Jews" and "non-Jews."

And this, I think, is interesting in that it suggests that responses to ghettoization, when it was first implemented in Budapest, were far from uniform. Now, I would be the first to admit that these ten contested sites I will examine are not representative of the 600 or so petitions submitted to the mayor in June 1944. As I've already noted, most—if not all—of those do fit with the breakdown of reactions into the classic categories of "non-Jews" calling for cancellation of yellow-star status and "Jews" calling for designation of their property as a yellow-star house. However, whilst not representative, these ten sites do provide an intriguing glimpse into the kinds of reactions generated by the implementation of a policy of ghettoization, which is significant source material of a qualitative nature. By dint of their lack of representativeness, studying them perhaps less answers questions than raises new questions—in particular, questions relating to the vexed issue of just what the responses of ordinary Hungarians were to the implementation of the Holocaust in Hungary in 1944.

In his opening address to the academic conference held in Budapest to commemorate the fiftieth anniversary of the Holocaust in Hungary, the historian Ferenc Glatz asked the question

> What did the ordinary citizen think about the situation existing in Hungary in April 1944? The ordering of all Jews to wear clothing on which a yellow star was displayed, the banning of Jews from the use of certain public transportation, and discrimination against them even in war rations, appeared as a still crueler continuation of the anti-Jewish laws. Not to speak of the large-scale political corruption involved in the transfer of Jewish property into "Christians hands."[6]

Glatz's question as to what the "ordinary citizen" thought is perhaps even more salient when asked of the month June 1944. By then, Hungary's "Jews" had been segregated in ghettos, and deportations from provincial Hungary to Auschwitz-Birkenau had commenced. However Glatz did not give an answer to his own—purely rhetorical—question of what ordinary Hungarians were thinking in April 1944, and the secondary literature on the Hungarian Holocaust is not much more forthcoming about the reactions of ordinary Hungarians during the spring and early summer of 1944. Whilst there have been explorations of collaboration by national and local officials in Hungary, reflections upon the reactions of the population at large to the implementation of the Holocaust in Hungary are largely restricted to isolated and rather general statements in the existing historiography and anecdotal references in survivors' memoirs.

Braham makes reference to "the generally passive, if not openly hostile, attitude of the Christian population,"[7] which he explains as a result of decades of antisemitic propaganda and a desire to profit from the attacks upon the "Jews."[8] However, he never fully develops popular responses to the implementation of the Holocaust. Rather, Braham—like other historians of the Hungarian Holocaust—pays more attention to the collaboration of Hungarian officials and institutions at both the national and the local levels. From the influential postwar writings of István Bibó onward, the role played by government ministries, county administrators, city mayors, and the gendarmerie have remained key questions. Not only do the names of native collaborators permeate Braham's narrative but the role of administrators in the locality has been examined by Karsai, Molnár, and myself amongst others.[9] In part, of course, the relative silence about the behavior and attitudes of ordinary citizens—"non-Jewish" neighbors and friends—in the historiography reflects problems of sources.

Whilst not generally referred to within the host of administrative documents available from both the national and the local levels, the actions and attitudes of ordinary Hungarians do crop up in oral history interviews, survivor memoirs, and postwar fiction. However, these references to the behavior of "non-Jewish" neighbors are largely anecdotal. For example, in Judith Isaacson's memoir of the implementation of the Holocaust in the town of Kaposvár in southwest Hungary, there are references to a variety of responses by "non-Jewish" neighbors. These run the gamut from school friends who hide both her bicycle and typewriter, to a former apprentice of her grandfather's who comes to measure up their home in the ghetto and tells them, "the house and the bakery'll soon be mine," to a former teacher who brings her a book when she is in the ghetto.[10]

Such a range of responses, from helping "Jewish" neighbors to seizing "Jewish" property, appears time and time again in memoir and fictional accounts. Interestingly, in her survivor memoir, Georgia Gabor attempts to quantify the segments of the population involved in these differing responses, claiming that

> at most a fifth were anti-Semitic by conviction. Perhaps another fifth aided the Gestapo and our quisling government for personal gains, such as promotions, favors, and rewards. About a third did not get involved; they disassociated themselves from the persecuted elements, and continued making the best of their status quo. The remaining fourth, however helped our people to a lesser or greater degree. Their aid ranged from loaning money, keeping valuables or occasionally giving food to one of their unfortunate friends, to actually hiding Jews for months in their own homes.[11]

However, such a definitive breakdown of the reactions of the Hungarian population is, of course, impossible for one city, let alone the entire country.

Now, as I've already suggested, the petitions submitted by "Jews" and "non-Jews" in the case of these ten contested sites are sources with severe limitations. It would be foolish to suggest that the reactions to ghettoization in these petitions reflect the attitudes of all petitioners in June 1944, let alone all inhabitants of Budapest or Hungary as a whole. I am taking the contesting of only ten properties within the specific context of the implementation of one element of the Holocaust in Hungary: ghettoization. But what these ten sites of contestation do suggest is that there were multiple responses by ordinary Hungarians—both "Jews" and "non-Jews"—to ghettoization in Budapest, and this raises interesting questions which deserve to be asked of other sources.

FIVE SITES OF CONTESTATION BETWEEN "JEWS" AND "NON-JEWS"

Half of these ten contested sites in mid-June 1944 were contested between "Jewish" and "non-Jewish" tenants and owners along the lines that Braham spells out. At V Koháry u. 16, which had not been designated for "Jewish" use on 16 June, it was the "Jewish" owners and tenants who were first off the blocks in petitioning the mayor for designation. The letter written by the "Jewish" owners in the name of the twenty-six "Jewish" tenants arrived in the City Hall on 19 June.[12] Two days later, a letter arrived from the "non-Jewish" tenants after they had heard a rumor that the "Jewish" inhabitants of the apartment building had presented an application for yellow-star status.[13] The rumor was, as the first letter shows, entirely true.

These two letters reveal a tussle over the status of this apartment block, which was mirrored throughout the city in the aftermath of the 16 June ghettoization decree. By the designation at the level of the apartment building, "Jewish" and "non-Jewish" tenants were brought into conflict with each other as they both sought to stay put in their apartments. Because segregation of "Jewish" and "non-Jewish" living space was being undertaken at the level of the apartment building, tenants seeking to remain in their own apartments had to fight over the status of the entire building. And thus, the "Jewish" tenants of Koháry u. 16 petitioned for "Jewish" status for the entire building (to ensure that they could stay put) and the "non-Jewish" tenants counterpetitioned to ensure that they could stay put.

With a view to staying put, both groups of petitioners noted the difficulties that being forced to move out would present. The "Jewish" tenants highlighted the problems that the building's three "Jewish" doctors—a scarce commodity in the city at war—would face in locating new surgeries if they had to move out.[14] The "non-Jewish" tenants pointed to the sheer costs of moving that would specifically impact a number of "non-Jews," including victims of bombing who had recently moved into apartments in the house and thus could not afford to move again.[15] But alongside these concerns with pragmatics were interwoven other strands of the discourses surrounding ghettoization that I have noted in previous chapters. For the "Jewish" tenants, it was the discourse of majority occupation—they could claim twenty-six out of the thirty-four tenants—and "Jewish" ownership.[16] For the "non-Jewish" tenants it was the quality of the apartment building—centrally heated and with average rents—and the status of some of the "non-Jewish" tenants—lawyers, bank managers, business leaders, and the like—that were deemed strong arguments against designation.[17]

It is striking in reading these petitions that the differing discourses being articulated in, for example, official press statements or more widely in the press in 1944 are utilized to make the case for designation or the cancellation of designation. Foremost amongst these is the discourse of majority occupation, which as I've suggested does seem to have been of significance in determining the shape of the ghetto. But the discourse of majority occupation is also joined by socioeconomic and geostrategic discourses. These can be seen being articulated by petitioners contesting VI Eötvös u. 42, not designated for "Jewish" use on 16 June. A group of "Jewish" tenants called for yellow-star status for their property in a letter arriving at the City Hall on 20 June.[18] The next day, a letter from a "non-Jewish" tenant sought to counter what he described as a campaign started by a "Jewish" lawyer living in the house that the "Jews" remain and the "non-Jews" be forced out of the property.[19] He justified the continuation of the house's "non-Jewish" status on the grounds of both the status of the tenants—some of whom were senior civil servants—and the length of their tenure in the property—some had lived there for several decades. In contrast, the "Jewish" lawyer argued the case for "Jewish" status on the grounds of majority occupation—fifteen of the twenty-six tenants were "Jewish" and only nine of the twenty-six flats did not have any "Jewish" interest. This argument for designation on the grounds of majority occupation was combined with an argument that can be seen as broadly geostrategic, although in rather different terms from the broader discourse I noted in the last chapter.

As I've already suggested, the idea that the Allies were sparing "Jewish" properties and therefore a dispersed form of ghettoization should be implemented in Budapest was widely held in 1944. In this "Jewish" petition, however, there was a different twist to the linkage between ghettoization and Allied bombing, and one that raises a somewhat problematic question. For a number of the "Jewish" tenants of Eötvös u. 42, an additional reason for designation of their property as a ghetto house was its proximity to the western railway station in the city, which placed it in danger of bombing raids.[20] In essence, these "Jewish" petitioners argued for the designation of their apartment building in part on the grounds that its potentially dangerous situation made it the kind of place where "Jews" rather than "non-Jews" should live.

The logic behind this statement was clear: It was more acceptable for the "Jew" to be susceptible to bomb attacks than the "non-Jew," and therefore it would be better to designate this house for "Jewish" rather than "non-Jewish" use, given its vulnerable location. In this example—and it is an example repeated in different ways in other petitions—it is clear that an antisemitic discourse was being articulated by "Jewish" petitioners. What is unclear is what we should make of this. Was this an essentially instrumental use of antisemitic discourse, with "Jews" utilizing such arguments for their own purposes? Or was this was an effective buying into antisemitic discourse on the part of "Jews"?

Whether antisemitic discourses were adopted by petitioners in merely instrumental ways is a question which needs asking not only of "Jewish" but also of "non-Jewish" petitioners. As I have suggested, the press offered a host of factors determining the choice of properties as ghetto houses, and these could be—and were—drawn upon by petitioners in framing their arguments. Indeed, explicit reference is made to this by the "non-Jewish" petitioners calling for the cancellation of the yellow-star status of VI Király u. 82, in their extensive correspondence.[21] There they reference the "principles . . . asserted many times and made public through the press" about which houses would qualify for yellow-star status, and it is clear from reading the petition that these principles are self-consciously picked up on—albeit selectively.

Their petition came after the designation of their apartment building for "Jewish" use on 16 June. Interestingly, prior to designation, the "Jewish" tenants of the house had already written—on 13 June—to the City Hall to call for "Jewish" designation for their property in the forthcoming list of ghetto houses.[22] This was justified in terms of majority occupation—thirty-one of the forty-six tenants were "Jewish." However, they were keen to ensure the accuracy of the figures submitted in the 1–2 June survey. Their assertion was that three flats had been mistakenly classified as "non-Jewish." The "non-Jewish" owner of the property had promised to correct this mistake, but you get the sense in reading the letter that these "Jewish" tenants were not entirely convinced that he was going to do this and so wrote to ensure that the correct proportion of "Jewish" to "non-Jewish" tenants was known by the city officials designating properties.

After the property was designated for "Jewish" use, the "non-Jewish" house air-raid warden wrote on behalf of the "non-Jewish" owner, tenants, and inhabitants requesting cancellation of yellow-star status.[23] In part this request was justified on the basis of majority occupation, albeit of a different kind from that argued by the "Jewish" tenants. They could not claim "non-Jewish" majority occupation in terms of tenants, but the air-raid warden was keen to note that there was clear "non-Jewish" majority occupation in terms of inhabitants—specifically the stationing of approximately 100 soldiers in the house. Alongside articulating a discourse of majority occupation, this "non-Jewish" petition for cancellation of the property also stressed the "non-Jewishness" of the owner and the status of a number of the "non-Jewish" tenants—civil servants, industrialists, businessmen.

In a lengthy letter, these justifications for cancellation were joined by socioeconomic and geostrategic discourses. Not only was the house the most modern on the street, but the south-facing balconies were described as sunny and healthy, and the flats had cheap rents. Moreover, the house had the very best air-raid shelter in the neighborhood, a fact that was backed up with the presentation of a newspaper clipping asserting just that. The assumption was that the house with "the best air-raid shelter" in the neighborhood should not be designated for "Jewish" use, given that Jews were prohibited from using air-raid shelters.

Now, in many ways, such an argument paralleled that articulated by the "Jewish" petitioners at Eötvös u. 42.[24] For both sets of petitioners—"Jewish" and "non-Jewish"—the "Jew" should be subjected to bombing attacks and the "non-Jew" shielded from them. In short, both adopt an antisemitic discourse. However, what is hard to ascertain is whether the articulation of such antisemitic discourses amounted merely to instrumentality on the part of *both* "Jews" and "non-Jews." Was it the case that in their desire to stay put both "Jewish" and "non-Jewish" tenants were willing in mid-June to draw upon whatever discourses were seen to have official sanction, including those that were blatantly antisemitic? In short, were the "non-Jews" of Király u. 82 antisemitic in their attitudes, or were they simply playing at it? And were the "Jews" of Eötvös u. 42 buying into a dominant antisemitism or attempting to utilize it for their own purposes? In the case of Király u. 82, the "non-Jewish" petitioners argued that the "Jew" was not simply more expendable but also deserving of less decent apartments. What is striking is that the very same discourse is adopted by "Jewish" petitioners, as can be seen in the case of VI Lendvay u. 15 that I examine below.[25] And thus the same questions of whether antisemitic discourse was merely being used in instrumental ways by both "Jews" and "non-Jews" in Budapest are again raised.

As I have suggested, a number of discourses being articulated in the context of the implementation of ghettoization reemerge in the pages of the petitions. As I noted in chapter 4, in the initial plans for ghettoization, a central concern was with clearing "Jews" from the main streets of the city. Not surprisingly perhaps, this concern is rearticulated within the petitions, albeit in a changed context. For, as I noted in chapter 5, this concern was no longer a priority when ghettoization was implemented in mid-June. It did, however, play a central role in the petitioning of a "non-Jewish" inhabitant of VII Erzsébet körút 15.[26] This building was not designated for "Jewish" use on 16 June, and it was that nondesignation which this petitioner was keen to protect. In a letter written the day after the publication of the list of ghetto houses, he made reference to "Jewish" campaigns to add further "Jewish" properties on the street. He called for the declining of these petitions and the maintenance of the original designations of "non-Jewish" properties on the street.

This request that no further properties be designated for "Jewish" use was justified on the grounds that Erzsébet körút was one of the main streets in the city, forming part of the main ring in Budapest. Writing as a self-proclaimed "Hungarian historian," the petitioner claimed that the main streets of a city gave a sense of the city's "general character" and therefore attaching yellow stars to houses on this major street was an act of symbolic value. Noting that the "non-Jewish" residents of the street had painfully witnessed the designation of sixteen houses for "Jewish" use, he asked that no further properties on the entire street be designated.

However, his petition was contested—as he noted was the case up and down the street—by a request for designation from the "Jewish" inhabitants.[27] In a telegram sent on 16 June, and a later letter, designation was called for on the grounds of majority occupation. The tenants were described as 76 percent "yellow star wearing" and the owners 80 percent "Jewish." During petitioning in direct opposition to a tenant from the same building, evidence appeared of a degree of coalition building with "non-Jewish" petitioners from a neighboring property. As was the case in a number of petitions, there seemed to be an assumption that the absolute number of "Jewish" properties would remain constant, and therefore any call for designation must be matched with a call for cancellation. So the petitioners offered a designation swap of sorts. They suggested that Erzsébet körút 15 be designated for "Jewish" use in place of Erzsébet körút 9–11. This latter property had been designated a yellow-star house on 16 June, and yet the tenants of Erzsébet körút 15 pointed out that it had a majority of "non-Jewish" inhabitants and was also home to the Hunnia film company, a government propaganda organ.

This suggested yellow-star swap was not the sum total of the initiative shown by the "Jewish" tenants of Erzsébet körút 15. They cleverly offered a solution to the problem raised in the counterpetition submitted by their "Hungarian historian" fellow occupant. With a clear eye to neutralizing the impact of the argument that it was on a main street, they suggested that if the property was designated, the yellow star could be placed on the entrance to the property from the side street Miksa u, rather than on the main entrance on Erzsébet körút. It was a stroke of genius. Not only did they have a building on the same street that was ready to swap designations with them, but they also had a ready solution to the complaint voiced about the location of their property on a main street. In effect, their solution offered the opportunity to have one less yellow star showing on a doorway on Erzsébet körút, whilst still allowing them to remain in their apartments.

As I have suggested, in the above four cases the concern of "Jewish" residents was with remaining in their apartments. Because designation took place at the scale of the apartment building, rather than the individual apartment, staying put meant petitioning for yellow-star status for the whole property. In short, their concern was that the ghetto would come to them. These petitions were countered by "non-Jewish" residents, intent on remaining in their apartments, and thus also concerned with influencing the status of the entire apartment building. However, ghettoization at the scale of the apartment building did more than bring "Jewish" and "non-Jewish" tenants into conflict. Ghettoization impacted not simply tenants but also owners, and often in very different ways. In the final property where contestation divides neatly along the lines of "Jew" versus "non-Jew," this division was not one between tenants but between owner-occupiers and nonresident owners. This division over ghettoization between inhabitants and owners was one that divided not only "Jews" and "non-Jews" but also "non-Jews." Ghettoization could mean very different things to those living in a designated building and those simply owning that building.

The apartment building at V Szent István Park 10 was not designated for "Jewish" use on 16 June. Therefore, the following day, the "Jewish" owner-occupiers wrote requesting yellow-star status on the grounds of majority occupation.[28] The fact that fifteen of the eighteen apartments were inhabited by "Jews" was stressed, along with the faultless record of loyalty to the nation of these pensioners. They had scraped together their life savings to purchase these freehold apartments, and being forced to move would be a major financial blow. As was the case with the petitioning over V Koháry u. 16, forced relocation had costs, not the least of which were financial costs.

However, for the nonresident "non-Jewish" owners of apartments in the buildings, ghettoization also had costs: not the costs of forced relocations but the costs of the overcrowding implicit to ghettoization. The petition presented by two nonresident "non-Jewish" owners came in the aftermath of the issuing of a second definitive list of yellow-star houses on 22 June.[29] In this list, which I want to look at in much more detail later on in this chapter, Szent István Park 10 was designated for "Jewish" use, no doubt to the delight of the "Jewish" owner-occupiers who penned the 17 June petition. However, this new designation was challenged in a letter that arrived at the mayor's office on 28 June. What is striking is that in this later letter, a remarkably similar discourse is adopted, although with a very different view in mind.

Like the "Jewish" owner-occupiers, these "non-Jewish" owners stressed that they had scraped together enough money to buy apartments in this building, which they rented out. For them, financial concerns over ghettoization were preeminent. These were not the costs of forced relocations central to the petitioning of tenants, but the costs of property damage central to the petitioning of owners. They were well aware that ghettoization involved the overcrowding of apartments, which they feared would result in the dirtying of "the beautifully painted white doors" of their apartments, amongst other things, and these apartments being left "wormy." For them, ghettoization meant overcrowding, and overcrowding meant material damage, which someone would have to pay for. Given that their petition was written after the deadline for "Jews" to move into properties, they stated that they would need to claim compensation from the authorities for the damage already caused by large numbers of "Jews" moving into their apartments.

What is striking is that their petition reveals a consciousness on the part of owners of designated properties about both the nature of ghettoization and the implications of ghettoization for property owners—as opposed to tenants and inhabitants. The designation of privately owned properties as ghetto houses by the authorities was seen by owners as incurring considerable costs. In some cases of course this could mean a coalition between "non-

Jewish" owners and "non-Jewish" tenants, with both wanting the property to remain nondesignated, albeit for different reasons. However, this was not always the case. Rather, the differing concerns of owners and tenants could—and did—result in contestation between "non-Jews" over the status of a particular property, as can be seen in the case of Pannonia u. 44.

TWO SITES OF CONTESTATION BETWEEN "NON-JEWS"

Designated for "Jewish" use on 16 June, V Pannonia u. 44 saw its status contested in the following days by the "non-Jewish" owner of the property and one of the "non-Jewish" tenants. The owner's request to the mayor on 19 June was for cancellation of the house's ghetto status, on the grounds that he was not a "Jew."[30] He pointed out that the neighboring houses—numbers 42 and 46—were both owned by "Jews," had the same proportion of "Jewish" tenants to his building, and yet had not been designated for "Jewish" use. His suggestion was clear: his property should be canceled from the list of yellow-star houses and one or both of these neighboring properties should be designated instead.

His request for cancellation was countered by a request that the designation remain.[31] Written by one of the tenants of the apartment building, the justificatory discourse was one of the pragmatics of relocation, albeit in a different form from that adopted by the "Jewish" tenants considered earlier. Whereas in the case of V Koháry u. 16 their concern was with the pragmatics and cost of moving out of a nondesignated property, the concern in the case of Pannonia u. 44 was with the pragmatics and cost of moving back *into* the earlier vacated property.

The petitioner had already moved into a new apartment in a nondesignated building on a nearby street and thus was opposed to the expense and inconvenience of having to move yet again. And he was clearly not alone in already having moved out of the designated property and arranged an exchange of apartments with a neighboring "Jewish" family. In a supporting letter from the air-raid warden in the building, it is clear that five of the "non-Jewish" tenants in the building either had already moved out or were in the process of exchanging apartments with "Jews" in the neighborhood. For these "non-Jewish" tenants—and they were not alone in this—ghettoization offered the opportunity to move from their present apartments into apartments vacated by "Jews," and this opportunity was seized and subsequently defended. In these cases, the costs of relocation were outweighed by the benefits of relocation in terms of attaining better living space. Ghettoization was seen as an opportunity rather than a cost, and indeed in a number of cases, designation was sought by "non-Jewish" tenants precisely on the grounds that it presented the opportunity to acquire more advantageous living conditions. In short, ghettoization was seen by some "non-Jews" as an opportunity for social mobility.

However, as the case of VIII Rákoczi út 51 demonstrates, there was not always consensus on the part of "non-Jewish" tenants over the question of whether designation presented an opportunity for social mobility or the unwelcome costs of forced relocation. Upon the designation of the property as a yellow-star house on 16 June, twelve of the "non-Jewish" tenants petitioned for cancellation of this status on 18 June.[32] In self-conscious opposition to this petition, nine of the "non-Jewish" tenants requested, on 20 June, that the designation stand.[33] For both, there was a concern with the costs of relocations. For twelve of the tenants, moving out of the property would entail financial and health costs. However, for nine of the tenants who had already begun to exchange their apartments for "Jewish" apartments in non-designated buildings, it was moving back that would be costly

What is striking in the case of this particular building is that the "non-Jewish" tenants were divided on whether they saw designation as a cost or an opportunity. For twelve petitioners, moving into "Jewish" apartments presented not a route to better living conditions but all the costs of moving into "extremely dirty, damaged, and in their present condition completely uninhabitable" living conditions which promoted "infectious diseases."[34] Thus, far from designation presenting the possibility for social mobility, it presented the very opposite. It was seen to entail costs both financial and medical. These petitioners' clear preference was to remain in what they saw as their existing comfortable and stylish apartments. In contrast, for nine petitioners, ghettoization presented the opportunity to change apartments with "Jews," and once those exchanges had taken place there was no desire to go back on them.[35]

It would seem that behind these radically different perceptions of ghettoization lay very different perceptions of the "Jew." For the former twelve petitioners, the "Jew" was constructed as a bearer of disease, and thus the idea of exchanging apartments with a "Jew" was anathema. However, for the latter nine petitioners, not only was the idea of exchanging apartments thinkable, but it was already something they were actively engaged in doing. Although the point is not explicit in their petition, I think it is possible to argue that for them the "Jew" was constructed as a member of a privileged elite, rather than as a bearer of disease. Thus not only was exchanging apartments admissible, but it also offered a chance for upward mobility. Here we see two opposing (antisemitic) discourses of the "Jew" being adopted, with ghettoization being variously perceived as an opportunity or a threat in terms of these radically different ways of constructing the "Jewish" Other.

THREE SITES OF COALITION BETWEEN "JEWS" AND "NON-JEWS"

For those "non-Jews" who saw ghettoization as an opportunity for social mobility, there could be—and were—possibilities for coalitions to be developed with "Jewish" tenants. For the "Jew" desiring to remain in their apartments and the "non-Jew" desiring to leave their apartments and exchange them for "Jewish" apartments elsewhere, there was the potential for a meeting of interests. Such a coalition can be seen in the case of VI Lendvay u. 15. Designated for "Jewish" use on 16 June 1944, this status was contested in a petition written the following day. In what is one of the more unusual justifications for the cancellation of "Jewish" status, the petitioner argued in terms of the cultural significance of the property.[36] Neither a tenant nor owner of the property, the petitioner's only connection with the property was that he was the son of a former resident. But this former resident was the esteemed artist Gyula Benczúr.

It was the artist Benczúr who had commissioned the building of the property, complete with lamps from Zurich, wall paintings, a rococo fireplace, and—according to the petitioner—one of the most beautiful Renaissance tiled stoves in Hungary, and had lived there from 1890 until his death in 1920. After his death, there had been plans—which ultimately did not come to fruition—to open a museum in the house. It was on these grounds of the perceived significance of the building in Hungarian cultural history that designation as a ghetto house was deemed incompatible. Indeed, the petitioner expressed a degree of disbelief that designation could be imagined, especially in the year—1944—that was the centenary of his father's birth. He noted the irony that in the same year, marble plaques were being erected on the houses in Szülöváros and Kassa where his father was born and grew up, and yet a large yellow star was to be placed on this building where his father had lived for some thirty years.

The petitioner's concerns with safeguarding cultural treasures mirrored in many ways the concerns of "non-Jewish" owners with safeguarding their properties from the effects of overcrowding. In some senses the petitioner can be seen as an "owner" of the property, certainly in terms of "owning" the memory of the property, and therefore it is not surprising that the discourse adopted is one shared by other "non-Jewish" owners of properties designated for "Jewish" use. And thus it is not that surprising that his petition was countered by one drawn up by a "Jewish"/"non-Jewish" coalition of inhabitants.

This coalition of "Jews" and "non-Jews" living in the property wrote to the mayor on 21 June in direct opposition to the appeal launched by Benczúr's son.[37] The present "Jewish" owner of the property spearheaded this counterpetitioning. His concern was to stress that a large number of "non-Jewish" tenants had already moved out of their primitive apartments in the building into more comfortable apartments in another property. In an attached letter supporting the continuation of "Jewish" status for the building, eight "non-Jewish" tenants confirmed that they had already relocated, and reading between the lines it is clear that they had no intention of moving back. For both these "non-Jewish" tenants and for the "Jewish" owner, the property was not the cultural gem that Benczúr's son referred to, but an apartment building with poor facilities. There is no mention of one of the finest Renaissance tiled stoves in Hungary, but only of the fact that twelve apartments shared a common bathroom. Thus for the "non-Jewish" tenants, designation of their property offered the opportunity to exchange their existing poor apartments for better apartments previously occupied by "Jews." And this desire for social mobility coincided with the "Jewish" owner's desire to stay put. However, in staying put, he was staying put in an apartment building with little to recommend it in terms of comfort.

One of the central elements of the owner's justification of designation of this property for "Jewish" use was not simply that he himself was "Jewish" along with a majority of the tenants after the relocations of the last few days. Alongside these discourses is the articulation of one that accepted a principle of poorer-quality apartments for "Jewish" use. It was in part precisely because these apartments were so poor, so the logic of the petition went, that the building should remain for "Jewish" use. Once again, this raises the question of whether such an argument points to the unwitting buying into antisemitic attitudes by this "Jewish" owner or the instrumental use of antisemitic discourse for his own purposes—in this case to stay put. What is striking is that his desire to stay put meshed with the desire of the "non-Jewish" tenants to escape, and thus both had an interest in the original designation's remaining. Therefore both joined in counterpetitioning the appeal against designating Lendvay u. 15 with a yellow star.

The other two examples of coalitions being formed between "Jews" and "non-Jews" were rather different. As I've noted in the case of Lendvay u. 15, the "Jewish" owner-occupier's desire to stay fitted neatly with the "non-Jewish" tenants' desire to leave. However, in the case of VII Hársfa u. 57 and IX Ráday u. 37, both "Jewish" and "non-Jewish" tenants wanted to remain in their apartments. Now normally this would involve conflict between "Jews" and "non-Jews," given that implementing ghettoization at the scale of the apartment building meant that a desire to stay within your own apartment necessitated fighting for the status of the entire building. To some extent at least that was the case with these two properties. There was conflict between "Jews" and "non-Jews" over the status of the buildings, but there was also coalition. And what is particularly interesting is that this coalition was based around the petitioning for a new category of designation: the "mixed house."

Neither property had been designated for "Jewish" use on 16 June. In the case of Hársfa u. 57, the "Jewish" inhabitants wrote to the mayor on 19 June requesting that the house be designated a mixed house on the grounds that the number of tenants was split 50:50 between "Jews" and "non-Jews."[38] Their concern was to stay put—they noted that none of them had yet moved out into other apartments—and thus the designation of the property had to change. However, rather than requesting "Jewish" status, their request was in essence for an entirely unchanged situation for everyone. This property was in reality mixed, and they requested that such status be officially recognized. The request would seem to have had some support from "non-Jewish" tenants in the building. Certainly that is suggested in a letter written by a "non-Jewish" tenant in response to "Jewish" petitioning.[39] In this letter of 19 June, one of the "non-Jews" living in the building notes that a number of "non-Jewish" tenants filed a petition on behalf of the "Jews" that day. His request was that his wife's signature be removed from that earlier petition, which he mentioned only just finding out about that evening. Contestation of the status of this property took place not simply at the level of the apartment building but at the level of the apartment— within this particular "non-Jewish" family.

At Ráday u. 37, there was a similar picture of contestation between "non-Jews" and a coalition of "Jews" and "non-Jews" over the status of the building. Again, with no designation on 16 June for "Jewish" use, the building's "Jewish" owner and inhabitants requested mixed status on the day the list of yellow-star houses was published.[40] Their request was endorsed by six of the "non-Jewish" tenants. Mixed status made sense, in that it would allow both "Jews" and "non-Jews" to remain in the property. However, this request was self-consciously contested by one of the "non-Jewish" tenants writing, at least he thought, in the names of all fourteen of the "non-Jewish" tenants.[41] But it was clear that there was not a singular response on the part of the "non-Jewish" tenants in the building. Whilst for one, any "Jewish" moves for designation as a "Jewish" property were to be resisted, for others, "Jewish" moves for designation as a mixed property were perfectly acceptable.

It is striking that calls for mixed houses were not restricted to these two petitions, but could be found in other petitions submitted in the aftermath of the issuing of a list of yellow-star houses on 16 June. As I have noted, those designations marked out "Jewish" and "non-Jewish" living space at the scale of the apartment building. In calling for mixed status, therefore, petitioners were challenging the scale at which ghettoization was being implemented, and thus to some extent challenging the very nature of this territorial solution. Calling for mixed houses was calling for a whole new category that did not fit with the assumptions of ghettoization in mid-June 1944 (and was radically different from the assumption of early May, which I've thought about in chapter 4). It might be going too far to suggest that it was an act of resistance on the part of "Jewish" petitioners and coalitions of "Jewish" and "non-Jewish" petitioners, but it certainly did suggest a territorial solution at a new scale. And perhaps most significant, this was being suggested by ordinary "Jews" and "non-Jews" in Budapest.

Now that does beg the question of what notice was taken of these petitions. I think it is clear from the ten contested sites I have looked at in some detail that there was a complex array of responses to ghettoization by both "Jews" and "non-Jews" in June 1944. However, that does leave the question "so what?" The crucial decisions regarding ghettoization were being made not by these petitioners but by city officials—those doctors of space—implementing the policy and choosing which buildings to designate for "Jewish" and "non-Jewish" use. The critical question is whether this petitioning had any impact upon the decisions they made, and thus ultimately on the shape of the ghetto in Budapest.

Now, of course, with these ten contested sites I have looked at, there were bound to be both winners and losers, whether the status of the properties remained the same or changed. In the case of six of these properties, the status of the building remained unchanged following petitioning and counterpetitioning—three remaining for "Jewish" use,[42] three remaining not for "Jewish" use.[43] In the case of four of the properties, however, the status of the building changed in the new list of ghetto houses issued on 22 June. Three of the contested sites became "Jewish" houses on 22 June,[44] and one was canceled from the ghetto list.[45] Decisions about all ten seem to have been made on a case-by-case basis, ultimately by city officials, although with the input of district council officials engaged in the reinvestigations, and also Jewish Council officials (although their impact appears minimal). Petitions seemed to play a role in this. It was not the case that only the houses for which petitions were submitted were either canceled or added, but petitioning did play a role at a number of levels. It resulted not only in individual reinvestigation but in a more general reinvestigation of the original ghetto list. But it did more than that. It would seem that petitioning reawakened official sensitivities to the impact of ghettoization upon the "non-Jewish" population of the city, and this resulted in a quite marked changing of the shape and nature of ghettoization. Not only does it seem that contestation of ghettoization by both "Jews" and "non-Jews" impacted the shape of the ghetto as it was redefined on 22 June 1944, but, more significantly, that contestation created an entirely new category, the mixed house, and thus effectively changed the scale at which ghettoization was being implemented in Budapest.

THE IMPACT OF PETITIONING UPON THE DOCTORS OF SPACE

It would seem that there was a thoroughgoing reinvestigation of the designated yellow-star houses and a significant number of the properties suggested for designation in petitions on 20–21 June. Certainly reference to this reinvestigation is made in some of the petitions themselves. The "Jewish" owner of VI Lendváy u. 15 noted in his petition requesting the property continue to be designated for "Jewish" use that a representative of the VI district council had come round to the building on the evening of 20 June to collect data on the occupants in the building.[46] These data were added to the cover sheet of the other petition, submitted earlier by the son of the painter Gyula Benczúr.[47] It was in essence a retallying of the data collected in the citywide survey of properties undertaken at the beginning of June. Thus, the total number of "Jewish" and "non-Jewish" flats, the total number of "Jewish" and "non-Jewish" inhabitants, and the status of the owner were all jotted down.

This practice of essentially reinvestigating the data collected in the 1–2 June survey was undertaken not only for properties like Lendváy u. 15 that were contested in the aftermath of the designations. In the VI district of the city—where Lendváy u. 15 was sited—there was a thorough investigation, with the VI district council recommending properties to be added to and deleted from the list of "Jewish" houses. Thirty-nine apartment buildings were recommended for designation and nine recommended for cancellation, generally on the grounds of majority occupation. Another twenty-four apartment buildings were listed as proposed by the Jewish Council for designation, but not endorsed after investigation of the data.[48]

The contested site Király u. 82 was amongst the nine properties in the district investigated and recommended for cancellation. On the cover sheet of the petition from the house air-raid warden calling for cancellation, the council official jotted down the numbers of "Jewish" and "non-Jewish" tenants and inhabitants.[49] As the separate petitions from both "Jewish" and "non-Jewish" inhabitants made clear, the building had a majority of "Jewish" tenants (thirty-one compared with twenty) but a majority of "non-Jewish" inhabitants (161 compared with 95), including a unit of Hungarian soldiers. Thus, in terms of majority occupation, both could—and did—make a case for designation/cancellation of yellow-star status. In the end, it was the majority of "non-Jewish" inhabitants that was seen as more significant by the VI district council official, who recommended cancellation of the property from the ghetto list. On the list of "Jewish" houses published on 22 June, Király u. 82 was absent. The thirty-one "Jewish" tenants had lost the battle to stay put, and the twenty "non-Jewish" tenants had won the battle to stay put.

It was not only in the VI district that such a thoroughgoing reinvestigation of designated properties took place. Evidence from the XI district of the city suggests that this practice was far more widespread.[50] There all of the properties designated for "Jewish" use on 16 June were subject to reinvestigation on 20–21 June. The eighty-one yellow-star houses were divided up between seventeen inspectors, with each inspector surveying properties proximate to each other. In addition, four houses for which petitions requesting yellow-star status had been submitted were also investigated. From the reports returned by inspectors it seems that a number of criteria were being investigated, which both reconfirmed and supplemented the data gathered under the auspices of the 1–2 June registration. Inspectors checked the number of apartments within each property, the number of "Jewish" and "non-Jewish" tenants, and the nature of the property. However, they also noted down the number of "Jewish" and "non-Jewish" families moving in and out of the property since designation on 16 June. Coming as they did on 20–21 June, these inspections were undertaken just prior to the deadline of 8 P.M. on 21 June, by which time "Jews" were to move into yellow-starred properties.

The returns for individual properties were collated, and the results sent to the mayor on 21 June.[51] The total number of apartments, the number of "Jewish" and "non-Jewish" flats, the number of "Jewish" and "non-Jewish" families moving in and out,[52] and a brief description of the type of property were given for each house designated on the 16 June list.[53] As was the case with the VI district submission, specific attention was drawn to properties that were recommended for cancellation. In the case of the XI district, seven of the eighty-one properties were specifically recommended for cancellation. In part, it would seem that majority occupation was the reason. However, there was clearly more to suggesting cancellation than this.

Those at district level seemed certain that all "villas" or "family houses" were to be canceled and the city's "Jews" were to be housed only in larger apartment buildings. This understanding was shared by the Jewish Council officials charged with relocating families in the district. As I noted in the last chapter, an order was passed down to one of the Jewish Council officials in the XI district on 19 June that no "Jews" should move into houses with fewer than three apartments, and such relocations were halted. That principle can also be seen in the letter of 21 June from the XI district councilor to the mayor.[54] After discussion with Endre, the principle of ghettoization's application to larger apartment buildings and explicitly not smaller houses had clearly been taken on board in the locality.

As far as the principle of larger apartment buildings was concerned, the rule being applied from the center was that the "Jew" was to be housed in large apartment buildings where the "Jew" already accounted for over 50 percent of the inhabitants. Perhaps most significantly, these apartment buildings not only had a majority of "Jewish" inhabitants but also did *not* have a majority of "non-Jewish" inhabitants. However, as the XI district councilor made clear, such a rule did not work in a district such as his where the "Jew" made up a mere 5.5 percent of the population. He reckoned that at the most, "Jews" made up 20 to 30 percent of the inhabitants of any single apartment building.[55] In short, within his district, clear majority occupation within larger apartment buildings rather than villas was an impossible criterion. And thus, it was only the most glaring cases of low proportions of "Jews" in larger apartment buildings that were signaled for cancellation.

However, whilst justifying the maintenance of properties that went against the rule of majority occupation, the district councilor made it clear that the nature of the reinvestigations was to isolate properties for cancellation rather than adoption. He specifically noted that he did not advocate adopting any new properties for designation in the district, on the grounds that it would be "inconsistent" with Secretary of State Endre's wishes.[56] As far as the XI district councilor was concerned, therefore, the parameters within which the 20–21 June investigations were undertaken within his particular district prompted recommending houses for cancellation, and not adoption.

And first and foremost, cancellation of designation was to be applied according to property type in a district such as the XI, with a high proportion of smaller houses. It is clear that a decision had been made centrally to cancel villas and family houses from the ghetto lists, and that this decision had been disseminated down to both "Jewish" and "non-Jewish" officials in the locality. In turn, the policy was made public. *Esti Ujság*, in an article of 21 June titled "Tomorrow the Revision of Designations Will Take Place," noted "almost continual meetings in the Interior Ministry" on 19–20 June to examine petitions, and the Interior Ministry's decision that "in the shortest period of time . . . the yellow star will be removed from villas" to be "later put at the disposal of Christians."[57] In the aftermath of the issuing of a definitive ghetto list on 22 June, it would seem an official press statement was released explaining that villas and family houses had been exempted from designation, with only those apartment blocks with majority "Jewish" occupation being marked with a yellow star.[58]

It is striking, I think, that in the week following the initial listing of ghetto houses there was plenty of activity at a variety of scales. The precise shape of the ghetto was being contested by hundreds of tenants and owners, both "Jewish" and "non-Jewish." A decision was made in the Interior Ministry, at some point between 16 and 19 June, that villas and family houses were to be excluded from the ghetto list. And then a large-scale reinvestigation of properties was instituted at the local level. Although not on the scale of the citywide survey of 1–2 June, this second survey of properties was not inconsiderable. It was a busy few days in Budapest.

What is particularly interesting is the return of concerns with ghettoization as explicit "Jewish absence." As I've suggested earlier, in many ways 16 June marks a coming full circle from the earliest implementation of a form of ghettoization in early April, when "Jewish absence" was the priority. However, the return of a concern with "Jewish absence" was not motivated by a concern with providing housing for bomb victims as was the case in early April. Nor was it the concern with clearing the main streets of "Jews," so central to the ghettoization plans of 9 May. Indeed, it is striking that in the case of one of the contested properties I have thought about—Erszébet körut 15—the local official recommended nondesignation, partly on the grounds that the apartment building was located on a main street.[59] In essence, he was still motivated by the earlier concerns. However, the situation had changed. Not only was this property designated for "Jewish" use on 22 June—against the judgment of the district official concerned with clearing "Jews" from main streets—but more properties were designated in total on this main street on 22 June than 16 June (two were cancelled, but six were added).

The concern with achieving explicit "Jewish absences" through the territorial solution of ghettoization was now focused on excluding "Jews" from a certain type of property in the city: family houses and villas. This explicit absence worked two ways. On the one hand, it meant that the city's "Jews" were to be spatially more concentrated than was envisioned on 16 June, in a smaller number of larger buildings. Thus the degree of control over the "Jew" exerted through this territorial solution was heightened. But on the other hand, the creation of explicit "Jewish absences" needs also to be seen as a measure aimed at the "non-Jew" as well as the "Jew." As was very clear to the doctors of space involved in implementing ghettoization, the segregation of "Jewish" and "non-Jewish" living space impacted "non-Jews" as well as "Jews." That the majority of petitions submitted to the mayor in the aftermath of 16 June were from "non-Jews" challenging designation of their apartment buildings certainly reinforced this fact in the minds of local officials.

In that context, the decision to restrict "Jewish" access to the highly prized villa and family house accommodation in the outlying districts of the city can be seen, I think, as an attempt to win over "non-Jewish" opposition to ghettoization. In particular, it was an attempt to shift ghettoization from a cost to an opportunity, as far as the city's "non-Jews" were concerned. As is clear from the ten contested sites that I have looked at in some detail above, ghettoization could be—and was—interpreted by the "non-Jew" as a threat of forced relocation or a possibility for upward mobility. By placing vacated "Jewish" villas "at the disposal of Christians," there was a clear attempt to provide some form of compensation for the "non-Jew" forced to vacate a property designated for the "Jew." In part at least, this new concern was no doubt a sop to the "non-Jewish" protests articulated in the aftermath of the June 16 designations.

What is striking about the return of explicit "Jewish absence" is that it spelled, in short, a return to earlier socioeconomic concerns. As I have noted, the initial ghettoization decree issued nationally at the end of April explained ghettoization as a means to restructure access to scarce housing resources in favor of the "non-Jew," and this discourse of ghettoization as primarily about appropriation continued to find expression both within the press and petitions submitted. Whilst it seems to have been only marginal in determining the shape of the ghetto on 16 June, this discourse played a much more visible role in the reshaping of ghettoization in Budapest seen in the issuing of the 22 June definitive list of "Jewish" houses. And this return to socioeconomic concerns seems, in part at least, to have been a result of the petitioning against ghettoization that took place in the days after 16 June. In some ways, therefore, the shape of the ghetto itself was changed from the bottom up.

But perhaps more significantly, the very nature of ghettoization was changed. And this change would seem to have been, again at least in part, due to the petitioning against ghettoization by "non-Jews." As I have noted before, the shift from the imagining of ghettoization on 9 May to the implementing of ghettoization on 16 June was a shift in scale. In the 9 May plans, ghettoization was imagined at the scale of areas in the city. However, in the 16 June list of yellow-star houses, ghettoization was imagined at the scale of the apartment building. This was quite literally scaled-down ghettoization, motivated by largely pragmatic concerns. The result was that ghettoization was contested in mid-June not at the city scale but at the scale of the apartment building and house. In order to remain in one's own apartment, one had to fight over the status of the whole apartment building. And as the contested sites I have looked at show, individual apartment buildings were fought over in the days following the 16 June designations.

What is striking about the 22 June designations is that a marked shift took place in terms of the scale of implementation of segregation of "Jewish" and "non-Jewish" living space. Ghettoization was no longer to be implemented at the scale of the apartment building, but—at least as far as "non-Jews" were concerned—at the scale of the individual apartment. The category of mixed house—created during and through contestation of the original ghettoization designations—became not only tolerated but in a sense sanctioned by the city authorities, albeit in one direction only. "Non-Jewish" tenants were permitted to remain in "Jewish" houses after the second—definitive—designation of 22 June, although "Jews" were not permitted to remain in "non-Jewish" houses. Thus with the addition of Hársfa u. 57 to the list of "Jewish" houses, the "non-Jews" who had called for a mixed house were permitted to remain in the house. In the case of Ráday u. 37, however, the continuing nonappearance on the list of designated houses meant that the "Jews" had to relocate.

This practice of "non-Jews" remaining in "Jewish" houses and therefore in reality making them into mixed houses was officially acknowledged in regulations issued on 25 June, in the aftermath of the issuing of the second—and definitive—list. The eighth point of a series of regulations concerning the governing of ghettoization in the city forbade "Christians" from hiding "Jews" or allowing "Jews" admission "for no matter how brief a period into either Christian houses *or the Christian-tenanted portions of Jewish houses*."[60] Thus segregation was being accepted in practice at the scale of the individual apartment, not the apartment building.

And it would seem that the practice of "Jewish" houses being, in reality, mixed houses in the aftermath of the 22 June definitive designation was fairly widespread. Braham follows Lévai in stating that "close to 12,000" "non-Jews" remained in yellow-star houses, although it is hard to tell where Lévai got these figures.[61] What can be said with some confidence is that in the city's VII district at least, the number of "Jewish" houses that were in reality mixed houses was high. At the end of November 1944, 144 of the 162 yellow-star houses in the area that was made into the Pest ghetto were partially occupied by "non-Jewish" tenants.[62]

With the creation of the closed Pest ghetto at the end of November 1944, this practice of "Jewish" houses in reality being mixed houses ceased. However, between June and November 1944, the segregatory logic of ghettoization was subverted by the desire of "non-Jewish" tenants to remain in their apartments. Therefore, it is not just that ordinary Hungarians impacted the shape of ghettoization in Budapest, but in a significant way they also challenged the scale at which this territorial solution was being implemented. But more than that, there is a sense, I think, in which they challenged the very logic behind ghettoization. After all, the creation of mixed houses fitted much more with the history of assimilation than the segregatory logic of ghettoization.

The question that arises in my own mind is whether it is pushing things too far to describe the calls for mixed houses as acts of "resistance" (given that they were a challenge to the very nature and assumptions of ghettoization). Now obviously that raises a parallel question. Were calls for either "Jewish" or "non-Jewish" status acts of "collaboration" in that they adopted to some extent at least the (antisemitic) logic that sought to spatially separate the city's "Jewish" and "non-Jewish" populations? Using the loaded language of "resistance" and "collaboration" to describe this contestation is obviously problematic. However, there is a sense in which notions of "resistance" and "collaboration" are potentially useful in distinguishing between the manner and the nature of contestation.

Whether seen as acts of "resistance" or not, contestation of ghettoization brought about a toleration of "non-Jews" remaining in "Jewish" houses. The principle of separation of "Jews" and "non-Jews" at the scale of the building had been done away with, and the territorial solution of ghettoization was now applied at the lowest scale possible, the individual apartment. It is worth noting in passing that of course at the scale of the individual apartment, ghettoization had significant costs for those in mixed marriages. These costs featured in a significant number of petitions submitted in the aftermath of 16 June. For now, I think that what is striking is that the implementation of ghettoization at the lowest scale possible came as a result of recognition—in part at least triggered by ordinary Hungarians—of the costs of implementing a territorial solution. There was—and had always been—official sensitivity to the costs of ghettoization for the "non-Jewish" population. This after all can be seen in the earliest plans to implement a rolling program of relocations over a three-month period. On 22 June, that consciousness of the costs of ghettoization for the "non-Jewish" population of the city can be seen as playing a central role. There was an attempt to implement a cost-free territorial solution—at least cost-free for the "non-Jew." Ultimately of course, such a solution was far from cost-free for the city's "Jews."

THE DEFINITIVE MAPPING OF THE GHETTO, 22 JUNE 1944

With the issuing of the definitive list of designations on 22 June, the shape of the ghetto changed quite significantly from that envisioned less than a week earlier. In terms of sheer statistics, there were now fewer properties designated for the "Jew" in the city—quite a lot fewer. For the city as a whole, the close to 200,000 "Jews" were now to live in 1,948 apartment buildings, rather than the 2,639 designated on 16 June.[63] Behind these statistics of 691 fewer properties being designated for "Jewish" use lay a more complex geography of the reshaping of the ghetto. This reshaping was a result of the adding of properties to the ghetto list, as well as the canceling of properties from the ghetto list in the week following 16 June. A total of 149 properties were added to the list of "Jewish" houses issued on 22 June, yet this number was dwarfed by the 840 properties canceled from the list. Within a week, close to a third of the entire ghetto buildings had been cut from the ghetto. This amounted to nothing less than a radical reshaping of the ghetto, in large part as a result of the decision to designate with a view to property type.

In the decision to place the "Jew" in larger apartment buildings, rather than smaller villas, yellow-star houses were increasingly concentrated within the central districts of the city. It was the outlying districts—with their larger number of smaller properties—that saw the greatest reductions in the numbers of "Jewish" houses. In contrast, the central districts of the city— with their smaller number of much larger properties—saw additions to the numbers of "Jewish" houses located there. Overall, of course, cancellations outnumbered additions, but the uneven spread of these meant that the ghetto was increasingly located in the center of the city rather than the periphery, and increasingly in Pest rather than Buda.

As the breakdown of the sheer numbers of cancellations and additions by districts reveals, the overall reduction in the number of properties (from 2,639 to 1,948) was not implemented uniformly across the city. In the central districts of Pest—V, VI, and VII districts—the number of designated properties actually rose slightly. In all three, additions outnumbered cancellations at a ratio of well over two to one. Given that there was a concern to place "Jews" in larger apartment buildings where "Jews" were a majority (or perhaps more important, where "non-Jews" were a minority), these districts with their larger apartment buildings and traditionally high "Jewish" population, featured even more heavily in the final ghetto plans drawn up on 22 June. Whilst on 16 June, these three districts accounted for just over 40 percent of all of the ghetto houses designated, on the 22 June definitive list, these three districts made up just over 60 percent of all of the yellow-star houses in the city.[64]

District	Number of Properties Designated on 16 June	Number of Properties Designated on 22 June	
I	35	16	(19 canceled)
II	157	53	(105 canceled)
			(1 added)
III	226	117	(110 canceled)
			(1 added)
XI	81	18	(63 canceled)
XII	83	16	(67 canceled)
Buda	582	220	(364 canceled)
			(2 added)
IV	48	46	(9 canceled)
			(7 added)
V	372	379	(25 canceled)
			(32 added)
VI	321	340	(10 canceled)
			(29 added)
VII	439	483	(15 canceled)
			(59 added)
VIII	156	146	(23 canceled)
			(13 added)
IX	48	32	(17 canceled)
			(1 added)
X	67	17	(53 canceled)
			(3 added)
XIII	106	78	(31 canceled)
			(3 added)
XIV	500	207	(293 canceled)
Pest	2,057	1,728	(476 canceled)
			(147 added)
Budapest	2,639	1,948	(840 canceled)
			(149 added)

In direct contrast to this increasing concentration of the ghetto within these three central districts of Pest, the numbers of "Jewish" houses in Buda was slashed. Over 60 percent of the ghetto houses on the Buda side of the Danube were canceled in the week following 16 June.[65] The result was that the proportion of yellow-star houses in Buda fell dramatically. On 16 June, just over 20 percent of the ghetto was located in Buda.[66] By 22 June, this had fallen to just over 10 percent.[67] The scale of these cancellations is particularly marked when I examine the XI district of Buda—a district that I've chosen to focus on in large part because of the survival of sources.

EXPERIENCING GHETTOIZATION: THE XI DISTRICT

Here the 22 June definitive ghetto list saw the cancellation of sixty-three of the eighty-one yellow-star houses in the district (see figure 7 and cf. figure 4 on page 106). These cancellations essentially followed the recommendations of the XI district councilor, who drew upon the investigations undertaken on 20–21 June. All seven properties explicitly recommended for cancellation did not feature on the 22 June ghetto list, nor did any of the villa and family house properties in the district (apart from Györök u. 18, which was mistakenly omitted from the XI district councilor's list).[68] Those few houses that continued as yellow-star houses post–22 June—only eighteen in total—were mainly larger apartment blocks, plus a few non-villa smaller properties.

The result of the investigations and redesignations was that the district's "Jewish" population of 2,154 was now to be housed in a maximum of 194 apartments in eighteen buildings. This worked out at a ratio of 11.10 persons per designated apartment, compared with 4.53 persons per apartment under the 16 June designations. However, in reality, the degree of overcrowding was to be much higher, in large part because of the official toleration of "non-Jews" remaining in "Jewish" houses. Of the 194 apartments in these eighteen designated buildings, only 65 already had "Jewish" tenants. Thus some two-thirds—129 in total—had "non-Jewish" tenants, who could now, if they so chose, stay put. It is clear that some had already moved out of their apartments in the days following 16 June. Twenty-eight "non-Jewish" families had already exchanged their apartments in these eighteen buildings with "Jewish" families, and one can assume that they chose not to move back in. However, that left 101 "non-Jewish" families liv-

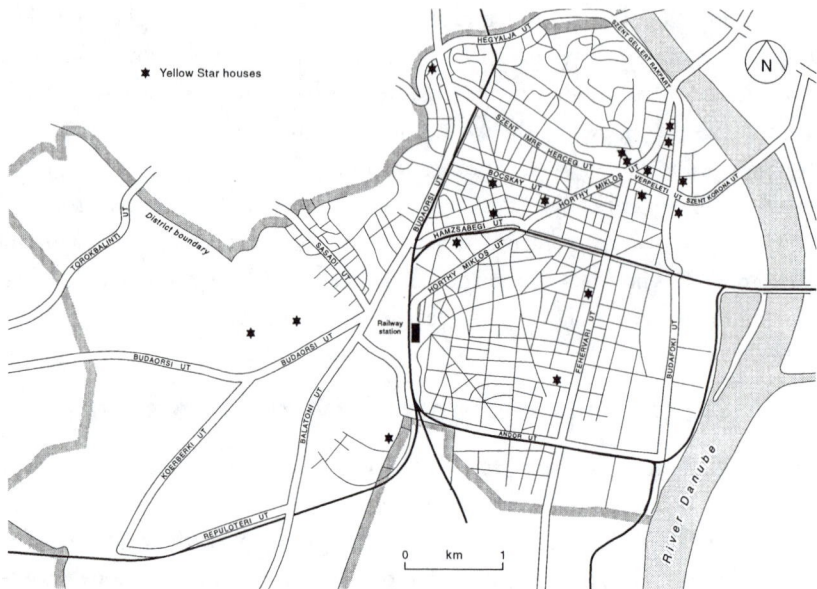

Figure 7. Ghettoization as implemented in the XI District (22 June 1944). © Tim Cole.

ing in these eighteen buildings now designated for "Jewish" use, and one can only assume that a relatively large number of these stayed put. As I have already noted, it would seem that "non-Jews" chose to live in the majority of apartment buildings in the VII district that later became part of the Pest ghetto. And it is safe to assume that was the case in XI district also. Now, as Braham notes, "many [of these "non-Jews" living in yellow-star houses] were of great assistance to the persecuted Jews. They were especially helpful during the curfew by shopping or doing errands for the Jews and by hiding or safekeeping their valuables."[69] But their presence also increased the extent of "Jewish" overcrowding. Thus the ratio of 11.10 persons per designated apartment in the XI district is in reality a severe underestimation. Overcrowding in the aftermath of the 22 June designations was no doubt far higher—and potentially double that figure.[70]

The costs of ghettoization in terms of heightened overcrowding post–22 June were compounded by the fact that many families who had already moved in the days following 16 June now had to move again. Of course, this impacted both "Jews" and "non-Jews" who had already moved, and a consciousness of this comes across in the petitions. In the XI district, the cancellation of sixty-three buildings meant that eighty-three "Jewish" families who had already moved into these buildings were now forced to move again within a matter of days. The corollary was that twelve "non-Jewish" families who had moved from these designated buildings were now free to return, in light of the cancellation of yellow-star status.[71] Whilst these "non-Jews" had a degree of choice over whether they did or did not return, no such degree of choice was available to "Jews."

With the increased levels of concentration implemented through the 22 June designations—heightened as it was by "non-Jews" remaining in their apartments in "Jewish" houses—ghettoization meant not only segregation of the Budapest "Jewry" but also serious overcrowding. In 1893, the city authorities had recognized a figure of more than four persons to a room as "unhygienic overcrowding."[72] Thus in housing the "Jew" at the ratio of one family per room, a conscious policy of "unhygienic overcrowding" was being pursued against the city's "Jews." The nature of this overcrowding was compounded by the fact that ghettoization amounted to not only less but worse. In particular, the cancellation of all villa and family house properties designated on 16 June restricted the "Jew" to the more crowded accommodation of larger apartment blocks.[73]

Now whilst the total number of properties designated for "Jews" decreased, the situation did, as I have pointed out, vary from district to district. As the following statistics show, the percentage of properties designated within a single district varied radically. To some extent, as I noted in the last chapter, this had been the case with the 16 June ghetto list. However, the discrepancies became sharper with the reshaping of the ghetto on 22 June. Whilst in a district like the XI district, less than 1 percent of all the buildings were marked with a yellow star on 22 June, in the VII district just over 30 percent of all the buildings were marked with a yellow star. In short, the city looked very different in the aftermath of 22 June. In some of the central districts of Pest, almost one in three buildings in the case of the V and VII districts, and one in five in the case of the VI districts, were marked with a yellow star. "Jewish" presence was highly visible. In contrast, in some of the outlying districts of both Buda and Pest, the "Jew" was almost invisible. In the XI and XII districts of Buda, only one in two hundred houses was marked with a yellow star. In the XIII and XIV districts of Pest, some one in thirty houses had a yellow star by the entrance doorway (see figure 8).

District	Total Number of Properties, 1941	Properties Designated, 16 June 1944 (total number and as % of properties)	Properites Designated, 22 June 1944 (total number and as % of properties)
I	788	35 (4.44)	16 (2.03)
II	2,597	157 (6.05)	53 (2.04)
III	4,342	226 (5.20)	117 (2.69)
XI	3,113	81 (2.60)	18 (0.58)
XII	3,551	83 (2.34)	16 (0.45)
Buda	14,391	582 (4.04)	220 (1.53)
IV	534	48 (8.99)	46 (8.61)
V	1,195	372 (31.13)	379 (31.72)
VI	1,546	321 (20.76)	340 (21.99)
VII	1,593	439 (27.56)	483 (30.32)
VIII	2,034	156 (7.67)	146 (7.18)
IX	1,484	48 (3.23)	32 (2.16)
X	2,581	67 (2.60)	17 (0.66)
XIII	2,067	106 (5.13)	78 (3.77)
XIV	6,458	500 (7.74)	207 (3.21)
Pest	19,492	2,057 (10.55)	1,728 (8.87)
Budapest	33,883	2,639 (7.79)	1,948 (5.75)

Now of course these discrepancies in the proportions of buildings designated did not take place within a demographic vacuum. There was, as I've shown in the previous chapter, a history of "Jewish" population presences and absences throughout the city. However, no neat tie-up existed between the proportion of "Jews" within a given district and the proportion of properties designated. This had not been the case on 16 June. It was even more clearly not the case on 22 June, given the matching of property type and majority occupation in the issuing of the definitive list of ghetto houses.

Overall, the proportion of properties designated fell. Whereas on 16 June, "Jews" who made up some 15.8 percent of the city's population were to live in 7.79 percent of the city's properties, on 22 June, this number fell to some 5.75 percent of the city's properties. Yet, in this context of ghettoization amounting to the allocation of living space for the "Jew" at a level

Figure 8. Entrance to a yellow-star house, Budapest, 1944. Yivo Institute for Jewish Research, courtesy of USHMM Photo Archives.

of around a third of that of the "Jewish" presence in the city, such under-provision was not uniform. Indeed, as I've already noted, in the V, VI, and VII districts, the proportion of properties designated rose and thus kept more or less in pace with the proportion of "Jews" in the district. In other districts, particularly the outlying districts in Buda and Pest, the situation was quite the opposite.

District	"Jewish" Population as % of Population in District (1941)	Properties Designated, as % of Properties in District (16 June)	Properites Designated, as % of Properties in District (22 June)
I	4.1	4.44	2.03
II	7.5	6.05	2.04
III	8.3	5.20	2.69
XI	3.8	2.60	0.58
XII	5.5	2.34	0.45
Buda	6.1	4.04	1.53
IV	14.3	8.99	8.61
V	34.4	31.13	31.72
VI	31.6	20.76	21.99
VII	35.5	27.56	30.32
VIII	16.6	7.67	7.18
IX	7.8	3.23	2.16
X	3.4	2.60	0.66
XIII	6.3	5.13	3.77
XIV	18.9	7.74	3.21
Pest	18.9	10.55	8.87
Budapest	15.8	7.79	5.75

The large-scale reduction in the proportion of properties designated in the Buda districts, and the increase in the proportion of properties designated in the central Pest districts, meant that the 22 June ghettoization decree set in process a Pest-wards drift of "Jews" in search of "Jewish" apartments. More than that, it set in process a shift in "Jewish" population from the periphery to the center. Now, Budapest's "Jews" had tended—as I've shown in the previous chapter—to live in the center of the city. After 22 June, this pattern was made all the more marked, with the mass cancellation of smaller properties in the outlying districts and the slight increases in real terms (and more marked increases in relative terms) of larger apartment blocks in the central districts of Pest. Such a move was, of course, interesting given the assumptions of geostrategic concerns shaping the Budapest ghetto, which I've outlined in the previous chapter. After 22 June, ghettoization became markedly more concentrated rather than more dispersed, which in geostrategic terms does not make sense. After all, the fac-

Figure 9. Moving into a yellow-star house, Budapest, 1944. Yad Vashem
Photo Archives, courtesy of USHMM Photo Archives.

tories which one discourse suggested needed protecting were situated on
the outskirts of the city, rather than in the V, VI, and VII districts.

For the city's "Jews" this increased concentration of yellow-star houses
within the central districts meant that more "Jews" had to relocate across
districts, thus making the practicalities of relocation more difficult. These
relocations had to take place within a very short timescale. When the definitive list of ghetto houses was issued, it was spelled out that all "Jews" were
required to move into these newly designated buildings by the evening of
Saturday, 24 June. The result was that from the day of the issuing of the new
list of "Jewish" houses, on Thursday, 22 June, until the Saturday when all
moves had to be completed, there were chaotic scenes in the city (see figure
9). As Munkácsi described it:

> June 24 fell on a Saturday. Budapest was the scene of such a sight as not seen for centuries. The children of Israel carried their bags and baggage, pieces of furniture and articles for personal use, whatever they needed most, by carriage, handcarts, and wheelbarrows, and those who found nothing better, in bundles on their back, to the houses indicated. . . . Breaking the sanctity of the Sabbath, thousands of people were obliged to carry their luggage on this last day.[74]

This massive process of relocations was overseen by the Jewish Council, which registered who had moved out of which building, and who had moved into which building.[75]

Immediately after relocations had taken place into these 1,948 properties, regulations were published restricting the "Jew" to remain in the yellow-star houses except for the hours of 2 to 5 P.M., when they were free to leave only for the purposes of shopping, cleaning, and medical treatment.[76] This curfew was relaxed later, with the "Jew" being free to leave their "Jewish" houses between 11 A.M. and 5 P.M. Thus the movement of the city's Jewish population was effectively restricted through the control of "Jewish" access to space. With the official manipulation of "Jewish" access to living space, the "Jew" was restricted to 1,948 places in the city for eighteen hours of the day. And for the remaining six hours, they were not free to go wherever they chose. As I want to examine in the next chapter, the public spaces of the city had already been metaphorically daubed with the same yellow stars attached to residential properties. The implementation of territorial solutions in Budapest in 1944 stretched much further than simply the regulating of "Jewish" living space.

Ghettoization allowed the Hungarian authorities to exercise the role of gatekeeper in allowing, or refusing, the "Jew" access to the living spaces of the city. The hegemonic control afforded by ghettoization assumed a new importance within the changing circumstances. As Braham notes, "the concentration and deportation of the Jews from Zone IV took place simultaneously with the concentration of the Jew of Budapest into special 'starred houses' . . . the central Jewish leadership had every reason to believe that the establishment of the starred houses was the prelude to the deportation and liquidation of the Jews of Budapest."[77] Indeed, the Jewish Council leadership petitioned Sztójay on 22 June, just as ghettoization was taking its final shape in Budapest.[78] The creation of yellow-star houses in Budapest was taken as a signal that the Budapest "Jewry" was the next to face deportation. The council leaders wrote, "After all this . . . it is with the greatest anxiety that we receive the news that the deportation of the Jews of the capital is also to begin within the next few days, so that the dejewification of all of Hungary will become a reality."[79]

The Jewish Council leaders were right to assume that the implementation of ghettoization in Budapest in late June 1944 was planned as the prelude to deportation. Plans were under way to mobilize the gendarmerie to collect the city's ghettoized "Jews" in order for the deportation of the "Budapest Jewry" to commence.[80] However, with the halting of deportations, the 22 June "dispersed ghetto" was not to be the prelude to deportation but the place of the "Jew" in the city, through to the winter of 1944. I want to examine that period in more detail in chapter 8, but before that I want to examine the broader context to ghettoization. The designating of "Jewish" and "non-Jewish" living space that took place in mid- to late June 1944 was one policy of spatial segregation, amongst a number, that sought to put Budapest's "Jews" in their place.

SEVEN

PUTTING THE "JEWS" IN THEIR PLACE, MAY–JUNE 1944

At the time in May 1944 when ghettoization was being planned in Budapest, there were a number of parallel attempts to create a whole series of distinct "Jewish" and "non-Jewish" places in the city. These plans to divide public space should be seen in the context of the 9 May imagining of ghettoization as a longish-term measure. In this context, pragmatics were not of prime importance. Rather, there was a utopian attempt by Budapest's doctors of space to radically reshape the entire geography of the city. The division of the spaces of the city along racialized lines would not impact just housing but the multiple spaces of the city. No longer was the city to be characterized by shared space, but divided space.

The first places in the city subjected to territorial solutions, dividing them into "Jewish" and "non-Jewish" spaces, were bathhouses. On 2 May 1944, the Interior Ministry issued regulations "concerning the prohibition on the attendance of public baths by Jews."[1] This nationally issued legislation empowered the chief municipal official in the locality—in the case of Budapest and other cities, this was the mayor—to designate bathhouses for "Jewish" use and, by corollary, those for "non-Jewish" use. This designation was to take place after consultation with the owners of the bathhouses themselves. Ten days after the national directives had been issued, the mayor in Budapest issued detailed instructions about "Jewish" access to bathhouses in the city.[2] From mid-May the city's "Jews" were to be admitted to only five of the city's more than fifteen bathhouses[3] (see figure 10).

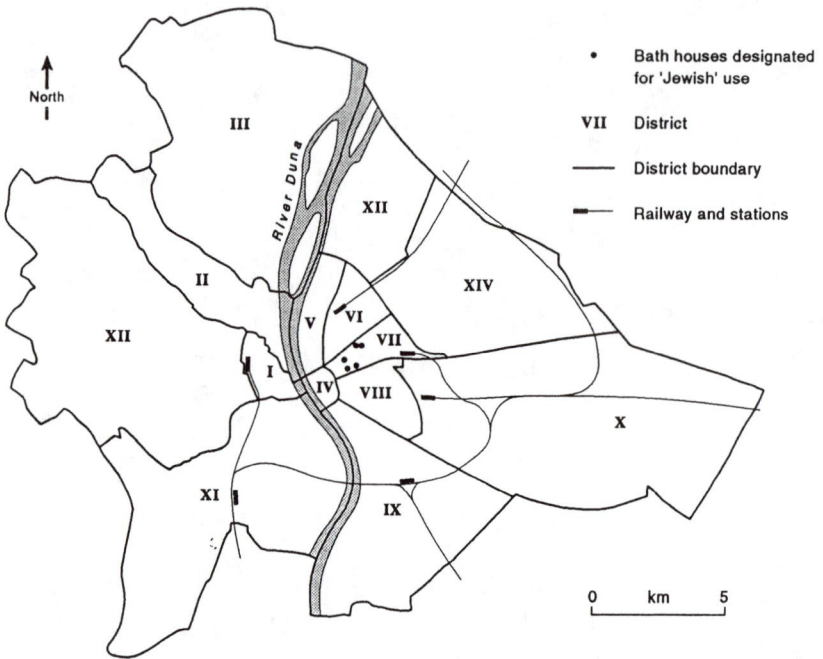

Figure 10. The division of Budapest's bathhouses (12 May 1944). © Tim Cole.

In the case of two of these—both Jewish ritual bathhouses—"Jews" were to have sole usage. In the case of the other three, "Jews" were to be permitted access at specified times on specified days.

A week later, the Interior Ministry sanctioned local authorities to divide the city's hotels and restaurants into those accessible to "Jews" and those barred to "Jews." As with the legislation concerning bathhouses, the specifics of which places were to be designated for "Jewish" use were to be worked out after consultation with hotel and restaurant owners and the competent trade federation.[4] On 23 May, a few days after the issuing of the national legislation, the mayor issued details of which hotels, inns, guest houses, and snack bars could be used by "Jews."[5] On the following day, lists of restaurants, coffeehouses, and bars open to the city's "Jews" were issued.[6] This division of the city's hotels and restaurants was to be put into effect from 25 May. After that date, Budapest's "Jews" were given access to eleven of the rooms in just three of the more than seventy hotels in the city and seventeen of the rooms in five of the city's inns. Of the city's more than one hundred forty guest houses, "Jews" were to use a maximum of sixty-six

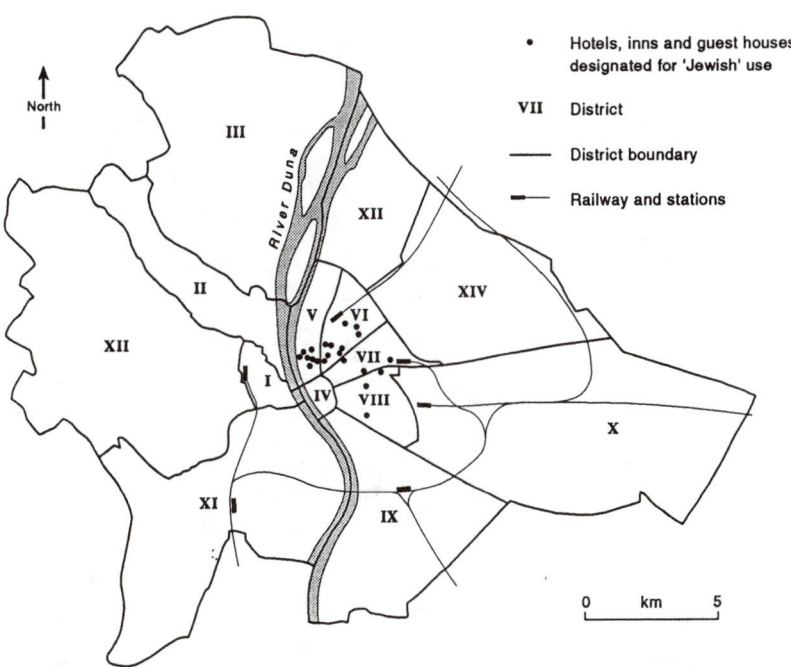

Figure 11. The division of Budapest's hotels, inns, and guest houses (23 May 1944).
© Tim Cole.

rooms in seven guest houses designated solely for "Jews" and twenty rooms in another seven guest houses to be shared by both "Jews" and "non-Jews"[7] (see figure 11).

Alongside this division of the city's hotels and guest houses, there was a division of the places in the city where people ate and drank. From 25 May onward, "Jews" could eat in fourteen snack bars designated exclusively for their use and in segregated rooms in a further eleven snack bars. The city's "Jewish" population was also permitted to eat in six kosher restaurants, as well as in a designated room in seven of the more than six hundred restaurants in the city.[8] Twenty-one of the city's approximately one hundred twenty coffeehouses and seven of the city's more than two hundred twenty-five bars were also designated for use, in part at least, by Budapest's "Jews"[9] (see figure 12). In these coffeehouses and bars, "Jews" were to drink in a room or part of the premises separated off from that used by "non-Jewish" customers.

Within a week, the city's cinemas had also been divided into those to be used by "Jews" and by "non-Jews." Again, the impetus came with the

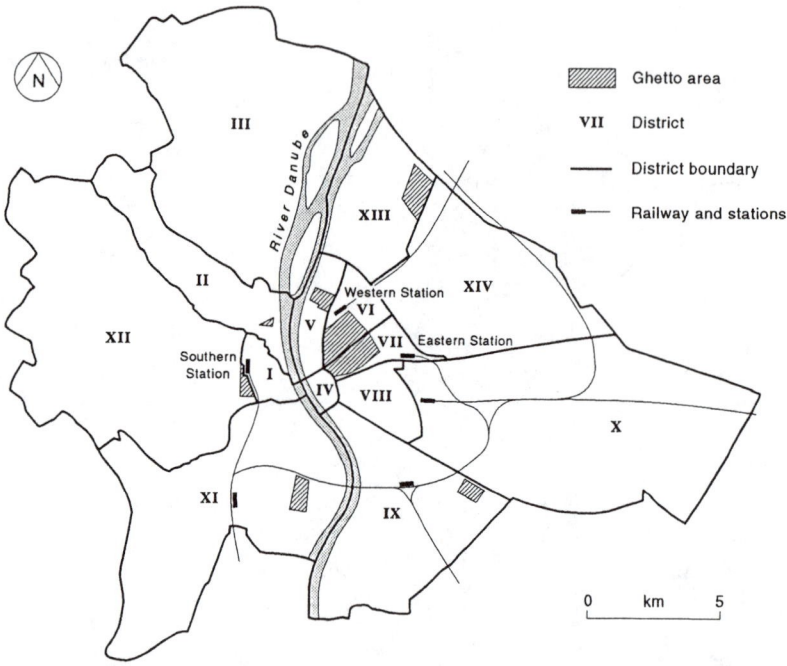

Figure 12. The division of Budapest's restaurants, coffeehouses, bars, and snack bars (23 and 24 May 1944). © Tim Cole.

issuing of Interior Ministry legislation "concerning the prohibition on the attendance of public entertainment places by Jews."[10] This empowered local officials to restrict "Jewish" access to specified performances in theaters and cinemas, following consultation with the relevant business federations. In Budapest, the "Jew" was permitted to attend a limited number of screenings at sixteen of the city's seventy-six cinemas[11] (see figure 13). Segregation of the city's cinemas took place at two scales at the very end of May 1944. At one scale, sixteen cinemas were accessible to "Jews" whilst some sixty were off-limits. At another scale, only thirty-five showings in those sixteen cinemas were accessible to "Jews." Rather than being permitted to attend any of the screenings at any of these sixteen yellow-star cinemas, "Jews" were permitted to attend only the first screening at five of these cinemas on a Monday, the first screening at all sixteen cinemas on a Wednesday, and the first screening at fourteen of these cinemas on a Friday. There was in effect the implementation of a temporal solution (specific times) within a territorial solution (specific places).

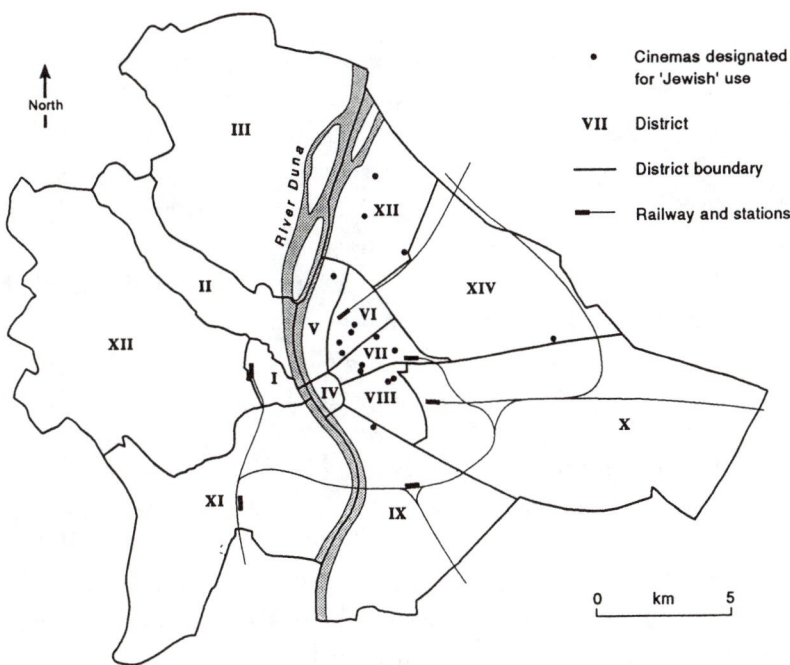

Figure 13. The division of Budapest's cinemas (31 May 1944). © Tim Cole.

The end result of this month of segregating the public spaces in Budapest was that by the time the division of housing space was implemented in June 1944, the city was already divided into places for "Jews" and places for "non-Jews." And that division shared some elements with the subsequent division of residential space, which I examined in chapter 6. Perhaps most strikingly, the division of public space was marked by an effective making of Buda *judenfrei*. By the end of May 1944, only one snack bar in Buda was accessible to the city's "Jews." All the bathhouses, hotels, inns and guest houses, restaurants, bars and coffeehouses, and cinemas "Jews" could frequent were located in Pest, and specifically in the central districts of Pest. In the case of the division of the city's bathhouses, this was perhaps especially surprising. By dint of the geology of the city, the majority of Budapest's bathhouses lay on the Buda side of the Danube. However, these bathhouses were declared *judenfrei* in May 1944, and the "Jew" was restricted to bathing in bathhouses located in the traditional "Jewish" quarter in Pest's VII district.

The segregation of public space in May 1944 can be seen—implicitly or explicitly—as an act of the "Pestization" of the Budapest "Jewry." Now, as

I have noted earlier, this did not take place within a vacuum, but within a history of "Jewish" demography. Pest *was* the home to the majority of the city's "Jews." However, with the effective exclusion of "Jews" from places of consumption and entertainment in Buda (apart from one snack bar), there was a codifying and hardening of the designation of Budapest's "Jews" as the Pest "Jewry." At least as far as the city's restaurants, bathhouses, cinemas, and the like went, "Jews" were only to frequent those in Pest, and thus this side of the river was being effectively made into the space of the "Jew." This process of "Pestization" was continued with the issuing of the definitive list of ghetto houses on 22 June, which was characterized by a marked shift "Pest-wards" in the evolving shape of the ghetto.

The ultimate "Pestization" of the city's "Jews" was to come in the winter of 1944, which I want to examine in the next chapter. By the winter of 1944, Pest had a growing significance in the context of the war. At that point it was most significantly the part of the city that lay in the path of the advancing Red Army. In the early summer of 1944, however, it was socioeconomic rather than geostrategic concerns that were to the fore. During May and June 1944, the hills of Buda, which were the most desirable sites in the city, were offered to the city's "non-Jews." In contrast, the "Jew" was given the central districts of Pest, both as places to live and places to bathe, eat, drink, watch movies, and so on. These were less desirable spaces from the viewpoint of resistance. Pest was the flat side of the river, in contrast to the hilly Buda, and as any student of resistance movements knows, such geography matters. However, socioeconomic concerns were more significant than geostrategic concerns as the spaces of entertainment were carved up.

That there was a socioeconomic dimension to these restrictions can be seen when you examine just which places in Pest were marked out for "Jewish" use. The minority of the hotels, restaurants, bathhouses, cinemas, and so on that the city's "Jews" were permitted to use did not simply amount to the provision of less, but the provision of worse. The division of public spaces in May 1944 resulted in the exclusion of the "Jew" from the most prestigious sites of consumption and entertainment in the city. The month-long process of division was intentionally aimed at undoing what was perceived by antisemites as "Jewish" access to prestigious sites by dint of "Jewish" wealth. This mirrored the subtext underlying the planned division of living space in the city in May 1944. In that case, ghettoization was seen to offer the opportunity to overturn perceived inequalities in housing provision. What antisemites perceived to be the unfair advantage that the city's wealthy "Jews" enjoyed in the housing marketplace was being done away with at one stroke through legislation. And this perception of an unfair advantage enjoyed by the city's "Jews" was carried into the sectors of spaces of consumption and entertainment. At a stroke, the city's "Jews" were to have access to merely a handful of places of consumption and entertainment, and those were far from the most salubrious in the city.

What is striking when looking at the places designated for "Jewish" customers in May 1944 is the extent to which the very best addresses in the city were quite consciously excluded. None of the most famous and prestigious bathhouses were accessible to the "Jew." None of the cream of the city's hotels, with their fashionable Mária Valéria u. addresses, were accessible to the "Jew." None of the city's very best restaurants or coffeehouses were accessible to the "Jew." And none of the best cinemas in the city were accessible to the "Jew." None of the cinemas designated were modern, none had an air-raid shelter, and none were the prime category a, "first run house" cinemas in the city that showed the new releases. Of the sixteen cinemas designated for "Jewish" use, only one was sufficiently prestigious to show movies the week after they had been released. The majority were small, old cinemas that got movies well after their release dates. In short, the city's "Jews" were being punished through the implementation of territorial solutions. After May 1944, they could still stay in hotels and eat in restaurants and use bathhouses and visit the cinema, but they could use only those places designated by the city's mayor. And the places designated were the least desirable sites of consumption and entertainment in the city. Space was redefined as "Jewish" and "non-Jewish" according to an antisemitic agenda of separate and unequal.

The power of the mayor to designate in May 1944 where the "Jew" bathed, stayed, ate, and watched movies gave local authorities considerable control over the "Jew." As can be seen, this control both effectively relocated the "Jew" within the spaces of Pest rather than Buda and restricted the "Jew" to less than luxurious surroundings. But there was more to the degree of control exercised by the local authorities through territoriality than this. The local authorities essentially assumed the role of a gatekeeper who policed "Jewish" access to public space (figure 14).

During the month of May, the territorial solutions that I have listed above combined to give city officials an extraordinary degree of control over the city's "Jews." There were no ghetto houses in Budapest at the end of May, let alone a closed ghetto. All of that was to come. By the end of June

Figure 14. Sign announcing that "Jews Can Visit This Place," Budapest, 1944. Hungarian National Museum Historical Photographic Archives, courtesy of USHMM Photo Archives.

1944, Budapest's "Jews" were restricted to 1,948 yellow-star houses dispersed throughout the city. They were permitted to leave these houses for only three hours in the afternoon, "exclusively for medical treatment, cleaning, and shopping."[12] By December 1944, the city's "Jews" were subjected to the extreme surveillance of life within the walls of a closed ghetto.

But already, by the end of the month of May, the city had been carved up, and the "Jew" was restricted to relatively few places in ghettoized Budapest. The city's almost 200,000 "Jews" were limited to a maximum of five bathhouses, three hotels, five inns, fourteen guest houses, twenty-five snack bars, thirteen restaurants, twenty-three coffeehouses,[13] seven bars, and sixteen cinemas. Of these 111 places of entertainment and consumption, all but one was in Pest. It was of course still possible to walk the city's streets, albeit marked with a canary-yellow star, but Budapest's "Jews" were effectively excluded from the majority of places in the city. In reality of course, on any individual day, the number of sites of consumption and entertainment accessible to the "Jew" was less than 111. As I have noted with regard to cinemas, only five were accessible on a Monday, the full sum of sixteen on a Wednesday, and fourteen on a Friday. None were open to the "Jew" for the majority of the week. This meant of course that there was the option of manipulating the images the city's "Jews" could see, limited as they were to thirty-five showings in sixteen cinemas each week.

TERRITORIAL SOLUTIONS, TEMPORAL SOLUTIONS

What the example of cinemas shows, and this is mirrored with the other sites, is that there were in effect two scales of control. At one level, there was a territorial solution, which limited "Jewish" access to 111 places in the city. However, within those 111 places there was further control exercised in both territorial and nonterritorial ways. The vast majority of hotels, inns, guest houses, snack bars, restaurants, coffeehouses, and bars operated in terms similar to the concept of the mixed house, which I have mentioned in the previous chapter. Thus in the same way that "Jews" were effectively limited to certain apartments within designated buildings that might also be occupied by "non-Jews," so in the majority of cases, "Jews" were limited to, say, a room in a restaurant that also continued to serve "non-Jews." In essence, the scale of the territorial solution applied to places of consumption was the room. "Jews" were permitted to eat and drink and stay in a limited number of rooms in three hotels, five inns, seven guest houses, eleven snack bars, seven restaurants, twenty-one coffeehouses, and seven bars. The exceptions were that in the case of a further seven guest houses, fourteen snack bars, and six kosher restaurants, "Jews" were given access to the entire premises.

Now, as I have suggested, a similar pattern of further limitations can be seen in the case of cinemas and bathhouses. Two ritual baths were available solely for "Jewish" use. But in the case of the other three, the situation was similar to that of the cinemas. These bathhouses were open to "Jews" on selected days or parts of days. Thus the Hungária fürdö was open to "Jews" on Thursdays, Fridays, and Saturdays, the Royal Köruti fürdö was open to "Jews" on Tuesday mornings and Friday afternoons, and the Teréz fürdö was open to "Jews" on Tuesdays and Thursdays. At the larger scale "Jewish" access was limited through a policy that was clearly territorial. However, within that broadly territorial solution, access was further defined along temporal lines. That control being exercised through a mixture of territorial and nonterritorial solutions can of course be seen in the aftermath of ghettoization in June 1944. The decision to house the city's "Jews" within apartments in 1,948 ghetto houses was clearly a territorial solution. The decision to restrict "Jews" to these ghetto houses for twenty-one hours of the day but permit them restricted access to the city was a nonterritorial solution that operated primarily in terms of time rather than space.

Such a restricting of "Jewish" access in terms of designated time rather than space can be seen in another arena. The territorial solutions I have outlined above restricted "Jewish" access to places of consumption and entertainment in the city. Within a week of the last of these being implemented, "Jewish" access to markets and shops in the city was restricted. But this was done not by designating certain shops and markets that "Jews" could and could not use, but by designating the hours when "Jews" could and could not shop. On 4 June, the Interior Ministry issued regulations "concerning the restriction on shopping by Jews to a specific period of the day,"[14] and the following day this was implemented in Budapest.[15] This limited "Jewish" access to Budapest's shops and markets to the hours between 11 A.M. and 1 P.M. to purchase foodstuffs, and 1 P.M. to 3 P.M. to purchase other items.[16]

TOP DOWN, BOTTOM UP

These restrictions on the number of hours when "Jews" could shop were not limited solely to Hungary. Similar restrictions had been introduced across Nazi-occupied Europe. In Germany, regulations—"initially locally ordered"—were issued to restrict "Jewish" shopping hours to specified hours in the afternoon.[17] Similar restrictions were applied in the Netherlands,[18] and, from 1942 onward, "Jews" in Paris were permitted to shop only between 3 and 4 P.M.[19] The (antisemitic) logic underlying this choice of the afternoon hours was that "otherwise Jews would 'grab up' the best and freshest produce and foods,"[20] and therefore they should be permitted access "when food stores . . . were already sold out."[21] And it is clear in the case of Budapest that the very same (antisemitic) logic was in operation.

However, whilst the restriction of shopping hours can be seen as being applied across Nazi-occupied Europe, including Hungary, for very similar reasons, it is wrong to simply assume—as Braham tends to—that this legislation was a Nazi German import. In the first edition of his study of the Hungarian Holocaust, Braham described the restrictions on "Jewish" shopping hours as but one element of what he terms "the Nazi-inspired 'legislative' programme of the quisling Sztójay government."[22] His assumption was that this measure was a Nazi idea, legislated at the center by the national government and then implemented in the locality by city mayors.[23] Yet this picture of implementation from the top down misses out on another part of the story of how this particular legislation came about. That other part of the story reveals clear evidence of initiative being taken by officials in Budapest.

Well before the issuing of national ministerial regulations restricting "Jewish" shopping hours, plans to restrict "Jewish" access to stores were already being hatched in Budapest.[24] On 11 May, the city's lord mayor wrote to the mayor suggesting that "Jews" be forbidden access to food stores before 10 A.M.[25] He cited increasing public disquiet about the fact that "Jews" were buying unrationed goods freely and to such a degree that "the Hungarian public have a sense of being disadvantaged."[26] The acting mayor replied on 16 May with the suggestion that the "Jew" be forbidden access before 11 A.M.[27] He reported that he had investigated the matter with the owners and managers of the markets, who claimed that the greatest problem and cause of complaints was that "Jews" were buying up the majority of the limited quantity of unrationed fish for sale. Their suggestion—which he saw as both suitable and justified—was to restrict "Jewish" access to the markets until after 11 A.M., giving "non-Jews" first options on unrationed goods. By 11 A.M., the very limited quantities of fish still available in market halls in mid-1944 would no doubt all be gone.

What is clear from the correspondence between the acting mayor and the lord mayor is that the intention behind introducing restricted shopping hours for "Jews" was to ensure that "Jewish" consumption was limited to the "Jewish" ration. On 22 April 1944 the Ministry of Food had legislated that "Jews" were to receive rationed foods at a far lower level than that of the "non-Jewish" population.[28] A week later, "Jews" in Budapest were ordered to register with the mayoral office before 1 May in order to receive new "Jewish" ration cards and coupons.[29] From 1 May 1944, this differential ration allowed "Jews" only 300 grams of sugar and 300·grams of sesame oil per month and 100 grams of beef or horse meat per week, in comparison to "non-Jews," who were to receive 1,400 grams of sugar and 600 grams of lard per month and 200g of meat per week.[30] Only "Jewish" women who were pregnant and "Jewish" children under the age of three could buy milk, and no "Jews" could buy rationed butter, eggs, rice, poppy seeds, and paprika.[31] As anyone who knows Hungarian cuisine will realize, such a list of restricted items was of considerable significance. Yet even given these severe restrictions implemented through a differential ration, there was recognition that unrationed goods provided a problem. "Jewish" access to these could not be restricted in the same way, and thus the idea of restricting

"Jewish" access to food stores was put forward by the lord mayor. It was an attempt to further reduce Budapest's "Jews" to essentially starvation rations.

The attraction of the lord mayor's plan to Acting Mayor Bódy was not only that it reduced the city's "Jews" to the "Jewish" ration. It was also attractive on more pragmatic grounds. Introducing separate shopping hours for "Jews" and "non-Jews" was seen as making for smaller queues outside the market halls. By keeping the city's large "Jewish" population at home until 11 A.M., Bódy imagined a city less overcrowded and therefore, from a civil-defense point of view, less dangerous. Alongside this, he clearly had an eye on "non-Jewish" opinion in the city, something that emerges even more strongly in later correspondence. As was the case with the segregation of housing, local officials were well aware of "non-Jewish" opinion. Their consistent aim was to ensure that implementing ghettoization would not harm the city's "non-Jews" but might positively benefit them.

There was, however, one problem. Despite the agreement of the lord mayor and the acting mayor that restricting "Jewish" access to market halls and food stores was a perfect solution, the acting mayor reported that after taking legal advice, he had been informed he lacked the necessary authority to implement such measures in the city. In his reply to the lord mayor, he advised him of the need for national authorization from the Interior Ministry. Upon being informed of this, the lord mayor wrote to the Interior Minister requesting just such authorization.[32] In essence what had started out as a solution to "non-Jewish" complaints in the locality was now being suggested to the Interior Minister as a piece of national legislation. This was a clear case of initiative coming from the bottom up.

But at the very same time as these proposals were coming from the bottom up, they were also coming from the top down, although from a different national source than the Interior Ministry. On 1 June, the question of "Jewish" shopping hours was bought up in the Council of Ministers meeting.[33] However, the subject was not placed on the agenda by the interior minister after his reading of the Lord Mayor's letter. Instead, the matter was raised by the minister of trade and transport affairs, whose concerns were rather different from those being articulated by the lord mayor and the acting mayor in Budapest. He did not argue for the introduction of separate shopping hours for "Jews" and "non-Jews" as a means of restricting "Jewish" access to nonrationed goods, as the lord mayor had done in his initial correspondence. Rather, he spoke of the dangers of "Jews" and "non-Jews" coming into contact with each other in the course of regular lengthy periods of time spent shopping. Such contact was seen to be undesirable because it presented the opportunity for disturbance and the spreading of rumors. To ensure that "Jews" and "non-Jews" were kept separate, the minister suggested limiting "Jewish" access to markets across the country to two hours each day.

Because his concerns were with segregation rather than ensuring that nonrationed goods had sold out, the trade and transport minister did not see the worth in specifying precisely when during the day those two hours would be. Rather, this was to be left to local officials, who would be empowered to specify when the "Jew" could shop in their city. These suggestions met with the approval of the Council of Ministers, and were issued under the signature of Prime Minister Sztójay on the same day. They were published—and came into force—on 4 June, with details of the punishments that both "Jewish" shoppers and ("non-Jewish") shopkeepers would face for infringements.

With the implementation of the ministerial decree of 4 June, the very authorization that the acting mayor was looking for was granted.[34] No time was wasted. The very next day, 5 June, mayoral regulations were issued restricting "Jewish" access to marketplaces and food stores in Budapest.[35] Such a speedy response makes sense in the light of the earlier correspondence. What also makes sense are the precise times of "Jewish" shopping hours chosen by the acting mayor. The two hours when foodstuffs could be bought were designated as 11 A.M.–1 P.M., the time slot initially suggested by the acting mayor in his earlier correspondence. The thinking behind the designation of these particular times was clearly that they would ensure that "non-Jews," rather than "Jews," would get access to unrationed goods.

What is striking here is that there is a sense of two meanings being given to the restriction on shopping hours for "Jews." For the trade and transport minister, this was a segregatory measure that would ensure mixing would not take place between "Jews" and "non-Jews." He thought of this legislation being enacted at a national scale, and this national context was one of ghettoization having *already* been enacted for most Hungarian "Jews" living anywhere outside of Budapest. In this national context, restrictions on "Jewish" shopping hours were seen as a continuation of the segregation associated with ghettoization. In those places where "Jews" were being permitted to leave the ghetto in order to shop, there was a clear desire to ensure that this did not afford them the opportunity to mix with "non-Jews."

However, the meanings given to restricting "Jewish" shopping hours were rather different in Budapest. For the acting mayor and the lord mayor, these restrictions were about ensuring that "non-Jews" were given free access to unrationed foodstuffs and "Jews" were restricted to their differential ration. Such thinking took place in a rather different context, most significantly an urban context that was not characterized by self-sufficiency. But more than that, there was, I think, a sense in which this thinking also took place in the context of the broader imagining of the city's "Jews" in May 1944. Such an imagining, as I have suggested, saw the opportunity to punish the wealthy "Jew" and overturn the history of "Jewish" and "non-Jewish" relations in the city. And so, it was out of this set of meanings that the acting mayor, charged with implementing this legislation in the locality, acted.

What I think is fascinating is that essentially the same piece of legislation could mean very different things to a national official and an official in the locality. The result was that this piece of legislation as it was enacted centrally meant one thing but then meant something radically different when it was implemented locally. In the act of specifying which two hours Budapest's "Jews" were to shop for foodstuffs, the acting mayor essentially reinterpreted this nationally issued act. This is clear from subsequent correspondence. A matter of days after "Jewish" shopping hours for foodstuffs had been fixed in Budapest, a letter from a self-styled "National Socialist housewife" to the lord mayor was passed on to Acting Mayor Bódy. What is significant is that the argument in this letter complaining about the hours chosen led to renewed investigation into the matter. According to the "National Socialist housewife," 11 A.M. was the worst possible time to allow "Jews" to shop, as it was precisely when supplies of vegetables arrived at the markets. Her suggestion therefore was that "Jews" be permitted to shop only in the afternoons, once all these fresh vegetables had gone.[36] If her claims were true, then the very intention of setting the hours for "Jews" to shop after 11 A.M. was being undermined. And therefore this single letter from a self-styled "National Socialist housewife" was taken very seriously. The matter was thoroughly investigated by mayoral officials who interviewed market owners and managers. However, they reported back that vegetables were generally delivered by 8 or 9 in the morning. The acting mayor therefore concluded that there was no need to alter the existing scope of the legislation as it was achieving its intended purpose.[37] And that purpose was clearly one of restricting "Jewish" access to nonrationed foodstuffs.

Now that purpose in the locality did not resonate with the intentions articulated by the minister of trade and transport at the national level. However, as I have already noted, it did resonate with the purposes behind introducing separate shopping hours for "Jews" in other places in Nazi-occupied Europe. This points, I think, to the need in the context of the Hungarian Holocaust to be aware of the complex interrelationship between three scales of power. These three scales—Nazi German, Hungarian national government, and Hungarian local government—interacted in much more complex ways than simply the top-down implementation and following of orders. And what is particularly interesting, I think, is that essentially the same piece of legislation could be—and was—seen rather differently at different scales. I think the meanings being given to ghettoization at the end of May 1944, which I have looked at in chapter 4, give another very clear example of this.

The implications are, I think, that there is a need to study—as I am aiming to do in this book—local implementation of policy and the vexed question of public opinion alongside the more German-centric and national government approaches that characterize Randolph Braham's numerous works on the Hungarian Holocaust. In short, the Holocaust was not implemented in Hungary solely from the top down. There is clear evidence of initiative in the locality and implementation of Holocaust measures from the bottom up. However, to say that there is clear evidence of local initiative is not to say that the meanings given to a particular Holocaust measure—say, ghettoization or restrictions on shopping hours—were identical at a variety of scales. I think that within the locality, measures that were clearly antisemitic could be—and were—viewed rather differently.

Such local initiative was not confined to Budapest alone. As the work of a number of scholars has shown—in particular, Judit Molnár's detailed study of the implementation of the Holocaust in the south of Hungary—there were a large number of bottom-up initiatives. To take just the regulation of "Jewish" shopping hours, in Szeged these were restricted to 10–11 A.M. by Deputy Chief of Police Buócz on 8 May 1944, well before the issuing of national legislation. Molnár suggests that this model may well have then been adopted by the mayor of Makó with the issuing of similar restrictions on 25 May.[38] In Győr, regulations were issued under the signature of Police Councilor Dr. Jenő Versényi on 13 May. Under these restrictions, the "Jew" was permitted to shop for groceries between 10 and 11 A.M. at the daily markets, 11 A.M. and 2 P.M. at the weekly markets, and 9 and 10 A.M. on Sundays and holidays. Domán notes that in reality, these regulations "almost made shopping at the markets impossible."[39] Further restrictions of shopping hours were issued locally in Pécs and Kőszeg prior to the issuing of national legislation in June 1944. In Pécs, the local authorities restricted "Jewish" access to markets to 11 A.M.–1 P.M., which "in practice meant that they could hardly get hold of groceries anymore."[40] In Kőszeg, a small number of "Jews" were permitted to leave the ghetto daily (except Saturday) between 10 A.M. and noon for the purpose of shopping in certain (designated) streets.[41]

Thus the discussion within municipal government circles in Budapest prior to the 4 June central issuing of legislation was by no means unique. What was perhaps unique in the case of Budapest was Bódy's reluctance to act without the necessary authority from the national level. Presumably these concerns were of less importance within provincial cities, some distance as they were from the seat of national government in Budapest. It is clear that it wasn't simply the issue of shopping hours that saw local initiative. In Szeged, "Jewish" access to steam baths was restricted prior to the national issuing of legislation by the Interior Ministry,[42] and the deputy mayor ordered (on his own initiative) the cutting off of electricity/gas from the ghetto area.[43]

Now of course such evidence of initiative being taken in the locality raises the question of where the motivation for these acts came from. This, in turn, raises the sensitive question of the extent to which antisemitism within the local Hungarian administration as well as the population at large played a role in the implementation of Holocaust measures. Of course, Nazi German officials could operate directly with local officials rather than working through national officials as seems to have been generally the case. Certainly an incident referenced by Karsai suggests German intervention in the locality over the question of the restriction of "Jewish" shopping hours. He claims that the initial decision of the chief constable of the district of Csorna to restrict "Jewish" shopping hours to 10 A.M.–noon was changed, to 11 A.M.–1 P.M., after the intervention of a "German security agent."[44] There is no evidence of Nazi Germany intervention in the specific Budapest case that I have examined in some detail above. But there is obviously a need to examine the implementation of territorial and nonterritorial solutions within the complex triadic relationship between German, national, and local officials.

CONTESTING THE DIVISION OF THE CITY

Of course both territorial and nonterritorial solutions involved more than simply this trio of actors. As I have suggested with the division of living space, ghettoization affected ordinary "Jews" and "non-Jews"—both owners and tenants. This was something not lost on those implementing ghettoization, and as I have suggested, concern with the impact of ghettoization upon "non-Jews" was of considerable significance. That concern with the impact of segregatory measures upon "non-Jews" can also be seen as playing a part in the context of the division of the city's places of consumption and entertainment. Within the text of the ministerial legislation, it was made explicit that local authorities were to consult the relevant owners and trade associations prior to designating specific premises. And as can be seen from the correspondence on restricting "Jewish" access to the place of the market and food store, not only were market owners consulted, but their expertise was actively drawn upon by mayoral officials.

It would seem that individual requests that premises be designated for "Jews," fed through trade federations, were taken on board by mayoral officials. In the case of a restaurant at Bulcsú út, the owner had requested through the restaurateurs association that a couple of regular "Jewish" customers continue to be allowed to eat in his premises.[45] This request no doubt led to the designating of a separate room in this restaurant for "Jewish" use on 24 May. Thus, in this case—and it seems not to have been an isolated case—the specifics of which places were designated for "Jewish" use were influenced in part at least by local restaurateurs.

However, in the case of the Bulcsú út restaurant there was a problem, as a reporter from *Esti Ujság* found out when he visited the premises. He discovered a small restaurant with only a single room, rather than separate rooms one of which could be designated for "Jews." The owner's intention in contacting his trade association had obviously been to ensure that a small number of regular "Jewish" customers be allowed to continue eating in his restaurant. What he had not planned on was that designation amounted to his premises becoming essentially a "Jewish" restaurant—the implementation of a territorial solution at the scale of the entire premises. But that was what had happened, much to his obvious displeasure. As he told the story to the *Esti Ujság* reporter, "At noon, when on the basis of the newspaper announcement, lots of Jews arrived . . . my Christian customers—without saying a thing—got up and left the premises. Simple workers come here and they are not willing to eat at a table with Jews."[46] His claim was that designation for "Jewish" use was ruining his business.

It is therefore not surprising that on 13 June, this Bulcsú út restaurant ceased to be accessible to "Jews," when a small number of cancellations and additions were issued, no doubt as a result of specific petitioning.[47] The concerns that this restaurateur had that designation would amount to financial ruin were shared by the owners of the hotel at Kenyérmezõ u. 4. In the 23 May list of hotels accessible to the city's "Jews," three rooms had been assigned for "Jewish" use in this property. This designation may well have been requested on similar grounds to those in the case of the Bulcsú út restaurant. After all, this hotel was home to seven permanent "Jewish" residents. However, designation in practice was not acceptable. These seven permanent residents would have to leave the hotel, as the three— "naturally not luxury"—rooms that had been designated for "Jewish" use were only available for use by temporary "Jewish" guests. No doubt with an eye to profits, the owners questioned whether they could fill these three rooms. Looking back at the guest book for the first months of the year, they noted that these seven permanent "Jewish" residents aside, only six of the 2,970 guests who stayed in the hotel from 1 January to 25 May had been "Jews."[48] For them, designation in practice was perceived as threatening their business.

However, not all owners saw designation as a cost. As with the designation of living space, designation was also seen as an opportunity. Thus alongside requests for cancellations, there were requests for additions. When the Bulcsú út restaurant was cancelled from the "Jewish" restaurant list on 13 June, the number of cancellations—two—was outnumbered by the number of additions—six. It would seem that at least two restaurateurs and four coffee shop owners saw designation for "Jewish" use as an opportunity. And it was not simply a case of nondesignated owners calling for designation. The owners of two of the bathhouses partially designated for "Jewish" use on 12 May requested that further days be added to those on which "Jews" could use the premises. The owners of the Hungária fürdõ asked the mayor on 7 September that "Jewish" access be increased to include Sunday and received a favorable response.[49] The argument of the owners was that members of "Jewish" labor battalions based in Budapest at present could only visit the bathhouse on Saturday afternoon. Similarly, access to the Royal Köruti fürdõ was increased with the addition of Tuesday afternoon on 3 October, upon the request of the owners.[50]

It is clear that as with the segregation of living space, the segregation of places of consumption and entertainment was actively contested. Thus, individuals were not simply subject to the decisions of Budapest's doctors of space but were, in a number of cases, active agents who impacted this reshaping of the city. As with the earlier contestation of ghettoization, this included requests for both additions and cancellations. Dividing the city's bathhouses, hotels, restaurants, and cinemas into "Jewish" and "non-Jewish" places brought the segregatory agenda of the doctors of space into contact with the commercial interests of owners and trade associations. And this contact could—and did—lead to conflict. This was clearly the case with regard to the division of the city's cinemas at the end of May 1944.

CONTESTING THE DIVISION OF CINEMA SPACE

What is striking about the case of the city's cinemas is that clearly the relevant trade association had already initiated its own segregatory measures in response to the 19 May Interior Ministry regulations. But conflict arose, because this interpretation of the thrust of the Interior Ministry regulations did not fit with that planned by mayoral officials. As I have noted, when the mayor issued the specifics of which cinemas could be used by "Jews" on 31 May, thirty-five screenings at sixteen cinemas were sanctioned. This did not match the measures being drawn up by the Cinema Proprietors Association. Their preference was that cinemas lying within expressly "Jewish"-inhabited areas would hold performances solely for "Jews," whilst other cinemas within the city were to designate screenings for "Jews" on different days of the week. This was intended, in part at least, to reflect what was already happening in the city, with "Jews" increasingly being reported as going only to the cinemas in the districts where they lived since the enforced wearing of the yellow star. In the case of cinemas in "non-Jewish" parts of the city, the desire was for self-regulation, with decisions of whether and when to designate performances being made at the scale of the individual cinema.[51]

So here were two alternative territorial solutions, one advocated by the trade association and one enacted by the city authorities. What is interesting is *Esti Ujság*'s suggestion that individual cinema owners rejected both. In an article of 1 June, headlined "Cinema Proprietors Do Not Want to Hold Separate Shows for the Jews," *Esti Ujság* reported the reactions of cinema proprietors to the 31 May regulations.[52] Their opposition to the mayoral details of segregation was, in the short term, rooted in a concern with currently declining cinema audiences—down 25 percent as a result of declining "Jewish" audiences. In this context, there were fears that designation as a "Jewish cinema" would alienate a large part of their "non-Jewish" audience, and so there was opposition to designation. Their preference was that a couple of second-rate cinemas in the "Jewish" Dob u. district of the city be designated, whilst the rest of the cinemas in the city were made completely *judenfrei*.

Such a territorial solution was far more radical than that envisioned by either the trade association or the Budapest mayor. And it was favorably reported by *Esti Ujság*, which applauded what it saw as the cinema owners' "determined right-wing stance." What is so striking is that such a radical short-term measure was grounded on an assumption of a much longer-term, and far more radical, agenda. The current downturn in cinema-going was seen to be only temporary. Once the "complete and permanent cutting off of the Jews" had been achieved, an economically empowered "non-Jewish" middle class would take the place of the "Jewish" cinema-going public. At present, the scene painted was one of a "non-Jewish" middle class "crowded into" second-rate cinemas in the outlying districts because of high seat prices in the city center cinemas serving a "Jewish" audience that "endeavored to be everywhere that meant entertainment, pleasure and ease." But such a situation was about to be overturned, so cinema owners were not making business decisions on the basis of the city's "Jews." They had seen the future, and they were pretty sure it was of a punished and impoverished "Jewry" and an economically powerful "non-Jewish" middle class. It was that "non-Jewish" audience which they clearly did not want to alienate.

Such attitudes raise the question of the responses of ordinary Hungarians to the antisemitic measures enacted in Hungary in 1944. Certainly *Esti Ujság*'s enthusiastic reporting of the response of cinema owners would suggest popular support for radical, long-term measures that would reconfigure the economic relationship of "Jews" and "non-Jews" in the city. For these cinema owners, the horizons of both the mayor and their trade associations were far too limited. They did not just want segregation, they wanted effectively to remove "Jews" from the city's cinemas as a result of removing "Jews" from the city's economic life. Of course, the extent to which such sentiments were those of the cinema owners or the writers at *Esti Ujság* is debatable.

However, there is, I think, a need to take ordinary Hungarians much more seriously in trying to understand what does and does not happen in terms of antisemitic measures in 1944. In short, ordinary Hungarians were not simply passive recipients of nationally or even locally issued legislation but could be—and were—active agents, as I've also suggested in the preceding chapter. One final example, again taken from the pages of *Esti Ujság*, points to this. The scene sketched out by the reporter was of entering the Zöldflaskó restaurant on Erzsébet királyné út, which had been designated, in part at least, for "Jewish" use. He described seeing a man walk in

> wearing a yellow-star badge, [who] looked round quietly and asked directions to the separate room.
>
> "I don't want to serve you," said the owner.
>
> "But . . . in the newspaper . . ."
>
> "It was an error . . . there is no service, I won't even serve a glass of soda water."
>
> The starred man went out of the door and the owner explained the situation in a few words.
>
> "There is a labor-battalion billeted in the Dance Hall of the restaurant. Because of that I asked the mayor—through the restaurateurs association—for permission to continue giving them food. After this they designated my restaurant, which was established under pure Christian management.
>
> "My customers are purely Christians and I don't want to go bust because of a few yellow-starred. They came here mistakenly today, and they didn't get a mouthful."[53]

As this incident shows, to see the implementation of policies of ghettoization as applied from the top down by the Nazi German–influenced Hungarian Interior Ministry is to miss more than half the story. There is not only a need to see mayoral officials as playing more than merely a passive role of implementation, but also a need to examine the reactions of individuals on the ground, as the previously shared spaces of the city were redefined and redesignated. Not only was there contestation of mayoral designation, but these designations could also be ignored. After all, whatever the rubric of regulations defining "Jewish" access to specified establishments, the owners of these establishments could simply choose not to serve the "Jew." Of course, to choose the opposite was a very different proposition. To serve the "Jew" in a place not designated for the "Jew" was an invitation to prosecution. So agency was not something that came solely from below. But recognizing that power was distributed unequally in Budapest in 1944 is not the same as seeing the division of the city into "Jewish" and "non-Jewish" places as purely implemented from the top down and forced onto an unwilling populace. There was after all a self-styled "National

Socialist housewife" who helpfully wrote to the mayor in mid-June 1944 with suggestions on how the city's "Jews" could be starved more effectively. And her letter was not simply discarded but taken very seriously. It was thoroughly investigated and carefully archived.

EIGHT

Planning and Implementing Hyphenated Ghettoization, July 1944–January 1945

During the spring and early summer of 1944, a series of territorial solutions were planned and implemented for Budapest's "Jews." These amounted to a thoroughgoing remapping of the city along racialized lines, with the separation of "Jewish" and "non-Jewish" space. The end result of this history of manipulating the spaces of the city was that by early July 1944, the city's "Jews" were housed in a ghetto made up of thousands of apartments in 1,948 "Jewish" apartment buildings, each marked with a large yellow star affixed by the entrance. In many ways, Budapest's "Jews" were lucky. While ghettoization had been planned and implemented in the capital, ghettoization had already been implemented in the remainder of Hungary, swiftly followed by deportations. Within a period of less than two months (15 May–9 July 1944), a total of 437,402 "Jews" were deported from ghettos across Hungary to Auschwitz-Birkenau.

The only "Jewish" community to ultimately be spared this fate was the largest in the country: the "Jews" of Budapest. That they would remain in Budapest in the summer of 1944, rather than being taken to Auschwitz, was due to the decision of Regent Horthy to halt deportations in early July. This decision, Braham suggests, "has emerged as one of the most controversial themes in post-war historiography."[1] That Horthy was able to prevent the mass deportation of Budapest's "Jews" to Auschwitz is read by Braham as evidence that Horthy could have stood against the earlier deportations of "Jews"—including Braham himself—from provincial Hungary. That he didn't is proof, Braham claims, of a lack of concern on the part of Horthy and Hungarian authorities with the hundreds of thousands of "Jews" living outside of the capital.[2] Underlying such a lack of concern was, according to Braham, an open dislike of the "Galician Jews" living outside the capital, who were seen as dispensable by Horthy, whereas those in Budapest were safeguarded and protected.[3]

However, of more impact than drawing distinctions between assimilated and unassimilated "Jews" was—as Braham himself recognizes—the changing military and geopolitical situation.[4] Alongside the rising implications of the Red Army's continued advance westward and the D-Day landings was growing diplomatic pressure on Hungary to halt the deportations. As soon as the deportations had begun in mid-May, Deputy Foreign Minister Arnóthy-Jungerth warned the Council of Ministers of the nature of foreign reactions. He was involved in monitoring foreign news coverage of the deportations and built up a sizable file of press clippings.[5] During June 1944, the issue of foreign reactions to the deportations was discussed at one council meeting after another.[6] On 21 June, just on the eve of the issuing of the final ghetto house list in Budapest, Arnóthy-Jungerth called upon government ministers to halt the deportations, citing foreign press reports that the "Jews" being deported to Auschwitz were being gassed and burned there. These reports were dismissed by Interior Minister Jaross, and the two undersecretaries responsible for implementing anti-Jewish measures, Baky and Endre, were invited to the 23 June council meeting to explain what the situation really was. After their reporting of the "true" situation,[7] the decision was made to ensure that any atrocities associated with the deportations were ended while the deportations themselves continued.

However, the foreign pressure on Hungary to halt deportations mounted at the end of June. Horthy was petitioned by Pope Pius XII on 25 June, President Franklin Roosevelt on 26 June, and King Gustav V of Sweden on 30 June.[8] In this context of growing foreign pressure, Horthy assumed a more active political role, chairing the Council of Ministers meeting on 26 June, when the issue of foreign protests against the deportations was again discussed. When precisely in early July the decision to halt deportations was made by Horthy is difficult to say conclusively.[9] On 6 July, Prime Minister Sztójay informed Veesenmayer of this decision,[10] who passed this news on to Ribbentrop on 8 July.[11] Veesenmayer also informed Ribbentrop of Hungarian wishes to allow a limited number of "Jews" to emigrate to Sweden and Palestine,[12] and recommended that this be permitted because "then the entire Jewish question could be solved quickly."[13] Hitler approved this recommendation on 10 July, "provided that Horthy is willing to allow the speedy resumption of deportations."[14] Hitler's decision was then discussed by the Council of Ministers on 12 July, with the decision being made to inform Hungarian legations abroad that "the dispatch of Jews abroad for the purpose of labor" was being temporarily suspended until the foreign emigration schemes had been implemented.[15]

So the broader context to the finalizing of ghettoization plans in Budapest, and then the first few weeks of the city's "Jews" living in the 1,948 yellow-star houses assigned for them, was a flurry of activity at the very highest political levels. Right at the point when ghettoization was finally implemented in the capital, the pressure to halt deportations began mounting. It was an uncertain time for the city's "Jews," with rumors of deportations being imminent and "conversion fever" in the capital, as ways were sought to escape the fate of the remainder of Hungary's "Jews."[16] However, Budapest's "Jews" ultimately escaped deportations.[17] The result was that they continued to live in the dispersed ghetto created on 22 June throughout the summer of 1944. The shape of this ghetto did change slightly. On 15 September, upon the Interior Ministry's request, fourteen yellow-star houses in five districts were vacated and transferred to the German military command for the purpose of billeting soldiers.[18] The "Jews" living there had to move out of the houses within twenty-four hours and into yellow-star houses assigned to them by the Jewish Council. However, these relocations did not go entirely smoothly. The owners or caretakers of five yellow-star houses refused to allow the "referred Jews" to occupy the apartments specified for them by the Jewish Council. Such intransigence was not to be tolerated, and the mayor wrote threatening criminal proceedings if these relocated "Jews" were not allowed immediate entry into these houses.[19] A further eight yellow-star houses in four districts were requested, also for the use of the German military, by the Interior Ministry on 27 October. Again the responsibility of assigning new living quarters lay with the Jewish Council.[20] But these changes to the shape of the ghetto were minor—only a total of twenty-two houses removed from the 1948 designated for "Jewish" use.

In broad terms, the city's "Jews" remained living in the ghetto centered on the central districts of Pest from its creation on 22 June through the summer and into the fall of 1944. By the end of August, the national situation had moderated somewhat, and it seemed that the city's "Jews" had weathered the storm. As early as 17 July 1944, Horthy had communicated to Veesenmayer demands that German occupation forces be recalled and the Szójay government be dismissed. During August there were significant personnel changes in the national government. On 7 August, Interior Minister Jaross was replaced by the former secretary of state in the Ministry of Justice Miklós Bonczos. Along with Jaross, Imrédy and Kunder were also dismissed from the cabinet, lessening the influence of the extreme right.[21] On 12 August, the convalescing Sztójay was temporarily replaced by Lajos Reményi-Schneller, who assumed the post of acting prime minister. A couple of weeks later, Horthy "forced Sztójay to submit his resignation,"[22] and on 29 August the former military chief General Géza Lakatos was installed as prime minister in Sztójay's place. A few days later, the two key individuals who had been involved in anti-Jewish measures in the Interior Ministry, Baky and Endre, were dismissed (on 2 and 8 September, respectively).[23] It was nothing less than a clearing out of the extreme right of M.É.P. and those associated closely with Imrédy.[24] However, in Budapest, both Keledy and Doroghi Farkas remained in their posts.

This change in government at the national scale did have an immediate impact on Budapest's "Jews." The appointment of the Lakatos government at the end of August 1944 resulted in the granting of a greater degree of freedom of movement. On the eve of Rosh Hashanah, "Jews" were permitted by the interior minister to leave their yellow-star houses between 5 and 7 P.M., and then on Rosh Hashanah itself between 9 A.M. and 7 P.M., in order to participate in services. Similar freedom of movement was granted for the Holy Days of Yom Kippur and Tabernacles.[25] "Jews" requiring greater freedom of movement to continue their work had already been informed on 27 July and again on 3 August that they could apply for papers allowing them to leave the yellow-star houses in the interests of maintaining production.[26] With the installation of the Lakatos government, the mobilization of "Jewish" labor was implemented on a mass scale. On 7 September, all able-bodied "Jews," both male and female, between the ages of fourteen and seventy, were to report for "defense work."[27]

In this period of flux over what would happen to the country's remaining "Jews," a whole series of plans were being discussed. These included plans to separate from the majority of "Jews" converted "Jews" and "Jews" slated for emigration to neutral nations. Whereas in the earlier period, the focus had been upon separating the "Jewish" and "non-Jewish" populations in the city, from the summer of 1944 onward, there were increasing concerns with differentiating between and separating out distinct categories of "Jews." What is particularly striking I think, is that there were territorial dimensions to these attempts at differentiating between one "Jew" and another. Although initially these territorial solutions remained at the level primarily of (contested) discussion, by the end of 1944, separate territorial solutions had been implemented for distinct groups of "Jews" in Budapest. It amounted to nothing less than the implementation of hyphenated ghettoization—with different ghettos being created for different categories of (hyphenated) "Jews."

PLANS TO SEPARATE "CHRISTIAN JEWS"

The physical separation of the "Jewish" and "non-Jewish" populations through ghettoization can be seen as an attempt to create a degree of clear water between the "Jew" and "non-Jew," and thus overturn the history of assimilation. As I have already suggested, this attempt to create clear water between the "Jew" and "non-Jew" had a particularly marked impact upon mixed marriages. It is not surprising that a large number of the petitions sent in the aftermath of the 16 June ghettoization decree in Budapest came from couples in mixed marriages requesting that partners (and their children) be permitted to remain together. Another group impacted by these attempts to separate the "Jew" and "non-Jew" was the rather ambiguous category of "Jews" who were converts to "Christianity." Their status was somewhat confusing. The yardstick was the 1941 legislation[28] according to which the status of the individual on the seventh birthday was the critical point in determining how "Jewish" an individual was. This law determined that only the converted Jew with two "Jewish" grandparents, who had been born a "Christian" or had converted before the seventh birthday was a "non-Jew."[29] For those whose conversion had come later on in life, they were still "Jews" rather than ("non-Jewish") Christians. But there was a sense in which all converts presented a liminal and ambiguous category that could quite literally go both ways.

Under pressure from both the churches and the newly formed Association of the Christian Jews of Hungary, the status and living space of "Christian-Jews" was questioned in mid-1944. On 11 July, the mayor ordered all those "Jews" aged between sixteen and sixty currently living in Budapest, who had converted to Christianity before 1 August 1941 (in Hungary, but outside Budapest) and been members of denominations since their conversion to register with their denominational authorities between 12 and 17 July.[30] This registration in some senses mirrored the 1–2 June registrations, in that it was intended as the basis for Interior Ministry–author-ized relocations of converted "Jews" into separate yellow-star houses. The denominational authorities were informed by Doroghi-Farkas as to the details they were to ascertain[31] and the manner of submission. All data were to be delivered by hand to the City Hall by midday on 31 July 1944. Relocations were to take place by 6 August.

During these first few weeks in July, plans to separate "Jew" and "Christian Jew" appear to have been of some importance. In his 8 July meet-ing with Veesenmayer, Horthy announced that he had ordered the separa-tion of the "converted Jews" prior to resuming the deportations of the "non-converted Jews."[32] The policy was spelled out in a letter sent to Hungarian legations on 18 July to explain the Hungarian government's stance on the "Jewish question" in the midst of foreign criticism.[33] Whilst "the dispatch of Jews abroad for the purpose of labor" was "temporarily sus-pended," "the dispatch of converted Jews for labor abroad" was to "cease." Moreover, legations were informed that "a review is under consideration about the matter of converted Jews sent to Germany for labor service." It was stated that pre–1 August 1941 converts were to remain in Hungary but "be separated from non-Jews." Thus, there were to be three categories: "Jew," "convert," and "non-Jew." Indeed, with relation to the second category, legations were informed that "a determination will be made in the shortest possible time as to who is to be considered a converted Jew." The "Jew" mar-ried to a "Christian" was to be exempt from the scope of "anti-Jewish" laws, as were "members of the immediate families of Christian clergymen," "holders of Church Orders" and "members of the Order of the Holy Grave."

In preparation for the planned date of relocations, a meeting was held in the Interior Ministry to discuss the separation of the converted "Jews," on the afternoon of 31 July. Representatives of the Jewish Council, Association of Christian Jews, the Interior Ministry, and the Gendarmerie[34] attended.[35] Székely-Molnár and Ferenczy, on behalf of the interior minister, informed the "Jewish" leaders present that all pre–1 August 1941 converts were to be relocated into separate houses by 8 P.M. on 6 August. However, this decision was contested by the leadership of both the Association of Christian Jews and the Jewish Council, although for very different reasons. For the leadership of the Association of Christian Jews, the relocations pre-sented practical problems.[36] They pointed to the lack of both the necessary means and time to implement relocations, and questioned how these yel-low-star houses would be differentiated from the others.[37] Ferenczy's response was that "orders were orders," and that the Jewish Council housing affairs department would be made available for use by the Association of Christian Jews. He did, however, agree to a two-week extension of the time period for relocations.

Whilst the response of the Association of Christian Jews leadership was to object at the level of practicalities, the Jewish Council response was one of objection in principle to the planned relocations. They raised fears that further relocations would result in panic among the city's "Jewish" population and "a new wave of suicides."[38] The Association of Christian Jews deputy president Sándor Török finally requested permission to utter "the word that had been in the air during the whole discussion: deportations."[39] There was no reply to his question as to whether the relocation of the converted "Jews" cleared the way for the deportation of the nonconverted "Jewry,"[40] and the meeting ended with some ill feeling in the air.

This sense of contestation between the "Jewish" and "Christian-Jewish" leadership over the ghettoization of "Jewish converts" emerges much more clearly in the notes on the meeting written by the Association of Christian Jews president György Auer.[41] It is clear, both from Auer's comments in these notes, and from Székely-Molnár's response to association objections in the 31 July meeting, that the plan to house the converts separately was largely initiated by the Association of Christian Jews and self-consciously seen by them as giving converts "an advantage" over the rest of the "Jews."[42] In essence, they were suggesting their own territorial solution. However, these plans initiated by the Association of Christian Jews were seen by Auer as being scuppered by the behavior of the Jewish Council representatives present at the 31 July meeting, who in "stressing the shocking consequences to come" got Székely-Molnár very worried.[43] The result was not simply the stalling of negotiations between the Association of Christian Jews and the Interior Ministry but ultimately the announcement on 1 August that the interior minister had decided to cancel the planned relocations in light of the potential for panic.[44] In essence, the Jewish Council had been successful. Mass relocations of "Christian-Jews" to their own distinct ghetto did not take place.

PLANS TO SEPARATE "PROTECTED JEWS"

Alongside these discussions about the implementing of a separate territorial solution for "Christian-Jews" were discussions over the separation of another distinct category of "Jews"—those protected by neutral nations. In the Council of Ministers meeting of 27 June, the Swedish Red Cross and Swiss offers of emigration for 300 to 400 and 7,000 Hungarian "Jews," respectively, were accepted upon the recommendation of Deputy Foreign Minister Arnóthy-Jungerth.[45] This was to be the start of increasing intervention by a growing number of neutral powers on behalf of a minority—albeit a sizable minority—of the Budapest "Jewry."[46] It would seem that the request for differentiated ghettoization for the "protected Jews" came from the neutral powers, in discussion with Foreign Ministry officials. Lévai certainly suggests that this was the case, writing with obvious disapproval that "the neutral legations were interfering, asking permission to accommodate their protégés in special houses."[47] However, in his 1948 book *Zsidósors Magyarországon*, Lévai argued that the idea for the setting up of "protected houses" first took shape during a meeting called by Dénes Csopey, head of the political department of the Foreign Ministry,[48] on 23 July.[49] At this meeting, Lévai suggests that the idea of concentrating all the "Jews" slated for emigration in the yellow-star houses on one street was raised, in the interests of "the simplification of arrangements." The "protected houses" were to be a preliminary gathering point on the journey from yellow-star house to transit camp, awaiting the necessary travel permits for emigration.

Braham—drawing on Mukácsi—claims that Kurzweil (from the Jewish Council housing department) was approached by Ferenczy "during the middle of July" and informed of the plans to allow 2,630 "Jews" to emigrate. It was at this meeting, Braham suggests, that Ferenczy "requested that 'for reasons of security' the Council make available a number of modern Yellow Star houses exclusively for these Jews."[50] In his memoirs, the Jewish Council member Petõ refers to a meeting with Ferenczy attended by himself, Kurzweil, and Gábor, but makes no reference to Ferenczy's demand that "modern Yellow Star houses" be made available for "Jews" awaiting emigration.[51] In his dispatch sent on 29 July, Wallenberg referenced Hungarian foreign ministry agreement "to secure high quality for our Jews."[52] The eventual choice of a number of houses on Pozsonyi út for the relocation of the Swedish-protected "Jews" clearly fitted the bill. Pozsonyi út was one of the major streets in the fashionable "Jewish" middle-class area of the V district, which had been developed since the turn of the century, with building continuing right to the outbreak of war.

On 23 August, the Jewish Council issued an order detailing the practicalities of moving "unprotected Jews" out of, and 3,000 Swedish-protected "Jews" into, a number of properties on Pozsonyi út.[53] The relocations were attributed to "the orders of Lieutenant Colonel Ferenczy," and were to take place by 26 August. A central housing affairs department was established under the leadership of Jenő Bleier and charged with liaising with the embassies of the neutral powers, arranging labor for the removals, and setting up and supplying an office in each house. It was at the individual house level that the practicalities of relocation were to be implemented, centered on the role of the manager of the individual house offices. Individual house managers were responsible for informing the central housing affairs department of the current inhabitants and the number and size of apartments in the yellow-star house. They would then decide centrally how many persons would be assigned to each individual house, with the office manager in each house assigning room space to families "appropriate to their life conditions and circumstances."

Those moving into the Pozsonyi út houses were to have their credentials checked by the office manager of the house they were assigned to. To gain entry, they had to possess both a *Schutzpass* issued by the Swedish Legation and a relocation certificate issued by the Jewish Council housing affairs department. On the basis of the latter, a simple exchange was to take place. The "unprotected Jew" forced out of their flat in a Pozsonyi út yellow-star house was to simply to take over the tenancy on the flat in a yellow-star house previously inhabited by the "protected Jew." If such an exchange was not possible, the housing affairs department undertook to designate flats in yellow-star houses for the use of those forced to relocate. What emerges in the Jewish Council order is an awareness of the sensitivity of the situation of enforced relocations. The relocation certificate was to be signed by both those "unprotected Jews" leaving their flats and those "protected Jews" replacing them. With an awareness of the potential for confrontation and disagreement that this exchange presented, the council called for the changeover to be handled in a spirit of "harmonious co-operation."

That moving "protected Jews" into, and "unprotected Jews" out of, yellow-star houses on Pozsony út was potentially problematic was acknowledged by Wallenberg. In his memorandum of 6 August, he wrote that

> this coming Wednesday or Thursday we will probably be able to empty the rental property Pozsony-utca 3 [*sic*], a Jewish house, of its present occupants and replace them with the same number of Jews under the embassy's protection. It would be most desirable if we could pay the moving costs and a small compensation to those Jews who are now suddenly vacating their homes in this way.[54]

His suggestion of the need for some form of compensation is recognition of the costs of implementing a separate territorial solution for "protected Jews" upon the city's "unprotected Jews" living in Pozsonyi út.

The creation of two categories of "Jews"—the "protected" and the "non-protected"—was contested within the Jewish Council, just as the creation of the two categories of "converts" and "unconverted" had been contested. Within the "Jewish" leadership, it is clear that major disagreement existed over the wisdom and desirability of drawing up different categories of hyphenated Jews within the city and then expressing these through the implementation of policies of hyphenated ghettoization. For the Jewish Council member Lajos Stöckler, the scheme to relocate the "protected Jewry" to the houses in Pozsonyi út was reprehensible.[55] Not only did he object in practice to the forced relocation of those "Jews" who had been relocated once before, a matter of two months previously, but he also objected in principle to individual rescue attempts. Indeed, he recommended that the council separate itself entirely from such rescue attempts and see the Budapest "Jewry" solely in terms of a "collective community."

Despite such internal debate, it would seem that the Jewish Council pressed ahead with preparing to implement the scheme to separate out "protected Jews," and in so doing opened itself up to charges of favoring "protected Jews" over "non-protected Jews." For the writers of a petition to the Jewish Council of 23 August 1944 it seemed that the Jewish Council had been influenced by those with "protected" status arguing against the interests of the Budapest "Jewry" as a whole.[56] As this petition reveals, it was not only within the Jewish Council that the implementation of separate territorial solutions was contested. Indeed, Lévai suggested that there was sufficient opposition on the ground to scupper the planned separation. His claim was that the August concentration of "protected Jews" into yellow-star houses on Pozsonyi út never took place,[57] "as the people staying in the houses nominated refused to hand them over."[58] That the opposition of "non-protected Jews" to planned separation had an impact certainly makes sense of Komoly's reference in his diary entry of 9 September 1944 that Rezsö Müller—head of the housing department and executive secretary of the Jewish Council—was speaking of plans to relocate those "Jews under foreign protection and on emigration lists" to houses on Asztalos Sándor út (in the city's X district) between 10 and 15 September.[59] It was a street with no yellow-star houses, and thus would not necessitate one category of "Jew" forcing the relocation of another.

However, from Wallenberg's comments, it would seem that it was the broader changing geopolitical solution that put these plans to separate out "protected Jews" on hold, rather than the protests of "non-protected Jews." In his report of 12 September, Wallenberg reported that "no money had been used to pay damages to those Jews, who were known to have been ousted from their apartments in Pozsonyi út, which was to have been transformed into a Swedish ghetto. This plan was never carried out due to the changes in the general situation."[60] Whatever the precise reason, it would seem that the plans to separate out "protected Jews" and "non-protected Jews" were put on hold, for a couple of months at least.

IMPLEMENTING HYPHENATED GHETTOIZATION DURING THE NYILAS PERIOD

Ultimately, the principle of separate territorial solutions for "protected Jews" and "unprotected Jews" was implemented in Budapest with the establishing of a distinct "International ghetto" and "Pest ghetto" in the winter of 1944, in the context of broader political changes in the autumn of 1944 (see figure 15). These came as Horthy again sought to withdraw from the war. A bungled attempt at withdrawing from the Axis on 15 October was thwarted as members of the Gestapo captured Horthy's son. The following day, Horthy was forced to nullify his proclamation of the end of the war and formally entrust the leader of the Nyilas Party, Ferenc Szálasi, with forming a new government. Horthy was then taken, with the rest of his family, to *Schloss* Hirschberg in Bavaria, where they remained for the duration of the war.[61]

It is clear that Veesenmayer had been in negotiation with members of the Nyilas Party for some time about the possibility of forming a government, and once it came to German attention that Horthy was attempting to withdraw from the war, there was a reassertion of Nazi German influence in Hungary. The government constituted on 16 October 1944 was essentially that agreed upon by Szálasi and Veesenmayer in discussions during the previous month.[62] The next day, 17 October, Eichmann returned to Budapest, with demands for the delivery, on foot, of 50,000 able-bodied "Jews."[63] The remaining able-bodied "Jews" were to be used to build fortifications around Budapest, whilst those "Jews" unable to work were to be concentrated in camps close to Budapest. Eichmann also demanded a thorough combing of the provinces, to isolate "Jews" in hiding and formerly

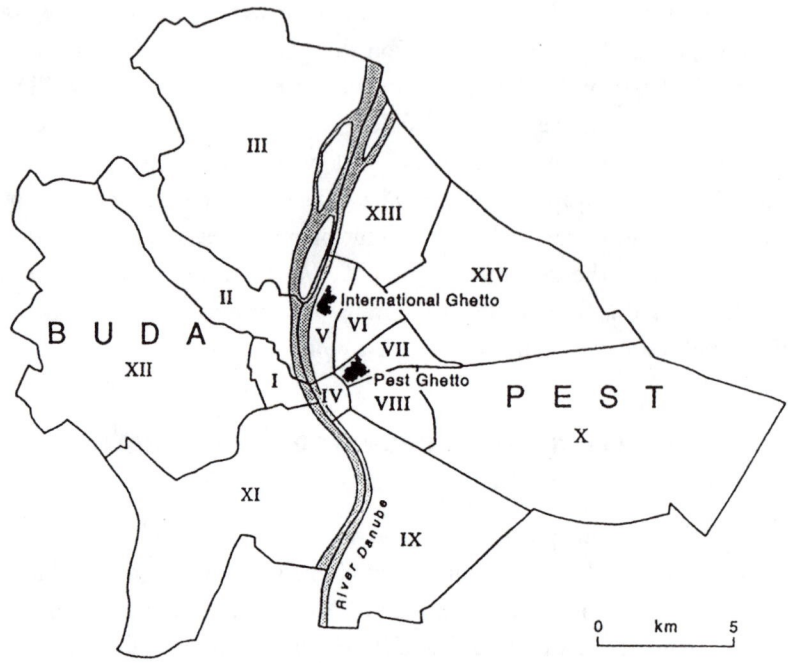

Figure 15. Implementing hyphenated ghettoization (November–December 1944). Reprinted from Tim Cole and Graham Smith, 1995, "Ghettoization and the Holocaust: Budapest 1944," *Journal of Historical Geography* 21(3), by permission of the publisher, Academic Press.

protected. No "Jews" were to be "protected" or "exempt" from these measures, as such categories were to be no longer relevant.

Eichmann met with the new interior minister, Gábor Vajna, on 18 October, when agreement was reached on most of these issues.[64] On the same day, Vajna issued a statement spelling out the official policy of the new government with regard to the "Jewish question."[65] Solving the "Jewish question" meant the implementation of measures against all "racial Jews," without distinction. In many ways this policy was an echoing of Eichmann's demands that there be no special categories. It was a marked break with the "special treatment" given to converts and foreign protected "Jews" by the Lakatos government, and resulted in immediate protests from representatives of the Vatican, neutral nations, and the International Red Cross, threatening the ending of any relations with Hungary.[66] A few days later the order was rescinded, and on 2 November, Szálasi reinstated the differentiation between "protected" and "unprotected" "Jews." The protective passes issued by the neutral legations were once again recognized, as was the extraterritoriality of the "protected" houses.

Whilst these negotiations were taking place between Eichmann and Vajna, the city's "Jews" were restricted to their yellow-star houses. In marked contrast to the increasing freedom of movement granted to the ghettoized "Jews" during the Lakatos period, yellow-star houses were sealed on October 16 for a period of ten days.[67] Four days later, Nyilas gangs and policemen entered yellow-star houses throughout the city and ordered all "Jewish" males aged between sixteen and sixty to be ready for departure within one hour. They were taken to the racetrack and KISOK sports field on Kerepesi út, from where they were formed into work groups and sent to build fortifications around the city in the path of the approaching Red Army. Ernö Szép, in his memoir, describes being woken at 5.30 A.M. and marched from his Pozsonyi út yellow-star house to Kerepesi út along with all the male inhabitants of his house, "some as old as 65, 70, 72 even."[68]

Two days later, an official request was made for all "Jewish" males aged between sixteen and sixty and all "Jewish" females aged between eighteen and forty to report for labor service. Braham estimates that some 25,000 men and 10,000 women had been recruited by 26 October.[69] Many were subjected to the often brutal treatment of their Nyilas guards.[70] Alongside this mass mobilization of "Jewish" labor within the country was mass mobilization of Hungarian "Jewish" labor for the Reich. On 23 October, Veesenmayer informed Berlin that Szálasi's government had agreed to provide 25,000 able-bodied "Jewish" males "for labor in the Reich for half a year."[71] This transfer got under way with the "death marches" toward Hegyeshalom from 8 November onward. By 13 November, Eichmann reported that 27,000 Hungarian "Jews" were en route, with another 40, 000 expected.[72] These so-called death marches were aptly named. As survivors have attested, and historians have recorded, the conditions faced by the marchers and the treatment meted out by the guards were severe.[73]

All of this renewed activity took place within the context of a Nyilas decision to divide the remaining "Jews" in the country (largely living in yellow-star houses in Budapest) into six distinct categories, each of which was to experience its own territorial solution. One category—"Jews" holding foreign protective passes—was to be relocated into what was to become the International ghetto. In contrast, those "Jews" to be lent to the German government "for the advancement of the common war effort" were to be removed from Hungary. Those "Jews" whose departure from Hungary was delayed were to be placed into ghettos. Separate measures were to be taken for "Jews" holding exemption certificates, "Jews" who were Christian clerics, and "Jews" who were foreign citizens.[74] The respective fates of all six categories of "Jews" were laid out in a "final plan" for the solution of the "Jewish question" published by Szálasi on November 17. For those "Jews" protected by neutral powers, there was recognition of a separate territorial solution, which was already being implemented. For those "unprotected Jews" who were to remain in the city, there was to be a distinct territorial solution.

Braham notes that when this "final plan" was forwarded to Berlin by Theodor Horst Grell, he stressed that the document was primarily intended for foreign consumption.[75] Thus, in Braham's opinion it was not so much a policy statement as a piece of propaganda. And yet the geographical reality of the winter of 1944 is that policies of hyphenated ghettoization were imposed upon the city's hyphenated Jewry. Arguably, by the winter of 1944, the homogenous category "Jew" no longer existed—if it ever had—and multiple categories of "Jews" were subjected to multiple territorial solutions. These distinct categories of "Jewishness" were inscribed in space.

In large part this book has focused upon the implementation of the destructive agenda of the Holocaust both in and through space. However, when the Holocaust city of Budapest in 1944–45 is examined, it was not simply a destructive agenda that was being exercised through territoriality. It was also policies of rescue, associated with the activities of the neutral legations in the winter of 1944. This is what I think is particularly striking about the Budapest example. Territoriality was something that worked two ways. On the one hand, control over the city's "Jews" was exercised spatially by local and national officials throughout 1944. On the other hand, control over the city's "protected Jews" was exercised spatially by members of neutral legations in the winter of 1944 through the creation of the so-called International ghetto. I am reminded of what the geographer Steve Pile wrote in a somewhat different context when he reminded his readers that "resistance, then, not only takes place in place, but also seeks to appropriate space, to make new spaces."[76] In the case of the rescue efforts implemented in Budapest in the winter of 1944, these same words can be rewritten. After all, Holocaust rescue . . . not only takes place in place, but also seeks to appropriate space, to make new spaces. The new space created in Budapest in the winter of 1944 was the space of the International ghetto.

THE MAKING OF THE INTERNATIONAL GHETTO

Plans to separate "protected" and "nonprotected" "Jews" were made known to the Jewish Council by Ferenczy on 7 November.[77] These plans were made public on 12 November, when Deputy Chief of Police Solymossy informed the caretakers and air-raid wardens of yellow-star houses that "Jews" under foreign protection were to be relocated to yellow-star houses in the V district near Pozsonyi út and Szent István Park. The onus was placed upon caretakers and air-raid wardens of the city's yellow-star houses to "remove from their buildings Jews in possession of provisional passports, safe-conduct passes, or protective certificates issued by the various neutral states so that they will occupy the apartments designated for them."[78] However, all queries relating to the relocations were to be addressed to the Jewish Council, which again found itself responsible for the implementation of the pragmatics of ghettoization. A deadline of 15 November was set for the completion of all relocations; in the end, it was extended to 17 November, on the request of the neutral legations.[79]

It is hard to say exactly how many protected "Jews" were to be relocated to what became known as the International ghetto in mid-November 1944. Lévai estimated that the total number was 15,600, although this would seem something of an underestimate.[80] A higher figure of 17,000 was given by the Swedish ambassador Carl Danielsson when he informed the Swedish Foreign Ministry by telegram on 12 November that "4,500 Swedish and 12,500 other Jews were moving into separate protected houses, awaiting emigration."[81] Wallenberg referred to this figure of 17,000, but suggested that in reality it was closer to 35,000.[82] Whatever the precise figure, "protected Jews" formed a sizable minority of the city's "Jews" in winter 1944.

Rather than being housed in a distinct, closed ghetto—as was the case with the remainder of the city's "Jews" as I will explore below—these thousands of "protected Jews" were assigned to specified houses within a roughly defined area of the V district. Spread over a limited number of streets in the Új Lipotváros part of the city, individual houses were assigned to specific neutral legations, or in a number of cases were to be shared by two legations. The historian Ágnes Ságvári estimates that a total of 122 houses were designated, with four of these being split between two legations:[83]

Swedish	31	(of which 2 double-designated)
Swiss	72	(of which 3 double-designated)
Portuguese	4	
Spanish	8	
Vatican	6	(of which 1 double-designated)
Governor & Interior Ministry	2	(of which 1 double-designated)
International Red Cross	2	
Swedish Red Cross	1	(of which 1 double-designated)
Total	126	(of which 8 double-designated)
		therefore total number of houses = 122

Her figures do, in part at least, find support elsewhere. For example, the figure of 31 houses designated for Swedish use, which Wohl gave,[84] is given also by Nina Langlet[85] and Leni Yahil,[86] with Freed counting 32 "Swedish-protected buildings," although he was perhaps double-counting Pozsonyi út 15–17.[87] And Ságvári's total of 72 Swiss-protected houses fits with Braham's comment that "the 7,800 Jews holding Swiss protective passes . . . were at first assigned only 60 buildings. Upon the intervention of the Swiss Legation, 12 additional buildings were added."[88]

The just over 120 International ghetto houses were centered on Pozsonyi út, which formed the core of this ghetto established at the scale of the individual apartment building. On this street, all of the yellow-star houses were designated for use by "protected Jews," with the majority designated for use by those under Swedish protection. Within the ghetto, whilst designation took place at the scale of the individual house, there were clear clusterings of houses within the ghetto area under the protection of individual countries. In the south of the ghetto, there was a cluster of Swedish-protected houses around Katona József u., Pozsonyi út, and Tátra u. In the north and west of the ghetto, there was a cluster of Swiss-protected houses around Szent István Park. Houses "protected" by other powers—which were far fewer in number—were scattered throughout the ghetto area. But here also some clustering was discernible, with three Spanish houses grouped in the northeast of the ghetto area, around Pannónia u. and Csanády u., and three Vatican houses in close proximity on Pozsonyi út.

Yet, the concept of extraterritoriality applied to individual buildings, rather than a distinct bounded ghetto area. Thus, on the gates of the "Swedish houses" a notice announced that "these premises and inhabitants possess extraterritoriality,"[89] giving them, theoretically at least, the same degree of extraterritoriality as an embassy building. And it seems that this principle of the extraterritoriality of individual buildings was applied beyond the rough boundaries of the V district international ghetto area in the winter of 1944. A degree of extraterritoriality appears to have been implemented by the neutral powers on an ad hoc basis. It seems that there were a number of "protected houses" outside of the International ghetto area, for example, two Swedish-protected houses in the VIII district at Esterházy u. 21 and the apartment block opposite, Esterházy u. 42.[90] Neither of these had been yellow-star houses under the June 16 or June 22 designations, nor do they appear on Wohl's list of 16 January 1945.[91] Wohl does list a number of "Swedish" houses—spread throughout the city— which were rented as office space and flats for embassy employees. "Protection" applied to individual flats in many cases, rather than the entire property.[92] It is clear that these properties were used to house "protected Jews."[93] Thus, the "protected Jew" was housed not only within the officially sanctioned International ghetto area but also within extraterritorial buildings throughout the city, protected by the neutral legations. Perhaps none was more important than the Swiss "Glass House" at Vadász u. 27, also in the V district.[94]

Whether outside or within the International ghetto area, it is clear that designation of a property for use by "protected Jews" was applied at the scale of the individual house, rather than to a continuous area. It was individual houses in the city's V district that were marked out as sovereign Swedish, Swiss, Portuguese, Spanish, Vatican, and Red Cross space. And in the case of the two Hungarian government houses for those granted exemptions by Horthy and the Interior Ministry, there was a sense of sovereign Hungarian space on Hungarian soil. The marking of specific buildings as extraterritorial spaces comes close to a hypothetical example posed by Allen Buchanan, in his book *Secession,* where he considers the morality of a contemporary claim to secession on the grounds of self-defense. It is an example worth citing at length:

> Suppose the year is 1939. Germany has inaugurated a policy of genocide against the Jews. Jewish pleas to the democracies for protection have fallen on deaf ears (in part because the Jews are not regarded as a nation—nationhood carrying a strong presumption of territory, which they do not possess). Leaders of Jewish populations in Poland, Czechoslovakia, Germany, and the Soviet Union agree

that the only hope for the survival of their people is to create a Jewish state, a sovereign territory to serve as a last refuge for European Jewry. Suppose further that the logical choice for its location—the only choice with the prospect of any success in saving large numbers of Jews—is a portion of Poland. Polish Jews, who are not being protected from the Nazis by Poland, therefore occupy a portion of Poland and invite other Jews to join them in a Jewish sanctuary state. They do not expel non-Jewish Poles who already reside in that area, but, instead treat them as equal citizens. . . . Unless one holds that existing property rights, including the right of Poland to keep all its territory intact, supersede all other considerations, including the right of an innocent people, utterly lacking in effective allies, to preserve its very existence from the depredations of mass murderers, one must conclude that the Jews would have been justified in appropriating the territory necessary for their survival.

The force of the self-defense argument derives in part from the assumption that the Polish Jews who create the sanctuary state are not being protected by their own state, Poland. The idea is that the state's authority over territory is granted to it so that it may provide protection for its citizens—all its citizens— and that its retaining authority is conditional upon its providing that protection. In the circumstances described, the Polish state is not providing protection to its Jewish citizens, and this fact voids its territorial authority.[95]

In many ways, if the year is changed from 1939 to 1944 and the place is changed from Poland to Hungary, one has something of the logic of the International ghetto. Whilst, unlike the hypothetical example forwarded by Buchanan, it is not possible to identify the International ghetto as a distinct foreign "sovereign territory" within the city, individual houses did operate in such terms. In essence, there was a reterritorialization of the existing ghetto houses in the ghetto (along with a number of other houses) as they were redesignated from the place of the "(unprotected) Jew" to the place of the "protected Jew."

But here lies a major difference with Buchanan's hypothetical example. In the case of the International ghetto, both the "non-protected Jew" and the "non-Jew" were to be excluded. They were not to be treated as "equal citizens." This exclusion of the "non-protected Jew" from the yellow-star houses within the newly designated International ghetto area had particularly serious consequences. It was concerns about these that had been at the forefront of earlier Jewish Council and more general popular "Jewish" opposition to plans to separate out converts and "protected Jews." Interestingly, the oral history memory of a "protected Jew" who moved into a Swedish house in the International ghetto "remembers" the houses being "empty" prior to occupation. She comments on the International ghetto area, "This was a new development, all very modern houses. It was only available because it was very Jewish and the Jews were all taken and they were empty houses. That's why Wallenberg was able to . . . to acquire those houses. Because about 95% they were Jewish and they were already deported . . . "[96]

And yet, in reality it was the other way round. Deportations of those "non-protected Jews" living within the International ghetto area took place as a result of the forced relocations made necessary by the implementation of a policy of hyphenated ghettoization. For "non-protected Jewish" males aged sixteen to sixty and females aged eighteen to forty, forced relocation was across the river to the brickyards in Óbuda. From this gathering point, these "non-protected Jews" joined the "death marches" westward to the border crossing of Hegyeshalom. Children and the elderly were relocated to yellow-star houses outside of the International ghetto area[97] and then were forced to relocate once more at the end of November into the place of the "non-protected" Pest ghetto.

It was not just the "non-protected Jew" who was relocated in the wake of the implementation of the International ghetto. "Non-Jews" living both within individual apartments in yellow-star houses were forced to relocate. As one survivor remembered it, "anyone who did not belong, these had to go whether he was a gentile person or a person with a Jewish—but did not have the passport . . . "[98] But in addition "non-Jews" living within previously non-designated properties were also forced to relocate. Although the 12 November order had specified that "protected Jews" were to relocate "to *the Yellow-Star buildings* allocated to them in the V district near Pozsonyi út and Szent István Park,"[99] it would seem that 24 of the houses that were ultimately occupied by "protected Jews" had never been a part of the existing ghetto. Whilst the majority of the just over 120 houses had been yellow-star houses since mid-June 1944, it is clear that not all yellow-star houses within the broad area designated for use by "protected Jews" were designated (44 seem not to have been) and not all the houses designated were already yellow-star houses. The designation of properties for inclusion in the International ghetto area did build upon the existing pattern of dispersed ghettoization in the V district, and yet it was not wholly constrained by that pattern.

In some cases, the omission of yellow-star houses appears to be for geostrategic reasons. Thus, it could be argued that the yellow-star houses at the Szent István körút end of Hollán u. (numbers 3 and 4) and Pannónia u. (numbers 4 and 6) were omitted in order to set the ghetto area back from the outer ring. Yet, not all omitted former yellow-star houses were at the ends of streets. The former yellow-star houses Pozsonyi út 1, 3, and 4—also proximate to the outer ring—were designated. In some ways, Pozsonyi út does seem to be exceptional. As is suggested by official descriptions of the International ghetto area—such as Solymossy's order referred to above— Pozsonyi út formed the heart of the ghetto area, accounting for 27 of the 128 houses appearing on all International ghetto lists. It was the only street within the International ghetto area on which *all* yellow-star houses were designated for occupation by "protected Jews."

The implications of the designation of both previously yellow-star and non-yellow-star houses as International ghetto houses was that *both* the "non-protected Jew" and "non-Jew" were forced to relocate to make way for the "protected Jew"—a group that was widely seen to be a privileged elite.[100] As I have suggested, these forced relocations had serious implications for "non-protected Jews" excluded from this particular territorial solution. But ghettoization also impacted the city's "non-Jews" in a way that the earlier measures ultimately had not, given that ghettoization had in reality been implemented at the scale of the individual apartment building. Those concessions to "non-Jewish" opinion were now cast aside, most significantly in the case of the establishing of the Pest ghetto. For the first time in Budapest, ghettoization was now implemented not at the scale of the individual apartment or apartment building, but at the scale of a number of sealed-off streets in the heart of the city.

THE MAKING OF THE PEST GHETTO

Following a number of meetings between Deputy Police Chief Solymossy and the Jewish Council in the latter half of November,[101] the precise shape of ghettoization was literally mapped out on 29 November 1944.[102] Alongside the text of the decree detailing the implementation of ghettoization, a map was issued showing the boundaries and gates of the ghetto and the subdivision of the ghetto into districts (see figure 16). According to Lévai, there were "multiple revisions" of this ghetto map, prior to its eventual publication on 29 November.[103] Indeed, even on the published map a last-minute revision appears to have been made with the altering of the ghetto boundary to exclude Csányi u. 4.

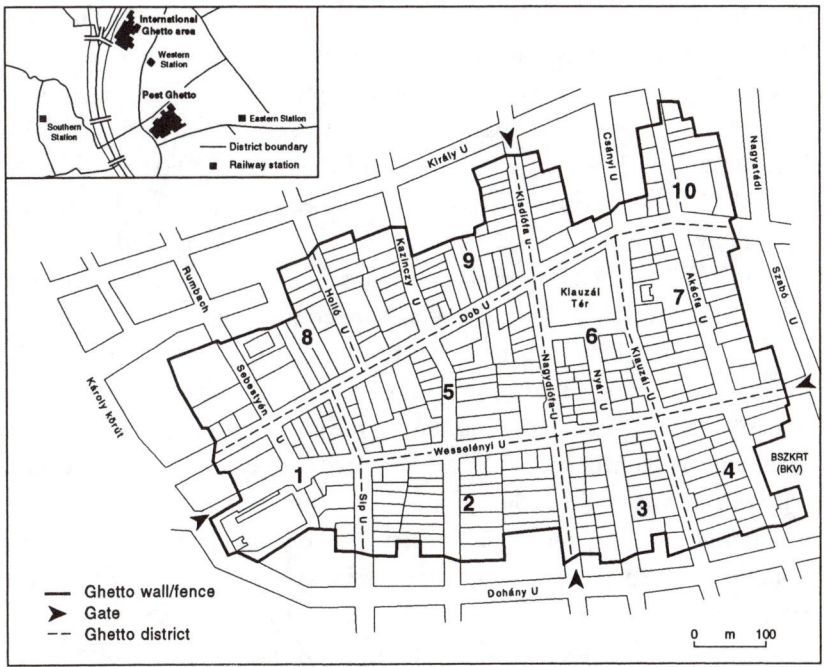

Figure 16. The Pest ghetto. © Tim Cole.

The area chosen for the ghetto was within the traditional "Jewish" VII district of Pest, and although more restricted in area, it fitted squarely with one of the seven ghettos drawn up by city officials on 9 May 1944 and the area "between Dob u. and Podmaniczy u.," which had been rumored as a ghetto area as early as April 1944. The choice of the precise boundaries of the ghetto was no doubt influenced by considerations about what lay both within and outside of the area finally designated. The ghetto was set back from the inner ring—Károly Király út—and the outer ring—Erzsébet körút—meaning that city traffic using these major thoroughfares, as well as the major road Rákóczi út, were not affected by the siting of the ghetto. In addition, the houses facing the streets bordering the ghetto were specifically restricted from being used by "Jews." They were to form a sort of no-man's-land between the world of the ghetto and the world of the city outside, where the trams kept running. Set back from the major surrounding streets, and making use only of houses facing away from the bordering streets, the ghetto was effectively an island looking in on itself.

The side streets within this "island" were, given the area's history of "Jewish" demography, already home to a large number of yellow-star houses. Indeed Solymossy noted, when meeting with Jewish Council members on 23 November, that of the 295 apartment blocks in the planned ghetto area, 162 were yellow-star houses.[104] On the basis of the definitive list of yellow-star houses of 22 June, it would seem that the number was 139 rather than the 162 claimed by Solymossy. Still, almost one-half of the buildings within the area designated as the ghetto were already "ghetto" houses. In part, then, the precise location chosen seems to have been determined by pragmatic concerns with taking the ghetto to a place where the ghetto, to some extent at least, already was. As was the case in June 1944, the attraction of taking the ghetto to the "Jew" was that it meant not taking the ghetto to the "non-Jew."

There remained awareness on the part of the authorities that ghettoization impacted the "non-Jewish" population, and Solymossy was very much aware of the numbers of "non-Jews" who would be forced to relocate from the ghetto area. Solymossy was conscious not only of the "non-Jewish" residents of the 133 non-yellow-star houses in the ghetto area, but also of the "non-Jewish" residents still living in 144 of the 162 yellow-star houses in the proposed ghetto area.[105] Whilst their presence had been tolerated under the 22 June ghettoization regulations that had separated living space at the scale of the individual apartment, the presence of "non-Jews" within the "Jewish" space of the ghetto was no longer to be tolerated. The Pest ghetto created at the end of November 1944 was to be, on the one hand, the place where "all Jews compelled to wear the yellow star" were ordered to relocate and, on the other hand, the place where "non-Jews" could *not* live or work and where public institutions and authorities could not have offices. The Pest ghetto was to be solely the place of the "Jew," and thus "Christian-*frei*" in a way that the yellow-star houses of earlier ghettoization measures had simply never been. The ghetto area was to be a place of explicit "non-Jewish absence" (see figure 17).

"Non-Jewish" institutions and businesses were specifically forbidden from maintaining offices within the newly designated ghetto area in central Pest, which was made up of a mixture of residential and nonresidential properties. Under the June regulations, the practice had generally been to designate only residential dwellings, but with the shift from designation at the scale of the individual building to designation at the scale of a number of streets (and in particularly streets right in the very center of the city), designation impacted business premises as well as apartment buildings. Amongst

Figure 17. Sign at the entrance to the Pest ghetto announcing, "Jewish Quarter. Entrance Forbidden to Christians," Budapest, 1944. Lilly Brust-Gach, courtesy of USHMM Photo Archives.

those institutions falling within the area designated for the ghetto were the city's Material Distribution Institute (Nagydiófa u. 14), central pharmacy and pharmacy warehouse for the city's hospitals (also at Nagydiófa u. 14), the offices of the technical department of the civil defense (Dob u. 51), the offices of the organization arranging temporary accommodation (also at Dob u. 51), one of the VII district tax offices (Klauzál u. 10), two of the city's schools (Wesselényi u. 38 and Nyár u. 9), and one of the city's market halls (Klauzál tér 11).[106] For those institutions and businesses forced to relocate, premises of similar size and value were to be allocated. These were, "as far as possible," to be vacated "Jewish" shops, workshops, and offices. The principle was that these properties would become the property of the relocated "non-Jew," with their vacated properties in the ghetto area becoming the property of the state. The loser in the exchange was the "Jew."

Whilst "non-Jewish" businesses and institutions were forced to relocate from the "Jewish" space of the ghetto, it is clear that in one case at least, the very shape of the ghetto was altered to ensure that a particularly high-profile "non-Jewish" institution could stay put. To look at the map of the ghetto, it is striking how the ghetto wall, which quite literally divided streets into "Jewish" absence and "Jewish presence," follows a somewhat circuitous route on the odd-numbered side of Akácfa u. The result of these twists and turns of the ghetto wall was that the Budapest central transport authority (BKV) building at Akácfa u. 15–23 remained outside of the ghetto, and thus was not effectively made "Christian-*frei*." With this shaping of the ghetto boundary, the Budapest transport authority headquarters continued to operate within the no-man's-land surrounding the ghetto during the winter of 1944.

The concessions made to the Budapest transport authority were not, of course, made to individual "non-Jewish" tenants and owners of apartments located within the ghetto. They were all to be relocated, and the practicalities of how this was to be achieved dominated the text of the 29 November ghettoization decree and subsequent regulations. Every effort was made to ensure as smooth a relocation for "non-Jewish" inhabitants of the ghetto area as possible. They were to receive vacated "Jewish" apartments in Pest, "equivalent" to those they had been forced to leave. Specific regulations were published on 24 November listing vacated, furnished "Jewish" apartments that "could be claimed or rather occupied" by "non-Jews" moving out of the newly designated area of the Pest ghetto.[107] These were, in the main, former yellow-star houses from the central districts of Pest, excepting the streets in the V and VII district designated for the international and Pest ghettos. However, the list did contain eleven houses that were not yellow-star houses,[108] as well as two house that had been canceled on October 27.[109]

The owners or caretakers of these former yellow-star houses were to make things easier for those searching for apartments by posting up the precise details of the newly available apartments, including the cost of the rent. As these apartments were already furnished, "non-Jews" forced to relocate were to make use of the furniture already there and store their materially or sentimentally valuable furniture in designated ground-floor apartments, former shops, and storerooms in twenty-one former yellow-star houses located on Dohány u., Király u., and Nagyatádi Szabó István u.[110] These streets effectively surrounded the ghetto on three sides (part of the no-man's-land around the ghetto), thus keeping furniture removal to a minimum in the wartime context of a shortage of the necessary transport. Those "non-Jews" forced to move were to provide their own transport but were entitled to claim financial help toward the costs of moving from the Mayoral IX section.[111] The girls' school at Dohány u. 32 became an inquiry office that could be used by those "non-Jews" to be relocated, from 2 to 5 December.

To make matters easier for "non-Jews" moving out of the Pest ghetto area, the city's "Jews" were required to vacate their apartments and relocate to the ghetto area prior to "non-Jewish" relocations taking place. Therefore, by the time that "non-Jewish" inhabitants were forced to vacate their properties between 2 and 7 December 1944, as specified in the November 29 regulations, vacant properties would be available for immediate occupation. Indeed according to Lévai, during negotiations in the run-up to the establishing of the ghetto, Solymossy had demanded the immediate vacating of "6000 Jewish dwellings for the Christians moving out of the ghetto."[112] In this context, it is worth noting that the list of ex-yellow-star houses for "non-Jewish" use predates the issuing of the ghettoization decree by five days. Presumably the "6000 Jewish dwellings" referred to by Lévai were those listed on the 24 November list. The "Jews" from these Pest apartments were to be taken to Klauzál tér for relocation in the ghetto area. The "non-Jew" was to be provided with apartments at the cost of "Jewish" homelessness.

Yet whilst the cooperation of "non-Jews" forced to relocate was being sought through the provision of alternative properties and limited compensation, their cooperation was also being guaranteed through a mixture of propaganda and threat. The ghettoization decree concluded with an appeal from the interior minister for "non-Jews" affected by the decree to play their part in the war effort: "I expect the Christian inhabitants to obey my decree with understanding and in a self-sacrificing spirit, thereby helping to solve finally the hitherto neglected Jewish question."[113] And this appeal was backed up with the threat of state-sanctioned punishment. For the "non-Jewish" inhabitant who failed to comply with state demands for relocation, the punishment was to be the transportation of the head of the family to a labor camp and the internment of all family members. Thus the forced relocation of "non-Jewish" inhabitants from the ghetto area was about both carrot and stick. This differed radically from the treatment of "non-Jewish" requests to remain in yellow-star houses in June 1944. At root this difference was that of different regimes. By November 1944, state-sanctioned violence was to be used against "Jew" and "non-Jew" in the pursuit of state aims, with little in the way of effective means of appeal. The opportunity for contestation of the shape of ghettoization had effectively been removed.

If the "non-Jew" found a suitable vacated "Jewish" apartment other than one of those listed, they could rent it with official authorization. However, in the text of the 29 November ghettoization decree it was explicitly stated that the "non-Jew" was only to move to flats *within Pest*. The only exception to this rule that the "non-Jew" living in the ghetto area was to relocate only to another address in Pest was if they already owned an apartment in a former yellow-star house in Buda. Otherwise, Buda was to be completely out of bounds. And here another important consideration underlying the locating of the ghetto in the VII district of Pest can be seen. Whilst the ghetto was about "Jewish presence," it was also about "Jewish absence" and in particular "Jewish absence" in Buda. With the creation of the Pest ghetto, Buda was made entirely *judenfrei*. And what is striking is that even prior to the creation of the ghetto at the end of November 1944, there were already claims being made for these newly *judenfrei* spaces in the former yellow-star houses of Buda.

Just over two weeks before the ghettoization decree was published, it would seem that district officials had already been given instructions to commence preparations for the redistribution of the soon-to-be-vacated yellow-star houses.[114] At this stage, some time before the shape of the ghetto had finally being decided upon, it is clear that there was already a rush by the new ruling elite to get their hands on soon-to-be-vacated "Jewish" houses in Buda. Thus in the III district, 74 of the 119 soon-to-be-vacated yellow-star houses had already "been reserved for the army, the German army and the Nyilas Party" by the end of November. And it was clear that these houses were intended to be used. One of the responsibilities of the III district councilor was to ensure that there was sufficient fuel to heat these apartments during the winter months.[115]

The attraction of Buda to members of the Hungarian army, the German army, and the Nyilas Party was obvious given the rapid advance of the Red Army from the east. Already in September and October a number of yellow-star houses had been assigned for use by the German military, many of whom had been in Buda. Now, however, there was a wholesale appropriating of the former yellow-star houses in Buda for use by the ruling elite, relocating to the western bank of the river Danube. In the winter of 1944, real estate in Buda was a geostrategically valuable commodity. And thus there was a concern during implementation of territorial solutions to clear property in this area of the city for use by Nyilas officials and members of the German military. In short, a concern with creating explicit "Jewish absence" in Buda was one element of the decision to create explicit "Jewish presences"—in the places of both the Pest and the International ghettos—in Pest.

But there was also a symbolic act in making a section of the VII district the place of the "(non-protected) Jew" in the winter of 1944. Certainly for the rightist press, this final act of ghettoization was heralded as the ultimate separation of the "Pest Jewry."[116] This was seen to be a final act overturning a history of assimilation, with the return of the Pest Jewry to their place in the city—the traditional "Jewish" quarter or ghetto. The VII district was therefore more than simply a pragmatic site. It was also a symbolic site. Here was the culmination of the process of "Pest-ization" initiated with the ghettoization policies of the early summer. With the official sanctioning of the Pest ghettos as the places of the "Jew" within the city, the "Pest Jewry" was finally constructed.

What was striking about this final act in a longer process of "Pest-ization" was that it amounted to bringing the city's "Jews" right into the very heart of the city, rather than removing them to the city's outskirts. That was, in some ways, rather surprising. As Sibley suggests, the tendency is for landscapes of exclusion to push minorities to the very edge, or even off the very edge, of the earth. He points to

> a history of imaginary geographies which cast minorities, "imperfect" people, and a list of others who are seen to pose a threat to the dominant group in society as polluting bodies or folk devils who are then located "elsewhere": This "elsewhere" might be nowhere, as when genocide or the moral transformation of a minority like prostitutes are advocated, or it might be some spatial periphery, like the edge of the world or the edge of the city.[117]

Certainly within the geography of apartheid, the racialized Other was restricted to the spatial periphery in South Africa. And yet, in the Holocaust city, the ghetto(s) were ultimately created at the very center of Budapest, rather than on its edge. This process of bringing the "Jew" into the center of the city, rather than pushing them to the periphery, can be seen in the increasing Pest-ization of both "Jewish" residential and public space in the summer of 1944. In the winter of 1944 the process was complete and the city's "Jews" were located in two ghettos in the heart of Pest. As I have suggested throughout, a number of factors determined these acts of Pest-ization from summer 1944 onward, and these reflected a concern with "Jewish absence" as well as "Jewish presence." Ultimately, of course, these territorial solutions that brought the "Jew" into the very center of the city were not "final solutions." In the case of the "Jewish" populations living in provincial Hungarian villages, towns, and cities, their experience was one of being brought to the center, before being expelled to the periphery, and ultimately to the genocidal "elsewhere" of Auschwitz-Birkenau.

But Budapest's "Jews" were spared this fate, and the Pest ghetto was liberated rather than liquidated. However, the few months of its existence during the winter of 1944–45 were harsh. The majority of Budapest's "unprotected Jews" were relocated to the place of the ghetto by the time the relocation of "non-Jewish" inhabitants commenced on December 2. "Jews" were given two hours to prepare to leave their apartments in the yellow-star houses that had been home for the last six months.[118] Once they had been informed of their relocation to the ghetto area, they were to gather in the courtyard within two hours, complete with bedding, clothing, food, and jewelry. The remainder of their property was to be stored in a designated ground floor flat in the apartment house. The gathered "Jews" were taken from their houses to Klauzál tér where they were assigned flats within the ghetto houses. Lévai reported that "during the removal into the ghetto, wholesale killings of Jews by Nyilas men took place."[119] This relocation of the city's "Jewish" population took place at the rate of ten to fifteen thousand "Jews" daily, until all of the city's yellow-star houses—outside of the places of the International and Pest ghettos—were emptied.[120] Once in the ghetto, "Jewish" freedom of movement was restricted to 9–11 A.M. from 2 to 7 December to enable "non-Jewish" inhabitants to move out of the ghetto area.[121] On 10 December, the ghetto was sealed.

Within the ghetto fence, a population of 44,416 "unprotected Jews," in December 1944, lived in just over 240 buildings.[122] Of the 291 buildings in the ghetto area approximately 50 were not to be used for residential purposes. These were both houses designated for "public use" within the ghetto and those that had been sealed. The 29 November ghettoization decree made provision for the sealing of apartments within the ghetto area rented by soldiers on active service who had no relatives living there and thus no one to claim a vacated yellow-star house. No doubt, the apartments described as "sealed" in the Jewish Council report belong to this category. From the Jewish Council report it would seem that the ghetto contained between 241 and 243 houses, containing a total of 4,513 apartments, with 7,726 rooms.[123] With a ghetto population at the time the survey was taken of 44,416, this meant an average population density of 5.75 persons per room.[124] There is no question that the ghetto amounted to officially sanctioned overcrowding. As has been noted before, a population density of more than four persons to a room had been recognized by city officials to amount to overcrowding. However, as was the case with the overcrowding associated with the implementation of dispersed ghettoization in June

1944, the experience of overcrowding varied quite markedly between districts within the ghetto.

Although they were spread over a number of streets—Akácfa u., Csányi u., Dob u., Holló u., Kazinczy u., Kisdiófa u., Klauzál u., Klauzál tér, Nagydiófa u., Nyár u., Rumbach Sebestyén u., Síp u., and Wesselényi u.— there was an attempt to segregate converted "Jews" within the ghetto area. In line with the statement in Szálasi's "final plan" for the solution of the "Jewish question" that "Christian Jews" were to be housed in separate buildings in the ghetto marked by crosses, Solymossy announced to Jewish Council members Lajos Stöckler, István Földes, and József Nagy in their 3 December meeting that "Christian Jews" were to be housed in a separate part of the ghetto.[125] They were to live in the area bordered by Csányi u., Dob u., and Nagyatádi Szabó u, which formed the majority of the tenth ghetto district.[126] Kemény's deputy in the Foreign Ministry, Zoltán Bagossy, had authorized 3,000 persons under Vatican protection, who were to be housed in this "in principle isolated" area of the ghetto.[127]

With the sealing of the ghetto on 7 December, the ghetto wall marked the physical separation of "Jewish presences" and "Jewish absences" in the city. The wall was breached by four gates, two situated at each end of Wesselényi u., one on Nagydiófa u., and one on Kisdiófa u. All four gateways were guarded by a mixture of Nyilas personnel and members of the city police. In response to Jewish Council petitioning following frequent unauthorized raids on the ghetto, the number of entrances was restricted, on 10 January 1945—to the two gates at each end of Wesselényi u. Only those holding permits issued by Kurt Rettmann, the chief Budapest district leader of the Nyilas Party, Lieutenant-Colonel Imre Nidossi, the party leader in the VII district, or Ministerial Councilor in Charge of Jewish Affairs István Lőcsey were now allowed to enter the sealed space of the ghetto.[128] The right to breach the wall operated both ways. A system of passes was created giving rights of entry and exit. The "non-Jew" holding a blue pass was permitted to enter the "Jewish" space of the ghetto. The "Jew" holding a green pass was permitted to enter the "non-Jewish" space of the city outside the ghetto wall.[129] These officially sanctioned entrances and exits were made through the ghetto gateways that served as the point of entry and exit of personnel, corpses,[130] commodities, and information. These walls and gateways were liminal spaces subject to policing and surveillance.

On 9 December 1944, the Red Army broke through the Friesner Line and by 27 December had effectively laid siege to Budapest.[131] Despite rumors of Nyilas and German plans to destroy the Pest ghetto prior to flee-ing westward,[132] the Pest ghetto was liberated intact on 17–18 January 1945, and what remained of the International ghetto shortly afterward. Seven months of ghettoization of the "Budapest Jewry" had come to an end.

In many ways, therefore, Budapest was not typical of all Holocaust cities. The territorial solution of ghettoization to which Budapest's "Jews" were subjected ended with liberation rather than deportation. However, even given that atypicality, there is, I think, a place to ask the kinds of ques-tions that I have been asking about the physicality of the implementation of the Holocaust in this particular Holocaust city, of other Holocaust cities. Holocaust ghettoization was a profoundly spatial measure. It quite literally meant the reshaping of the city along segregated lines. By dint of their very nature, the implementation of territorial solutions impacted not only the city's "Jews" but also the "non-Jewish" population of this Holocaust city.

UNCOVERING THE
TRACES OF GHETTOIZATION,
1945 TO THE PRESENT

By dint of the physicality of the implementation of the Holocaust, this event has left traces upon the European landscape. That traces would remain was, however, something those implementing the "Final Solution of the Jewish Question" sought to negate. The razing to the ground of the death camps at Chelmno, Belzec, Treblinka, and Sobibor, and the dynamiting of the gas chambers at Auschwitz-Birkenau, all point to Nazi attempts to eradicate the traces of the architecture of the Holocaust. Yet whilst these factories of death were intended to have a short-lived existence and then be wiped from the face of the earth, the monumental architecture of Nazism was self-consciously built for longevity.

Not only was the monumental architecture built with materials intended to last for centuries, but there was also a concern with how these buildings would look as ruins in thousands of years' time. Speer's development of a theory of ruin value self-consciously aimed at an architecture that would ultimately result in ruins to rival those of imperial Rome. The result was that modern building materials such as steel and concrete were rejected in favor of granite, which was seen to guarantee monumental ruins.[1] But the irony is that perhaps the most symbolic ruins of Nazism are the twisted steel and fractured concrete slabs of the dynamited gas chambers of Auschwitz-Birkenau. These ruins have emerged as the ultimate trace of Nazi architectural practice. However, there was nothing inevitable about the twisted ruins of Auschwitz-Birkenau emerging as iconic traces of the Nazi past. As

James Young has noted, the concentration camps and death camps were, at the end of the war, places which were

> blood-soaked but otherwise mute. While in operation, the death camps and the destruction of people wrought in them were one and the same: sites and events were bound to each other in their contemporaneity. But with the passage of time, sites and events were gradually estranged. While the sites of killing remained ever-present, all too real in their physical setting, time subtly interposed itself between them and their past. Events that occurred in another time seemed increasingly to belong to another world altogether. Only a deliberate act of memory could reconnect them, reinfuse the sites with a sense of their historical past.[2]

As Young suggests, there was a need for decisions to remember, if the sites of Holocaust history were to be turned into sites of Holocaust memory.

Of course, the corollary was also true. It is not simply the case that decisions to remember are critical for ensuring that sites of history become sites of memory. The decision, either self-consciously or unconsciously, to forget is crucial in ensuring that sites of history are silenced and remain very much places of the past rather than places that intrude upon the present. As Kenneth Foote has suggested, writing in a different context, "obliteration" is an alternative strategy to "sanctification" in dealing with sites of traumatic history.[3]

Something of that parallel history of "obliteration" and "sanctification" can be seen, I think, in the case of the turning of Auschwitz-Birkenau into a site of memory. I have written much more about this subject elsewhere, so my comments here will be brief.[4] What is striking in the case of Auschwitz is the way in which this death camp was deliberately chosen above other Polish death camps as the site of memory. Now, as I've mentioned already, there were ruins at Auschwitz. This was not the case at those death camps—Chelmno, Belzec, Treblinka, and Sobibor—which were razed to the ground by the Nazis in a clear attempt to obliterate their memory. However, it was not only the camp at Auschwitz which partially survived the war relatively unscathed. This was also the case at Majdanek, which like Auschwitz combined both wartime death and labor camps. Thus Majdanek would seem to have as much claim on being turned into a place of memory as Auschwitz. That it was not was due to more than simply the fact that there were fewer victims at Majdanek and that they tended to be Polish "Jews" rather than "Jews" from a number of countries—including

Hungary—as was the case with Auschwitz. Rather, there were geopolitical considerations underlying the decision of the Polish government to make Auschwitz into "a Monument of the Martyrdom of the Polish Nation and of Other Nations."[5]

As the historical geographer Andrew Charlesworth argues, the attraction of Auschwitz over Majdanek in 1947 was that Auschwitz looked westward and therefore pointed to German aggression. In looking eastward, Majdanek did point to Soviet liberation, but it also pointed to a darker side of Polish-Soviet relations, as immediately after liberation, the camp had been turned into a concentration camp for prisoners of the Soviet secret police.[6] Such a history was not shared by Auschwitz, making it a less problematic choice as a site for remembering Polish martyrdom at the hands of the Germans only. This suggests, I think, that the history of these two sites had a bearing upon the decisions to remember one place and forget the other.

However, whilst there is clearly a link between Auschwitz as site of history and Auschwitz as site of memory, that link is far from straightforward. There have been clear acts of manipulation and reinterpretation in transforming this site of wartime history into a site of postwar memory. Although particularly marked in the case of Auschwitz, and in particular during the Communist era, there is nothing unique about this story of reinterpretation. The act of turning places of history into places of memory is not simply about uncovering traces, but is also supremely an act of creation. To take an example from an entirely different time and place, the geographer Jane Jacobs reflects upon a recent product of the heritage industry in Melbourne, Australia: the "Another View Walking Trail." She suggests that "like other recent urban place-making projects with an Aboriginal theme, this trail intended to (re)Aboriginalise the city space. It did not necessarily uncover pre-existing sites of significance to Aborigines, but charted a new geography of Aboriginality in the city."[7]

That sense of the charting of a new geography in the process of creating sites of memory on top of sites of history is not restricted to Holocaust sites alone. Far from it, However, the case of Auschwitz is a particularly dramatic example. Here, the postwar creation of a singular site of memory involved a telescoping of the complex geography of the historical places of Auschwitz. In the town renamed Auschwitz, a number of different camps were created during the course of the Second World War. Foremost amongst these from the perspective of the Hungarian Holocaust was the death camp at Auschwitz-Birkenau, which was where Hungarian "Jews" arrived in summer 1944. It was here that selections were made, with large numbers of those coming in on the trains from Hungary being sent straight to their deaths in the gas chambers. Those deemed young and healthy enough to work were sent, in the case of Elie Wiesel, to the labor camp at the IG Farben Buna works.

However, from a Polish perspective, of more importance than either Auschwitz-Birkenau or Auschwitz-Buna was the original Auschwitz concentration camp. It is this site which saw the imprisoning and execution of thousands of Poles and Soviet POWs during the war. And it is this site of history which became the prime site of memory when a memorial museum was established in Auschwitz to remember Polish martyrdom above anything else. In the siting of the museum there, the "Jewish" memory of Auschwitz-Birkenau was downplayed, within a broader context of Warsaw bloc rejection of the "Jewish" specificity of the Holocaust. And the various elements of the entire Auschwitz complex were brought into this one place. The climax of the museum tour became a reconstructed gas chamber and crematoria which had been used as an experimental gas chamber. Later it was converted into an air-raid shelter before being destroyed by the Red Army after liberation. In 1948, it was rebuilt as part of the broader transformation of the original Auschwitz concentration camp into a site of memory. As van Pelt and Dwork reflect, it "was reconstructed to speak for the history of the incinerators at Birkenau."[8] Thus a site whose history included the experimental gassing of Soviet POWs became a site of memory expanded to include the mass gassings undertaken a mile or so down the road at Birkenau. But the "Jewishness" of these victims was unstated in this site of Polish rather than "Jewish" memory.

As this very brief survey of the early history of the transformation of Auschwitz from a site of history into a site of memory suggests, this process was about much more than simply the recovering of the traces of the past. Not only was that recovery selective, but it also involved (re)creation. And I think those ideas are useful ones to explore when reflecting upon what happened in postwar Budapest to the sites of Holocaust history. In this final chapter, I want to examine the postliberation history and geography of the physical sites of this Holocaust city. Because there was a physicality to the implementation of the Holocaust in Budapest, this event left its traces in the postwar landscape of the city. What I am interested in examining here is what has happened to those traces over the last five decades or so.

I am particularly interested in the extent to which organized memory work has been enacted in the places in the city—such as the Pest and International ghettos—which can clearly be seen as places of Holocaust history. The question I want to ask is: To what extent have these sites of Holocaust history been turned into sites of Holocaust memory? My focus is going to be largely upon more formalized acts of memory, connected in particular with the erection of physical memorials and monuments. Of course, there is so much more to acts of memory than simply memorials,[9] but memorials provide one way into thinking about how attempts have been made to (selectively) transform historical sites such as the wartime Pest ghetto into sites of Holocaust memory.

As a number of writers have noted, the siting of memorials is of critical importance in impacting the meanings given to that memorial. Strikingly, Pierre Nora had suggested quite the opposite, arguing that "statues or monuments to the dead, for instance, owe their meaning to their intrinsic existence; even though their location is far from abitrary, one could justify relocating them without altering their meaning."[10] However, such an interpretation has been criticized, quite rightly I think, by the geographer Nuala Johnson, who argued that "the space which . . . monuments occupy is not just an incidental material backdrop but in fact inscribes the statues with meaning."[11] As not only Johnson herself noted, a clear example of the importance of place in determining the meanings given to memorials and monuments can be seen in contemporary Budapest. Since the fall of communism, a number of the most prominent communist statues that were removed from the public places of Budapest have been relocated to a rather kitsch "Staute Park" for tourists on the outskirts of the city.[12] When I was last there, amongst the drinks that you could buy at the snack bar were "Molotov cocktails"! Within such a setting, it is clear that those monuments that were originally located in prominent places in the city have been given radically different meanings.

This is a rather extreme example, but it is clear that location makes a difference to the meanings attributed to a memorial. To some extent at least, the decision where to locate a memorial can be in part pragmatic. The question of ownership of the space is crucial. There may also be concerns with visibility (as well as the opposite concern with hiddenness). But what I think remains rather understudied is the ways in which the locating of memorials does or does not take into account what happened there in the past. In short, it is to examine the awareness of space as almost sacred space, given its particular history. And it is to explore how—and why—the past is selectively drawn upon in the shaping of places of memory in the present.

THE PEST GHETTO AS SITE OF HISTORY
AND SITE OF MEMORY

In the immediate postwar period, a fraction of the site of the Pest ghetto was transformed into a site of memory. A plaque erected close to the place where one of the gates to the former ghetto had stood revealed the articulation of a memory that was striking in its partiality (see figure 18). It was clear that what was being remembered was not the construction and existence of the ghetto and its victims, but the liberation of the ghetto and the liberators. This can be seen in the siting of the memorial plaque, not in the very heart of the ghetto, but right at the very edge. But it is most clearly seen in the text of the plaque itself, which announced: "In the Fascist period one of the gates to the Budapest ghetto stood here. The liberating Soviet Army broke down the ghetto walls on 18 January 1945."[13]

The concern with the ghetto, which both the siting and the text of the plaque revealed, was with the outer boundaries of the ghetto. The significance of the ghetto gate and ghetto walls was not so much that they acted as a boundary keeping the city's "Jews" within this death space, but that they were the boundary that was breached by the liberators. It was the breaching of the ghetto walls that was remembered (18 January 1945), rather than the sealing of the ghetto (10 December 1944). And it was the breachers of those walls (the "liberating Soviet Army") who were being remembered, rather than the sealers of those walls (the Hungarian Nyilas government).

A similar concern with the boundaries of the ghetto and the breaching of those boundaries by the Soviet liberators can be seen in the next major act of memorialization in the space of the Pest ghetto. The date of the unveiling of this memorial, 18 January 1985, was highly significant. It was the fortieth anniversary of the liberation of the ghetto. This concern with liberation can be seen, as with the earlier plaque, in the choosing of a periperal location on the very edge of the former ghetto. However, this time the memorial plaque was not placed on any wall, but on a reconstructed fragment of ghetto wall in the courtyard of the Dohány u. synagogue. Again, the text made clear that it was the breaching of the ghetto walls on 18 January 1945 and the breachers of those walls (the "Soviet Army, liberators of our homeland") that were being remembered. It read: "As an eter-

Figure 18. Wall plaque at the site of one of the gates of the former Pest ghetto. © Tim Cole.

nal reminder of the day forty years ago when the walls surrounding the only ghetto remaining in Europe were broken down by the Soviet Army, liberators of our homeland. 18 January 1945–18 January 1985."[14]

This concern with the broken-down walls of the ghetto, and those who did that breaking down, is marked. In both plaques, it was the Soviet Army that was stressed in the text. It was they who were being remembered. On the one hand they were remembered as liberators of this particular ghetto. On the other hand, they were remembered as liberators of the entire nation from Fascism. Any notions of "Jewish" specificity were squeezed out by this monolithic juxtaposition of the Fascists, the creators of ghettos, and the Soviets, the liberators of ghettos. That absence of "Jews" from these memorials within the space of the Budapest ghetto reflected the wider trend within the Soviet bloc of erasing the "Jewish" specificity of the Holocaust.[15] This broader political agenda impacted memorialization in Budapest, given that such acts were sponsored by the central state.[16]

In the shifting political climate of the late 1980s, however, official agreement was given to erect a specifically "Jewish" memorial within the space of the former Pest ghetto.[17] This Memorial of the Hungarian Jewish Martyrs was finally unveiled on 8 July 1990, the anniversary not of libera-

Figure 19. Holocuast memorial in the courtyard of the Dohány u. synagogue. © Tim Cole.

tion by the Soviet army but of the halting of the deportations by Horthy (see figure 19). Although located within the area of the Pest ghetto, this memorial was also self-consciously located within the pre-Holocaust "Jewish" space of the Dohány u. synagogue courtyard. That these two layers of history in this one place—"Jewish" history and Holocaust history—were being drawn upon was made explicit in a fund-raising leaflet that justified the proposed siting of the memorial on the grounds that

> that spot is hallowed ground—*Admath Kodesh*—to all of us, the place where our next of kin, our relatives came to a miserable end, whose common grave still is there. It is the one common grave in Hungary in which solely those massacred in the Holocaust are buried. It is the site, therefore, where a memorial that befittingly proclaims their memory should be erected. At that very place, too, Raoul Wallenberg and his associates did their utmost to save people who were being persecuted, fighting desperately to frustrate the murderers' plans.
>
> That very spot, close by the gate of the ghetto . . . was the daily scene in times past of a considerable proportion of Jewish life.
>
> There, from synagogues and meeting-houses prayers would go up and rise heavenward, and *bokhers*, Talmud Torah pupils would hurry to seminaries and schools.
>
> This memorial must be erected on that spot, site of the World War II horrors.[18]

That self-conscious drawing upon a site of Holocaust history and a site of Jewish religious history was also echoed within the sculpture itself, which is part weeping willow and part upturned menorah.

Although this site drew upon a Holocaust past, it was not the complex history of the Budapest ghetto. Rather, this particular place was being re-created as essentially generic Hungarian Holocaust space. The memory being offered by the memorial was not the memory of the Holocaust in Budapest, let alone the Budapest ghetto, but the memory of the entire Hungarian Holocaust. And yet in many ways, this was simply the wrong place to try to remember the Hungarian Holocaust in its entirety. After all, the majority of Hungarian "Jews" murdered in 1944 were gassed and burned at Auschwitz-Birkenau. There is something ironic about their being remembered here, on the site of the only ghetto in Hungary—aside from the International ghetto—to be liberated rather than liquidated. However, the mass grave at the edge of the Budapest ghetto has been reinterpreted through this act of memorialization as a symbolic site of the "martyrdom" of the entire Hungarian "Jewry."

More recently, the fenced-off space surrounding this memorial has become a site of multiple Holocaust memory. No longer does the weeping willow memorial stand alone in the midst of the synagogue courtyard. It has been joined by a number of other memorials, which are also the product of the fund-raising activities of the U.S.-based Emanuel Foundation, named in memory of the father of the Hollywood actor Tony Curtis. Indeed, now the weeping willow memorial is situated not simply within the synagogue courtyard but within what has been designated the "Raoul Wallenberg Memorial Park" (see figure 20). According to the plaques in both Hungarian and English, this memorial park has been created in order to "commemorate as an exclamation mark for the post-Holocaust generations the name of the Swedish diplomat Raoul Wallenberg who saved the lives of tens of thousands of Hungarian Jews. May it also remind all of the hundreds of thousands of Jewish martyrs, of the labour-camp inmates who died unknown, and of all those righteous men and women who putting their own lives at risk, saved persecutees of certain death."[19]

Within the fenced-off space of this memorial park, now accessible only through the Jewish Museum and Syngagoue, multiple Hungarian Holocaust memories each have their own memorial. Close to the street is a tombstonelike memorial set up on 6 July 1997, upon which is engraved the words from the Talmud made famous in *Schindler's List*, that whoever saves

Figure 20. The Raoul Wallenberg Memorial Park. © Tim Cole.

one life saves the whole world. This focus upon rescue is personalized in another tombstonelike memorial on the far side of the memorial to the martyrs. Here, Raoul Wallenberg's name takes precedence, but it is joined with the names of nineteen other foreign and Hungarian rescuers and surrounded by the names of tens of other Hungarian "righteous gentiles."

Rescuers thus jostle with martyrs in this Hungarian Holocaust memorial space. Although still assuming a central position, the memorial to the martyrs is changed by the later addition of these memories of rescue. It is almost as if evil is countered with good: Hitler is tempered by Wallenberg.[20] This more recent focus upon the rescuers within this memorial space reflects a broader shift, of which Spielberg's movie *Schindler's List* was a striking example. Yet this overlaying of the memory of the victims of the Hungarian Holocaust with the memory of the rescuers of Hungarian "Jews" is not the sum total of the recent shifts within this memorial space. In July 1998, another memorial plaque, which remembers those who died in Jewish labor battalions during the war, was added to this increasingly crowded courtyard. Although included within the figure of 600,000, these male "Jews" were not subjected to deportation to Auschwitz but were placed in labor battalions that served alongside Hungarian army units on the Eastern Front, where many suffered brutal treatment. In the neighboring space of the courtyard of the Hösök temple, a recently erected memorial mirrors the Memorial of the Hungarian Jewish Martyrs by remembering all those deported from Hungary, "only because they were Jews."[21]

So there is a restating of "Jewish" victimhood in the midst of the celebration of rescue, and in particular the rescue work of the most iconic figure associated with the Holocaust in Hungary, Raoul Wallenberg. As I will explore in more detail below, Raoul Wallenberg has been remembered in the site of the former International ghetto. He has, also, since 1997, made it into the site of the former Pest ghetto. His memory thus joined that of the Swiss rescuer Carl Lutz, who had been remembered within the former Pest ghetto since 1991. In that year, the Swiss Carl Lutz Board, with the support of the City Council, erected a sculpture by Tamás Szabó in the heart of the former eighth district of the Pest ghetto.[22] This was a memorial to Lutz as rescuer, rather than a memorial to the "Jewish" victims of the Holocaust in general or in the Pest ghetto in particular. Indeed, the very text on the sculpture, symbolizing the rescuer reaching out to offer salvation, made no mention of the "Jewish" specificity of those "saved" by Lutz in 1944. It spoke only of "those thousands of Nazi persecuted saved through the leadership of Swiss Consul Carl Lutz in 1944," rather than of "Jews."[23]

Now it is surprising to find Lutz being remembered here, right in the heart of one of the districts of the former ghetto. Lutz, like Wallenberg and other consular officials from neutral countries, did act to protect thousands of Budapest "Jews" in the latter half of 1944. But he didn't do it here. The major action of the neutral legations was focused on the International ghetto area. But there is no memorial to Lutz there. Nor is there a memorial to Lutz at the so-called Glass House at 29 Vadász u., where the Swiss legation sheltered "Jews." Rather, the site of the former Pest ghetto was chosen as a site of Lutz's memory. This may well be, in part at least, because the site of the former International ghetto had already been, to some extent, Wallenberg-ized.

THE INTERNATIONAL GHETTO AS SITE OF HISTORY AND SITE OF MEMORY

Immediately after the end of the war in 1945, the City Council in Budapest renamed one of the streets in the former International ghetto area Raoul Wallenberg u.[24] (see figure 21). The choice of street was in many ways an unusual one. After all, the street chosen—Phönix u.—whilst being within

Figure 21. Wall plaque on Raoul Wallenberg u. © Tim Cole.

the International ghetto area, had not included any Swedish-protected houses. For the journalist Jenö Lévai, the nearby Tátra u. was a more obvious choice, given that the majority of houses in that street had been under Swedish protection. However, Phönix street it was, and Lévai diplomatically concluded that the city authorities had simply made "no doubt a well intentioned error."[25] But rather than an error, it was likely the self-conscious choice of a small side street well away from the main Pest thoroughfare, Szent István körút. By contrast, Tátra u., which was Lévai's suggestion, joined onto this boulevard which forms the outer ring of central Pest. Such a street was deemed too visible for Wallenberg's memory, and so a minor side street that had contained no Swedish houses was renamed.

Although the precise choice of street was clear evidence of the marginalizing of Wallenberg's memory, the act of renaming did mean that Wallenberg's name was attached to the site of the former International ghetto. Indeed, through this early privileging of Wallenberg's name, rather than those of any of the other consulate officials involved in acts of rescue, the complex history and geography of the International ghetto was essentially Wallenberg-ized. Indeed, as the wall plaque erected beneath the new street sign made clear, it was not the place of the International ghetto that was being remembered in this space, but the personality Wallenberg. It was his name that was attached to the street, and he who was celebrated in the wall plaque as the heroic figure, "who saved ten thousand lives during the Nyilas Terror with his courageous actions and his zealous self-sacrifice" and "vanished during the siege of Pest."[26] As with many other of the memorials erected in Budapest, this one also denied the "Jewish" specificity of those Wallenberg "saved." Moreover, it made no reference to the broader context within which Wallenberg operated. In particular, the implementation, not simply by Wallenberg, of a territorial attempt at rescue in the place of the International ghetto is strikingly absent. Although the street was located in the former area of the International ghetto, it is Wallenberg the man who was being remembered, rather than the International ghetto the place. And Wallenberg was being remembered not simply as heroic rescuer but also as the man who disappeared.

The wartime disappearance of Wallenberg, and his unknown fate in the Soviet Union, ultimately emerged within the context of the Cold War as of significance equal to, if not greater than, Wallenberg's wartime activities on behalf of Budapest's "Jews." What is particularly striking is that the postwar disappearance of a statue of Wallenberg became symbolic of the disappearance of Wallenberg himself in 1945. The statue in question was commissioned by the Budapest Wallenberg Memorial Committee in the immediate postwar period. The work of the sculptor Pál Patzay, this monument was placed in 1949 in a visible location right at the center of Szent István Park, on the edge of the former International ghetto area (see figure 22). Patzay's sculpture showed a naked bronze figure—Wallenberg—fighting a swastika-covered serpent symbolizing Nazism. Although city officials had approved the location, this decision was overruled by the Soviet authorities who removed the statue and plinth on the eve of its unveiling in April 1949. Some years later, the bronze statue of the figure and serpent—now minus the swastika—reappeared in front of a pharmaceutical factory in Debrecen

Figure 22. Raoul Wallenberg Memorial, Szent István Park, 1949, prior to removal. Hungarian National Museum Historical Photographic Archives, courtesy of USHMM Photo Archives.

where it symbolized "the triumph of medical science over disease,"[27] rather than the triumph of Wallenberg over Nazism.[28]

This history of the disappearance of Wallenberg's statue became, during the subseqent decades, a symbol of the disappearance of Wallenberg himself in 1945. Such a linking of the Soviet erasure of Wallenberg's memory and the Soviet capture of Wallenberg himself was perhaps most explicitly presented in Cold War America. In 1989, forty years after the memorial's disappearance, the Wallenberg Committee of New York installed a copy of the disappearing statue on the grounds of the Soviet dacha in Glen Cove, New York.[29] The link had also been made in a memorial erected in Budapest two years previously.

Figure 23. 1987 Raoul Wallenberg Memorial, Buda. © Tim Cole.

Designed by Imre Varga and donated by the former American ambassador to Hungary Nicolas Salgo, the 1987 memorial quite self-consciously echoed Patzay's earlier disappearing sculpture. On the pillars of Swedish marble that stand on either side of the figure of Wallenberg, Varga etched the image of a man striking a swastika-covered serpent[30] (see figure 23). This allusion to both the disappearing memorial and the disappearing man was heightened by the location of the 1987 memorial, not in the vicinity of the former International ghetto but at the site in Buda where Wallenberg's abandoned car was discovered. Although for Harvey Rosenfeld, it was "by sheer coincidence, [that] the site chosen for the monument was the spot where Wallenberg's *Studebaker* was found abandoned in February 1945,"[31] it is clear that the location of this memorial was more than simply fortuitous.

Locating the memorial on this site meant that a site of Cold War rather than Holocaust history had been chosen for Wallenberg's memory. That the history of the Cold War rather than the history of the Holocaust was being remembered in the person of Wallenberg was also made clear on the text of the memorial itself. Rather than making reference to Wallenberg's wartime activities on behalf of the city's "Jews," the text alluded instead to Wallenberg's disappearance. The Latin text on the memorial, translated as "While good fortune stands by your side, friends are plentiful. But should grey clouds gather, you are alone to withstand the storm,"[32] pointed to Wallenberg not as the rescuer of "Jews" but as a—if not the—Cold War victim.

That such allusions were made in a memorial that clearly sought to reverse the Soviet erasure of Wallenberg's memory reflected the increased freedom being exercised by the Hungarian government vis-à-vis Moscow in the late 1980s. The year before the erection of this memorial was permitted by the Budapest authorities, the Hungarian ambassador to Britain had publically admitted that the statue outside the pharmaceutical factory in Debrecen had originally been created as a tribute to Wallenberg. But such official sanctioning of Wallenberg's memory in the late 1980s was tentative.[33] The unveiling ceremony of Varga's statue on 2 May 1987 was a "small and discreet" affair not attended by any senior members of the Hungarian government.[34] However, evoking the memory of Wallenberg's disappearance was clearly seen by the Hungarian authorities as a way by which a much bigger history of Soviet aggression—supremely, the history of 1956—could start to be remembered. For the Hungarian authorities in the late 1980s who began to sanction the memory of Wallenberg, as well as those such as the former American ambassador who commissioned the memorial, Wallenberg was ultimately being remembered as a victim of Soviet "totalitarianism" rather than as a victor against Nazi "totalitarianism." In the context of the Cold War, his position of Holocaust hero was downplayed, and his own victimhood was deemed of more significance and was remembered in non-Holocaust space.

Wallenberg's return to the heart of Holocaust space—the courtyard of the Dohány street synagogue—in 1997 marked the end of the Cold War and the increased interest in the Holocaust as the defining event of the twentieth century. The location of the Raoul Wallenberg Memorial Park suggested the memory of Wallenberg as rescuer of Hungarian "Jews" rather than as a victim himself. His heroic status was returned to him here, as the place of memory shifted from the Buda side of the Danube back to the Pest side. Literally just a few meters from a plaque that remembers the Soviet Army as liberators, Wallenberg is remembered as a fellow Holocaust hero "who saved the lives of tens of thousands of Hungarian Jews."

There was a sense of history coming full circle two years later, with the unveiling of a Wallenberg memorial in Szent István Park (see figure 24). Locating a memorial to Wallenberg there, on the edge of the International ghetto, can be seen as the reassertion of Wallenberg as Holocaust rescuer. Indeed, the text on the memorial refers to Wallenberg's rescue efforts in

Figure 24. Raoul Wallenberg Memorial, Szent István Park, 1999. © Tim Cole.

1944 and 1945. However, it was clear from the memorial itself, as well as its location, that this memorial was less about the winter of 1944 than about Wallenberg's disappearance in 1945 and the disappearance of his memorial in 1949.

The memorial erected in 1999 was not simply any old Wallenberg memorial in any old spot close to the International ghetto. It was the return of the disappearing memorial fifty years after its disappearance. Well, not quite the return of the actual disappearing memorial. The pharamaceutical company that had the original refused to allow it to be relocated once more. They did, however, allow a casting to be made, and it was this copy that was unveiled in April 1999 on the site of the 1949 memorial. Putting a copy of the original memorial back was nothing less than a self-conscious act of symbolic restitution, paid for by both private donors and the city authorities. Whilst it had not been possible to restore Wallenberg himself, here was the opportunity to restore the disappearing memorial that had assumed such importance as representative of the disappearing man. As the text beside the statue made explicit, the original statue had been taken down by the "Communist dictatorship," and its origins "deliberately silenced" when it reappeared in Debrecen some years later. Thus the memorial is not simply one to Wallenberg and his activities in 1944–45, but also a memorial to the suppression of Wallenberg's memory, specifically in 1949 but also in the subsequent decades. By self-consciously referencing the earlier destruction and silencing of the true nature of this statue, the memorial acts as, in part at least, a memorial of a memorial.

However, as well as remembering the disappearance of the statue—and, by implication, the man—during the "Communist dictatorship," the reinstatement of this memorial also remembers Wallenberg explicitly as the rescuer of Hungarian "Jews." Although on the memorial itself, the original 1949 text made no reference to the "Jewishness" of those saved, on the accompanying contemporary plaques, this is explicitly stated. Wallenberg as rescuer of Hungarian "Jews" is not the only foreign diplomat to be remembered in the space of the former International ghetto. A short walk away, the Italian Giorgio Perlasca is remembered on a wall plaque erected in 1993,[35] and just around the corner there is a plaque to the Spaniard Angel Sanz-Briz.[36] Whilst both are remembered for saving "Jews" during 1944–45, the numbers saved are not as great as those attributed to Wallenberg's memory. Perlasca and Sanz-Briz saved "several thousand," but Wallenberg is credited with saving "many tens of thousands." In short, the area of the former International ghetto is still dominated by Wallenberg's memory.

OTHER SITES OF HISTORY AND MEMORY

As is clear, elements of the former sites of both the Pest and the International ghettos have been, selectively, transformed into sites of memory over the last five or so decades. However, the sites of Holocaust memory in the city have by no means been restricted to these two sites of Holocaust history alone. Others involved in rescue activities in 1944 have been remembered throughout the city. In 1992, a plaque was erected at 4–5

Figure 25. Memorial for Jewish Martyrs at the Central Jewish Cemetery, Pestlörinc. © Tim Cole.

Dísz tér in memory of the papal nuncio Angelo Rotta. However, the text recording that "He faithfully served his church during the hard years of the war and he took an active part in helping foreign refugees and those persecuted" makes no reference to the "Jewishness" of those being rescued.[37]

But the "Jewishness" of the victims has been remembered elsewhere, with the transformation of traditional "Jewish" sites outside of the ghetto areas into sites of Holocaust memory. The most significant was the erection of a Memorial for Jewish Martyrs in 1949 in the Central Jewish Cemetery at Pestlörinc[38] (see figure 25). In the largest "Jewish" cemetery in the country, located on the outskirts of Budapest, the memorial created was the only one that stressed the "Jewish" specificity to the Holocaust during the

Figure 26. Evidence of acts of reinterpretation of the Memorial for Jewish Martyrs. © Tim Cole.

Communist period. Siting a Holocaust memorial in the place of "Jewish" mourning in the city did make sense. However, permitting the erection of such a monument at the periphery, rather than in the center, can be seen as an act of marginalizing the specifically "Jewish" memory of the Holocaust in Budapest.[39]

Within the place of the major "Jewish" cemetery in the capital, the memorial itself picks up on funereal architecture. A simple black marble sarcophagus acts as a symbolic grave for those whose names are listed on the memory wall. Above the symbolic tombstone, there is text in both Hungarian—"Murdered by hatred. May love cherish their memory"—and Hebrew—"God be mindful of the soul of our Jewish brothers who gave their lives for the hallowing of God"s name."[40] Certainly the memorial itself is interpreted as a virtual tomb for Hungary's Holocaust victims by those who visit. Flowers and stones are placed both on the black sarcophagus and along the bottom of the memory wall (see figure 26). These ritualistic actions reflect what James Young has called "the constant give and take between memorials and viewers."[41] Whilst common to all memorials, here physical evidence remains of that process of interpretation and reinterpretation.

Such evidence suggests the need to think of memorials not simply in the rather instrumental terms of who created them, when, and where.

Rather, there is a need for an anthropological concern with how these memorials have been, and are, used. Of course, it is much harder to uncover usage of memorials. But there is clearly much more to memorials than simply the intentions of those who set them up. What is ultimately equally, if not more, significant is how those memorials are then used and (re)interpreted. Although memorials are clearly given meaning by dint of, for example, location, they are also given potentially very different meanings by those who visit them. In the case of the Memorial for Jewish Martyrs in the Pestlôrinc Cemetery, those meanings do cohere with the intentions inherent in both the location and architecture of the memorial. This is clearly intended as a symbolic tomb and is interpreted by visitors in just such terms.

However, as well as laying flowers and stones along the base of the wall of names, visitors have also engaged in what could be seen as acts of "graffiti" (see figure 27). A large number of individual names engraved into the stone have been painted in to ensure their continued legibility and the continuing memory of those remembered. More strikingly, additional names of victims have been added in pen and pencil. This memorial, although in some ways fixed in 1949, is continually evolving through acts of emphasis and addition by individual visitors. As new names are added and existing names reemphasized, the memorial and who it remembers is changed. This is not a memorial that is policed and is to be viewed only, but one that is open to the intervention of the visitor. And the visitor does not need to pay to add the name of a family member or friend. All they need do is bring a pencil.

The memorial spaces at the cemetery on the very edge of the city and in the synagogue courtyard in the heart of the city couldn't be more different. Although stones can be laid on the symbolic tombstones at both, there is continual policing of the use of the latter space by docents and security guards. No doubt concerns with antisemitic attacks are at the forefront of such activity. However, there are clearly also monetary concerns at play in the synagogue courtyard Holocaust memorial space. Memory has to be paid for. Whilst at one level the tree memorial remembers the "600,000 martyrs," at another level it remembers those who are named. The corollary is that at one level, it forgets those who are not named. And the difference between being named and not named is—or certainly was back in 1988 when the memorial was planned—$125 "or the value of that sum in forints."[42] That memory in this space can be—and must be—bought can also be seen in the donors' plaques on the memorial tombstone set up in 1997 in the Raoul Wallenberg Memorial Park.

Figure 27. Evidence of acts of reinterpretation of the Memorial for Jewish Martyrs. © Tim Cole.

There is clearly self-policing of memory within this central Holocaust memorial space in the city. However, as I have suggested, the Communist period saw considerable official policing of memorial space. The disappearance of Wallenberg's statue in April 1949 is of course the prime example of this. But the lack of reference to the "Jewish" specificity of the Holocaust within central Pest prior to 1990 also points to the effective policing of Holocaust memory. With the collapse of communism, the policing of this memory was relaxed and there was something approaching a free market of memorialization.

In this context, the Hungarian Zionist Federation and the Hungarian Office of the Jewish Agency for Israel erected a simple memorial in the grounds of an apartment block on the Pest bank of the Danube in April

1994. Erected on the fiftieth anniversary of the Hungarian Holocaust, the small *gal-ed*—a witness heap of stones, as in Genesis 31:45–48—was dedicated to the "memory of those sacrificed and the heroes of the Zionist resistance." The reference to "Jewish" heroes as well as victims drew upon a Zionist and Israeli memory of the Holocaust,[43] which contrasts with the American Diasporic memory of the Holocaust in terms of "Jewish" martyrs and "non-Jewish" rescuers that characterizes the Dohány street synagogue courtyard.

The location of this Zionist memorial is significant in drawing upon another site of Holocaust history in the city, outside of the dominant sites of the Pest and International ghettos. This memorial is one of a number which have been part of the transforming the Danube riverbank into a place of memory. In the winter of 1944, Budapest "Jews" were shot into the river by Nyilas gangs, and this history has been selectively remembered. Along the riverbank in Angyalföld, at the very edge of the city, a memorial was erected in 1986 by the City Council and the national antifascist resistance organization. This memorial adopted the dominant discourse of resistance; not only did the text refer to the persecuted only in the abstract (rather than the "Jewish" particular), but it was clearly more concerned with celebrating members of the Resistance. They are explicitly referred to along with army deserters who were shot into the river, and the memorial itself is one that is heroic in form.

Another example of this transformation of the Pest bank of the Danube into a place of memory can be seen in the memorial tiles by the artist Anna Stein, set into the ground in the middle of a road junction at the end of the Margit bridge in 1990. Dedicated "as a token of remembrance to those Hungarians who in the winter of 1944–45 fell victim to the Nyilas terror," this memorial did not focus on the early spring and summer of 1944. It is those dates which are dominant in the Zionist memorial self-consciously erected in April of 1994. In contrast, Stein's tiles remember the later chapter of the Hungarian Holocaust and the actions of the Nyilas puppet government.

What is striking about the remembrance of this period is the lack of any reference to "Jewish" specificity. Rather, there is a nationalizing of memory here. The memory of the period and place is "Magyarized," with the "Jewish" victims of the Holocaust being replaced by the "Hungarian" victims of the Nyilas. Now, what is striking is that rather than the use of the generic language of Fascism, there is specific reference to the native Fascist party the Nyilas. Thus, implictly at least, the Hungarian-ness of the perpetrators is referenced. However, this is countered by the explicit stressing of the Hungarian-ness of the victims. And I think the choice of both the place and the dates adds to this sense of the Magyarization of victimhood.

By the winter of 1944, when Nyilas gangs were shooting Budapest "Jews" into the icy waters of the Danube, there was clearly a sense in which the "normal" order had broken down. But a few months earlier, in the late spring of 1944 when municipal officials were creating ghettos in Hungarian towns and cities with a population of more than 10,000, and when Hungarian gendarmes were loading "Jews" onto deportation trains, it is far more difficult to claim that "normal" order had broken down. These officials and gendarmes cannot be dismissed simply as Nyilas ("Fascist"). Most of them were—as I have suggested—in post well before the German occupation of March 1944, and many of them stayed in post after 1945. They were more clearly ordinary Hungarians than extraordinary Nyilas.

Yet, it is in many ways much easier to confront that latter memory, rather than the former, in contemporary Hungary. It is easier to paint a picture of shared Hungarian victimhood, which does not discriminate between "Jews" and "non-Jews," at the hands of the Nyilas in the winter of 1944. It is harder to know quite what to do with the late spring and early summer of 1944 when the whole state apparatus was geared to enact anti-Jewish measures. And of course, as I've noted, anti-Jewish measures predated March 1944. The conflict between those two memories—of spring–summer 1944, and autumn–winter 1944—can be seen as playing out in the context of two Budapest museums, one already open and one in the planning stage.

TWO MUSEUMS, TWO MEMORIES

In February 2002, a museum called The House of Terror opened in Budapest (see figure 28). The museum, with both the financial and the political backing of the center-right government of Viktor Orbán,[44] was heavily criticized by the Hungarian left. Located at 60 Andrássy út, the museum self-consciously occupies a space with a complex and controversial history. It was there that the Nyilas had their headquarters, and also interrogated and tortured large numbers of opponents. In the postwar period, the Communist secret police—the Á.V.H.—took the building over as their headquarters and continued the practice of interrogating and torturing

Figure 28. The House of Terror, Budapest. © Tim Cole.

political opponents there. The premises chosen for the museum therefore have the dubious distinction of being a site of both Fascist and Communist brutality. Thus the museum offers what is in essence a telling of twentieth-century history in terms of totalitarianism.

Now the danger with such an approach is that the specificity of "Jewish" suffering during the Holocaust is subsumed within a broader category of Hungarian victims of totalitarianism. At The House of Terror, the "Jewish" victims of the Holocaust are essentially equated with the "Hungarian" victims of the Communist dictatorship. It is striking that the text on the Memorial of the Hungarian Jewish Martyrs in the courtyard of the Dohány street synagogue states, "In memory of the 600, 000 Hungarian Jewish martyrs who can never be forgotten, who were innocent victims of an evil unparalleled in history." And yet the claim of The House of Terror is that the evil of the Fascist era *was* paralleled during the Communist era. It is not perhaps entirely coincidental that in the Gulag Hall in the museum, the cattle cars that took 600,000 Hungarians to the Soviet Union in the 1940s and 1950s are portrayed.

Not only does the museum essentially claim the equivalency of the victims of Fascism and Communism, but indeed the emphasis in the museum would suggest that the Communist era was the more significant. Only two rooms in the museum are devoted to telling the story of the Fascist era, compared with seventeen rooms that outline in great detail the brutality of the Communist dictatorship. For critics on the left, such an emphasis was convenient to a center-right government seeking to discredit opposition politicians on the left.[45] Whilst this may be the case, of more concern is the attempt to subsume the specific history of the Holocaust within a much more monolithic history. This more monolithic history of Hungary from 1944 to 1989 is essentially told as a history of Hungarian victimhood at the hands of outside forces. Both the Hungarian "Jews" and the Hungarians are portrayed within such a telling of the past half century as victims of totalitarianism. The "Jews" were the victims of Nazi Germany and the native exponents of the foreign doctrine of Fascism, the Nyilas. The "Hungarians" were the victims of the Communist Soviet Union and their Á.V.H. collaborators. Such an approach neither takes the specificity of the Holocaust seriously nor comes to terms with the complex history of Hungarian collaboration in 1944, which I have attempted to explore to some extent at least in this book.

More of that specific history of the Hungarian Holocaust is being planned for exhibition in a forthcoming Budapest Holocaust Museum and Education Center. The intention to locate this museum within the area of the former Pest ghetto points to the self-conscious drawing upon this site of Holocaust history, albeit in rather generic ways. As with the Holocaust memorial complex in the courtyard of the Dohány street synagogue, the memory articulated by the museum is intended to be that of the "600,000" Hungarian Holocaust victims, rather than the more specific and atypical memory of the Budapest ghetto. And again like the Holocaust memorial complex in the courtyard of the synagogue, it is not just the Holocaust history of the site that is being drawn upon in generic ways but also the "Jewish" history of the site. This duality can be clearly seen in the museum's fund-raising literature, which states: "The museum will open at the end of 2002 in the historic 7th district of Budapest, where the ghetto was situated during the war, and which continues to be a vibrant Jewish neighborhood. Our aim is to place this important institution in a high traffic area, close to other Jewish attractions and memorial sites."[46]

When this museum is built, it is clear that it will ask difficult questions about Hungarian collaboration in the Holocaust in a way that The House of Terror simply does not do. And it is also clear that it will focus on specifically "Jewish" victimhood rather than generic "totalitarian" victimhood. With only a short walk between them, it will be possible to take in both museums in one day, and so take in two very different readings of the place of the Holocaust in contemporary Hungarian memory, housed in two very different places.

But both places are in many ways atypical sites as far as the Hungarian Holocaust goes. This is in large part due to the atypicality of Budapest. The Pest ghetto was liberated, not liquidated like every other ghetto within the wartime Hungarian borders. And those hundreds of provincial ghettos were liquidated well before the coming to power of the Nyilas government in mid-October 1944. By then, every "Jewish" community outside of Budapest had been deported from Hungary to Auschwitz-Birkenau. And the critical decisions about these deportations were not made at the almost demonic site of Andrássy út 60, but in the far more "respectable" offices of national, regional, and local government (offices which, by and large, are still used by the organs of government at a variety of scales).

Focusing upon the period and places associated with Nyilas rule allows for a sidestepping of the difficult questions about the complicity of the Hungarian state apparatus in implementing the Holocaust. The House of Terror is quite simply the wrong place to attempt to come to terms with the Holocaust. But the Pest ghetto—another Nyilas product—is also the wrong place. As I've examined in this study, the Budapest parallel to the nationwide implementation of ghettoization was not the VII district Pest ghetto but 1,948 yellow-star houses dispersed throughout the city. Those are perhaps better places to try to remember what happened across Hungary in the fateful months in late spring and early summer 1944. But the yellow stars have long been taken down from the entrances to this dispersed ghetto. And uncovering the Holocaust history of these ordinary apartment buildings might be just too uncomfortable.

I am reminded of the memorial artwork undertaken by the artist

Shimon Attie in an entirely different Holocaust city. In 1992, Attie projected images of the Jewish district of Schenenviertel in Berlin from the 1920s and 1930s onto the present-day locations. His aim was "to give this invisible past a voice, to bring it to light, if only for some brief moments."[47] However, some local residents were less happy with this reconnection of these present sites with their past. As Young recounts, "While Attie was installing the *Buchhändler* (bookseller) slide projection, for example, a fifty-year-old man suddenly came running out of the building shouting that his father had bought the building 'fair and square' from Mister Jacobs in 1938. 'And what happened to this Mr. Jacobs?' Attie asked the man. 'Why, of course, he was a multi-millionaire and moved to New York.' Of course."[48] With some sites of history, it seems so much more preferable to forget rather than to remember—to leave them as mute sites of history rather than transforming them into sites of memory. But there is surely a need to uncover the complex histories and geographies of Europe's cities, including their Holocaust history. In the case of one Holocaust city—Budapest—this book has been just such an attempt.

My aim has not been to uncover the traces of the Holocaust geography of this city in order to offer simple moral lessons from this complex past. After trying to get inside the heads of the doctors of space who implemented ghettoization policies during 1944, as well the heads of ordinary Hungarians—both "Jewish" and "non-Jewish"—who contested those policies, I am struck by the complexity of the events of 1944 and the multiplicity of motives that seem to mark the shaping of this Holocaust city. I am left, with the words of Primo Levi echoing around in my head.

In *The Drowned and the Saved*, Levi saw the place of the concentration camp to be a "gray zone" that resisted being reduced to the simplistic binaries of "victims" versus "perpetrators"—"good" versus "evil."[49] Entering into this place was, Levi suggested,

indeed a shock because of the surprise it entailed. The world into which one was precipitated was terrible, yes, but also indecipherable: it did not conform to any model; the enemy was all around but also inside, the "we" lost its limits, the contenders were not two, one could not discern a single frontier but rather many confused, perhaps innumerable frontiers which stretched between each of us. One entered hoping at least for the solidarity of one's companions in misfortune, but the hoped for allies, except in special cases, were not there . . .[50]

Not only did Levi refuse to paint the "victim" as a homogenous group characterized by "goodness," but he also refused to paint the "perpetrator" as a homogenous group characterized by "evil." Writing of one SS officer—who orders the killing of a girl who manages to survive the gassings—Levi concludes that

> this man Muhself was not a compassionate person; his daily ration of slaughter was studded with arbitrary and capricious acts, marked by his inventions of refined cruelty. He was tried in 1947, sentenced to death and hung in Krakow and this was right, but not even he was a monolith. Had he lived in a different environment and epoch, he probably would have behaved like any other common man.[51]

The power of Levi's work is his resistance to a monolithic telling of the Holocaust. My hope is that my attempt to uncover the traces of the Holocaust city of Budapest is similarly resistant of monolithic tellings. There is a sense in which monolithic tellings provide closure to this past which refuses to go away—hence their attraction. But I wonder if there isn't something profoundly disturbing in a past that resists such easy categorization. At the end of his essay on the "gray zone," Levi reflects on the controversial figure Chaim Rumkowski, who led the Jewish Council in Lódz. His closing words on Rumkowski seem to me to be appropriate closing words to this book on another Holocaust city.

> We are all mirrored in Rumkowski, his ambiguity is ours, it is our second nature, we hybrids molded from clay and spirit. His fever is ours, the fever of our Western civilization that "descends into hell with trumpets and drums," and its miserable adornments are the distorting image of our symbols of social prestige. His folly is that of presumptuous and mortal Man . . . Like Rumkowski, we too are so dazzled by power and prestige as to forget our essential fragility. Willingly or not we come to terms with power, forgetting that we are all in the ghetto, that the ghetto is walled in, that outside the ghetto reign the lords of death, and that close by the train is waiting.[52]

NOTES

PREFACE

1. N. L. Kleeblatt (ed.), *Mirroring Evil. Nazi Imagery/Recent Art* (New York: The Jewish Museum, 2001), ix.

2. E. van Alphen, "Playing the Holocaust," in Kleeblatt, *Mirroring Evil*, 75.

3. See Kleeblatt, *Mirroring Evil*, plates 17–19, between pages 78–79, for photographs of Libera's work.

4. Kleeblatt, *Mirroring Evil*, 129, is right to describe the scenes on the LEGO boxes exhibited by Libera as "nothing less than the most horrific and morally debased architectural complexes ever built."

5. E. H. Spitz, "Childhood, Art, and Evil," in Kleeblatt, *Mirroring Evil*, 49.

6. J. E. Young, "Foreword: Looking into the Mirrors of Evil," in Kleeblatt, *Mirroring Evil*, xvi.

7. C. R. Browning, *Ordinary Men. Reserve Police Battalion 101 and the Final Solution in Poland* (New York: HarperCollins, 1992), 188–89.

8. On my use of quotation marks when writing of the "Jew," see my comments at the end of chapter 2, and also T. Cole, "Constructing the 'Jew,' Writing the Holocaust: Hungary 1920–45," *Patterns of Prejudice* 33, No. 3 (1999), 19–27.

CHAPTER ONE

1. From the movie *The Last Days* (1998). For more on Alice Lok Cahana's story see S. Spielberg & Survivors of the *Shoah* Visual History Foundation, *The Last Days* (London: Weidenfeld & Nicolson, 1999), 58–75.

2. S. Schama, *Landscape and Memory* (London: HarperCollins, 1995), 26.

3. J-C. Pressac, *Auschwitz: Technique and Operation of the Gas Chambers* (New York: The Beate Klarsfeld Foundation, 1989), R. J. van Pelt & D. Dwork, *Auschwitz 1270 to the Present* (New Haven: Yale University Press, 1996).

4. R. J. van Pelt & C. W. Westfall, *Architectural Principles in the Age of Historicism* (New Haven: Yale University Press, 1993), 120.

5. USHMM Archives, 1997. A.0294 Microfilm I. 33—sketch maps of the location of the

ghettos in Tolna county. These sketch maps of the ghettos in Bonyhád, Dombóvár, Dunaföldvár, Högyész, Paks, Pincehely, Tamási, and Tolna are drawn by different hands. This microfilm is also available in the Hungarian National Archives [hereafter O.L.], I collection.

6. M. Berenbaum & A. J. Peck (eds.), *The Holocaust and History. The Known, the Unknown, the Disputed, and the Re-examined* (Bloomington: Indiana University Press, 1998), xii.

7. Van Pelt & Westfall, *Architectural Principles*, 121.

8. B. M. Lane, *Architecture and Politics in Germany 1918–1945* (Cambridge, Mass.: Harvard University Press, 1968), R. Taylor, *The Word in Stone: The Role of Architecture in the National Socialist Ideology* (Berkeley: University of California Press, 1974).

9. Van Pelt & Westfall, *Architectural Principles*, 369.

10. A. Charlesworth, "Towards a Geography of the *Shoah*," *Journal of Historical Geography* 18, No. 4 (1992), 469.

11. German Library of Information, *A Nation Builds: Contemporary German Architecture* (New York: German Library of Information, 1941).

12. T. Cole, *Selling the Holocaust: From Auschwitz to Schindler. How History Is Bought, Packaged, and Sold* (New York: Routledge, 1999), esp. chs. 1 & 4.

13. G. Broadbent, "Neo-Classicism," *Architectural Design* 49, Nos. 8–9 (1979), 39.

14. A. Scobie, *Hitler's State Architecture. The Impact of Classical Antiquity* (University Park: Pennsylvania State University Press, 1990), 130.

15. Ibid., 137.

16. Van Pelt & Dwork, *Auschwitz*, 11.

17. Ibid., on second page of plates, between pp. 320–21.

18. Van Pelt & Westfall, *Architectural Principles*, 72.

19. Ibid., 355–56.

20. *A Nation Builds*, 89.

21. Van Pelt & Westfall, *Architectural Principles*, 373.

22. F. Aldor, *Germany's 'Death Space,' The Polish Tragedy* (London: Francis Aldor, 1940), 141—"The fate of Poland since the German occupation shows only too clearly that what the Germans mean by German living space is at the same time the dying space of other peoples." See also the stress upon the interrelationship between *Lebensraum* and *Entfernung* [elimination of Jews from the German lifeworld] in D. B. Clarke, M. A. Doel & F. X. McDonough, "Holocaust Topologies: Singularity, Politics, Space," *Political Geography* 15, Nos. 6–7 (1996), 485, who "demonstrate how the Nazi's quest for *Lebensraum* was necessarily and not simply contingently related to their desire for *Entfernung*."

23. Van Pelt and Westfall, *Architectural Principles*, 356.

24. P. B. Jaskot, *The Architecture of Oppression. The SS, Forced Labor and the Nazi Monumental Building Economy* (London: Routledge, 2000), 121.

25. Ibid., 127.

26. Ibid., 130.

27. Ibid., 134. Jaskot notes, 135, "of course, unlike the castles of Henry I, SS concentration camps were designed not to keep attackers out but prisoners in."

28. Ibid., 134.

29. Ibid., 131.

30. G. J. Horwitz, "Places Far Away, Places Very Near. Mauthausen, The Camps of the *Shoah*, and the Bystanders" in Berenbaum & Peck, *The Holocaust and History*, 413–14.

31. Ibid., 413.

32. H. Lefebvre, *The Production of Space* (translated by D. Nicholson-Smith) (Oxford: Blackwell, 1991), 37.

33. Ibid., 99.

34. Ibid., 303.

35. M. T. Allen, *The Business of Genocide: The SS, Slave Labor and the Concentration Camps* (Chapel Hill: University of North Carolina Press, 2002).

36. Jaskot, *The Architecture of Oppression*, 1.

37. Ibid., 140–45.

38. G. D. Rosenfeld, "The Architects' Debate. Architectural Discourse and the Memory of Nazism in the Federal Republic of Germany, 1977–1997," *History and Memory* 9, Nos. 1–2 (1997), 189.

39. Cited in ibid., 205.

40. Cited in ibid., 205.

41. Cited in ibid., 205.

42. Cited in ibid., 199.

43. Cited in Z. Bauman, *Modernity and the Holocaust* (Cambridge: Polity Press, 1989), 8.

44. See especially Bauman's *Modernity and the Holocaust*.

45. *A Nation Builds*, 113.

46. Van Pelt & Westfall, *Architectural Principles*, 121.

47. Ibid., 365.

48. R. Hilberg, "The Bureaucracy of Annihilation" in F. Furet (ed.), *Unanswered Questions. Nazi Germany and the Genocide of the Jews* (New York: Schocken Books, 1989), 120–21.

49. Van Pelt sees these chimneys to be "the symbol of the architectural contribution to the Nazi destruction of the Jews," in Van Pelt & Westfall, *Architectural Principles*, 363.

50. Lefebvre, *The Production of Space*, 99—"In connection with the city and its extensions (outskirts, suburbs), one occasionally hears talk of a 'pathology of space,' of 'ailing neighborhoods,' and so on. This kind of phraseology makes it easy for people who use it—architects, urbanists or planners—to suggest the idea that they are in effect 'doctors of space.'"

51. Questions of functionality and intentionality dominated writing on the Holocaust in the 1980s and into the 1990s. For a good survey, and the sense of shift away from such earlier concerns, see C. R. Browning, *The Path to Genocide. Essays on Launching the Final Solution* (Cambridge: Cambridge University Press, 1992) and C. R. Browning, *Nazi Policy, Jewish Workers, German Killers* (Cambridge: Cambridge University Press, 2000).

52. Van Pelt & Westfall, *Architectural Principles*, 121.

53. Ibid., 121.

54. Cited in ibid., 121.

55. The study draws mainly on archival material from the Hungarian National Archives and Budapest City Archives, rather than on oral history interviews. In large part these sources have been chosen because they best allow me to answer the kinds of questions—of motivation—that I am asking.

56. See R. Hartmann, "Dealing with Dachau in Geographic Education," in H. Brodsky (ed.), *Land and Community: Geography in Jewish Studies* (Bethesda: University of Maryland Press, 1997), 357, who notes that "historical and political geographers have examined concepts about Nazi Germany and other fascist and autocratic regimes in Europe, but, with few exceptions, geographers have shied away from a discussion of the material expressions of Nazi landscapes of fear and terror in the concentration camps."

57. Charlesworth, "Towards a Geography of the *Shoah*," 469. See also A. Charlesworth, "Teaching the Holocaust through Landscape Study: The Liverpool Experience," *Immigrants and Minorities* 13, No. 1 (1994), 66 & 75.

58. R. Breitman, "The 'Final Solution'" in G. Martel (ed.), *Modern Germany Reconsidered, 1870–1945* (London: Routledge, 1992), 207.

59. D. Massey, *Spatial Divisions of Labor: Social Structures and the Geography of Production* (London: Macmillan, 1984), 52.

60. R. Hilberg, *The Politics of Memory. The Journey of a Holocaust Historian* (Chicago: Ivan R. Dee, 1996), 40–41, where Hilberg notes a childhood fascination with maps and geography, and states, 41, that "geography, however, became for me something more than an array of place names. I was beginning to think in spatial terms. When I studied international law I understood without need for explanation what 'territory' meant in the context of that law, and when I delved

into the German Reich, its occupied areas and satellite states, I saw it in a specific space, widening and extending its measures against the Jews."

61. Although note Breitman's comments that "Hilberg . . . showed greater interest in the unfolding of the basically similar elements in each location than with the differences in timing or substance from country to country," Breitman, "The 'Final Solution,'" 199.

62. R. Hilberg, *The Destruction of the European Jews* (Chicago: Quadrangle Books, 1961). A revised edition (3 volumes) was published in 1985 (New York: Holmes and Meier, 1985).

63. Cited in M. Heffernan, *The Meaning of Europe. Geography and Geopolitics* (London: Arnold, 1998), 172. See also Andrew Charlesworth's comments on the film *Shoah*, in "Teaching the Holocaust through Landscape Study," 68, that "Lanzmann constantly re-locates the camps of Chelmno and Treblinka by his shots of the movement of the gas vans and the death trains through the surrounding landscapes and their eventual arrival at the sites of the camp. The repetition allows the viewer no escape from the conclusion that the camps were set in living landscapes, not in Siberian wastes. He makes the point more discursively for the ghettos but it is made all the same. The ghettos were in the centers of Polish cities, not distant suburbs. The geography of the bystander is brought into sharp focus by Lanzmann." See also Hilberg, *Politics of Memory*, 39–40, where he notes that "my cognizance of trains has affected my work, and for a long time I was preoccupied with them in a research project. Specifically I was interested in the transport of Jews to their deaths. Germany relied on railways not only for moving supplies and troops, but also for the so-called Final Solution, which entailed the transfer of Jews from all parts of Europe to death camps or shooting sites."

64. See H. Fein, *Accounting for Genocide: National Responses and Jewish Victimization during the Holocaust* (New York: The Free Press, 1979) for an early—and problematic—study of these questions.

65. B. Moore, *Victims and Survivors. The Nazi Persecution of the Jews in the Netherlands 1940–1945* (London: Arnold, 1997), 2.

66. M. Gilbert, *Atlas of the Holocaust* (London: Michael Joseph Limited, 1982).

67. USHMM, *Historical Atlas of the Holocaust* (New York: Macmillan Publishing USA, 1996).

68. M. Gilbert, *Holocaust Journey. Travelling in Search of the Past* (New York: Columbia University Press, 1997).

69. Cf. M. Gilbert, *The Holocaust. The Jewish Tragedy* (London: Collins, 1986).

70. Gilbert, *Holocaust Journey*, 400.

71. Massey, *Spatial Divisions of Labor*, 68.

72. Although that is an important issue—see for example the transportation of "Jews" from Athens to Auschwitz toward the end of the war, when the rail network was under considerable strain. See Gilbert, *Atlas*, map 232, 180.

73. S. Pile "Introduction" in S. Pile & M. Keith (eds.), *Geographies of Resistance* (London: Routledge, 1997), 4.

74. Massey, *Spatial Divisions of Labor*, 56.

75. Lefebvre, *The Production of Space*, 44.

76. Ibid., 219.

77. E. W. Soja, "The Spatiality of Social Life: Towards a Transformative Retheorization" in D. Gregory & J. Urry (eds.), *Social Relations and Spatial Structures* (London: Macmillan, 1985), 95.

78. D. Gregory, *Ideology, Science and Human Geography* (London: Hutchinson, 1978), 120.

79. M. Freeman, *Atlas of Nazi Germany. A Political, Economic and Social Anatomy of the Third Reich*. Second Edition (London: Longman, 1995), 3.

80. See my critique of Freeman in a "Review of Atlas of Nazi Germany," *Political Geography* 16, No. 6 (1997), 538–39.

81. W. A. D. Jackson, *The Shaping of Our World. A Human and Cultural Geography* (New York: John Wiley & Sons, 1985), 309, 311, 318.

82. Ibid., 309.

83. Hartman, "Dealing with Dachau," 366.

84. Jackson, *The Shaping of Our World*, 311.

85. D. Sibley, *Geographies of Exclusion* (London: Routledge, 1995), ix.

86. Ibid., 49.

87. Ibid., ix.

88. Pile, "Introduction," 16.

89. Ibid., 29.

90. Ibid., 16.

91. Ibid., 29.

92. Kleeblatt, *Mirroring Evil*, 129–30, notes, in relation to Libera's artwork mentioned above, that "for Libera, like Foucault, benign institutions such as the school, the cloister, the military barracks, or the factory are modeled on disciplinary institutions and buildings. Reaching further, Libera grasps the ultimate paradigm of disciplinary models and one overlooked by Foucault: the concentration camp." Kleeblatt is surely right to suggest that the concentration camp is the ultimate space of control.

93. See Jackson, *The Shaping of Our World*, 324, who sees the 1950 Group Area Act which "divided the land into segregated areas of which only members of a designated race could live or own property" as instituting "pariah landscapes."

94. See J. Crush, "The Discourse of Progressive Human Geography," *Progress in Human Geography* 15, No. 4 (1991), 395–414.

95. J. Robinson, *The Power of Apartheid. State, Power and Space in South African Cities* (Oxford: Butterworth-Heinemann, 1996), 1.

96. G. S. Elder, "The South Africa Body Politic: Space, Race and Heterosexuality," in H. J. Nast & S. Pile (eds.), *Places through the Body* (London: Routledge, 1998), 153.

97. J. Crush, "Scripting the Compound: Power and Space in the South African Mining Industry," *Environment and Planning D: Society and Space* 12, No. 3 (1994), 307.

98. J. Robinson, " 'A Perfect System of Control?' State Power and 'Native Locations' in South Africa," *Environment and Planning D: Society and Space* 8, No. 2 (1990), 135–62.

99. S. J. Smith, *The Politics of "Race" and Residence: Citizenship, Segregation and White Supremacy in Britain* (Cambridge: Polity Press, 1989). Jackson, *The Shaping of Our World*, 309, notes that "social geographers in Britain tend, on the whole, to be in forefront of the study of spatial expressions of discrimination, but the framework of analysis tends to view the social landscape in neo-Marxist terms."

100. D. Sibley, "Survey 13: Purification of Space," *Environment and Planning D: Society and Space* 6, No. 4 (1988).

101. P. Jackson (ed.), *Race and Racism: Essays in Social Geography* (London: Allen & Unwin, 1987).

102. Ibid., 14.

CHAPTER TWO

1. S. Gringauz, "The Ghetto as an Experiment of Jewish Social Organization," *Jewish Social Studies* XI (1949), 3.

2. Ibid., 3–4.

3. Cf. for example the approaches adopted in D. Ofer, "Everyday Life of Jews under Nazi Occupation: Methodological Issues," *Holocaust and Genocide Studies* 9, No. 1 (1995), 42–69 and C. R. Browning, "Genocide and Public Health: German Doctors and Polish Jews, 1939–41," *Holocaust and Genocide Studies* 3, No. 1 (1988), 21–36.

4. Gringauz, "The Ghetto," 5.

5. Ibid., 20.

6. S. Gringauz, "Some Methodological Problems in the Study of the Ghetto," *Jewish Social Studies* XII (1950), 67.

7. See, for example, P. Novick, *The Holocaust in American Life* (Boston: Houghton Mifflin, 1999), esp. ch. 5, and Cole, *Selling the Holocaust*, esp. ch. 1.

8. H. Arendt, *Eichmann in Jerusalem. A Report on the Banality of Evil* (Harmondsworth: Penguin, 1977), see esp. 117–25.

9. I. Trunk, *Judenrat. The Jewish Councils in Eastern Europe under Nazi Occupation* (New York: Macmillan, 1972).

10. D. Cesarani, "Introduction" in D. Cesarani (ed.), *The Final Solution: Origins and Implementation* (London: Routledge, 1994), 16, and see his bibliographical notes in footnotes 54 & 55, 28.

11. For a recent example of this approach, see G. Corni, *Hitler's Ghettos. Voices from a Beleaguered Society 1939–1944* (London: Arnold, 2002).

12. Hilberg, *The Destruction*, 16–17.

13. M. Gilbert, "Introduction" in A. Tory, *Surviving the Holocaust. The Kovno Ghetto Diary* (London: Pimlico, 1991), xvi.

14. See Corni, *Hitler's Ghettos*, 1. The most significant work on the Warsaw ghetto is that of Gutman—see Y. Gutman, *The Jews of Warsaw, 1939–1943. Ghetto, Underground, Revolt* (Brighton: The Harvester Press Limited, 1982), ix, where he notes that "the purpose of this work is to examine the character and conduct of the Jewish community of Warsaw in face of the persecutive tactics of the Nazi occupation regime; to throw light on the means that were adopted to cope, both intellectually and psychologically, with the grave problems of the period; and to analyze the development of the armed resistance movement and the armed struggle of the Jews of Warsaw."

15. Cole, *Selling the Holocaust*, 122–26.

16. See also H. Fein, *Accounting for Genocide*, figure 3–2, 63, where Fein essentially adopts the process-oriented approach of Hilberg, seeing ghettoization as one element of a fivefold "chain of Jewish victimization": "definition, stripping, segregation, isolation, concentration."

17. Hilberg, *The Destruction*, 152–53.

18. Ibid., 106–7.

19. Ibid., 150.

20. P. Friedman, "The Jewish Ghettos of the Nazi Era," *Jewish Social Studies* XVI (1954), 61. This essay was reprinted in P. Friedman, *Roads to Extinction. Essays on the Holocaust* (edited by A. J. Friedman) (New York: The Jewish Publication Society of America, 1980), ch. 3.

21. Ibid., 61.

22. Ibid., 62.

23. Ibid., 63.

24. L. S. Dawidowicz, *The War against the Jews, 1933–45* (Harmondsworth: Penguin, 1990), 258.

25. H. Mommsen, *From Weimar to Auschwitz. Essays in German History* (translated by Philip O'Connor) (Cambridge: Polity Press, 1991), 243, where he claims that "there is no doubt that the resettlement program agreed to in the Nazi-Soviet Non-Aggression Pact, whereby ethnic Germans living in the Soviet Union were to be settled mainly in the *Wartheland*, provided the impetus for the large-scale deportation program, which affected Poles as well as Jews."

26. M. Broszat, "Hitler and the Genesis of the 'Final Solution': An Assessment of David Irving's Theses," *Yad Vashem Studies* 13 (1970), 97.

27. Ibid., 119.

28. Ibid., 120.

29. C. R. Browning, "Nazi Ghettoization Policy in Poland: 1939–1941," *Central European History* XIX, No. 4 (1986), 344–45. This essay was reprinted in Browning, *The Path to Genocide*, ch. 2.

30. Ibid., 346.

31. Ibid., 347–48.

32. Ibid., 348.

33. Ibid., 355.

34. Ibid., 355.

35. Ibid., 346–48. On Warsaw see also, Browning, "Genocide and Public Health," 23–24.

36. See, e.g., U. Herbert, "Labor and Extermination: Economic Interest and the Primacy of *Weltanschauung* in National Socialism," *Past and Present* 138 (1993), 160, who argues that the rational discourse adopted in the implementation of ghettoization was a form of justification belying the real motivation, and then suggests that once implemented, ghettoization "became a kind of self-fulfilling prophecy" whereby conditions in the ghettos acted as a form of proof of the "rational" arguments used in their construction. For example, overcrowding led to epidemics.

37. L. Dobroszycki (ed.), *The Chronicle of the Lódz Ghetto 1941–1944* (New Haven: Yale University Press, 1984), xxxvi.

38. Gutman, *The Jews of Warsaw*, 55.

39. Friedman, "The Jewish Ghettos," 73.

40. Browning, "Genocide and Public Health," 24.

41. C. G. Roland, *Courage under Siege. Starvation, Disease, and Death in the Warsaw Ghetto* (Oxford: Oxford University Press, 1992), ch. 7, suggests the usefulness of examining the specific rationalizations being articulated within a broader study of the discourse of typhus.

42. Friedman, "The Jewish Ghettos," 73–74.

43. Ibid., 75.

44. Ibid., 75 [emphasis mine].

45. J. Robinson & P. Friedman (eds.), *Guide to Jewish History under Nazi Impact* (Jerusalem & New York: Yad Vashem & YIVO, 1960), 74.

46. Browning, "Genocide and Public Health," 26.

47. Gilbert, *Atlas*, map 204, 158.

48. Gilbert, *Holocaust Journey*, maps 18, 28, 42 & 47, 421, 429, 442 & 447.

49. USHMM, *Historical Atlas*.

50. J. Szekeres, *A Pesti Gettók 1945 Januári Megmentése* (Budapest: Nemzeti Kulturális Alap, 1997), 95 & 154–55.

51. J. Molnár, *Zsidósors 1944–ben az V. (Szegedi) Csendőrkerületben* (Budapest: Cserépfalvi Kiadó, 1995), 210–14.

52. Hilberg, *The Destruction*, 222. See also, on the location of the Lódz ghetto, D. M. Smith, *Geography and Social Justice* (Oxford: Blackwell, 1994), 258–61.

53. This reading of the ghetto landscapes supports Browning's reading of the texts produced by the officials planning and implementing ghettoization in Lódz.

54. Hilberg, *The Destruction*, 241–42.

55. Ibid., 107.

56. Ibid., 168.

57. Ibid., 171.

58. Ibid., 205.

59. Ibid., 205.

60. See K. R. Cox, "Comment. Redefining 'Territory,'" *Political Geography Quarterly* 10, No. 1 (1990), 6–7, who notes that "territory is a central concept in political geography, perhaps *the* defining concept without which the field would not exist," and yet, "oddly, and despite some notable contributions such as that of Sack [see below], it had not received the explicit attention one might have expected." For an early study on territoriality see E. W. Soja, *The Political Organization of Space*, Commission on College Geography Resource Paper No. 8 (Washington, D.C.: Association of American Geographers, 1971), 19, where Soja defines territoriality as "a behavioral phenomenon associated with the organization of space into spheres of influence or clearly demarcated territories which are made distinctive and considered at least partially exclusive by their occupants or definers." He suggests that "its most obvious geographical manifestation is an identifiable patterning of spatial relationships resulting in the *confinement* of certain activities in particular areas and the *exclusion* of certain categories of individuals from the space of the territorial individual and group."

61. R. D. Sack, *Human Territoriality. Its Theory and History* (Cambridge: Cambridge University Press, 1986), 1. For a somewhat different perspective on territory, which lays less stress than Sack on the spatial exercise of political power, see J. Gottmann, *The Significance of Territory* (Charlottesville, Va.: The University Press of Virginia, 1973), esp. 1–15.

62. Sack, *Human Territoriality*, 26.

63. Ibid., 15–16.

64. Ibid., 5.

65. Soja, *The Political Organization of Space*, 39.

66. Sack, *Human Territoriality*, 22.

67. R. Hilberg, "The Ghetto as a Form of Government: An Analysis of Isaiah Trunk's *Judenrat*," in Y. Bauer & N. Rotenstreich (eds.), *The Holocaust as Historical Experience. Essays and a Discussion* (New York: Holmes & Meier, 1981), 157.

68. Sack, *Human Territoriality*, 20.

69. Ibid., 19.

70. J. Améry, "In the Waiting Room of Death. Reflections on the Warsaw Ghetto" in J. Améry, *Radical Humanism. Selected Essays* (translated and edited by S. & S. Rosenfeld) (Bloomington: Indiana University Press, 1984), 23.

71. Y. Tuan, *Landscapes of Fear* (Oxford: Blackwell, 1980), 6.

72. Browning, "Genocide and Public Health," 26.

73. E. Apfelbaum cited in R. Bertell, *No Immediate Danger. Prognosis for a Radioactive Earth* (London: The Women's Press, 1988), 4.

74. On the contradictory role of smuggling see Corni, *Hitler's Ghettos*, 332–33.

75. Cited in Dawidowicz, *The War against the Jews*, 265.

76. Cited in ibid., 272.

77. Hilberg, *The Destruction*, 48.

78. R. L. Braham, *The Politics of Genocide. The Holocaust in Hungary* (New York: Columbia University Press, 1981), vol. 1, 30. A revised edition was published in 1994 (New York: Columbia University Press, 1994). Where there are significant changes, I have tended to cite from the revised edition. Otherwise, I have tended to cite from the original 1981 edition.

79. N. Katzburg, *Hungary and the Jews. Policy and Legislation, 1920–1943* (Ramat Gan: Bar-Ilan University Press, 1981), 62.

80. See full text in L. Gonda, *A Zsidóság Magyarországon 1526–1945* (Budapest: Századrég Kiadó, 1992), 276–79.

81. See Cole, "Constructing the 'Jew,'" 23.

82. See full text in Gonda, *A Zsidóság*, 279–92.

83. On the Nuremberg Laws see J. Noakes, "The Development of Nazi Policy towards the German-Jewish '*Mischlinge*,' 1933–1945," *Leo Baeck Institute Yearbook* 34 (1989), 353.

84. See the full text of 1240/1944 Me. in I. Beneschofsky & E. Karsai (eds.), *Vádirat a Nácizmus Ellen 1. 1944 Március 19–Május 15* [hereafter *Vádirat* 1] (Budapest: A Magyar Izraeliták Országos Képviselte Kiadása, 1958), 53–54.

85. See for example the text of 500/1944 Bm. (legislation restricting "Jewish" access to hotels and restaurants) in I. Beneschofsky & E. Karsai (eds.), *Vádirat a Nácizmus Ellen 2. 1944 Május 15–Június 30* [hereafter *Vádirat* 2] (Budapest: A Magyar Izraeliták Országos Képviselte Kiadása, 1960), 86, which I will deal with in more detail in chapter 7.

86. H. L. Gates Jr. (ed.), *"Race," Writing and Difference* (Chicago: University of Chicago Press, 1985), 4.

87. Ibid., 5.

88. For more on Radnóti's story, see D. Dwork & R. J. van Pelt, *Holocaust. A History* (London: John Murray, 2002), xvii–xx.

89. A. Benjamin, *Present Hope. Philosophy, Architecture, Judaism* (London: Routledge, 1997), 111–12.

CHAPTER THREE

1. Hilberg, *The Destruction*, 509.

2. I. Deák, "Could the Jews Have Survived?," *The New York Review of Books* (4 February 1982), 24.

3. Braham, *Politics of Genocide*, vol. 1, 225.

4. N. Kállay, *Hungarian Premier: A Personal Account of a Nation's Struggle in the Second World War* (New York: Columbia University Press, 1954), 114.

5. R. L. Braham, "The Holocaust in Hungary: A Retrospective Analysis" in R. L. Braham with S. Miller (eds.), *The Nazi's Last Victims. The Holocaust in Hungary* (Detroit: Wayne State University Press, 1998), 36.

6. I. Deák in "Genocide in Hungary: An Exchange," *The New York Review of Books* (27 May 1982), 55.

7. See R. L. Braham (ed.), *The Destruction of Hungarian Jewry: A Documentary Account* (New York: World Federation of Hungarian Jews, 1963), vol. 1, document 110, 254–95.

8. I. Deák, "A Fatal Compromise? The Debate over Collaboration and Resistance in Hungary," *East European Politics and Societies* 9, No. 2 (1995), esp. 224, where Deák suggests that "the Final Solution was too important for the Germans to let so many Jews stay alive and even thrive in Central Europe."

9. R. L. Braham, *Eichmann and the Destruction of Hungarian Jewry* (New York: World Federation of Hungarian Jews, 1961), 13.

10. Braham, *Politics of Genocide*, vol. 1, 362.

11. Braham, *Politics of Genocide*, revised edition, vol. 1, 385–86.

12. J. S. Conway, "The Holocaust in Hungary: Recent Controversies and Reconsiderations" in R. L. Braham (ed.), *The Tragedy of Hungarian Jewry: Essays, Documents, Depositions* (New York: Columbia University Press, 1986), 1.

13. C. A. Macartney, *October Fifteenth. A History of Modern Hungary* (Edinburgh: Edinburgh University Press, 1957), vol. 2, 223.

14. Braham, *Destruction*, vol. 1, document 70, 135–42.

15. Ibid., vol. 1, document 78, 160, and Braham, *Politics of Genocide*, vol. 1, 233.

16. Ibid., vol. 1, document 83, 168–69.

17. See the comments of Kállay and Baranyi in ibid., vol. 1, document 86, 175–82, and Braham, *Politics of Genocide*, vol. 1, 230–31.

18. Ibid., vol. 1, document 86, 175–82.

19. Ibid., vol. 1, document 92, 199–200, and Braham, *Politics of Genocide*, vol. 1, 236–37.

20. Braham, *Politics of Genocide*, vol. 1, 239, and B. Vágo, "Germany and the Jewish Policy of the Kállay Government," in R. L. Braham (ed.), *Hungarian-Jewish Studies* II (New York: World Federation of Hungarian Jews, 1969), 195.

21. Cited in Braham, *Politics of Genocide*, vol. 1, 241.

22. Braham, *Destruction*, vol. 1, document 104, 229–42, and Braham, *Politics of Genocide*, vol. 1, 242–43. See also Macartney, *October Fifteenth*, vol. 2, 148.

23. Braham, *Destruction*, vol. 1, document 110, 254–95.

24. J. K. Hoensch, *A History of Modern Hungary 1867–1986* (London: Longman, 1989), 154.

25. Braham, *Politics of Genocide*, vol. 1, 245–6.

26. Ibid., vol. 1, 366.

27. Ibid., vol. 1, 514–5, where Braham also points to the fact that "one of the unpublicized objectives of the German occupation of Hungary was the maximum economic exploitation of the country and the subordination of its industrial and agricultural productive capacity to the interests of the Third Reich."

28. Ibid., vol. 1, 246–47.

29. Ibid., vol. 1, 368.

30. J. F. Montgomery, *Hungary, the Unwilling Satellite* (New York: Devin-Adair, 1947). See

this approach is taken in the postwar memoirs of the interwar political elite—e.g., Kállay, *Hungarian Premier*, xxxiii, who wrote of the German occupying force as "usurpers of power" who "defiled" the nation's ideals along with their "hirelings."

31. T. Sakmyster, "The Search for a *Causus Belli* and the Origins of the Kassa Bombing," *Hungarian Studies Review* X, No. 1 (1983), 54.

32. See I. Pintér, *Hungarian Anti-Fascism and Resistance 1941–1945* (Budapest: Akadémiai Kiado, 1986), 7–8, who refutes the idea that Hungary was forced into a prewar alliance with Germany. Note also the comment of Gy. Juhász, *Hungarian Foreign Policy 1919–1945* (Budapest: Akadémiai Kiado, 1979), 135, that "determined opposition to pro-German policy would have meant co-operation with and reliance on the left-wing, democratic forces, but this was unthinkable to any group of the ruling classes." Gy. Száraz, "The Jewish Question in Hungary: A Historical Retrospective" in R. L. Braham & B. Vago (eds.), *The Holocaust in Hungary: Forty Years Later* (New York: Columbia University Press, 1985), 23, writes of this "last ally" historiography that "it did not matter that Miklós Horthy's regime had not sprouted from the soil of the people, that it had been forced on the nation by foreign arms, and that Szálasi's rule was the end-product of that regime. It seemed pointless to refer to past achievements to counterbalance the recent memory of the Arrow Cross Party. Hungarians had to accept that theirs was the first pre-Fascist regime in Europe and that they were Hitler's last satellites."

33. See J. Erös, "Hungary" in S. J. Woolf (ed.), *European Fascism* (London: Weidenfeld & Nicolson, 1968), 117, who argues that the "Horthy regime began and until its end functioned as a pluralistic system of competing groups and organizations forming an uneasy coalition, yet at the same time engaged in non-violent struggles with each other."

34. Macartney, *October Fifteenth.*, vol. 1, 52.

35. N. Horthy, *Memoirs* (New York: Robert Speller, 1957), 203–4.

36. Hilberg, *The Destruction*, table 64, 511.

37. Braham, *Politics of Genocide*, vol. 1, 222, who writes that "with Kállay's appointment as Prime Minister on March 9, 1942, the political pendulum of the nation began to swing back from Bárdossy's openly pro-German position to Teleki's cautiously Anglophile line."

38. R. L. Braham, "The Jewish Question in German-Hungarian Relations during the Kállay Era," *Jewish Social Studies* XXXIX, No. 3 (1977), 183.

39. Hilberg, *The Destruction*, 511.

40. The impact of the Trianon Treaty upon interwar Hungary was considerable, with revision of the hated treaty the central aim of Hungarian foreign policy—see below.

41. S. B. Vardy, "The Impact of Trianon upon Hungary and the Hungarian Mind: The Nature of Interwar Hungarian Irredentism," *Hungarian Studies Review* X, No. 1 (1983), 29.

42. Ibid., 29–30.

43. E. S. Balogh, "Peaceful Revision: The Diplomatic Road to War," *Hungarian Studies Review* X, No. 1 (1983), 44, notes that between November 1938 and April 1941 "Hungary took full advantage of German patronage, and, in four different stages, doubled her size."

44. N. F. Dreisziger, "Part I The Road to War—Introduction," *Hungarian Studies Review* X, No. 1 (1983), 13.

45. Cited in F. S. Wagner, "Diplomatic Prelude to the Bombing of Kassa: Reflections and Recollections of a Former Diplomat," *Hungarian Studies Review* X, No. 1 (1983), 69–70.

46. Dreisziger, "The Road to War," 14.

47. R. M. Bigler, "*Heil Hitler und Heil Horthy!* The Nature of Hungarian Racist Nationalism and Its Impact on German-Hungarian Relations 1919–1945," *East European Quarterly* VIII, No. 3 (1975), 267, goes as far as to suggest that "the gamble of trying to use Hitler for their purposes resulted in Hungary's involvement and defeat in World War II and its occupation by the Soviet Army."

48. Although there was a dominant postwar conspiracy theory which claimed that the bombing was initiated by a group of Hungarian officers and Germans eager to see Hungary's entry into the war. For the debate on this see Sakmyster, "The Search for a *Causus Belli*," 55–56, and

N. F. Dreisziger, "The Kassa Bombing: The Riddle of Ádám Krúdy," *Hungarian Studies Review* X, No. 1 (1983).

49. Hilberg, *The Destruction*, 511.

50. Braham, *Politics of Genocide*, revised edition, vol. 1, 200.

51. Katzburg, *Hungary and the Jews*, 216.

52. Ibid., 216–18.

53. S. Kertesz, *Diplomacy in a Whirlpool: Hungary between Nazi Germany and Soviet Russia* (Notre Dame, Indiana: University of Notre Dame Press, 1953), 60, argues that the 1939 and 1941 acts were Hungarian attempts "to take some of the wind out of the Nazi sails."

54. V. Ranki, *The Politics of Inclusion and Exclusion. Jews and Nationalism in Hungary* (New York: Holmes and Meier, 1999), 2.

55. R. Patai, *The Jews of Hungary. History, Culture, Psychology* (Detroit: Wayne State University Press, 1996), 489.

56. Cole, "Constructing the 'Jew,'" 22.

57. Ibid., 22–24.

58. Ranki, *Politics of Inclusion*, 2 [emphasis mine].

59. Ibid., 136.

60. Ibid., 209.

61. Gy. Ránki, "The Germans and the Destruction of Hungarian Jewry" in Braham & Vago, *Forty Years Later*, 88.

62. A. Cohen, "Continuity in the Change: Hungary, 19 March 1944," *Jewish Social Studies* XLVI, No. 2 (1984), 139.

63. See the impact of these in Y. Don, "Economic Implications of the Anti-Jewish Legislation in Hungary" in D. Cesarani (ed.), *Genocide and Rescue. The Holocaust in Hungary 1944* (Oxford: Berg, 1997), 47–76.

64. Kállay cited in M. Y. Herczl, *Christianity and the Holocaust of Hungarian Jewry* (translated by J. Lerner) (New York: New York University Press, 1993), 146. See 146–64 for more on this legislation. For Kállay's speech advocating the "removal of the Jews," see 152.

65. T. Majsai, "A Körösmezei Zsidódeportálás 1941-ben," *A Ráday-Gyüjtemény Évkönyve* (1986) and J. Fejes, "On the History of the Mass Deportations from Carpatho-Ruthenia in 1941" in R. L. Braham & A. Pók (eds.), *The Holocaust in Hungary. Fifty Years Later* (New York: Columbia University Press, 1997).

66. For more details, see R. L. Braham, *The Hungarian Labor Service System, 1939–1945* (Boulder: East European Quarterly and Columbia University Press, 1977).

67. Braham, *Politics of Genocide*, vol. 1, 509.

68. Ibid., vol. 2, 743.

69. Ibid., vol. 2, 743.

70. Y. Jelinek, "The Holocaust and the Internal Policies of the Nazi Satellites in Eastern Europe: A Comparative Study" in M. R. Marrus (ed.), *The Nazi Holocaust. Historical Articles on the Destruction of European Jews 4. The "Final Solution" Outside Germany* (Westport, Conn.: Meckler, 1989), vol. 1, 291. He also suggests, 293, that "the Holocaust in the satellite states was an outgrowth of the local needs no less than Nazi pressure (or dictate)."

71. Hilberg, *The Destruction*, 527, writes of "an army of German policy makers, supervisors, co-ordinators, and advisers" who "*swarmed* into the country" [emphasis mine].

72. Braham, *Politics of Genocide*, vol. 1, footnote 8, 397.

73. Ibid., vol. 1, 387, and Braham, *Destruction*, vol. 1, document 113, 302–4.

74. Ibid., vol. 1, 388, e.g., *Legationsrat* Adolf Hezinger (until May 1944—his place was taken by Grell from May onwards)—expert on treatment of "foreign" Jews, Franz von Adamovic-Waagstaetten, SS *Hauptsturmführer* Ballensiefen—expert on antisemitic propaganda.

75. Braham, *Eichmann*, 14.

76. Ibid., 14.

77. Ibid., 7.

78. Ibid., 8.

79. Ibid., 18–19.

80. In these later writings, Braham also pays attention to the role of the Jewish leadership in Hungary, no doubt in part as a result of Arendt's comments made in the wake of the Eichmann trial.

81. R. L. Braham, "Foreword" in Ranki, *Politics of Inclusion*, xii.

82. Ránki, "The Germans," 77.

83. Cited in Herczl, *Christianity and the Holocaust*, 185.

84. E. Karsai, "Deportation and Administration in Hungary," in Braham & Vago (eds.), *Forty Years Later*, 109.

85. B. Vago, "The Hungarians and the Destruction of the Hungarian Jews," in Braham & Vago, *Forty Years Later*, 94.

86. Braham, *Politics of Genocide*, vol. 1, 533.

87. Ibid., vol. 1, 532.

88. Vago, "The Hungarians," 97.

89. Karsai, "Deportation and Administration," 121.

90. Molnár, *Zsidósors*, 54.

91. Ibid., 54.

92. R. W. Seton-Watson, *Racial Problems in Hungary* (London 1908), 239. Law XLII of 1870 lays the basis for county autonomy in post-Compromise Hungary.

93. Ibid., 245, who writes of the increasing power of central government "to override local opinion." See also A. C. Janos, *The Politics of Backwardness in Hungary 1825–1945* (Princeton, Princeton University Press, 1982), 96, where he describes the 1886 legislation as "reducing the elective principle to a sham."

94. Karsai, "Deportation and Administration," 107.

95. Á. Ságvári (ed.), *Budapest. The History of a Capital* (Budapest: Corvina Press, 1975), 55.

96. J. Szekeres (ed.), *Források Budapest Történetéhez III. 1919–1945* (Budapest: Budapest Főváros Levéltárának Kiadványa, 1972), document 255, 534.

97. Ibid., document 252, 530.

98. Ibid., 608.

99. See, e.g., *Függetlenség* XII (16 April 1944).

100. *Magyarság* XX (16 April 1944), 4.

101. P. Sipos, "Hungary: The Occupied Satellite" in W. Benz, J. H. ten Cate & G. Otto (eds.), *Anpassung, Kollaboration, Widerstand. Kollecktive Reaktionen auf die Okkupation* (Berlin: Metropol Verlag, 1996), 255–56, who notes that "the Germans were satisfied with personnel changes in top positions; through the *Gleichschaltung* of political life they were able to operate the Hungarian state apparatus according to their own needs. The Lord Mayor of Budapest was replaced, two-thirds of the mayors of all Hungarian towns . . . "

102. Karsai, "Deportation and Administration," 109. Keledy himself was replaced as lord mayor in the aftermath of the 15 October Nyilas coup by Gyula Mohay who was appointed lord mayor on November 9. This practice of the replacement of lord mayors was not mirrored at the mayoral/deputy mayoral scale. Thus Doroghi Farkas continued as mayor of Budapest after the 15 October coup.

103. Cited in Molnár, *Zsidósors*, 39.

104. Ibid., 39.

105. Ibid., 77.

106. Ibid., 39.

107. Ibid., 39–40.

108. *Függetlenség* XII (21 May 1944). That Doroghi Farkas was appointed, rather than elected, points to the increased power of the center.

109. Braham, *Politics of Genocide*, vol. 1, 500.

110. Szekeres, *Források*, document, 224, 477.

111. *Új Magyarság* XI, No. 139 (22 June 1944).

112. Ibid.

113. Szekeres, *Források*, 609.

114. O.L., P1434 16 cs. (Endre László) 1944 IV/15 (15 April 1944).

115. "Diary of Ottó Komoly" in R. L. Braham (ed.), *Hungarian-Jewish Studies* III (New York: World Federation of Hungarian Jews, 1973), 230.

116. Cited in Vago, "The Hungarians," 102.

117. M. Lackó, *Arrow-Cross Men, National Socialists 1935–1944* (Budapest: Akadémiai Kiadó, 1969), 44.

118. I. Bibó, "The Jewish Question in Hungary after 1944" in I. Bibó, *Democracy, Revolution, Self-Determination. Selected Writings* (edited by Károly Nagy, translated by András Boros-Kazai) (New York: Columbia University Press, 1991), 163.

119. Ibid., 164.

120. Ibid., 165.

121. Braham, *Politics of Genocide*, vol. 1, 535.

122. Cohen, "Continuity in the Change," 131.

123. Braham, *Destruction*, vol. 1, xviii.

124. Braham, "A Retrospective Analysis," 38.

125. Braham, *Politics of Genocide*, vol. 1, 529, notes that "since Endre would not be formally appointed Secretary of State until 9 April, the document (no. 6163/1944. res. of the Ministry of Interior) was issued secretly under the signature of Baky."

126. Decree no. 1.610/1944 M.E., 28 April 1944.

127. Budapest's "Jews" ultimately escaped mass deportation to Auschwitz—see below, chapter eight.

128. For more on this see T. Cole, "Budapest 1944: Changing the Shape of the Ghetto" in J. K. Roth (ed.), *Remembering for the Future. The Holocaust in an Age of Genocide. Vol. 1. History* (Houndmills: Palgrave, 2001), esp. 198–201.

129. Macartney, *October Fifteenth*, vol. 2, 285.

130. Ibid., vol. 2, 279 [emphasis mine].

131. Ibid., vol. 2, 285.

132. Ibid., vol. 2, 280.

133. Braham, *Politics of Genocide*, vol 1, 529. See also M. D. Fenyo, *Hitler, Horthy and Hungary. German-Hungarian Relations, 1941–1944* (New Haven: Yale University Press, 1972), 183, who describes it as "the order for the deportation of the Hungarian Jews."

134. Braham, *Politics of Genocide*, vol. 1, 529–30.

135. Cf. J. Lévai, *Black Book on the Martyrdom of Hungarian Jewry* (Zurich: The Central European Times Publishing Company, 1948), 112–13 and J. Lévai, *Eichmann in Hungary. Documents* (Budapest: Pannonia Press, 1961), 72–73.

136. Lévai, *Eichmann*, Preface.

137. Ibid., 71.

138. Although it would seem that limited deportation was envisaged—presumably the limited supply of Hungarian Jewish labor that was agreed upon by German and Hungarian political elites—Braham, *Destruction*, vol. 1, document 134, 342.

139. See Fenyo, *Hitler*, 183, who cites selectively from the document in support of his thesis that it amounts to "the order for the deportation of the Hungarian Jews."

140. Braham, *Politics of Genocide*, vol. 1, 529–31.

141. The exception was to be the housing of "Jews dangerous from the point of view of state security" in special camps rather than urban ghettos.

142. Braham, *Politics of Genocide*, vol. 1, 558.

143. Ibid., vol. 1, 558.

144. Ibid., vol. 1, 558.

145. See text in *Vádirat* 1, 244.

146. O.L., K27, box 260 (Council of Ministers minute book, 26 April 1944), 95.

147. Ibid., 94.

148. *Esti Ujság* 9, (28 April 1944), 2.

149. The war compounded a prewar housing shortage, especially in Budapest—see Raoul Wallenberg Project Archive [hereafter R.W.P.A.], FC2/22–554.

150. Patai, *The Jews of Hungary*, 520.

CHAPTER FOUR

1. The paperwork of the perpetrators regarding these events does not survive in the archives. There is one document—610926/1944.XVII—dated 4 April 1944 and signed by Dr. József Szentmiklósy of the city's housing department, reproduced in *Vádirat* 1, 100–101. This, however, is reproduced from Munkácsi's postwar writings rather than from the missing original. Both Munkácsi's and Lévai's postwar works are problematic. Whilst intended as part histories and part collections of documents, the "documents" presented need to be handled carefully, as a number of historians have pointed out. Vágo described both as "works partly based on questionable documentary evidence"—B. Vágo, "Budapest Jewry in the Summer of 1944: Otto Komoly's Diaries," *Yad Vashem Studies* VIII (1970), 81–82. See also my comments in chapter 5, below. Both Munkácsi and Lévai are best treated as postwar accounts with all of the associated problems of recall and interpretation. Those issues need to be borne in mind when assessing the other postwar accounts, which I have used to re-create the events of 4 April. See footnote 3 below.

2. B. Klein, "The *Judenrat*," *Jewish Social Studies* XXII, No. 1 (1960), 32.

3. There is agreement over the figure of 500 within 24 hours in the postwar account of Council President Samu Stern—S. Stern, " 'A Race with Time': A Statement" in Braham, *Hungarian-Jewish Studies* III, 23—and the report written by the leaders of the Orthodox community Diámant, Freudiger, and Link who escaped to Romania in August 1944—S. Diámant, F. Freudiger & Gy. Link, "Report on Hungary: March 19–August 9, 1944" in Braham, *Hungarian-Jewish Studies* III, 89. These details are also in Lévai, *Black Book*, 95–97 and E. Munkácsi, "Hogy Történt?," *Új Élet* II, No. 5 (31 January 1946) & II, No. 6 (7 February 1946) cited in *Vádirat* 1, 99–102. A figure of 500 apartments in 24 hours is given in K. Frojimovics, G. Komoróczy, V. Pusztai & A. Strbik, *Jewish Budapest. Monuments, Rites, History* (Budapest: Central European University Press, 1999), 374, but the date given is 12 April. It is clear that in being given the role of identifying which apartments were to be handed over, the Jewish Council was popularly seen as active in appropriation. See T. D. Kramer, "From Utility to Catastrophe. Aspects of Hungarian Jewry's Responses to the Holocaust Process with Particular Reference to the 'Jewish Question' in Hungary" (Ph.D. thesis submitted to the Department of Semitic Studies, The University of Sydney, 1994), 280, who notes that "the intensity of bitterness directed at the Jewish Council because of its requisition activity is indicated by the following grievous joke, which contemporaneously swept the Jewish community: At 3 A.M. a furious hammering erupts on the door of a Jewish household in Budapest. '*Achtung*! Open immediately, It's the Gestapo.' 'Oh, thank goodness,' sighs the householder fumbling with his key. 'For a moment I was terrified it was the Jewish Council.' "

4. Macartney, *October Fifteenth*, vol. 2, 262, suggested that the "psychological and political effects of the raids" were "profound."

5. *Fuggetlenség* XII, No. 82 (13 April 1944).

6. The requisitioning groups were to be made up of two "Jewish" employees of one of the communal organizations, one policeman, and one teacher. The teacher was specifically given the task of ensuring that the apartment was appropriately furnished and equipped. See 610 926/1944. XVII, *Vádirat* 1, 100–101.

7. Munkácsi cited in *Vádirat* 1, 102 and Diámant, Freudiger & Link, "Report," 89, although Lévai, *Black Book*, 94–97, and Klein, "The *Judenrat*," 32, give a total figure of 2,500. Stern, "Race," 23, suggests that the new total was 1, 000. Diámant, Freudiger & Link go on to claim that ultimately "4,500 Jewish dwellings were requisitioned in this manner," 89.

8. *Függetlenség* XII, No. 79 (7 April 1944).

9. Ibid.

10. Diámant, Freudiger & Link, "Report," 89.

11. O.L., I 19, letters to the mayoral housing affairs division from the VIII and IX district councilors—the latter is designated 33.820/1944 (21 July 1944).

12. *Magyarság* XX (16 April 1944), 4.

13. Ibid., 4.

14. O.L., K 148, 3410 cs. See also *Vádirat* 1, 301–3. The copy in *Vádirat* is unsigned and therefore reckoned by the editors to be compiled by a committee—probably that of the Budapest housing affairs department. The cover of the original, however, is signed by Endre, showing that it was received and checked by him in the Interior Ministry on 10 May 1944.

15. It is somewhat surprising that Braham—*Politics of Genocide*, vol. 2, 733–34—does not reference these plans, despite the document relating to them being reproduced in *Vádirat* 1.

16. For the term "dispersed ghettoization" see T. Cole & G. Smith, "Ghettoization and the Holocaust: Budapest 1944," *Journal of Historical Geography* 21, No. 3 (1995), 301, 305–10.

17. Braham, *Politics of Genocide*, vol. 1, 538–87.

18. Ibid., vol. 2, table 19.1, 607.

19. Siting ghetto areas close to railway stations can of course be interpreted rather differently. For Braham, the initial ghettoization plans adopted in Hungary—at the 4 April meeting—drew on the Polish model. He argues—ibid., vol. 1, 529—that "In launching the ghettoization and deportation program, the participants at the meeting were partially guided by the Nazi experience in other parts of German-occupied Europe, which reflected the directives of Reinhard Heydrich of 21 September 1939. Heydrich's directives, addressed to the *Einsatzgruppen* in occupied Poland, stipulated that the first prerequisite for the implementation of the 'ultimate goal' was the speedy 'concentration of the Jews from the country to the larger cities.' The number of concentration points was to be as low as possible and care was to be taken that they be 'located either at railroad junctions or at least along a railroad.'" However, Braham fails to offer explicit evidence to back up this claim. In the case of Budapest at least, it would seem that geostrategic concerns were more significant in determining siting close to railway stations and lines.

20. *Magyarság* XX (16 April 1944), 4.

21. O.L., K148, 3410 cs.

22. Ibid.

23. Ibid.

24. Ibid. The opening paragraph specifies that the end result should be that in one house only Christians or Jews will live.

25. Ibid. Four questions were to be asked of the census data: How many "Jewish" inhabitants lived in Budapest? How many "Jewish" flats were rented? How many rooms did these flats have? and, where were these flats situated in the city?

26. Braham, *Politics of Genocide*, vol. 1, 558.

27. O.L., I 17, Letter from the Lord Mayor to the Interior Minister—Biz. 323.1944 (31 May 1944), 2. See also *Vádirat* 2, 113, 114–19.

28. Ibid., 1.

29. O.L., I 17, Letter from the Lord Mayor to the Mayor (1 June 1944).

30. Ibid.

31. Macartney, *October Fifteenth*, vol. 2, 285–86.

CHAPTER FIVE

1. The official government news agency, M.T.I., made an announcement to that effect. See *Esti Ujság* 9 (1 June 1944) and posters pasted up in the city spelling out how and why registration was taking place. See *Vádirat* 2, 113–14, and photograph facing 97.

2. The number of apartments within the building were to be recorded, along with the num-

ber of rooms within each apartment and whether apartments faced onto the street or onto the courtyard.

3. See, e.g., the forms attached to B.F.L., IX/2786.1944/147793 (17 June 1944) re. IV Váci u. 7, and 147794 (17 June 1944) re. IV Váci u. 50. See the photograph of the form for IV Irányi u. 1 in *Vádirat* 2, facing 112.

4. *Esti Ujság* 9 (13 June 1944), which reported that the choice of approximately 2,800 apartment blocks was made "on the basis of the information" gathered in the 1–2 June mass registration.

5. B.F. L., IV/1402b.1944—498, (10 June 1944) and see also *Vádirat* 2, 162–64.

6. *Esti Ujság* 9 (16 June 1944).

7. *Vádirat* 2, 162–64.

8. See footnote 3 above. It has thus far not been possible to locate the original registration forms, nor confirm whether they have or have not been destroyed.

9. See in another context the use of the marks "-", "+", and "?" penned onto forms by "experts" involved in selecting patients for euthanasia; see D. de Mildt, *In the Name of the People: Perpetrators of Genocide in the Reflection of Their Post-war Prosecution in West Germany. The "Euthanasia" and "Aktion Reinhard" Trial Cases* (The Hague: Martinus Nijhoff Publishers, 1996), 57–58.

10. B.F.L., IX/2786.1944/147794 (17 June 1944).

11. O.L., K148, 1200 cs.

12. 14 of the 20 tenants were "Jewish" according to the Jewish Council list.

13. 18 of the 25 tenants were "Jewish" according to the Jewish Council list.

14. Braham's observation—in *Politics of Genocide*, vol. 2, 734—that the selection of properties for "Jewish" use "was based on a number of criteria, of which the most important was the percentage of Jews residing in them: a building in which close to 50% of the tenants were Jewish was to be identified as a Yellow-Star house. Other major criteria were the condition and location of the buildings, and the background and influence of their Christian tenants" would seem to be about right, although the last criteria are unsubstantiated.

15. *Esti Ujság* 9 (13 June 1944).

16. The total is my calculation drawn up after comparing all existing lists in the press, on posters and in *Budapesti Közlöny*. In the press, a figure of 2,681 houses was reported in *Függetlenség* XII, No. 134 (16 June 1944).

17. See for a parallel example S. Liszewski, "The Role of the Jewish Community in the Organization of Urban Space in Lódz," *Polin. A Journal of Polish-Jewish Studies* 6 (1991), 30.

18. For the 1941 census results, see *Budapest Székesfõváros Statisztikai Évkönyve* XXXII (Budapest: Budapest Székesfõváros Statisztikai Hivatalának Kiadása, 1944). Note that "Jew" was used as a religious category in the interwar censuses and thus did not equate fully with the racialized category of "Jew" ("yellow-starred") being used with ghettoization.

19. In 1941, Pest was home to just over three-quarters of the city's total population.

20. The VI and VII district "Jewish town" had been home to 80.4% of the Pest "Jewry" in 1820 and 70% in 1870. By 1910, it was the home to 60% of Budapest's "Jews" and 46% in 1941—see Gy. Zeke, "A Budapesti Zsidóság Lakóhelyi Szegregációja a Tõkés Modernizáció Korszakában (1867–1941)" in P. Horváth (ed.), *Hét Évtized a Hazai Zsidóság Életében* I (Budapest: M.T.A. Filozófiai Intézet Kiadása, 1990), 169–70, and P. Bihari, "A Magyarországiv Zsidóság Helyzete a Zsidótörvényektõl a Deportálásig" in P. Horváth (ed.), *Hét Évtized a Hazai Zsidóság Életében* II (Budapest: M.T.A. Filozófiai Intézet Kiadása, 1990), 31–32. The lower figure for the VI and VII district in 1941 can be seen as largely a result of the growth of the "Jewish" V district population. These four districts—the V, VI, VII, and VIII—were home to a little over four-tenths of the city's total population.

21. See the statistics from 1920 at a subdistrict level in *Budapest Székesfõváros Statisztikai Évkönyve*. At this date, the city was divided into 10 rather than 14 main administrative districts.

22. The average "Jewish" population density in Buda in 1920 was 9.5%

23. The average "Lutheran" population density in Buda in 1920 was 5.6%.

24. The average "Reformed" population density in Buda in 1920 was 11.1%.

25. The average "Catholic" population density in Buda in 1920 was 71.9%.

26. The average "Jewish" population density in Pest in 1920 was 26.7%.

27. The average "Lutheran" population density in Pest in 1920 was 4.6%.

28. The average "Reformed" population density in Pest in 1920 was 10.8%.

29. The average "Catholic" population density in Pest in 1920 was 55.6%.

30. Compare for example the central VII and outlying XIV districts of Budapest. In 1941, the majority of the 1,593 apartment buildings in the VII district housed 51–150 persons. In comparison, in the XIV district, the majority of the 6,458 buildings housed 3–10 persons. *Budapest Székesföváros Statisztikai Évkönyve* XXX (Budapest, 1942), table 8, 4.

31. This figure must be taken as a rough estimate given that the statistics of numbers of properties date from 1941. It is safe to assume that the number of properties in 1944 was not identical, although the degree of new building taking place during the course of the war was surely not as marked as in the interwar period.

32. The comparison of course does not work fully, given the different dates. See footnote 31 above.

33. See the text of Bp. Szék. Polg. 147501/1944.IX, *Vádirat* 2, 203–8.

34. B.F.L., IV/1402b.1944/147616 (16 June 1944) and attached notes.

35. N. M. Nagy-Talavera, "The Second World War as Mirrored in the Hungarian Fascist Press," *East European Quarterly* IV, No. 2 (1971), 201.

36. P. Róbert, "A Holokauszt a Magyar Sajtóban" in R.L. Braham (ed.), *Tanulmányok a Holokausztról* (Budapest: Balassi Kiadó, 2001), 54.

37. See *Magyarság* (5 July 1944), cited in ibid., 54.

38. Braham, *Politics of Genocide*, vol. 1, 486, noted that "the first air attacks on Budapest brought forth a wave of anti-Jewish feeling, which made it easier for the authorities to bring about the mass evacuation of Jewish apartments for the benefit of the Christian raid victims. Leaflets were scattered throughout the capital calling for the execution of 100 Jews for each Hungarian killed by bombing." See also reference to this in Veesenmayer's second report of 14 December 1943 in Braham, *Destruction*, vol. 1, document 110, 254–95.

39. *Esti Ujság* 9, No. 77 (5 April 1944), 3.

40. Frojimovics et al., *Jewish Budapest*, 374.

41. Article of 15 May 1944 cited in Nagy-Talavera, "The Second World War," 202. See also *A Nép* (20 July 1944) cited in Róbert, "A Holokauszt a Magyar Sajtoban," 55.

42. Macartney, *October Fifteenth*, vol. 2, 263; Braham, *Politics of Genocide*, vol. 1, 486.

43. I. Domán, *A Györi Izraelita Hitközség Története 1930–47* (Budapest: A Magyar Izraeliták Országos Képviseletének Kiadása, 1979), 51; J. Schweitzer, *A Pécsi Izraelita Hitközség Története* (Budapest: A Magyar Izraeliták Országos Képviseletének Kiadása, 1966), 143.

44. *Magyarság* XX (16 April 1944), 4.

45. Ibid., 4.

46. *Esti Ujság* 9 (13 June 1944).

47. Ibid.

48. Stern, "A Race with Time," 23–24 [emphasis mine]. Stern's words are adopted uncritically by Kramer, "From Utility to Catastrophe," 249–50, who claims that "In their defensive measures, the Council also successfully utilized the commonly accepted element of Nazi ideology which claimed that the Allies were fighting the war on behalf of the Jews. By convincing the authorities that creation of a ghetto in Budapest would permit the Allies to bomb the rest of the metropolis with impunity, the creation of a dangerous concentration of Jews in the city was delayed for some five months, until the Szálasi junta's inescapable order of 29 November."

49. Klein, "The *Judenrat*," 32.

50. Diamánt et al., "Report on Hungary," 90–91.

51. Ibid., 112—"As the naive idea prevailed that the English and Americans would bombard only the quarters not inhabited by Jews, the plans had to include so-called Jewish houses in every quarter of the town."

52. R. Wallenberg, *Letters and Dispatches 1924–1944* (translated by K. Board) (New York: Arcade Publishing, 1995), 237.

53. Kramer, "From Utility to Catastrophe," footnote 235, 425, Kramer notes that "agreeing with Dr. Cohen's assessment, [see below] this writer has restricted Lévai to confirmation purposes or where no alternative source exists. As expected, Gergely deprecates Lévai's publications, calling them 'journalistic quick-books, money making operations.'"

54. A. Cohen, *The Halutz Resistance in Hungary 1942–1944* (New York: Columbia University Press, 1986), footnote 1, 249.

55. E. Munkácsi, *Hogyan Történt? Adatok és Okmányok a Magyar Zsidóság Tragédiájához* (Budapest: Renaissance Kiadás, 1947), 129–30.

56. Braham, *Politics of Genocide*, vol. 2, 732.

57. Lévai, *Black Book*, 184.

58. Macartney, *October Fifteenth*, vol. 2, 284–85.

59. Hilberg, *The Destruction*, 537.

60. Macartney, *October Fifteenth*, vol. 1, ix, notes that he was unable to footnote the relevant press reports as "to give the references each time in such cases would mean filling half my pages half-full with footnotes."

61. Hilberg, *The Destruction* (second edition), 1231

62. T. Berkes, "Napilapok a Zsidókérdésröl. 1944 Március-Július," *Világosság* XXXIV, No. 6 (1993), 69.

63. Gy. Juhász, "Some Aspects of Relations between Hungary and Germany during the Second World War," in Gy. Ránki (ed.), *Hungarian History—World History* (Budapest: Akadémiai Kiadó, 1984), 212.

64. Ibid., 211.

65. Macartney, *October Fifteenth*, vol. 2, 272.

66. Ibid., 273.

67. Cf. *Magyarság* XX (16 April 1944), 4, and *Magyarság* XX (9 July 1944) (the latter is cited in Nagy-Talavera, "The Second World War," 201, and also in Róbert, "A Holokauszt a Magyar Sajtóban," 55).

68. Article in *Nemzeti Figyelo* (11 July 1944), cited in Nagy-Talavera, "The Second World War," 201.

69. Article in *Magyarság* (9 July 1944), cited in ibid., 201.

70. Y. Bauer, "Conclusion: The Holocaust in Hungary: Was Rescue Possible?" in Cesarani, *Genocide and Rescue*, 203–4.

71. See e.g. M.T.I. press statement in *Függetlenség* XII, No. 131 (13 June 1944).

72. M.T.I. statement reported in *Esti Ujság* 9 (12 June 1944).

73. *Esti Ujság* 9 (13 June 1944).

74. B.F.L., IV/1480.1944/018325 (21 June 1944).

75. Ibid.

76. According to the 1941 census. In reality, the population in 1944 would no doubt have been less than this, particularly with the absence of "Jewish" males of military age serving in labor battalions.

77. B.F.L., IV/1480.1944/018325 (21 June 1944).

78. Ibid.

79. Braham, *Politics of Genocide*, vol. 2, 736–37, drawing upon J. Lévai, *Zsidósors Magyarországon* (Budapest: Magyar Téka, 1948), 182–83. See also *Vádirat* 2, 201.

80. *A Budapesti Egységes Hálózat Betürendes Távbeszélö Névsora* (Budapest: A Magyar Király Postavezérigazgatóság, January 1943), 522.

81. *Magyarországi Zsidók Lapja* 6, 25 (22 June 1944), 4 and *Vádirat* 2, 304–5.

82. B.F.L., IV/1480.1944/018325 (21 June, 1944)—attached report on XI Kikinda köz 9 compiled by Szepesváry.

83. Braham, *Politics of Genocide*, vol. 2, 736.

84. Stern, "Race against Time," 24. For more on the supposed role of Szentmiklóssy in tempering the nature of ghettoization in Budapest see Braham, *Politics of Genocide*, vol. 2, 733–34, Munkácsi, *Hogyan Történt?*, 130–31, Lévai, *Zsidósors*, 163. Such claims are seemingly impossible to either substantiate or dismiss from the documents available from the archives.

85. Diámant et. al., "Report on Hungary," 112. See also F. Freudiger, "Five Months" in Braham, *The Tragedy of Hungarian Jewry*, 265.

86. Lévai, *Zsidósors*, 182.

87. Á. Ságvári, *A Budapesti Zsidóság Holocaustja 1944* (Budapest: The Jewish Agency for Israel, 1994), see text on p. 8 and lists on pp. 18–20. In combining the two lists, Ságvári ignores the differences between the two, and fails to note that the sheets for the XIV district are missing from one list, which contains only 458—and not 525—houses. Sagvári fails to reproduce the ratios of "starred" flats included on the original lists, which is perhaps the most useful material in the lists.

88. *Esti Ujság* 9 (20 June 1944).

89. Ibid.

90. *Esti Ujság* 9 (20 June 1944) & (21 June 1944).

91. *Esti Ujság* 9 (21 June 1944).

CHAPTER SIX

1. Lévai, *Zsidósors*, 166.

2. *Új Magyarság* XI (22 June 1944). See J. Lévai, *Fekete Könyv a Magyar Zsidóság Szenvedéseiről* (Budapest: Officina, 1946), 155, writes of "scores of complaints" being submitted, and Braham, *Politics of Genocide*, vol. 2, 852, of the city office dealing with the designations being "besieged by petitioners requesting changes from the original designations." Although a significant number, this total should be set in the context of the sheer size of the city—as I've noted, there were some 36,000 separate buildings in Budapest—as well as the scope of the policy of dispersed ghettoization. For the surviving petitions see B.F.L., IX/1867.1944, IX/1870.1944, IX/2026.1944, IX/2027.1944, IX/2030.1944, IX/2031.1944, IX/2035.1944, IX/2037.1944, IX/2040.1944, IX/2041.1944, IX/2042.1944, IX/2048.1944, IX/2102.1944, IX/2105.1944, IX/2114.1944, IX/2115.1944, IX/2116.1944, IX/2339.1944, IX/2747.1944, and especially IX/2781.1944, IX/2782.1944, IX/2783.1944, IX/2784.1944, IX/2785.1944, IX/2786.1944, IX/2787.1944, IX/2789.1944, IX/2790.1944, IX/2791.1944, IX/2792.1944. See also O.L., I collection—films I 15–17.

3. Braham, *Politics of Genocide* (revised edition), vol. 2, 852.

4. B.F.L., IV/1402b.1944/148484 (22 June 1944).

5. B.F.L., IX/1867.1944/147519, 2027/148332, 2031/148369, 2116/148095, 2781/147845, 2782/147966, 2783/148001, 2783/148075, 2784/148115, 2784/148128, 2784/148129, 2784/148145, 2784/148191, 2785/147686, 2785/147696, 2787/147983, 2787/148091, 2789/148403, 2789/148414, 2789/148419, 2791/148794.

6. F. Glatz, "Hungary, 1944: Questions of Historical Science and of the Citizen" in Braham & Pók (eds.), *Fifty Years Later*, 27.

7. Braham, *Politics of Genocide* (revised edition), vol. 2., 1058.

8. Ibid., 1058–60.

9. See my comments on this historiography in chapter 3 above.

10. J. M. Isaacson, *Seed of Sarah. Memoirs of a Survivor* (Urbana: University of Illinois Press, 1990), 42–46, 53–54.

11. G. M. Gabor, *My Destiny. Survivor of the Holocaust* (Arcadia, Calif.: Amen Publishing Company, 1981), 25.

12. B.F.L., IX/2783.1944/148001 (19 June 1944).

13. B.F.L., IX/2789.1944/148414 (21 June 1944).

14. B.F.L., IX/2783.1944/148001 (19 June 1944).

15. B.F.L., IX/2789.1944/148414 (21 June 1944).

16. B.F.L., IX/2783.1944/148001 (19 June 1944).

17. B.F.L., IX/2789.1944/148414 (21 June 1944).

18. B.F.L., IX/2784.1944/148145 (20 June 1944).

19. B.F.L., IX/2031.1944/148369 (21 June 1944).

20. B.F.L., IX/2784.1944/148145 (20 June 1944).

21. B.F.L., IX/2787.1944/147983 (19 June 1944).

22. B.F.L., IX/1867.1944/147519 (13 June 1944).

23. B.F.L., IX/2787.1944/147983 (19 June 1944).

24. B.F.L., IX/2784.1944/148145 (20 June 1944).

25. B.F.L., IX/2789.1944/148419 (21 June 1944).

26. B.F.L., IX/2784.1944/148129 (19 June 1944).

27. B.F.L., IX/2782.1944/147966 (19 June 1944).

28. B.F.L., IX/2785.1944/147686 (17 June 1944).

29. B.F.L., IX/2791.1944/148794 (28 June 1944).

30. B.F.L., IX/2787.1944/148091 (19 June 1944).

31. B.F.L., IX/2116.1944/148095 (19 June 1944).

32. B.F.L., IX/2789.1944/148403 (21 June 1944).

33. B.F.L., IX/2027.1944/148332 (21 June 1944).

34. B.F.L., IX/2789.1944/148403 (21 June 1944).

35. B.F.L., IX/2027.1944/148332 (21 June 1944).

36. B.F.L., IX/2784.1944/148128 (19 June 1944).

37. B.F.L., IX/2789.1944/148419 (21 June 1944).

38. B.F.L., IX/2784.1944/148115 (19 June 1944).

39. B.F.L., IX/2784.1944/148191 (19 June 1944).

40. B.F.L., IX/2783.1944/148075 (19 June 1944). See also IX/2785.1944/147696 (17 June 1944).

41. B.F.L., IX/2781.1944/147845 (19 June 1944).

42. V Koháry u. 16, VI Eötvös u. 42, IX Ráday u. 37.

43. V Pannonia u. 44, VI Lendvay u. 15, VIII Rákoczi út 51.

44. V Szent István Park 10, VII Erzsebet körut 15, VII Hársfa u. 57.

45. VI Király u. 82.

46. B.F.L., IX/2789.1944/148403 (21 June 1944).

47. B.F.L., IX/2784.1944/148145 (20 June 1944).

48. O.L., I. 18. See also *Vádirat* 2, 290–93.

49. B.F.L., IX/2787.1944/147983.

50. B.F.L., IV/1480.1944/018325 (21 June 1944) plus attached reports.

51. Ibid.

52. In the report, the heading for the column of "Christian" relocations is "Christian families moving in" despite the individual reports compiled by investigators detailing "Jewish" families moving in and "Christian" families moving out.

53. Although for some reason, two of the designated properties—Ercsi út 96 and Györök u. 21—were omitted from the list despite investigations being undertaken.

54. B.F.L., IV/1480.1944/018325 (21 June 1944).

55. Ibid.

56. Ibid.

57. *Esti Ujság* 9 (21 June 1944).

58. See the almost identical statements printed in *Függetlenség* XII, No. 140 (23 June 1944) and *Összetartás* II, No. 140 (23 June 1944).

59. B.F.L., IX/2782.1944/147966 (19 June 1944)—see notes on cover.

60. Braham's translation of the legislation in Braham, *Politics of Genocide*, vol. 2, 737–38 [emphasis mine].

61. Lévai, *Fekete Könyv*, 156; Braham, *Politics of Genocide*, vol. 2, 735.

62. New Hungarian Central Archives [hereafter Ú.M.K.L.], XXXIII–5–c–1, XI.23.

63. The total is my calculation drawn up after comparing all existing lists in the press, on posters and in *Budapesti Közlöny*.

64. The figure on 16 June is 42.90%. Cf. 61.70% on 22 June.

65. The figure is 62.54%.

66. The figure is 22.05%.

67. The figure is 11.29%. In the 1941 census, 9.31% of the city's "Jewish" population lived in Buda and 90.69% in Pest.

68. B.F.L., IV/1480.1944/018325 (21 June 1944).

69. Braham, *Politics of Genocide*, vol. 1, 735.

70. If all 101 "non-Jewish" families chose to stay put—as they were entitled to after 22 June—then the remaining apartments would have an average of 23.16 "Jews" per apartment.

71. B.F.L., IV/1480.1944/018325 (21 June 1944).

72. J. Lukacs, *Budapest 1900. A Historical Profile of a City and Its Culture* (New York: Weidenfeld & Nicolson, 1988), 56. Lukacs notes that in 1900 the average population density in Budapest was 2.6 persons per room.

73. Although it should be noted that whilst most of the recommendations of the VI district councilor for adopting properties as "Jewish" houses were taken on board, they were not when justification was based on the poor quality of the building rather than majority occupation.

74. Cited in Frojimovics et al., *Jewish Budapest*, 382.

75. Ú.M.K.L., XXXIII–5–c–11, the registration form, dated 24 June, details the relocation of the 80-year-old Klein Jakabné from her flat on Budafoki út 16–18 to the yellow-star house at Váli u. 6.

76. See the text of the legislation is translated by Braham, *Politics of Genocide*, vol. 2, 737–38.

77. Ibid., vol. 2, 654.

78. See the text of the petition translated in ibid., vol. 2, 654.

79. Ibid., vol. 2, 655.

80. Macartney, *October Fifteenth*, vol. 2, 285–86, citing document N.G. 2190.

CHAPTER SEVEN

1. A M. Kir. Belügyminiszter 444/1944 Bm. (1 May 1944, published 2 May 1944), *Vádirat* 1, 285–86.

2. O.L., I 18, Bp. Szék. Polg. 224156/1944.XI (12 May 1944).

3. The figure is taken from the 1943 telephone directory, *A Budapesti Egységes Hálózat Betűrendes Távbeszélő Névsora*, 319. This source is of course limited by dint of only listing those premises with a telephone. It thus provides an underestimate of the total number of premises, in particular with smaller premises such as snack bars.

4. A M. Kir. Belügyminiszter 500/1944 Bm. (20 May 1944), "Concerning the restriction on the visiting of restaurants and restaurant-related enterprises by Jews," *Vádirat* 2, 86–87.

5. O.L., I 17, Bp. Szék. Polg. 294507.1944. XV (23 May 1944), 294508.1944. XV. (23 May 1944).

6. O.L., I 17, Bp. Szék. Polg. 294509.1944. XV (24 May 1944).

7. The total numbers of hotels and guest houses are drawn from the 1943 telephone directory. See the comments on the limitations of this source above.

8. A total of 612 restaurants are listed in the 1943 telephone directory. However, six of those designated do not appear in this list. These could be new premises; however, that is highly unlikely. It is much more likely that they were establishments without a telephone. This points to the limitations of the telephone directory as a source.

9. See similar reservations to above. Of the designated coffeehouses, four do not appear in the 1943 telephone directory. Of the designated bars, only one appears in the 1943 telephone directory.

10. A M. Kir. Belügyminiszter 510/1944 Bm. (19 May 1944), *Vádirat* 2, 89–90.

11. See Bp. Szék. Polg. 224. 597/1944. XI (31 May 1944), signed by Deputy Mayor Bódy,

Vádirat 2, 89–91. From an examination of the 1943 city telephone directory and contemporary newspaper cinema columns, it would seem that 76 cinemas were functioning within the city (excluding Újpest, Kispest, etc.) during the period.

12. See translation of regulations of 25 June in Braham, *Politics of Genocide*, vol. 2, 737–38.

13. The number of coffeehouses rose on 13 June from 21 to 23. See below.

14. A M. Kir. Minisztérium 1990/1944 Me. (4 June 1944), *Vádirat* 2, 126–27.

15. Bp. Szék. Polg. 295061/1944.XV (5 June 1944), *Vádirat* 2, 127–28.

16. On national holidays, the hours for purchasing foodstuffs were brought forward to 10 A.M. to noon.

17. A. Barkai, *From Boycott to Annihilation. The Economic Struggle of German Jews, 1933–1943* (Hanover: Brandeis University Press, 1989), 168–69.

18. Hilberg, *The Destruction*, 37, who notes that "Jewish" access to shops was restricted to 3–5 P.M.

19. J. Adler, *The Jews of Paris and the Final Solution. Communal Response and Internal Conflicts, 1940–1944* (Oxford: Oxford University Press, 1987), 41.

20. Barkai, *From Boycott*, 169.

21. Adler, *The Jews of Paris*, 41.

22. Braham, *Politics of Genocide*, vol. 1, 509, although Braham omits this phrase from the 1994 revised edition.

23. Ibid., vol. 1, 511—"On June 4 the Jews were limited to only two hours daily shopping, with the beginning and end of the period during which they would be allowed in stores determined by local authorities."

24. A similar picture of local initiative in Budapest prior to national legislation can be seen in the case of ghettoization. See above chapter 4.

25. B.F.L., IV/1402b.1944/936 (11 May 1944).

26. Ibid. His assumption was, of course, that "Jews" were not part of the "Hungarian public."

27. B.F.L., IV/1402b.1944/121600 (16 May 1944).

28. A M. Kir. Közellátásügyi Miniszter 108 500/1944 Km. (23 April 1944), *Vádirat* 1, 228–31.

29. Ibid., 232–34.

30. See this differential ration as reported by Wallenberg in his report of 29 July 1944—see Wallenberg, *Letters and Dispatches*, 242.

31. Braham, *Politics* of Genocide, vol. 1, 511.

32. Bp. Sz. Főpolg. 1067/1944. (27 May 1944), in *Vádirat* 2, 123–24, along with a photograph of the original between pp. 128–29.

33. O.L., K27, box 260 (1 June 1944). See also *Vádirat* 2, 125.

34. See the handwritten comment at the foot of the 27 May letter, added by an official in the Interior Ministry—Bp. Sz. Főpolg. 1067/1944. (27 May 1944), in *Vádirat* 2, 123–24.

35. Bp. Szék. Polg. 295061/1944.XV (5 June 1944), *Vádirat* 2, 127–28.

36. B.F.L., IV/1402b.1944/001184 (12 June 1944).

37. B.F.L., IV/1402b.1944/123015 (14 July 1944).

38. Molnár, *Zsidósors*, 55, who notes the issuing of such regulations one month prior to the official issuing of ministerial legislation as "evidence of Buócz's zeal."

39. Domán, *A Győri*, 54.

40. Schweitzer, *A Pécsi*, 143. Unfortunately Schweitzer does not date the issuing of this local legislation.

41. L. Harsányi, *A Kőszegi Zsidók* (Budapest: A Magyar Izraeliták Országos Képviseletének Kiadása, 1974), 203–4.

42. Molnár, *Zsidósors*, 54.

43. Karsai, "Deportation and Administration," 117.

44. Ibid., footnote 21, 125–26.

45. *Esti Ujság* 9 (1 June 1944).

46. Ibid.

47. O.L., I 17, Bp. Szék. Polg. 295187/1944.XV (13 June 1944).

48. *Esti Ujság* 9 (1 June 1944).

49. O.L., I 17, Bp. Szék Polg. 225909/1944.XI (7 September 1944).

50. O.L., I 17, Bp. Szék Polg. 226079/1944.XI (3 October 1944).

51. *Esti Ujság* 9 (1 June 1944).

52. *Esti Ujság* 9 (1 June 1944).

53. *Esti Ujság* 9 (26 May 1944), 8.

CHAPTER EIGHT

1. Braham, *Politics of Genocide*, vol. 1, 372.

2. Ibid., vol. 1, 374.

3. Ibid., vol. 1, 375.

4. Ibid., vol. 2, 754—Braham writes that "the most important reason for his decision to do something about mitigating if not entirely ceasing the anti-Jewish persecutions was the swiftly deteriorating military situation, which threatened the collapse of Hungary together with its Nazi allies."

5. See the newspaper clippings that form a part of the Foreign Ministry archive—O.L., K84, 296 cs. IX-5.

6. See the minutes for the Council of Ministers meetings in O.L., K27, boxes 260–62.

7. See Braham's translation of Endre's statement in Braham, *Politics of Genocide*, vol. 2, 745–51.

8. Ibid., vol. 2, 754, 1070–71, 1110, 1213. See also *Vádirat* 3, 57–60, B. Vágo, "The Horthy Offer. A Missed Opportunity for Rescuing Jews in 1944" in R.L. Braham (ed.), *Contemporary Views on the Holocaust* (Boston: Kluwer Nijhoff, 1983), 25, Z. Erez, "The Jews of Budapest and the Plans of Admiral Horthy, August-October 1944," *Yad Vashem Studies* XVI (1984) 190, and P. A. Levine, *From Indifference to Activism. Swedish Diplomacy and the Holocaust; 1938–1944* (Uppsala: Acta Universitatis Upsalaiensis, 1996), 274.

9. Arnóthy-Jungerth claimed that Horthy called for an end to deportations at the 26 June Council of Ministers meeting. For more details of the timescale see Braham, *Politics of Genocide*, vol. 2, 755–59, and also document 183 in Braham, *Destruction*, vol. 2, 414.

10. Braham, *Destruction*, vol. 2, document 187, 425–29.

11. Ibid., vol. 2, documents 190–1, 437–40.

12. See the discussion of these Swedish and Swiss proposals at the 27 June Council of Ministers meeting, in *Vádirat* 3, 199–204.

13. Braham, *Destruction*, vol. 2, documents 190–91, 437–40.

14. Ibid., documents 324–76, 695–701.

15. See text of note sent to Hungarian legations abroad on 18 July in Lévai, *Zsidósors*, 233–34. This is translated in Braham, *Politics of Genocide*, vol. 2, 767–68.

16. Braham, *Politics of Genocide*, vol. 2, 779–80.

17. Less fortunate were the more than 1,000 "Jews" deported from the Kistarcsa camp some 15 miles northeast of Budapest to Auschwitz in mid-July. See ibid., vol. 2, 771–74.

18. B.F.L., IX/2915.1944/151929 (15 September 1944). See also *Vádirat* 3, 549–50.

19. B.F.L., IX/3354.1944/529342 (27 September 1944), the apartments in question were IV Magyar u. 26 II floor, 2, V Szent István körut 4 III floor, 4, VI Hajós u. 16–18 I floor, 2, VI Teréz körut 34 II floor, 1, VII Wesselényi u. 4 IV floor, 27. See also B.F.L., IX/3354.1944/152396 (5 October 1944).

20. B.F.L., IX/3535.1944/153346 (28 October 1944), and 153650 (9 November 1944).

21. Braham, *Politics of Genocide*, vol. 2, 770.

22. P. Gosztony, "Horthy, Hitler and the Hungary of 1944," *Canadian-American Review of Hungarian Studies* II, No. 1 (1975), 51.

23. Vágo, "A Missed Opportunity," footnote 91, 45.

24. Braham, *Politics of Genocide*, vol. 2, 799.

25. *Vádirat* 3, 545.

26. Ibid., 274, 344–45 and Braham, *Politics of Genocide*, vol. 2, footnote 154, 817–18.

27. *Vádirat* 3, 510–11, which reproduces the article "Honvédelmi munka!" from *Mayarországi Zsidók Lapja* 6, No. 36 (7 September 1944).

28. See my brief comments on this law at the end of chapter 2.

29. Braham, *Politics of Genocide*, vol. 1, 194–95.

30. *Vádirat* 3, 156–57, and original order reproduced facing p. 160.

31. The following information was required: Christian name and surname, Date and place of birth, Present religion, Parents' names, Occupation, Yellow-star house address, Date of christening and details of christening registry.

32. Braham, *Politics of Genocide*, vol. 2, 766.

33. See translation of Lévai, *Zsidósors*, 233–34 in Braham, *Politics of Genocide*, vol. 2, 767–68.

34. Gendarmerie Lieutenant Colonel Ferenczy was given full jurisdiction over the solution of the "Jewish question" at the end of August 1944.

35. *Vádirat* 3, 305–8, for an Association of Christian Jews report on the meeting.

36. Ibid., 305–6.

37. Note Ferenczy's response was to suggest that later, "some sort of cross"-like sign may be placed over the star, ibid., 306.

38. Ibid., 306.

39. Ibid., 307.

40. Although Auer claimed that Székely-Molnár replied that this was not the plan, ibid., 307.

41. Ibid., 308–10.

42. Ibid., 309.

43. Ibid., 308–9.

44. Ibid., 307.

45. Braham, *Politics of Genocide*, vol. 2, 756.

46. The intervention of neutral powers on behalf of the Budapest "Jewry" forms the focus for a quite sizable literature. Braham's survey includes a discussion of foreign rescue efforts. Fuller treatments can be found in J. Lévai, *Raoul Wallenberg. Regényes Élete, Hősi Küzdelmei, Rejtélyes Eltűnésének Titka* (Budapest: Magyar Téka, 1948), the collection of documents edited by P. Bajtay (ed.), *Emberirtás, Embermentés. Svéd Követjelentések 1944–ből Az Auschwitzi Jegyzőkönyv* (Budapest: Katalizátor Iroda, 1994), Levine, *From Indifference to Activism*, T. Tschuy, *Dangerous Diplomacy. The Story of Carl Lutz, Rescuer of 62,000 Hungarian Jews* (Grand Rapids: William B. Eerdmans Publishing Co., 2000). On the rescue work of the Hungarian Dr. György Gergely, see T. D. Kramer, *From Emancipation to Catastrophe. The Rise and Holocaust of Hungarian Jewry* (Lanham, Md.: University Press of America, 2000).

47. Lévai, *Black Book*, 316.

48. Braham, *Politics of Genocide*, vol. 2, 791.

49. Lévai, *Zsidósors*, 245.

50. Braham, *Politics of Genocide*, vol. 2, 788, drawing on Munkácsi, *Hogyan*, 191.

51. E. Petõ, "Statement by Ernõ Petõ," in Braham (ed.), *Hungarian-Jewish Studies* III, 60–1.

52. Wallenberg, *Letters*, 245.

53. *Vádirat* 3, 428–31

54. Wallenberg, *Letters*, 249.

55. *Vádirat* 3, 427–28.

56. *Vádirat* 3, 431–32.

57. Lévai, *Raoul Wallenberg*, 120.

58. Lévai, *Black Book*, 316.

59. Komoly, *Diary*, 221–22.

60. L. Yahil, "Raoul Wallenberg—His Mission and His Activities in Hungary," *Yad Vashem Studies* XV (1983), 34.

61. Juhász, *Hungarian Foreign Policy*, 299–330 and N. M. Nagy-Talavera, *The Green Shirts and the Others. A History of Fascism in Hungary and Rumania* (Stanford: Hoover Institution Press, 1970), 226–32.

62. Braham, *Politics of Genocide*, vol. 2, 823, and footnote 11, 876, drawing on Macartney, *October Fifteenth*, vol. 2, 370.

63. Braham, *Destruction*, vol. 2, document 226, 506, and Braham, *Politics of Genocide*, vol. 2, 834.

64. Ibid., document 227, 507, and ibid., 834.

65. See the statement is reproduced by Braham, *Politics of Genocide*, vol. 2, 832–33, from Lévai, *Eichmann in Hungary*, 145–46.

66. Braham, *Politics of Genocide*, vol. 2, 833.

67. See Lévai, *Zsidósors Magyarországon*, 302. Braham follows Lévai's account—unacknowledged—more or less word for word in *Politics of Genocide*, vol. 2, 830.

68. E. Szép, *The Smell of Humans. A Memoir of the Holocaust in Hungary* (translated by J. Bátki) (Budapest: Central European University Press, 1994), 4.

69. Braham, *Politics of Genocide*, vol. 2, 836.

70. Ibid., vol. 2, 838, and Szép, *Smell of Humans*, 82–83.

71. Braham, *Destruction*, vol. 2, documents 232–33, 512–13, document 237, 521, and document 239, 526.

72. Braham, *Politics of Genocide*, vol. 2, footnote 58, 879, and Braham, *Destruction*, vol. 2, document 240, 527.

73. See Braham, *Politics of Genocide*, vol. 2, 838–43, and on the subsequent history of these deportees, see E. Lappin, "The Death Marches of Hungarian Jews through Austria in the Spring of 1945," *Yad Vashem Studies* XXVIII (2001).

74. Translated in Braham, *Politics of Genocide*, vol. 2, 845–46.

75. Ibid., vol. 2, 846.

76. Pile, "Introduction," 16.

77. Lévai, *Raoul Wallenberg*, 121.

78. Braham's translation in Braham, *Politics of Genocide*, vol. 2, 845–46, of the order reproduced by Lévai, *Zsidósors*, 322–23.

79. Lévai, *Zsidósors*, 323.

80. His figures for "Spanish protected" appear to be somewhat on the low side—see the lists running into the hundreds in I. Harsányi, "A Budapesti Spanyol Követség által az 1944 Évi Üldözések Idején Védelemben részesített Magyar Zsidók Névsora," *Holocaust Füzetek* 3 (1993).

81. Bajtay, *Emberirtás*, document 49, 155.

82. Wallenberg, *Letters*, 265.

83. Ságvári, *A Budapesti Zsidóság Holocaustja*, 9.

84. Wohl's 16 January 1945 list of Swedish houses—he was office manager at the Swedish Embassy Tátra u. branch—is reproduced in Lévai, *Raoul Wallenberg*, 252.

85. N. Langlet, *A Svéd Mentőakció, 1944* (Budapest: Kossuth Könyvkiadó, 1988), 42.

86. Yahil, "Raoul Wallenberg," 40.

87. G. B. Freed, "Humanitarianism vs. Totalitarianism: The Strange Case of Raoul Wallenberg," *Papers of the Michigan Academy of Science, Arts, and Letters* 46 (1961), 509.

88. Braham, *Politics of Genocide*, 848.

89. Lévai, *Raoul Wallenberg*, 278.

90. Frojimovics et al. *Jewish Budapest*, 404.

91. Lévai, *Raoul Wallenberg*, 252.

92. Ibid., 279.

93. See R.W.P.A., FC2/1—003, FC2/1—004 by way of examples.

94. For further details, see K. Frojimovics, "A Zsidó Budapest. Pest: Gettó, 1944," in Cs. Králl (ed.), *Holocaust Emlékönyv. A Vidéki Zsidóság Deportálásának 50 Évfordulója Alkalmából* (Budapest: Teljes Evangéliumi Diák és Ifjúsági Szövetség, 1994) 252–55 and Braham, *Politics of Genocide*, vol. 2, 979–82.

95. A. Buchanan, *Secession: The Morality of Political Divorce from Fort Sumter to Lithuania and Quebec* (Boulder, Colo.: Westview Press, 1991), 66–67.

96. R.W.P.A., FC2/21—532.

97. Cf. Braham, *Politics of Genocide*, vol. 2, 847, who writes that they "were moved to other Yellow-Star buildings, mostly in the area which later became the Ghetto of Budapest" and Lévai, *Zsidósors*, 323, who writes that they were relocated into yellow-star houses outside of the area designated for the International ghetto, giving as examples the streets Visegrádi u. and Csáky u. Both of these streets were within the V district, just bordering on the International ghetto area.

98. R.W.P.A., FC2/21–531.

99. Translated in Braham, *Politics of Genocide*, vol. 2, 847 [emphasis mine].

100. R.W.P.A., FC/3–118, FC/5—144 & FC/16—342.

101. See the text of the letter reproduced in J. Lévai, *A Pesti Gettó. Csodálatos Megmenekülésének Hiteles Története* (Budapest: Officina, 1946), 43, requesting the attendance of members of the Jewish Council at a meeting on 18 November to discuss the concentration of the capital's "Jews" in a "certain area" in the VII district.

102. Reproduced in Braham, *Politics of Genocide*, vol. 2, 852.

103. Lévai, *A Pesti Gettó.*, 61.

104. Ú.M.K.L., XXXIII–5–c–4, XI. 23.

105. Ibid.

106. 1943 Budapest Telephone Directory.

107. Ú.M.K.L., XXXIII–5–c–10, copy of 142/4 Zs. ü—1944.

108. V Honvéd u. 18, Személynök u. 2/c, VI Bencur u. 2, VII Károly kir. u. 9, Rákóczi út 8/a-b, Király u. 65, Király u. 57, Miksa u. 11, Erzsébet krt 40–42, VIII Baross u. 18, Szigetvári u. 25/b.

109. IV Haris bazár 5, VI Andrássy út 77.

110. Ú.M.K.L., XXXIII–5–c–10, copy of 142/5 Zs. ü—1944.

111. A sliding scale was specified: tenants of a one-roomed flat could claim 450 pengő, tenants of a two-roomed flat 600 pengő, tenants of larger flats 750 pengő, single subtenants 100 pengő, married subtenants 200 pengő and family subtenants 300 pengő. To put these figures into context it is worth comparing them with the official price of bread in the winter of 1944, which Braham gives as 1.5 pengő, and the black market price of bread, which he gives as 10–12 pengő— Braham, *Politics of Genocide*, vol. 2, 862.

112. Lévai, *Black Book*, 375.

113. Ibid., 377.

114. O.L., I 18—Letter from III district councilor to the Mayor (24 November 1944).

115. Ibid.

116. *Harc* I, No. 30 (16 December 1944), 6.

117. Sibley, *Geographies of Exclusion*, 49.

118. Ú.M.K.L., XXXIII–5–c–10, copy of 142/1 sz. Zs. ü. 1944. Those who were sick were to be taken to a designated ground floor apartment, from which they were to be transported to the ghetto by the Jewish Council within 24 hours.

119. Lévai, *Black Book*, 377.

120. Ibid., 375.

121. See the text of the order in Lévai, *A Pesti Gettó*, 65.

122. Ú.M.K.L., XXXIII–5–c–2. See this figure of 44,416 from this undated Jewish Council report would fit with Braham's estimate that the ghetto population at the beginning of December was approximately 33,000, reaching a total of 55, 000 by the end of December and a peak of 70,000 in January 1945. See Braham, *Politics of Genocide*, vol. 2, 854. See also Sz. Szabolcs, "A Pesti Gettó Küzdelme a Túlélésért," *Valóság* XXXVIII, No. 3 (1995), 69–70. See he also gives figures of 52,688 for 2 January and 62,949 for 8 January.

123. Compare this to the statistics drawn from the Miksa Domonkos family ghetto writings given in Szabolcs, "A Pesti Gettó," 69, which give a total of 4,513 flats with 7,565 rooms.

124. Cf. Lévai, *A Pesti Gettó*, 137, who estimates an average population density of 14 persons per room, which is repeated by Braham.

125. Ú.M.K.L., XXXIII–5–c–1, XII. 3.

126. Lévai, *A Pesti Gettó*, 68.

127. Braham, *Politics of Genocide*, vol. 2, 1076.

128. See the text of the order in Lévai, *A Pesti Gettó*, 123–24.

129. Braham, *Politics of Genocide*, vol. 2, 853, 859 & footnote 87, 881.

130. Ibid., 865.

131. Macartney, *October Fifteenth*, vol. 2, 463.

132. Braham, *Politics of Genocide*, 874.

CHAPTER NINE

1. Scobie, *Hitler's State Architecture*, 94.

2. J. E. Young, *The Texture of Memory. Holocaust Memorials and Meaning* (New Haven: Yale University Press, 1993), 119.

3. K. E. Foote, *Shadowed Ground. America's Landscapes of Violence and Tragedy* (Austin: University of Texas Press, 1997), 24–25. Foote notes that "whereas sanctification leads to the permanent marking of a site and its consecration to a cause, martyr, or hero, effacement demands that all evidence of an event be removed and that consecration never take place. Whereas sanctification is spurred by the wish to remember an event, obliteration stems from a desire to forget."

4. Cole, *Selling the Holocaust*, ch. 4.

5. K. Smolen, *Auschwitz 1940–1945. Guidebook through the Museum* (fifth edition) (Oswiecim: Panstwowe Muzeum, 1974), 114.

6. A. Charlesworth, "Contesting Places of Memory: The Case of Auschwitz," *Environment and Planning D: Society and Space* 12 (1994), 581–83.

7. J. J. Jacobs, "Resisting Reconciliation. The Secret Geographies of (Post)Colonial Australia" in Pile & Keith, *Geographies of Resistance*, 210.

8. Van Pelt & Dwork, *Auschwitz*, 364.

9. See my reflections in T. Cole, "Review Article: Scales of Memory, Layers of Memory: Recent Works on Memories of World War Two and the Holocaust," *Journal of Contemporary History* 37, No. 1 (2002), 129–38.

10. P. Nora, "Between Memory and History: *Les Lieux de Mémoire*," *Representations* 26 (1989), 22, criticized in N. Johnson, "Cast in Stone: Monuments, Geography, and Nationalism," *Environment and Planning D: Society and Space* 13 (1995), 55.

11. Johnson, "Cast in Stone," 51.

12. Ibid., 51, and S. Levinson, *Written in Stone. Public Monuments in Changing Societies* (Durham, N.C.: Duke University Press, 1998), 71–73.

13. Text of wall plaque, VII Wesselényi u., Budapest.

14. Text of wall plaque, in courtyard of Dohány u. synagogue close to the Jewish Museum.

15. See W. Korey, "In History's 'Memory Hole': The Soviet Treatment of the Holocaust" in Braham (ed.), *Contemporary Views on the Holocaust*.

16. S. Milton, *In Fitting Memory. The Art and Politics of Holocaust Memorials* (Detroit: Wayne State University Press, 1991), 10.

17. L. Keller, *Küldestésem. A zsidó Tradíciók Szolgálatában* (Budapest: Távlat Kiadás, 1994), 146–47.

18. Emanuel Foundation, *Don't Forget the Victims!* (undated pamphlet), 2–3.

19. Text of the English plaque. This is the first time, at least that I know of, that a Holocaust memorial plaque in English has been erected in Budapest.

20. For more on the masculinized heroism of Wallenberg's memory see T. Cole, "Turning the Places of Holocaust History into Places of Holocaust Memory: Holocaust Memorials in Budapest, Hungary 1945–1995" in S. Hornstein & F. Jacobowitz (eds.), *Image and Remembrance: Representation and the Holocaust* (Bloomington: Indiana University Press, 2003), 272–87.

21. Text on memorial in Dohány synagogue courtyard.

22. Frojimovics et al., *Jewish Budapest*, 396.

23. Text on sculpture on VII Dob u.

24. Frojimovics et al., *Jewish Budapest*, 400, notes that the street was initially named Wallenberg street, but then changed to Raoul Wallenberg street in 1946.

25. Lévai, *Raoul Wallenberg*, 260.

26. See photograph between pages 169–70 in A. Adachi, *"Child of the Winds." My Mission with Raoul Wallenberg* (Chicago: Adams Press, 1989), for original wall plaque. This was replaced in 1989 with a new plaque (see figure 21).

27. H. Rosenfeld, *Raoul Wallenberg* (New York: Holmes & Meier, 1995), 122.

28. The original statue, retitled The Snake Killer, can be found outside the Biogal Pharmaceutical Works at 13 Pallagi út in Debrecen.

29. Rosenfeld, *Raoul Wallenberg*, xv.

30. H. Kamm, "Wallenberg: Statue Rises in Budapest," *New York Times* (15 April 1987), Section A, 2.

31. Rosenfeld, *Raoul Wallenberg*, xxii.

32. Translation in J. Eisenhammer, "The Search Goes Back to Moscow for the Truth about Wallenberg," *The Independent* (12 October 1989), 12.

33. Rosenfeld, *Raoul Wallenberg*, xxii.

34. J. Bierman, *Righteous Gentile. The Story of Raoul Wallenberg, Missing Hero of the Holocaust* (Harmondsworth: Penguin, 1995), 201.

35. See wall plaque on the north end of V Szent István Park.

36. See wall plaque on the corner of V Ujpest Rakpart, close to Szent István Park.

37. Frojimovics et al., *Jewish Budapest*, 396.

38. Ibid., 442, although A. Rieth, *Monuments to the Victims of Tyranny* (New York: Frederick A. Praeger, 1969), 82, gives the date as 1948.

39. A similar marginalizing of memory is noted in Foote, *Shadowed Ground*, 11–14, with reference to remembering the Haymarket Riot of 1886 in Chicago: "The business community claimed the site of the bombing to erect a policemen's monument and prevented labor from memorializing its martyrs within the city limit. The memorial to the labor martyrs was placed at their grave in Waldheim Cemetery, across the city line in Forest Park."

40. Translation of Hebrew text from Rieth, *Monuments*, 24.

41. Young, *Texture of Memory*, ix.

42. Emanuel Foundation, *Don't Forget the Victims!* (New York: Emanuel Foundation, 1988), 7.

43. See Cole, *Selling the Holocaust*, 121–27.

44. It should be noted that it was the Orbán government which instituted a National Holocaust Memorial Day in Hungary on 16 April, the day that deportations from Hungary started. The choice of this date—rather than a date related to e.g. an aspect of the Nyilas period—is significant. It certainly raises the question of collaboration by e.g. the Hungarian gendarmerie.

45. See J. Cote, "Hungarians Relive Painful Era in 'House of Terror.' Museum a Powerful Reminder of Nazi, Communist Atrocities," *San Francisco Chronicle* (14 June 2002).

46. Budapest Holocaust Museum and Education Center, *About the Past. In the Present. For the Future* (undated pamphlet).

47. Cited in J. E. Young, *At Memory's Edge. After-Images of the Holocaust in Contemporary Art and Architecture* (New Haven: Yale University Press, 2000), 67.

48. Ibid., 72.

49. P. Levi, *The Drowned and the Saved* (translated by R. Rosenthal) (London: Abacus, 1989); see ch. 2, esp. 22–23.

50. Ibid., 23.

51. Ibid., 40.

52. Ibid., 50–51.

BIBLIOGRAPHY

PRIMARY SOURCES
Unpublished
Hungarian National Archives, Budapest (O.L.)

K27, Box 260 (Council of Ministers minute book, April–June 1944).
  Box 261 (Council of Ministers minute book, June–July 1944).
  Box 262 (Council of Ministers minute book, July–August 1944).
  Box 263 (Council of Ministers minute book, August–September 1944).
K84, 296 cs. IX—5 (Foreign Ministry correspondence and press cuttings on the "Jewish Question").
K148, 1200 cs. 112–176 (Jewish Council lists of "Jewish" houses).
K148, 3410 cs. (9 May ghettoization plans).
K150 XXI k. 4517 cs. (Confidential writings 1943/1944/1945).
P1434 (Endre László correspondence).
I Collection (especially reels 15–21) [also available at USHMM archives].

New Hungarian Central Archives, Budapest (Ú.M.K.L.)

XXXIII–5–c–1 (Jewish Council diary).
XXXIII–5–c–2 (Jewish Council report on distribution of ghetto houses and the number of inhabitants).
XXXIII–5–c–4 (List of International protected houses).
XXXIII–5–c–8 (Papers relating the establishing of the Pest ghetto).
XXXIII–5–c–10 (Posters and leaflets relating to the establishing of the Pest ghetto).
XXXIII–5–c–11 (Posters and leaflets relating to the establishing of the Pest ghetto).

Budapest City Archives, Budapest (B.F.L.)

II/1480.1944 (Correspondence).
IV/1402b.1944 (Correspondence).
IV/1409c.1944.
IV/1480.1944 (XI district councilor's reports).

IX/1867.1944 (Correspondence).
IX/1870.1944.
IX/2026.1944.
IX/2027.1944.
IX/2030.1944.
IX/2031.1944.
IX/2035.1944.
IX/2037.1944.
IX/2040.1944.
IX/2041.1944.
IX/2042.1944.
IX/2048.1944.
IX/2102.1944.
IX/2105.1944.
IX/2114.1944.
IX/2115.1944.
IX/2116.1944.
IX/2339.1944.
IX/2747.1944.
IX/2781.1944.
IX/2782.1944.
IX/2783.1944.
IX/2784.1944.
IX/2785.1944.
IX/2786.1944.
IX/2787.1944.
IX/2789.1944.
IX/2790.1944.
IX/2791.1944.
IX/2792,1944.
IX/2915.1944.
IX/3354.1944.
IX/3535.1944.

University Library, Uppsala

Raoul Wallenberg Project Archive.
FC2/1–22 (transcripts of 172 interviews).

Published

Newspapers

Esti Újság 9 (1944*).
Függetlenség XII (1944).
Harc I (1944).
Magyar Front XIII (1944).
Magyar Futár IV (1944).
Magyarországi Zsidók Lapja 6 (1944).
Magyarság XX (1944).
Összetartás II (1944).
ÚjMagyarság XI (1944).

BIBLIOGRAPHY 281

Official Publications

A Budapesti Egységes Hálózat Betűrendes Távbeszélő Névsora (Budapest: A Magyar Király Postavezérigazgatóság, January 1943).

Budapesti Közlöny 135 (1944).

Budapest Székesfőváros Statisztikai Évkönyve XXX (Budapest: Budapest Székesfőváros Statisztikai Hivatalának Kiadása, 1942).

Budapest Székesfőváros Statisztikai Évkönyve XXXII (Budapest: Budapest Székesfőváros Statisztikai Hivatalának Kiadása, 1944).

Books, Memoirs, Pamphlets

Adachi, A., *"Child of the Winds." My Mission with Raoul Wallenberg* (Chicago: Adams Press, 1989).

Budapest Holocaust Museum and Education Center, *About the Past. In the Present. For the Future* (undated pamphlet).

Diámant, S., F. Freudiger & Gy. Link, "Report on Hungary: March 19–August 9, 1944" in R. L. Braham (ed.), *Hungarian-Jewish Studies* III (New York: World Federation of Hungarian Jews, 1973).

Emanuel Foundation, *Don't Forget the Victims!* (New York: Emanuel Foundation, 1988).

————, *Don't Forget the Victims!* (undated pamphlet).

Freudiger, F., "Five Months" in R. L. Braham (ed.), *The Tragedy of Hungarian Jewry: Essays, Documents, Depositions* (New York: Columbia University Press, 1986).

Gabor, G. M., *My Destiny. Survivor of the Holocaust* (Arcadia, Calif.: Amen Publishing Company, 1981).

German Library of Information, *A Nation Builds: Contemporary German Architecture* (New York: German Library of Information, 1941).

Horthy, N., *Memoirs* (New York: Robert Speller, 1957).

Isaacson, J. M., *Seed of Sarah. Memoirs of a Survivor* (Urbana: University of Illinois Press, 1990).

Kállay, N., *Hungarian Premier: A Personal Account of a Nation's Struggle in the Second World War* (New York: Columbia University Press, 1954).

Komoly, O., "Diary of Ottó Komoly" in R. L. Braham (ed.), *Hungarian-Jewish Studies* III (New York: World Federation of Hungarian Jews, 1973).

Levi, P., *The Drowned and the Saved* (translated by R. Rosenthal) (London: Abacus, 1989).

Petö, E., "Statement by Ernő Petö" in R. L. Braham (ed.), *Hungarian-Jewish Studies* III (New York: World Federation of Hungarian Jews, 1973).

Smolen, K., *Auschwitz 1940–1945. Guidebook through the Museum* (fifth edition) (Oswiecim: Panstwowe Muzeum, 1974).

Stern, S. " 'A Race with Time': A Statement" in R. L. Braham (ed.), *Hungarian-Jewish Studies* III (New York: World Federation of Hungarian Jews, 1973).

Szép, E., *The Smell of Humans. A Memoir of the Holocaust in Hungary* (translated by J. Bátki) (Budapest: Central European University Press, 1994).

Collections of Documents

Bajtay, P. (ed.), *Emberirtás, Embermentés. Svéd Követjelentések 1944–ből. Az Auschwitzi Jegyzőkönyv* (Budapest: Katalizátor Iroda, 1994).

Beneschofsky, I. & E. Karsai (eds.), *Vádirat a Nácizmus Ellen 1, 1944 Március 19–Május 15* (Budapest: A Magyar Izraeliták Országos Képviselete Kiasása, 1958).

————, *Vádirat a Nácizmus Ellen 2, 1944 Május 15—Június 30* (Budapest: A Magyar Izraeliták Országos Képviselete Kiasása, 1960).

Braham, R. L. *The Destruction of Hungarian Jewry: A Documentary Account* (New York: World Federation of Hungarian Jews, 1963).

Harsányi, I., "A Budapesti Spanyol Követség által az 1944 Évi Üldözések Idején Védelemben részesített Magyar Zsidók Névsora," *Holocaust Füzetek* 3 (1993).

Karsai, E. (ed.), *Vádirat a Nácizmus Ellen 3, 1944 Május 26–Október 15* (Budapest: A Magyar Izraeliták Országos Képviselete Kiasása, 1967).

Szekeres, J. (ed.), *Források Budapest Történetéhez III. 1919–1945* (Budapest: Budapest Fõváros Levéltárának Kiadványa, 1972).

Wallenberg, R., *Letters and Dispatches 1924–1944* (translated by K. Board) (New York: Arcade Publishing, 1995).

SECONDARY SOURCES

Adler, J., *The Jews of Paris and the Final Solution. Communal Response and Internal Conflicts, 1940–1944* (Oxford: Oxford University Press, 1987).

Aldor, F., *Germany's "Death Space." The Polish Tragedy* (London: Francis Aldor, 1940).

Allen, M. T., *The Business of Genocide: The SS, Slave Labor, and the Concentration Camps* (Chapel Hill: University of North Carolina Press, 2002).

Améry, J., *Radical Humanism. Selected Essays* (translated and edited by S. & S. Rosenfeld) (Bloomington: Indiana University Press, 1984).

Arendt, H., *Eichmann in Jerusalem. A Report on the Banality of Evil* (New York: Viking Press, 1963).

Balogh, E. S., "Peaceful Revision: The Diplomatic Road to War," *Hungarian Studies Review* X, No. 1 (1983).

Barkai, A., *From Boycott to Annihilation. The Economic Struggle of German Jews 1933–1943* (Hanover: Brandeis University Press, 1989).

Bauer, Y., "Conclusion: The Holocaust in Hungary: Was Rescue Possible?" in D. Cesarani (ed.), *The Final Solution: Origins and Implementation* (London: Routledge, 1994).

Bauman, Z., *Modernity and the Holocaust* (Cambridge: Polity Press, 1989).

Benjamin, A., *Present Hope. Philosophy, Architecture, Judaism* (London: Routledge, 1997).

Berenbaum, M., & A. J. Peck (eds.), *The Holocaust and History. The Known, the Unknown, the Disputed, and the Re-examined* (Bloomington: Indiana University Press, 1998).

Berkes, T., "Napilapok a Zsidókérdésröl. 1944 Március-Július," *Világosság* XXXIV, No. 6 (1993).

Bibó, I., "The Jewish Question in Hungary after 1944" in I. Bibó, *Democracy, Revolution, Self-Determination. Selected Writings* (edited by K. Nagy, translated by A. Boros-Kazai) (New York: Columbia University Press, 1991).

Bierman, J., *Righteous Gentile. The Story of Raoul Wallenberg, Missing Hero of the Holocaust* (Harmondsworth: Penguin, 1995).

Bigler, R. M., "*Heil Hitler und Heil Horthy!* The Nature of Hungarian Right Nationalism and Its Impact on German-Hungarian Relations 1919–1945," *East European Quarterly* VIII, No. 3 (1975).

Bihari, P., "A Magyarországi Zsidóság Helyzete a Zsidótörvényektõl a Deportálásig" in P. Horváth (ed.), *Hét Évtized a Hazai Zsidóság Életében* II (Budapest: M.T.A. Filozófiai Intézet Kiadása, 1990).

Braham, R. L., *Eichmann and the Destruction of Hungarian Jewry* (New York: World Federation of Hungarian Jews, 1961).

―――― (ed.), *Hungarian-Jewish Studies* II (New York: World Federation of Hungarian Jews, 1969).

―――― (ed.), *Hungarian-Jewish Studies* III (New York: World Federation of Hungarian Jews, 1973).

――――, *The Hungarian Labor Service System, 1939–1945* (Boulder: East European Quarterly & Columbia University Press, 1977).

"The Jewish Question in German-Hungarian Relations during the Kállay Era," *Jewish Social Studies* XXXIX, No. 3 (1977).

――――, *The Politics of Genocide. The Holocaust in Hungary* (New York: Columbia University Press, 1981).

—— (ed.), *Contemporary Views on the Holocaust* (Boston: Kluwer Nijhoff, 1983).

—— (ed.), *The Tragedy of Hungarian Jewry: Essays, Documents, Depositions* (New York: Columbia University Press, 1986).

——, *The Politics of Genocide. The Holocaust in Hungary* (revised edition) (New York: Columbia University Press, 1994).

—— (ed.), *Tanulmányok a Holokausztról* (Budapest: Balassi Kiadó, 2001).

Braham, R. L., & B. Vago (eds.), *The Holocaust in Hungary: Forty Years Later* (New York: Columbia University Press, 1985).

Braham, R. L., & A. Pók (eds.), *The Holocaust in Hungary. Fifty Years Later* (New York: Columbia University Press, 1997).

Brahan, R. L., with S. Miller (eds.), *The Nazi's Last Victims. The Holocaust in Hungary* (Detroit: Wayne State University Press, 1998).

Breitman, R., "The 'Final Solution' in G. Martel (ed.), *Modern Germany Reconsidered, 1870–1945* (London: Routledge, 1992).

Broadbent, G., "Neo-Classicism," *Architectural Design* 49, Nos. 8–9 (1979).

Broszat, M., "Hitler and the Genesis of the 'Final Solution': An Assessment of David Irving's Theses," *Yad Vashem Studies* 13 (1970), 97.

Browning, C. R., "Nazi Ghettoization Policy in Poland: 1939–1941," *Central European History* XIX, No. 4 (1986).

——, "Genocide and Public Health: German Doctors and Polish Jews, 1939–41," *Holocaust and Genocide Studies* 3, No. 1 (1988).

——, *The Path to Genocide. Essays on Launching the Final Solution* (Cambridge: Cambridge University Press, 1992).

——, *Ordinary Men. Reserve Police Battalion 101 and the Final Solution in Poland* (New York: HarperCollins, 1992).

——, *Nazi Policy, Jewish Workers, German Killers* (Cambridge: Cambridge University Press, 2000).

Buchanan, A., *Secession. The Morality of Political Divorce from Fort Sumter to Lithuania and Quebec* (Boulder, Colo.: Westview Press, 1991).

Cesarani, D. (ed.), *The Final Solution: Origins and Implementation* (London: Routledge, 1994).

—— (ed.), *Genocide and Rescue. The Holocaust in Hungary 1944* (Oxford: Berg, 1997).

Charlesworth, A., "Towards a Geography of the *Shoah*," *Journal of Historical Geography* 18, No. 4 (1992).

——, "Teaching the Holocaust through Landscape Study: The Liverpool Experience," *Immigrants and Minorities* 13, No. 1 (1994).

——, "Contesting Places of Memory: The Case of Auschwitz," *Environment and Planning D: Society and Space 12* (1994).

Clarke, D. B., M. A. Doel & F. X. McDonough, "Holocaust Topologies: Singularity, Politics, Space," *Political Geography* 15, Nos. 6–7 (1996).

Cohen, A., "Continuity in the Change: Hungary, 19 March 1944," *Jewish Social Studies* XLVI, No. 2 (1984).

——, *The Halutz Resistance in Hungary 1942–1944* (New York: Columbia University Press, 1986).

Cole, T., "Review of M. Freeman, Atlas of Nazi Germany," *Political Geography* 16, No. 6 (1997).

——, "Constructing the 'Jew,' Writing the Holocaust: Hungary 1920–45," *Patterns of Prejudice* 33, No. 3 (1999).

——, *Selling the Holocaust: From Auschwitz to Schindler. How History Is Bought, Packaged, and Sold* (New York: Routledge, 1999).

——, "Budapest 1944: Changing the Shape of the Ghetto" in J. K. Roth (ed.), *Remembering for the Future. The Holocaust in an Age of Genocide. Vol. 1. History* (Houndmills: Palgrave, 2001).

——, "Review Article: Scales of Memory, Layers of Memory: Recent Works on Memories of World War Two and the Holocaust," *Journal of Contemporary History* 37, No. 1 (2002).

———, "Turning the Places of Holocaust History into Places of Holocaust Memory: Holocaust Memorials in Budapest, Hungary 1945–1995" in S. Hornstein & F. Jacobowitz (eds.), *Image and Remembrance: Representation and the Holocaust* (Bloomington: Indiana University Press, 2003).

Cole, T., & G. Smith, "Ghettoization and the Holocaust: Budapest 1944," *Journal of Historical Geography* 21, No. 3 (1995).

Conway, J. S., "The Holocaust in Hungary: Recent Controversies and Reconsiderations" in R. L. Braham (ed.), *The Tragedy of Hungarian Jewry: Essays, Documents, Depositions* (New York: Columbia University Press, 1986).

Corni, G., *Hitler's Ghettos. Voices from a Beleaguered Society 1939–1944* (London: Arnold, 2002).

Cote, J., "Hungarians Relive Painful Era in 'House of Terror.' Museum a Powerful Reminder of Nazi, Communist Atrocities," *San Francisco Chronicle* (14 June 2002).

Cox, K. R., "Comment. Redefining 'Territory,'" *Political Geography Quarterly* 10, No. 1 (1990).

Crush, J., "The Discourse of Progressive Human Geography," *Progress in Human Geography* 15, No. 4 (1991).

———, "Scripting the Compound: Power and Space in the South African Mining Industry," *Environment and Planning D: Society and Space* 12, No. 3 (1994).

Dawidowicz, L. S., *The War against the Jews, 1933–45* (Harmondsworth: Penguin, 1990).

De Mildt, D., *In the Name of the People: Perpetrators of Genocide in the Reflection of Their Post-war Prosecution in West Germany. The "Euthanasia" and "Aktion Reinhard" Trial Cases* (The Hague: Martinus Nijhoff Publishers, 1996).

Deák, I., "Could the Jews Have Survived?," *The New York Review of Books* (4 February 1982).

———, "Genocide in Hungary: An Exchange," *The New York Review of Books* (27 May 1982).

———, "A Fatal Compromise? The Debate over Collaboration and Resistance in Hungary," *East European Politics and Society* 9, No. 2 (1995).

Dobroszycki, L. (ed.), *The Chronicle of the Lódz Ghetto 1941–1944* (New Haven: Yale University Press, 1984).

Domán, I., *A Györi Izraelita Hitközség Története 1930–47* (Budapest: A Magyar Izraeliták Országos Képviseletének Kiadása, 1979).

Don, Y., "Economic Implications of the Anti-Jewish Legislation in Hungary" in D. Cesarani (ed.), *Genocide and Rescue. The Holocaust in Hungary 1944* (Oxford: Berg, 1997).

Dreisziger, N. F., "Part I. The Road to War—Introduction," *Hungarian Studies Review* X, No. 1 (1983).

———, "The Kassa Bombing: The Riddle of Ádám Krúdy," *Hungarian Studies Review* X, No. 1 (1983).

Dwork, D., & R. J. van Pelt, *Holocaust. A History* (London: John Murray, 2002).

Eisenhammer, J., "The Search Goes Back to Moscow for the Truth about Wallenberg," *Independent* (12 October 1989).

Elder, G. S., "The South African Body Politic: Space, Race and Heterosexuality" in H. J. Nast & S. Pile (eds.), *Places through the Body* (London: Routledge, 1998).

Erez, Z., "The Jews of Budapest and the Plans of Admiral Horthy, August–October 1944," *Yad Vashem Studies* XVI (1984).

Erös, J., "Hungary" in S. J. Woolf (ed.), *European Fascism* (London: Weidenfeld & Nicolson, 1968).

Fein, H., *Accounting for Genocide: National Responses and Jewish Victimization during the Holocaust* (New York: The Free Press, 1979).

Fejes, J., "On the History of the Mass Deportations from Carpatho-Ruthenia in 1941" in R. L. Braham & A. Pók (eds.), *The Holocaust in Hungary. Fifty Years Later* (New York: Columbia University Press, 1997).

Fenyo, M. D., *Hitler, Horthy and Hungary. German-Hungarian Relations, 1941–1944* (New Haven: Yale University Press, 1972).

Foote, K. E., *Shadowed Ground. America's Landscapes of Violence and Tragedy* (Austin: University of Texas Press, 1997).

Freed, G. B., "Humanitarianism vs. Totalitarianism: The Strange Case of Raoul Wallenberg," *Papers of the Michigan Academy of Science, Arts, and Letters* 46 (1961).

Freeman, M., *Atlas of Nazi Germany. A Political, Economic and Social Anatomy of the Third Reich* (second edition) (London: Longman, 1995).

Friedman, P., "The Jewish Ghettos of the Nazi Era," *Jewish Social Studies* XVI (1954).

———, *Roads to Extinction. Essays on the Holocaust* (edited by A. J. Friedman) (New York: The Jewish Publication Society of America, 1980).

Frojimovics, K., G. Komoróczy, V. Pusztai & A. Strbik, *Jewish Budapest. Monuments, Rites, History* (Budapest: Central European University Press, 1999).

Gates, H. L. Jr. (ed.), *"Race," Writing and Difference* (Chicago: University of Chicago Press, 1985).

Gilbert, M., *Atlas of the Holocaust* (London: Michael Joseph Limited, 1982).

———, *The Holocaust. The Jewish Tragedy* (London: Collins, 1986).

———, *Holocaust Journey. Travelling in Search of the Past* (New York: Columbia University Press, 1997).

Glatz, F., "Hungary, 1944: Questions of Historical Science and of the Citizen" in R. L. Braham & A. Pók (eds.), *The Holocaust in Hungary. Fifty Years Later* (New York: Columbia University Press, 1997).

Gonda, L., *A Zsidóság Magyarországon 1526–1945* (Budapest: Századvég Kiadó, 1992).

Gosztony, P., "Horthy, Hitler and the Hungary of 1944," *Canadian-American Review of Hungarian Studies* II, No. 1 (1975).

Gottman, J., *The Significance of Territory* (Charlottesville, Va.: The University Press of Virginia, 1973).

Gregory, D., *Ideology, Science and Human Geography* (London: Hutchinson, 1978).

Gringauz, S., "The Ghetto as an Experiment of Jewish Social Organization," *Jewish Social Studies* XI (1949).

———, "Some Methodological Problems in the Study of the Ghetto," *Jewish Social Studies* XII (1950).

Gutman, Y., *The Jews of Warsaw, 1939–1943. Ghetto, Underground, Revolt* (Brighton: The Harvester Press Limited, 1982).

Harsányi, L., *A Kőszegi Zsidók* (Budapest: A Magyar Izraeliták Országos Képviseletének Kiadása, 1974).

Hartmann, R., "Dealing with Dachau in Geographic Education" in H. Brodsky (ed.), *Land and Community: Geography in Jewish Studies* (Bethesda: University of Maryland Press, 1997).

Heffernan, M., *The Meaning of Europe. Geography and Geopolitics* (London: Arnold, 1998).

Herbert, U., "Labor and Extermination: Economic Interest and the Primacy of *Weltanschauung* in National Socialism," *Past and Present* 138 (1993).

Herczel, M. Y., *Christianity and the Holocaust of Hungarian Jewry* (New York: New York University Press, 1993).

Hilberg, R., *The Destruction of the European Jews* (Chicago: Quadrangle Books, 1961).

———, "The Ghetto as a Form of Government: An Analysis of Isaiah Trunk's *Judenrat*" in Y. Bauer & N. Rotenstreich (eds.), *The Holocaust as Historical Experience. Essays and a Discussion* (New York: Holmes & Meier, 1981).

———, *The Destruction of the European Jews* (revised edition) (New York: Holmes & Meier, 1985).

———, "The Bureaucracy of Annihilation" in F. Furet (ed.), *Unanswered Questions. Nazi Germany and the Genocide of the Jews* (New York: Schocken Books, 1989).

———, *The Politics of Memory. The Journey of a Holocaust Historian* (Chicago: Ivan R. Dee, 1996).

Hoensch, J. K., *A History of Modern Hungary 1867–1986* (London: Longman, 1989).

Horowitz, G. J., "Places Far Away, Places Very Near. Mauthausen, The Camps of the *Shoah*, and the Bystanders" in M. Berenbaum & A. J. Peck (eds.), *The Holocaust and History. The Known, the Unknown, the Disputed, and the Re-examined* (Bloomington: Indiana University Press, 1998).

Horváth, P. (ed.), *Hét Évtized a Hazai Zsidóság Életében* I & II (Budapest: M.T.A. Filozófiai Intézet Kiadása, 1990).

Jackson, P. (ed.), *Race and Racism: Essays in Social Geography* (London: Allen & Unwin, 1987).

Jackson, W.A.D., *The Shaping of Our World. A Human and Cultural Geography* (New York: John Wiley & Sons, 1985).

Jacobs, J. J., "Resisting Reconciliation. The Secret Geographies of (Post)Colonial Australia" in S. Pile & M. Keith (eds.), *Geographies of Resistance* (London: Routledge, 1997).

Janos, A. C., *The Politics of Backwardness in Hungary 1825–1945* (Princeton: Princeton University Press, 1982).

Jaskot, P. B., *The Architecture of Oppression. The S.S., Forced Labor and the Nazi Monumental Building Economy* (London: Routledge, 2000).

Jelinek, Y., "The Holocaust and the Internal Policies of the Nazi Satellites in Eastern Europe: A Comparative Study" in M. R. Marrus (ed.), *The Nazi Holocaust. Historical Articles on the Destruction of European Jews 4. The "Final Solution" Outside Germany* (Westport, Conn.: Meckler, 1989).

Johnson, N., "Cast in Stone: Monuments, Geography, and Nationalism," *Environment and Planning D: Society and Space* 13 (1995).

Juhász, Gy., *Hungarian Foreign Policy 1919–1945* (Budapest: Akadémiai Kiadó, 1975).

———, "Some Aspects of Relations between Hungary and Germany during the Second World War," in Gy. Ránki (ed.), *Hungarian History—World History* (Budapest: Akadémiai Kiadó, 1984).

Kamm, H., "Wallenberg: Statue Rises in Budapest," *New York Times* (15 April 1987), Section A.

Karsai, E., "Deportation and Administration in Hungary" in R. L. Braham & B. Vágo (eds.), *The Holocaust in Hungary: Forty Years Later* (New York: Columbia University Press, 1985).

Katzburg, N., *Hungary and the Jews. Policy and Legislation, 1920–1943* (Ramat Gan: Bar-Ilan University Press, 1981).

Keller, L., *Küldetésem a Zsidó Tradíciók Szolgálatában* (Budapest: Távlat Kiadás, 1994).

Kertesz, S., *Diplomacy in a Whirlpool: Hungary between Nazi Germany and Soviet Russia* (Notre Dame, Indiana: University of Notre Dame Press, 1953).

Kleeblatt, N. L. (ed.), *Mirroring Evil. Nazi Imagery/Recent Art* (New York: The Jewish Museum, 2001).

Klein, B., "The *Judenrat*," *Jewish Social Studies* XXII, No. 1 (1960).

Korey, W., "In History's 'Memory Hole': The Soviet Treatment of the Holocaust" in R. L. Braham (ed.), *Contemporary Views on the Holocaust* (Boston: Kluwer Nijhoff Publishing, 1983).

Králl, Cs., *Holocaust Emlékkönyv. A Vidéki Zsidóság Deportálásának 50 Évfordulója Alkalmából* (Budapest: Teljes Evangéliumi Diák és Ifjúsági Szövetség, 1994).

Kramer, T., "From Utility to Catastrophe. Aspects of Hungarian Jewry's Responses to the Holocaust Process with Particular Reference to the 'Jewish Question' in Hungary" (Ph.D. thesis submitted to the Department of Semitic Studies, The University of Sydney, 1994).

———, *From Emancipation to Catastrophe. The Rise and Holocaust of Hungarian Jewry* (Lanham, Md.: University Press of America, 2000).

Lackó, M., *Arrow-Cross Men, National Socialists 1935–1944* (Budapest: Akadémiai Kiadó, 1969).

Lane, B. M., *Architecture and Politics in Germany 1918–1945* (Cambridge, Mass.: Harvard University Press, 1968).

Langlet, N., *A Svéd Mentőakció* (Budapest: Kossuth Könyvkiadó, 1988).

Lappin, E., "The Death Marches of Hungarian Jews through Austria in the Spring of 1945," *Yad Vashem Studies* XXVIII (2001).

Lefebvre, H., *The Production of Space* (translated by D. Nicolson-Smith) (Oxford: Blackwell, 1991).

Lévai, J., *A Pesti Gettó Csodálatos Megmenekülésének Hiteles Története* (Budapest: Officina, 1946).

———, *Fekete Könyv a Magyar Zsidóság Szenvedéseiről* (Budapest: Officina, 1946).

———, *Black Book on the Martyrdom of Hungarian Jewry* (Zurich: The Central European Times Publishing Company, 1948).

———, *Zsidósors Magyarországon* (Budapest: Magyar Téka, 1948).

———, *Raoul Wallenberg. Regényes Élete, Hősi Küzdelmei, Rejtélyes Eltűnésének Titka* (Budapest: Magyar Téka, 1948).

———, *Eichmann in Hungary. Documents* (Budapest: Pannonia Press, 1961).

Levine, P.A., *From Indifference to Activism. Swedish Diplomacy and the Holocaust 1938–1944* (Uppsala: Acta Universitatis Upsaliensis, 1996).

Levinson, S., *Written in Stone. Public Monuments in Changing Societies* (Durham, N.C.: Duke University Press, 1998).

Liszewski, S., "The Role of the Jewish Community in the Organization of Urban Space in Lódz," *Polin. A Journal of Polish-Jewish Studies* 6 (1991).

Lukacs, J., *Budapest 1900. A Historical Profile of a City and Its Culture* (New York: Weidenfeld & Nicolson, 1988).

Macartney, C. A., *October Fifteenth. A History of Modern Hungary* (Edinburgh: Edinburgh University Press, 1957).

Majsai, T., "A Körömezei Zsidódeportálás 1941–ben," *A Ráday Gyüjtemény Évkönyve* (1986).

Massey, D., *Spatial Divisions of Labor: Social Structures and the Geography of Production* (London: Macmillan, 1984).

Milton, S., *In Fitting Memory. The Art and Politics of Holocaust Memorials* (Detroit: Wayne State University Press, 1991).

Molnár, J., *Zsidósors 1944–ben az V. (Szegedi) Csendőrkerületben* (Budapest: Cserépfalvi Kiadó, 1995).

Mommsen, H. S., *From Weimar to Auschwitz. Essays in German History* (translated by P. O'Connor) (Cambridge: Polity Press, 1991).

Montgomery, J. F., *Hungary, the Unwilling Satellite* (New York: Devin-Adair, 1947).

Moore, B., *Victims and Survivors. The Nazi Persecution of the Jews in the Netherlands 1940–1945* (London: Arnold, 1997).

Munkácsi, E., *Hogyan Történt? Adatok és Okmányok a Magyar Zsidóság Tragédiájához* (Budapest: Renaissance Kiadás, 1947).

Nagy-Talavera, N. M., *The Green Shirts and the Others. A History of Fascism in Hungary and Rumania* (Stanford: Hoover Institution Press, 1970).

———, "The Second World War as Mirrored in the Hungarian Fascist Press," *East European Quarterly* IV, No. 2 (1971).

Noakes, J., "The Development of Nazi Policy towards the German-Jewish '*Mischlinge*,' 1933–1945," *Leo Baeck Institute Yearbook* 34 (1989).

Nora, P., "Between Memory and History: *Les Lieux de Mémoire*," *Representations* 26 (1989).

Novick, P., *The Holocaust in American Life* (Boston: Houghton Mifflin, 1999).

Ofer, D. "Everyday Life of Jews under Nazi Occupation: Methodological Issues," *Holocaust and Genocide Studies* 9, No. 1 (1995).

Patai, R., *The Jews of Hungary. History, Culture, Psychology* (Detroit: Wayne State University Press, 1996).

Pile, S., & M. Keith (eds.), *Geographies of Resistance* (London: Routledge, 1997).

Pintér, I., *Hungarian Anti-Fascism and Resistance 1941–1945* (Budapest: Akadémiai Kiadó, 1986).

Pressac, J.-C., *Auschwitz: Technique and Operation of the Gas Chambers* (New York: The Beate Klarsfeld Foundation, 1989).

Ránki, Gy., "The Germans and the Destruction of Hungarian Jewry" in R. L. Braham & B. Vágo (eds.), *The Holocaust in Hungary: Forty Years Later* (New York: Columbia University Press, 1985).

Ranki, V., *The Politics of Inclusion and Exclusion. Jews and Nationalism in Hungary* (New York: Holmes and Meier, 1999).

Rieth, A., *Monuments to the Victims of Tyranny* (New York: Frederick A. Praeger, 1969).

Róbert, P., "A Holokauszt a Magyar Sajtóban" in R. L. Braham (ed.), *Tanulmányok a Holokausztról* (Budapest: Balassi Kiadó, 2001).

Robinson, J., " 'A Perfect System of Control?' State Power and 'Native Locations' in South Africa," *Environment and Planning D: Society and Space* 8, No. 2 (1990).

———, *The Power of Apartheid. State, Power and Space in South African Cities* (Oxford: Butterworth-Heinemann, 1996).

Robinson, J., & P. Friedman (eds.), *Guide to Jewish History under Nazi Impact* (Jerusalem & New York: Yad Vashem & Y.I.V.O., 1960).

Roland, C. G., *Courage under Siege. Starvation, Disease, and Death in the Warsaw Ghetto* (Oxford: Oxford University Press, 1992).

Rosenfeld, G. D., "The Architects' Debate. Architectural Discourse and the Memory of Nazism in the Federal Republic of Germany, 1977–1997," *History and Memory* 9, Nos. 1–2 (1997).

Rosenfeld, H., *Raoul Wallenberg* (New York: Holmes & Meier, 1995).

Sack, R.D., *Human Territoriality. Its Theory and History* (Cambridge: Cambridge University Press, 1986).

Ságvári, Á. (ed.), *Budapest. The History of a Capital* (Budapest: Corvina Press, 1975).

———, *A Budapesti Zsidóság Holocaustja 1944* (Budapest: The Jewish Agency for Israel, 1994).

Sakmyster, T., "The Search for a *Causus Belli* and the Origins of the Kassa Bombing," *Hungarian Studies Review* X, No. 1 (1983).

Schama, S., *Landscape and Memory* (London: HarperCollins, 1995).

Schweitzer, J., *A Pécsi Izraelita Hitközség Története* (Budapest: A Magyar Izraeliták Országos Képviseletének Kiadása, 1966).

Scobie, A., *Hitler's State Architecture. The Impact of Classical Antiquity* (University Park: Pennsylvania State University Press, 1990).

Seton-Watson, R. W., *Racial Problems in Hungary* (London, 1908).

Sibley, D., "Survey 13: Purification of Space," *Environment and Planning D: Society and Space* 6, No. 4 (1988).

———, *Geographies of Exclusion* (London: Routledge, 1995).

Sipos, P., "Hungary: The Occupied Satellite" in W. Benz, J. H. ten Cate & G. Otto (eds.), *Anpassung, Kollaboration, Widerstand. Kollektive Reaktionen auf die Okkupation* (Berlin: Metropol Verlag, 1996).

Smith, S. J., *The Politics of "Race" and Residence: Citizenship, Segregation and White Supremacy in Britain* (Cambridge: Polity Press, 1989).

Soja, E. W., *The Political Organization of Space*, Commission on College Geography Resource Paper No. 8 (Washington, D.C.: Association of American Geographers, 1971).

———, "The Spatiality of Social Life: Towards a Transformative Retheorization" in D. Gregory & J. Urry (eds.), *Social Relations and Spatial Structures* (London: Macmillan, 1985).

Spielberg, S., & Survivors of the Shoah Visual History Foundation, *The Last Days* (London: Weidenfeld & Nicolson, 1999).

Szabolcs, Sz., "A Pesti Gettó Küzdelme a Túlélésért," *Valóság* XXXVIII. No. 3 (1995).

Száraz, Gy., "The Jewish Question in Hungary: A Historical Retrospective" in R. L. Braham & B. Vágo (eds.), *The Holocaust in Hungary: Forty Years Later* (New York: Columbia University Press, 1985).

Szekeres, J., *A Pesti Gettók 1945 Januári Megmentése* (Budapest: Nemzeti Kulturális Alap, 1997).

Taylor, R., *The Word in Stone: The Role of Architecture in the National Socialist Ideology* (Berkeley: University of California Press, 1974).

Tory, A., *Surviving the Holocaust. The Kovno Ghetto Diary* (translated by J. Michalowitz, edited by M. Gilbert) (London: Pimlico, 1991).

Trunk, I., *Judenrat. The Jewish Councils in Eastern Europe under Nazi Occupation* (New York: Macmillan, 1972).

Tschuy, T., *Dangerous Diplomacy. The Story of Carl Lutz, Rescuer of 62,000 Hungarian Jews* (Grand Rapids: William B. Eerdmans Publishing Company, 2000).

Tuan, Y., *Landscapes of Fear* (Oxford: Blackwell, 1980).

USHMM., *Historical Atlas of the Holocaust* (New York: Macmillan Publishing USA, 1996).

Vágo, B., "Germany and the Jewish Policy of the Kállay Government," in R. L. Braham (ed.), *Hungarian-Jewish Studies II* (New York: World Federation of Hungarian Jews, 1969).

"Budapest Jewry in the Summer of 1944: Otto Komoly's Diaries," *Yad Vashem Studies* VIII (1970)

———, "The Horthy Offer. A Missed Opportunity for Rescuing Jews in 1944" in R. L. Braham (ed.), *Contemporary Views on the Holocaust* (Boston: Kluwer Nijhoff, 1983).

———, "The Hungarians and the Destruction of the Hungarian Jews" in R. L. Braham & B. Vágo (eds.), *The Holocaust in Hungary: Forty Years Later* (New York: Columbia University Press, 1985).

Van Pelt, R. J., & D. Dwork, *Auschwitz 1270 to the Present* (New Haven: Yale University Press, 1996).

Van Pelt, R. J., & C. W. Westfall, *Architectural Principles in the Age of Historicism* (New Haven: Yale University Press, 1993).

Vardy, S. B., "The Impact of Trianon upon Hungary and the Hungarian Mind: The Nature of Interwar Hungarian Irredentism," *Hungarian Studies Review* X, No. 1 (1983).

Wagner, F. S., "Diplomatic Prelude to the Bombing of Kassa: Reflections and Recollections of a Former Diplomat," *Hungarian Studies Review* X, No. 1 (1983).

Yahil, L., "Raoul Wallenberg—His Mission and His Activities in Hungary," *Yad Vashem Studies* XV (1983).

Young, J. E., *The Texture of Memory. Holocaust Memorials and Meaning* (New Haven: Yale University Press, 1993).

———, *At Memory's Edge. After-Images of the Holocaust in Contemporary Art and Architecture* (New Haven: Yale University Press, 2000).

Zeke, Gy., "A Budapesti Zsidóság Lakóhelyi Szegregációja a Tökes Modernizáció Korszakában (1867–1941)" in P. Horváth (ed.), *Hét Évtized a Hazai Zsidóság Életében* I (Budapest: M.T.A. Filozófiai Intézet Kiadása, 1990).

INDEX